T0183117

Lecture Notes in Computer Science 9425

Commenced Publication in 1973
Founding and Former Series Editors:
Gerhard Goos, Juris Hartmanis, and Jan van Leeuwen

More information about this series at http://www.springer.com/series/7409

Boris De Ruyter · Achilles Kameas
Periklis Chatzimisios · Irene Mavrommati (Eds.)

Ambient Intelligence

12th European Conference, AmI 2015
Athens, Greece, November 11–13, 2015
Proceedings

 Springer

Editors

Boris De Ruyter
Philips Research
Eindhoven
The Netherlands

Achilles Kameas
Hellenic Open University
Patras
Greece

Periklis Chatzimisios
Alexander Technological Educational
Institute of Thessaloniki
Sindos
Greece

Irene Mavrommati
Hellenic Open University
Patras
Greece

ISSN 0302-9743   ISSN 1611-3349   (electronic)
Lecture Notes in Computer Science
ISBN 978-3-319-26004-4   ISBN 978-3-319-26005-1   (eBook)
DOI 10.1007/978-3-319-26005-1

Library of Congress Control Number: 2015953240

LNCS Sublibrary: SL3 – Information Systems and Applications, incl. Internet/Web, and HCI

Springer Cham Heidelberg New York Dordrecht London

Printed on acid-free paper

Springer International Publishing AG Switzerland is part of Springer Science+Business Media
(www.springer.com)

Preface

The annual Ambient Intelligence conference is the prime venue for research on ambient intelligence, with an international and interdisciplinary character. It brings together researchers from the fields of science, engineering, and design working toward the vision of ambient intelligence. Over the past 20 years, the vision of Ambient Intelligence has gradually materialized into a plethora of technologies and devices, which are being introduced into almost every aspect of everyday life, thus affecting our abilities, activities, behavior, and, in the end, are shaping a new way of thinking.

Volume 9425 of Springer's LNCS series is the formal proceedings of the 12th event in the Ambient Intelligence series. The AmI 2015 conference was organized along a set of themes including among others:

- Ambient Intelligence and Health Care
- Ambient Intelligence and Well-Being
- Ambient Intelligence and Social Robots
- Ambient Intelligence and Evaluation
- Ambient Intelligence and City

AmI 2015 continued the tradition of AmI conferences in providing a venue for high-quality papers in a wide range of research areas in ambient intelligence. This year's edition of the AmI conference received 48 submissions for the full and short paper track. Each paper was carefully reviewed by at least three experts of the Technical Program Committee, which included external reviewers from a wide variety of academic, industrial, and research organizations around the world. With an acceptance rate of 54 %, a total of 21 full and five short papers were accepted for presentation at the conference and are included in this volume.

In addition to an exciting technical program, AmI 2015 included four very interesting and visionary keynote talks by the following distinguished speakers:

- James L. Crowley (Grenoble Institut Polytechnique, Inria Grenoble Rhône-Alpes Research Center, France): "An Ecological View of Smart Home Technologies"
- Panos Markopoulos (Department of Industrial Design, Eindhoven University of Technology, The Netherlands): "Ambient Intelligence: Visions Past and Future"
- Michail Bletsas (Research Scientist and Director of Computing, MIT Media Lab, USA): "Ubiquitous Connectivity for Ambient Intelligence"
- Jan van Zoest (CTO HealthSuite DigitalPlatform, Philips HealthTech, The Netherlands): "Philips HealthSuite Digital Platform"

Despite a general trend of declining conference attendance, we observed a strong interest in the ambient intelligence research and application field. Based on statistics provided by Springer, it is noted that (on average and based on statistics available since 2009) each annual edition of the conferences proceedings in the LNCS series results in nearly 20,000 chapter downloads. Clearly the community for ambient intelligence is very active and up to date!

We would like to express our gratitude to the authors who submitted their latest research results to AmI 2015. The realization of the technical program of AmI 2015 would not have been possible without the dedicated voluntary effort of the members of the Technical Program Committee and the Organizing Committee. The Technical Program Committee members offered their time and expertise in order to provide high-quality reviews, within a tight schedule, while thanks to the support by the Organizing Committee, we are able to offer you an interesting and varied program.

November 2015   Achilles Kameas
                                                        Irene Mavrommati
                                                        Boris De Ruyter
                                                     Periklis Chatzimisios

Organization

AmI 2015 was organized by the Hellenic Open University (School of Science and Technology and School of Applied Arts).

Committees

Honorary Chair

Emile Aarts   Tilburg University, The Netherlands

Conference Chairs

Achilles Kameas   Hellenic Open University, Greece
Irene Mavrommati   Hellenic Open University, Greece

Program Chairs

Boris De Ruyter   Philips Research, The Netherlands
Periklis Chatzimisios   Alexander TEI of Thessaloniki, Greece

Thematic Chairs

Massimo Zancanaro   Bruno Kessler Foundation, Italy
Reiner Wichert   Fraunhofer, Germany
Vassilis Kostakos   University of Oulu, Finland
Dimitris Charitos   National Kapodistrian University of Athens, Greece
Christos Goumopoulos   University of the Aegean, Greece
Ioannis Chatzigiannakis   University of Rome La Sapienza, Italy
Vanessa Evers   University of Twente, The Netherlands

Workshops Chairs

Andreas Komninos   University of Strathclyde, UK
Vassilis Koutkias   INSERM Paris, France

Posters and Demos

Petros Nikopolitidis   Aristotle University of Thessaloniki, Greece
Javed Vassilis Khan   Breda University of Applied Sciences, Netherlands

Academic Liaison

Athanassios Skodras   University of Patras, Greece

Industrial Liaison

Kieran Delaney   Cork Institute of Technology, Ireland
Alex Vakaloudis   Cork Institute of Technology, Ireland

Publicity Chair

Norbert A. Streitz   Smart Future Initiative, Germany

Local Secretariat

Spyridoula Kouna

Website

George Birbilis

Publicity

Eirini Lagiou

Additional Reviewers

Albert Salah   Bogazici University, Turkey
Achilles Kameas   Hellenic Open University, Greece
Stefano Chessa   University of Pisa, Italy
Reiner Wichert   Fraunhofer IGD, Germany
Javier Caminero   Telefonica R&D, Spain
Mitja Lustrek   Jozef Stefan Institute, Slovenia
Rob Van Kranenburg   Council theinternetofthings.eu
Maurits Kaptein   Eindhoven University of Technology, The Netherlands
Margherita Antona   ICS-FORTH, Greece
Stefano Valtolina   Università degli Studi di Milano, Italy
Vassilis Kostakos   University of Oulu, Finland
Otthein Herzog   TZI, Universitt Bremen, Germany
Kristof Van Laerhoven   University of Freiburg, Germany
Sarah Gallacher   UCL, UK
Matjaz Gams   Jozef Stefan Institute, Slovenia
Maria Ganzha   University of Gdańsk, Poland
David Lillis   University College Dublin, Ireland
Antonio Maa   University of Màlaga, Spain

Robbert Jan Beun	University Utrecht, The Netherlands
Marcelo Vasconcelos	Oswaldo Cruz Foundation, Brazil
Aske Plaat	Tilburg University, The Netherlands
Hans W. Guesgen	Massey University, New Zealand
Teck-Hou Teng	Nanyang Technological University, Singapore
Alexander Rosemann	Eindhoven University of Technology, The Netherlands
Dimitris Grammenos	FORTH-ICS, Greece
Carmelo Ardito	University of Bari Aldo Moro, Italy
Massimo Zancanaro	FBK-cit, Italy
Kostas Stathis	University of London, UK
Pedro Gamito	ULHT, Portugal
Vassilis-Javed Khan	NHTV University of Applied Sciences, The Netherlands
Kaori Fujinami	Tokyo University of Agriculture and Technology, Japan
Juan Carlos Augusto	Middlesex University, UK
Wei Chen	Eindhoven University of Technology, The Netherlands
Oscar Tomico	Eindhoven University of Technology, The Netherlands
Carmen Santoro	ISTI-CNR, Italy
Julia Kantorovitch	VTT Technical Research Centre of Finland
Marco Rozendaal	Industrial Design Engineering, TU Delft, The Netherlands
Lars Braubach	University of Hamburg, Germany
Joyce Lacroix	Philips Research, The Netherlands
Jaap Ham	Eindhoven University of Technology, The Netherlands
Babak A. Farshchian	SINTEF ICT, Norway
Sean Russell	University College Dublin, Ireland
Thomas Schlegel	TU Dresden, Germany
Rosa Lanzilotti	University of Bari, Italy
Fabio Paterno	CNR-ISTI, Italy

Sponsoring Institutions

Hellenic Open University
National and Kapodistrian University of Athens
IEEE, Greece section

Contents

An Ecological View of Smart Home Technologies

James L. Crowley[1,2(✉)] and Joelle Coutaz[2]

[1] INRIA Grenoble Rhone-Alpes Research Center, Université Grenoble Alpes,
38000 Grenoble, France
James.Crowley@inria.fr
[2] Laboratoire Informatique de Grenoble (LIG), Université Grenoble Alpes,
38000 Grenoble, France

Abstract. In this paper we propose an ecological view in which a smart home is seen as an interconnected collection of smart objects that work together to provide services to inhabitants. We review home technologies in a historical context in which the home is a personal habitat that provides services to inhabitants, and draw lessons from the profusion of new services that were made possible by the introduction of electricity in the home during the 20th century. We examine possible metaphors for smart homes, including the smart home as an inside-out autonomous robot, and the smart home as an ecosystem of smart objects providing services. We propose a taxonomy for smart home services and discuss examples for each class of service. We conclude with a discussion of required system qualities and potential show-stoppers.

Keywords: Smart objects · Smart home · Ecological view · Domotics · Intelligent home services · Human computer interaction · Ambient intelligence

1 Introduction

Continued advances in information and communication technologies, coupled with progress in machine learning, sensors, actuators and human computer interaction make it increasingly easy to embed technologies for perception, action, communication and interaction in ordinary human objects. The result is an enabling technology for smart objects and smart environments with the potential to provide revolutionary new services. In this paper we discuss how this technology can be used to create new forms of intelligent services for the home.

We begin by discussing historical barriers to Home Automation, and propose an alternative ecological view of the home as a personal habitat that provides services such as personal protection and shelter from the elements. We examine the profound rupture in the nature of services that resulted from the introduction of electricity in the home at the beginning of the 20th century and draw lessons from the adoption of different forms of electric appliances. We then examine the nature of services that are made possible by the introduction of ambient intelligence in the home.

We propose a taxonomy for smart home services in terms of tools, housekeepers, advisors, and media. For each class, we explore forms of services for different functional

© Springer International Publishing Switzerland 2015
Kameas et al. (Eds.): AmI 2015, LNCS 9425, pp. 1–16, 2015.
DOI: 10.1007/978-3-319-26005-1_1

areas of the home. We conclude by discussing required system qualities and potential show-stoppers. We argue that establishing proper legal and ethical foundations may be as important as technological research to the long-term acceptance of smart home technologies.

2 Domotics as Home Automation

Much of the early work in smart home technologies has been directed towards automating common tasks such as cleaning, environmental control and energy consumption. More recently, we have seen a big push in the area of health monitoring, particularly for the area of providing autonomy for healthy aging. In most cases, work has been primarily directed towards automating established processes rather than providing a new perspective for how smart technologies can affect the organization of the home.

For many years, smart home technologies were considered to be part of the field of home automation, sometimes referred to as Domotics [1]. The dominant approach was to automate regulation of Heating, Ventilation and Air Conditioning (HVAC) equipment, control of energy consuming appliances such as water heaters, control of lighting, and automatic control of shutters and awnings. Intelligence was provided by analog timers, sensors and finite state machines wired into the home electrical system. Communication signals were based on cables, or in some cases, communication over power lines (CPL). Configuration required a certified electrician. While the high cost of installation was a barrier to such technologies, the biggest obstacle was lack of user control. Programming the behavior of home automation systems based on timers and finite state machines required intervention by a certified technician who generally had little or no understanding of the preferences of inhabitants. Such systems quickly earned a reputation for inappropriate, almost comical behavior.

The arrival of personal computers and wireless communications provided the potential for a technological rupture in home automation. In theory, it became possible to provide home-owners with a computer based "control panel" running on a personal computer, providing information and control of environmental conditions throughout the home. However, to date there has been little penetration of such technology in the home. Frequently cited reasons for this lack of success include

(1) The proliferation of closed proprietary standards and protocols,
(2) The high cost of installation of sensors and actuators,
(3) Dependence on technologies that evolve on time scales that are very different than buildings,
(4) Incomprehension of the technology and its use by both architects and classically trained electricians.

In addition to these obvious reasons, a more subtle obstacle also exists. Simply replacing analog timers and finite state automata with centralized digital controls provides only marginal improvements in quality of life. The real gains in quality of life require rethinking the role of intelligent systems in terms of the ecology of the home.

3   The Ecology of the Smart Home

Ecology is the scientific field that deals with the relationships between groups of living things and their environments [2]. An ecological approach is increasingly important to scientific domains such as Biology, Anthropology, Sociology, Economics, Psychology and the Environmental Sciences. Human Ecology, in particular, is the study of the relations between humans and their natural, social, and artificial environments [3]. Human ecology has a fragmented academic history with publications dating back to the mid 19th century, and developments spread throughout a range of disciplines. For example, the term "human ecology" was used in 1907 in a study on the effects of sanitation [4] in terms of the interaction between city sanitation services and domestic hygiene. An ecological approach provides important insights into smart home technologies.

To understand the ecology of the smart home, we need to examine the relation between the habitat and inhabitants. A habitat is the place or environment where a plant or animal normally lives and grows [5]. The term is also used to refer to artificial human environments where people can survive under inhospitable conditions such as on other planets or under the sea. An inhabitant is any plant or animal that lives in a habitat. In this paper we will refer to persons who regularly inhabit a home as inhabitants.

Habitats provide services to inhabitants [6]. For natural habitats, such services can range from providing shelter and security to providing food, water, facilitating biodiversity. We propose to examine the smart home as an ecosystem of smart objects that can individually or collectively provide services to inhabitants. Examining the home as a provider of services reveals a multitude of interesting and attainable possibilities for smart homes, most of which are natural extensions of the historical role of the home. This ecological notion of service should not be confused with Service Oriented Computing.

3.1   A Smart Home Is not a HaaS

It would be tempting to write that we are proposing the concept of "Home as a Service" (HaaS), however this would be both inaccurate and misleading. In the technical area of "Service oriented computing", a service is defined as a "logical representation of a repeatable activity that has a specified outcome". Services obey a contract. Software services are self-contained, may be composed of other services, and operate as a "black box" to consumers [7].

The notion of service used in ecology is much closer to the natural language notion of service as "an activity or process that provides something of value". In particular, we are concerned with intelligent services that provide value to inhabitants. In this sense, smart home services cannot be constrained by a contract and may not comply with the accepted definition of a "software service". So, while these definitions may have some overlap, the notion that we are proposing may not be recognizable to the scientific community of service oriented computing, and the concepts and techniques required are not necessarily relevant to that domain.

3.2 Traditional Home Services

From prehistoric times, humans have depended on a home as a personal habitat. Prehistoric homes provided protection of persons and possessions, both from nature and from other species. Homes provide heat and shelter in cold climates, allowing the human species to migrate over much of the planet, with the home providing shelter and protection of possessions, as well as a protected place for grooming, cooking, eating and sleeping. In more modern times, the home has provided light at night through use of tallow lamps and candles followed by gas lamps and electric lighting [8].

In the late 19th century, the introduction of electricity in the home provoked a rupture in the nature of services that the home could provide. The arrival of electric distribution networks (1883) made possible electric light and electric heat in the home. These were soon followed by vacuum cleaners (1908), the electric iron (1909), clothes washing machines (1910), air conditioners (1911), the refrigerator (1913), electric toasters and hot-plates (1919), home radio (1920), the dishwasher (1922), electric ovens (1930), television (1948), electric can openers (1956), microwave ovens (1967), and the Home Computer (1977). Each of these appliances augmented the services provided to inhabitants by the home.

Bowden and Offer [9] examine the penetration of durable household appliances in the US and UK during the early 20th century, modeling the diffusion of technologies as a logistics "S" curve. They examine a number of technologies that were introduced to households following the widespread introduction of electricity and rank these based on the number of years between adoption by 20 % and 75 % of all households. They observe differences in adoption rates for two distinct classes of appliances, referred to as time-saving appliances and time-using appliances.

Time-saving appliances, such as electric irons, vacuum cleaners and washing machines increase the quantity of discretionary time of inhabitants, typically by automating or improving the efficiency of common household tasks. Time-using appliances, such as TV, Radio and the Video Cassette Recorder bring a new function to the home, at the cost of a commitment of discretionary time. Bowden et al. show that, contrary to intuition, time-using appliances are typically adopted more rapidly than time-saving appliances. They argue that this is because modern households already have sufficient disposable time and are more interested in improving quality than increasing quantity. One exception is the telephone, whose 75 % penetration required 67 years, despite its evolution from a time-saving appliance to a time-using appliance, a phenomena explored in great detail in [10].

The take home message is that inhabitants are more likely to adopt smart objects and smart home services that improve quality of life, rather than increase available leisure time. This argument is reinforced by the observation that many supposedly time-saving appliances such as washing machines and vacuum cleaners have not actually reduced the time spent on chores. Rather they are commonly used to improve hygiene by increasing the frequency of cleaning. The message for smart home technologies is clear. Automating existing processes is not the most effective approach. Smart home technologies that improve quality of life are likely to be adopted much faster than technologies that seek to save time.

3.3   The Smart Home as an Inside-Out Autonomous Robot

We propose to rethink the changes to the role of the home made possible by technologies for ambient intelligence. One obvious approach would be to see the home, itself, as an inside-out intelligent autonomous robot. Just as with autonomous robots, the first task for an intelligent autonomous home would be to observe and protect its own integrity. In biological systems, integrity is maintained by autonomic processes. A primary function for such processes is to maintain homeostasis [11]. For the smart home, homeostasis requires regulating internal environmental conditions, as well as maintaining stable supplies of energy, liquids and consumables. In this sense, starting with regulation of environmental comfort and smart energy are reasonable first steps toward the smart home. The inside-out autonomous robot analogy suggests a number of other fundamental services that are quite attainable with current technology, including maintaining integrity of the infrastructure of the home and its appliances, evacuation of waste, cleaning and management of consumable supplies and fluids.

Autonomy and homeostasis suggest that the environmental conditions and state (opening and closing of windows and doors) of each room in the house should be instrumented to give a better understanding of comfort. Monitoring the energy used by individual appliances and rooms can provide a wealth of information to allow consumers to understand their consumption of energy in order to operate as informed participants in the smart grid. We call this "making energy visible", and a variety of products and services are currently under development in this area. Similar efforts are possible concerning consumption of water and production of waste-water and sewage, particularly in drought stricken regions. Homeostasis also suggests that the smart home participate in managing the integrity of home appliances, as well as the immediate environment such as lawn and gardens. These are potential areas of rapid progress for the near future.

Similar ideas can be applied to management of cleaning and detection and removal of recyclable trash and organic waste. It should be relatively easy to build sensors that detect cleaning activities for floors, surfaces, windows, walls, furniture and appliances, to provide a summary of the current state of each surface, and indicate when surfaces require cleaning. An objective record of cleaning activities can help with planning for both manual and automatic cleaning, particularly in areas where hygiene is important such as kitchens and bathrooms. Similar information can be collected about the state of trash and garbage.

Beyond simple hygiene, homeostasis also suggests managing logistics for consumables. Maintaining inventory of food and cleaning stocks in the kitchen can help avoid cluttering storage areas and refrigerators with long expired foodstuffs and inedible leftovers, and provide automated shopping lists. Current technologies can be used to equip kitchen cabinets, refrigerators and drawers with low-cost image sensors. Computer vision techniques can be used to keep a record of current inventory including when each item was placed or removed. From this, it is relatively easy to inform users about where utensils can be found, and which foods should or should not be consumed.

This idea can be extended from the kitchen to all storage areas of the home. Closets, pantries, cabinets and dressers can be augmented with visual sensors for contents to provide a record of when items are placed and removed and when it is time to do the laundry. A particularly ripe area for inventory control is the medicine cabinet. Placing small micro-cameras in the sides and doors would make it possible to identify different medicines and health products and even to obtain key information from bar-codes or QR codes. This information could then be used to maintain an inventory to observe when medicines are taken and when they pass their expiration date. It can also be used to maintain a log of when medicines are taken and replaced as an aid to persons with memory problems.

Autonomic maintenance for smart homes should also include detection and removal of waste and trash. Human waste is currently handled quite effectively by toilets, showers and wash basins, without need for information technologies. However removal of solid waste (packaging, used articles, etc.), and organic waste from meal preparation remains a manual task. Trashcans can be augmented with sensors to aid in sorting for recycling.

Cleaning robots for floors already exist as stand alone products operating on preprogrammed timers. Such devices could be operated as peripheral cleaning appliances to be awoken and directed by the smart home as needed. Cleaning of eating and living areas, floors and furniture is more challenging and will likely require substantial robotics engineering. Similarly, automatic cleaning of bathrooms, toilets, sinks and kitchen surfaces are likely to be higher payoff but at a substantially larger investment in engineering effort. On the other hand, as discussed above, available technology can be used to observe such surfaces and note when they have been cleaned and detect when they need to be cleaned. This can be of strong interest for hospitals, hotels and assisted living facilities. These examples can be seen as "low-hanging fruit" that have become feasible at reasonable price using recent advances in machine learning, sensing, computer vision and robotics.

The analogy of smart home as an inside-out autonomous robot can only take us so far in understanding the range of possibilities for innovation. Beyond autonomic control for homeostasis, it is increasingly feasible to endow a home with a form of intelligence. Robots are considered to be intelligent if they are autonomous, embodied and exhibit situated behavior [12]. An embodied robot must be able to act on the world. For a smart home, this can be as simple as control of HVAC equipment, or as complex as controlling internal robotic devices cleaning and waste removal. Situated behavior is behavior that is appropriate to the goals and environment of the robot. For a smart home this would mean behaving in a manner that complies with the expectations and requirements of inhabitants. In addition to the simple autonomic services described above, intelligence requires that services understand inhabitants and behave in a socially appropriate manner. To better understand how smart systems can behave in an appropriate "situated" manner, we propose to consider the nature of the interaction that services can have with inhabitants.

4   Intelligent Services for the Smart Home

In human societies, powerful people surround themselves with servants. Servants perform activities that provide value, such as cooking, cleaning, logistics and security. All of these activities depend on the visual, manual and cognitive abilities of the servant.

For the most part, such abilities have remained beyond the state of the art in robotics and intelligent systems. However, this is rapidly changing with continued advances in the technologies of machine perception, machine learning, actuators, materials, and spoken language interaction. A popular consensus is that these technologies will eventually lead to intelligent humanoid robots that can take on the role of servants. However, this may not be the most appropriate or the most effective manner to bring intelligent services to the home.

Rather than trying to replace human servants with humanoid robots, it may be more appropriate to consider the kinds of services that can be provided by a smart home. In this section, we propose four categories of smart home services: tools, housekeepers, advisors, and media. These categories are defined by the way in which they interact with inhabitants [13]. For each category, we propose a definition and then describe several examples of possible services, most of which can be attained with existing technology. We conclude with a discussion of relative potential for penetration. In the following section, we will discuss qualities that can affect the acceptability and rate of adoption of smart home services.

4.1 Tool Services

A tool is a device or implement used to achieve a goal. Historically, human tools were mechanical artifacts, such as kettle that could be placed on a fire to heat water. The arrival of electricity made it possible to augment tools with energy. The kettle could now be equipped with its own heating element, obviating the need for a fire. Replacing analog controllers with digital controls makes it possible to dramatically increase the range of functions, and the precision of the tool. The kettle can now be equipped with a digital thermometer and offers preprogrammed modes to heat water for the exact temperature required for coffee, tea or instant soup. Augmenting tools with abilities to perceive, learn, communicate and interact offers even greater range of functions, but poses particularly difficult challenges. Allowing the kettle to adapt to each inhabitants' preference for the temperature of tea raises a real danger of rendering the kettle unusable.

The kitchen can be a rich domain for smart objects. For example, the mechanical can opener is a classic tool. Adding electricity gives us an electrical can opener, reducing the need for human force. Adding sensors and digital controls makes it possible to create a digital can opener that can adapt its shape and force to automatically penetrate and open cans of any size and material. Adding computing and sensors to recognize the can (peaches or pears), gives us a smart can opener that keeps track of what was opened and when.

Interconnected smart objects can be orchestrated to create a variety of new services for which there are no current analogs. For example, instrumenting cabinets and storage closets makes it possible to create a memory prosthesis tool that we refer to as "Where is my stuff?". Augmenting a refrigerator with recognition contents would enable a service that adjusts temperature to contents for optimum freshness.

The nature of "tool-ness" is not in the function, but in the way in which the device is used by inhabitants. Tools should perform a specific task or function as robustly as possible under the control of an inhabitant. They should be reliable and invariant.

Any intelligence should be used to enable the service to provide exactly the expected behavior under changes in operating conditions. The user interface and interaction with users should be perfectly predictable.

4.2 Housekeeping Services

Housekeeping services perform the chores involved in running a household, such as cleaning, cooking, home maintenance, shopping, and laundry. As with a human servant, housekeeping services should fade into the background and perform their task unobtrusively as a form of calm technology as proposed by Weiser [14]. Services for evacuation of waste, cleaning, management of consumable supplies and maintaining integrity of home and its appliances, discussed above, are examples of Housekeeping services.

Housekeeping Services automate existing processes and thus can be seen as similar to time-saving appliances. While they can result in some improvements in quality of life, inhabitants may be less willing to invest time and money in their adoption. Penetration rates are likely to remain modest for reasons discussed above in Sect. 3.2.

As with human servants, housekeeping services operate with knowledge of the most intimate details of each inhabitants' activities. Placing the information for such services on a cloud computer potentially reveals such details to companies and government services that happen to have the cryptographic keys. For this reason, privacy and trustworthiness are essential for Housekeeping Services.

4.3 Advisor Services

Advisor services observe the inhabitants and their activities in order to propose information on possible courses of actions. Advisors are analogs to experts such as doctors, culinary chefs or personal coaches for health, grooming or fashion. Advisors should be completely obedient and non-disruptive. They should not take initiatives or actions that cannot be overridden or controlled by the user. They should not create an unwanted distraction (nagging). Rather than saving time, advisors serve to improve the quality and effectiveness of inhabitants' activities.

An obvious example is a service that advises inhabitants on how to make more effective use of energy and the smart grid. Such a service would observe inhabitants' daily routines and patterns of energy consumption in order to suggest ways in which the inhabitant could reduce energy consumption with little or no change to comfort or personal habits. This information could be combined with information from the smart grid on current and expected pricing to advise users on how to minimize their electricity bill.

More generally, Advisor Services can be constructed to inform inhabitants on how to reduce their overall cost of living. A kitchen advisor could provide suggestions for meals based on current contents and expiration dates of food in the pantry and refrigerator. A cooking advisor would observe inhabitants' actions in preparing meals, and offer suggestions on how to improve taste or nutritional quality, or reduce cost of meals. An entertainment advisor could draw information from the Internet on television and cable schedules, as well as cultural events and movies. This could be combined with information about inhabitants' tastes and preferences to suggest possible leisure activities. A security advisor could be constructed to observe an inhabitant's routines to warn of potential dangers to person or property.

A number of research laboratories and companies are currently working on advisor services for sports training, weight loss and active healthy aging. Such services can be augmented with information from wearable activity sensors and models of the "quantified self" to provide advice and encouragement concerning physical activity and meals. Services can be devised to guide recovering patients about prescribed and proscribed activities during recovery from surgery. We have recently worked on an emotional coach that can monitor emotions of seniors and act to stimulate affection to prevent depression.

An important, unsolved, challenge for advisor services is how to enable such services to communicate in an unobtrusive manner, respecting the user's attention. Nanny bots that nag do not provide an improvement to quality of life, and are not likely to be adopted by anyone who controls their own habitat. Weiser's notion of a Calm Technology is once again relevant.

An even more critical issue is the problem of legal responsibility. Who is responsible when an advisor service gives incorrect or harmful advice? Can consumers be protected from services that give advice that surreptitiously leads to undue profit by companies? The potential for abuse is enormous.

4.4 Media Services

Media services provide extensions to perception and experience, including entertainment, communications, and non-obtrusive peripheral display of information. Music and art in the home are historical forms of media. Radio, television, and the telephone are examples of media made possible by the arrival of home electricity. The world-wide web is an extremely rich form of media made possible by the Internet. Ambient intelligence will enable an explosion of new media services with no obvious analogs to the past.

The arrival of inexpensive interactive displays will make it possible to augment every surface with interactive access to information via the web. It is already possible to embed interactive displays in glass[1]. Low cost wall-paper that includes color display and tactile interaction should soon be possible using technologies such as OLED or Graphene. When every surface is an interactive display, avoiding sensory overload of inhabitants may become a real challenge. Such a technology would enable the home to become a form of augmented reality blending the physical and virtual in a seamless experience. This can make possible, for example, a sense of presence with remote family members and loved ones. It can offer ubiquitous access to social media such as Twitter and Facebook, as well as immediate access to internet search. Video communications and entertainment can follow the inhabitant anywhere in the house.

Tangible and peripheral displays [15, 16] are another example of media made possible by ambient intelligence. Ordinary objects can be augmented with motion, light and sound

---

[1] Corning - A day made of Glass: https://www.youtube.com/watch?v=jzLYh3j6xn8.

to provide information about weather, traffic, or the activity of close family members. Internet-enabled lamps, such as the Philips Hue have been used to unobtrusively display information such as the cost of electricity [17] or energy consumption [18]. Similar services have been proposed to announce imminent arrival of family members or changes in weather conditions.

Episodic memory is a form of media service for which there is currently no analog. Such memory can take many forms. For example, engineers at INRIA Grenoble recently constructed a "refrigerator time machine" that uses micro-cameras to keep a visual record of items that are placed and removed from a refrigerator, combined with an interactive tablet interface that allowed an inhabitant to browse the visual history of the interior. This could be combined with visual recognition to identify and record individual items as they are placed or removed. The identity of the inhabitant that operated the refrigerator door could be used to record who, what, and when for every item. Similar systems could be constructed for cabinets and storage areas, making it possible to maintain a dynamic inventory.

Episodic memory can also be used to augment work surfaces. Low cost RGBD sensors can be used to observe ordinary objects as well as the human hands that manipulate them. Techniques currently exist to geometrically model the configuration of the hand and to detect common actions such as pick, place, turn, pour, stir, etc. [19, 20]. Recent progress in computer vision and machine learning make it possible to robustly detect and recognize ordinary objects from arbitrary view points and lighting conditions [21, 22]. Combining these techniques makes it possible to create episodic memories for kitchen work surfaces, dining tables, and bathroom surfaces. Visual recordings can be segmented and organized with event detection to provide a searchable record of actions and activities that occur at surface. These can be made available to inhabitants through interactive displays. Such tools provide a promising new approach to helping seniors avoid over medication, monitoring eating habits and offering interactive cooking advice.

4.5 Categories of Service Are Based on Interaction

The proposed categories of smart services are defined by the way they interact with inhabitants rather than by the domain in which they operate. For example, episodic memory, discussed in the previous section, can be used to construct a tool ("Where is my stuff"), an advisor ("How can I make a better cake?") or a media ("display of recent events"). These categories do not provide an unambiguous partition of the space of possible services. Indeed, in some cases, some services can be seen as belonging to more than one category, depending on which facet of the service is examined and the goal for which it used. It is likely that other categories can be defined.

5 Qualities and Show Stoppers for Smart Home Services

In this final section, we discuss required qualities and possible "show-stoppers" for smart home services. A quality defines the behavior of a system or service, and can be key in determining acceptability and rate of adoption. Qualities should ideally be defined as measurable attributes. For example, in the domain of Service Oriented Software, important qualities include Availability, Assurance, Usability and Adaptability. Each of these can be defined by measurable quantities.

Qualities are often defined as hierarchies, with general categories of quality made up with more detailed sub-categories. For example, Boehm defined a hierarchical model for software quality in which the highest-level qualities are Utility, Maintainability, and Portability [23]. Each of these is composed of a number of more detailed qualities. Show-stoppers are critical qualities with the potential to impede or even prevent adoption of technology. We begin with discussion of qualities that can affect the rate of adoption and the degree of satisfaction of inhabitants. We continue with examples of show-stoppers that could impede or prevent the emergence of smart home services if not properly addressed.

5.1 Controllability

Quality of life (QoL) is the general well-being of individuals and societies. In healthcare, a common metric of Quality of Life is the degree to which a person enjoys the opportunities of their life to achieve Being, Belonging, and Becoming. Control of ones' personal habitat is an important component of general well being, and will be an important factor in the rate with which individuals will invest time and money in smart home services.

A Smart Home can be seen as a micro-cloud composed of specialized CPUs, data storage units, sensors, actuators and interaction devices. The result is a complex heterogeneous ecosystem with a very large space of possible services. Mastering this complex ecosystem is a difficult challenge, especially if each home harbors a unique collection of devices.

In [24] the authors consider two approaches to providing smart home services in such a space: Smart Home Apps (Apps) versus End User Development (EUD). The Apps approach is attractive because it frees users from having to think about what they want. Users can opportunistically retrieve Apps from an App Store, even when they are looking for something else. While this model has proven popular for smart phones, the smart home differs from a smart phone in many critical aspects. The technical components of a smartphone are well defined whereas those of Smart Homes are diverse and unpredictable. Apps for Smart Homes must accommodate a great variety of underlying hardware. Smart phones tend to be used by one task at a time, while scenarios for Smart Homes envision a large number of services running in parallel. Finally, the smartphone is the intimate property of one owner, while a home, in general, is a shared spaces inhabited by a family or small group.

The End User Development (EUD) approach allows inhabitants to craft the behavior of their homes in accordance with their tastes and needs. This approach is well suited to the distributed collection of heterogeneous devices likely to populate a smart home, and allows users to opportunistically create new services and new uses for existing services. EUD allows inhabitants to remain masters of their home and the services that it provides, thus deriving a sense of personal satisfaction, contributing to quality of life.

5.2 Reliability and Maintainability

Home services are critical services [25]. They must be reliable and maintainable. Failures must be graceful with built-in safeguards and backups so as not to threaten health or property. This would seem to be antagonistic with a requirement for controllability and End User Development, particularly given the heterogeneous nature of a smart home infrastructure. Thus, reliability and maintainability of end-user developed smart home services appears to be one of the key research challenges to the development of smart home technologies. So far, this research challenge has not been widely recognized.

5.3 Usability

Smart home services must also be usable [26]. The contextual nature of usability has recently been recognized by the International Organization for Standardization/International Electrotechnical Commission (ISO/IEC) 9126 standards developed in the software community with the overarching notion of "quality in use." Unfortunately, usability is viewed as only one independent contribution to quality in use. Thus, the temptation is high for engineers to assimilate usability with cosmetic qualities of the user-interface, forgetting that system latency, reliability, missing functions, and inappropriate sequencing of operations can have a strong impact on the system "use worthiness."

Use worthiness is central to Cockton's argument for the development of systems that have value in the real world [27, 28]. In value-centered approaches, software design starts with the explicit expression of an intentional creation of value for a selected set of target contexts of use. Intended value for target contexts are then translated into evaluation criteria. Evaluation criteria are not necessarily elicited from generic intrinsic features such as time for task completion, but are contextualized. They are monitored and measured in real usage to assess the achieved value. Achieving this for smart homes is a critical challenge.

5.4 Durability

Smart Home Technologies must be durable. They should have technological life cycles that are on the same temporal scale as the home. Programmed obsolescence is not an option. This quality can be particularly challenging during times of rapid technological evolution. It would encourage novel uses of mature technologies rather than adapting emerging technologies to existing uses.

Durability is yet another reason that closed proprietary standards are incompatible with smart home services, particularly when employed by startups and small enterprises with limited expected life spans. Long-term durability argues for open standards and open source software and hardware designs.

5.5 Security, Privacy and Trustworthiness

The potential for abuse of smart home services by companies and governments constitutes the biggest danger for their development. Such services will operate with very intimate details of daily life that go beyond anything imagined by George Orwell in his novel 1984 [29]. Even without video or audio recording, smart home services can acquire detailed records of daily routines for eating, sleeping and bathing. Personal tastes in clothing, entertainment, food and social interaction would all become transparent. Once recorded, such information can potentially be eternal.

Personal information has value. Without legal restraints, it is very tempting for companies to base a business plan on the hidden value of customer information, particularly when it is "protected" by overly complex "user agreements" written in legal jargon. Many consumers are likely to be seduced by offers of inexpensive or free smart objects and services whose true cost is paid with the personal information that is harvested and exploited by companies. It is difficult to overstate the potential for abuse if current practices concerning collection of personal information on the web are allowed to proliferate into smart home technologies.

In most Western countries, personal information is protected by legal guarantees. However, recent history has shown that such guarantees are easily ignored in times of crisis. Government powers for surveillance of citizens imposed for specific needs in a crisis are easily made permanent and gradually adopted for everyday use by law enforcement. Certain governments have declared that any information that transits the Internet can be collected and used for surveillance. This should raise warnings for anyone considering using smart home services based on cloud computing. Obviously, smart devices and smart home services must be secure by design. However, even the best cryptographic coding can be undone by careless behavior, misleading user agreements or brute-force computing.

Legal restraints on corporate and governmental collection and use of personal data are important to the future of the smart home. However, even if companies and government bodies agree to obey legal restraints, how can inhabitants trust smart home services? A few cases of abuse can easily blossom into widespread suspicion and distrust. Clear rules and aggressive legal protection of privacy are essential.

6   Concluding Remarks

Throughout history, humans have relied on a personal habitat for protection and shelter from the elements. As human technology has evolved, the home has increasingly become a source of services. Mastery of fire enabled the home to provide heat, light and preparation of food. Bronze and iron enabled new forms of lamps and stoves. Technologies for candle wax and kerosene provided increasingly cleaner light. Electricity triggered a revolutionary expansion of services as ordinary objects were augmented with electrical power, and new media such as telephones and radio were invented.

Information and communications technologies are poised to trigger a new revolution in services provided by the home. In this paper, we examined this revolution in the larger historical context. We have proposed an ecological view in which the home is seen as a personal habitat that provides services to inhabitants. We have examined the smart home using the metaphor of an inside-out autonomous robot providing autonomic services that maintain stability in the internal environment. We have defined four categories of smart home services: Tools, Housekeepers, Advisors and Media and given examples of possible services in each category. We have reviewed qualities that can be used to describe and compare smart home services, and discussed potential show stoppers that could prevent the emergence of the smart home.

Two competing approaches emerge for the development of smart home technologies. In one view, users are passive consumers who willingly trade their data in exchange for the convenience of smart services. This approach is compelling both because it frees the user from the challenge of configuring and maintaining systems, and because it makes it possible for established companies to apply modern machine learning and big data analysis to construct smart home systems. The challenge to companies is to provide services that are so compelling and easy to use that end-users surrender control of both system behavior and personal data. The danger is that end-users will become prisoners of closed ecosystems of smart home services subject to the dictates of the large companies.

An alternative is that end-users retains local control of data and services, at the cost of investing the effort required to configure and manage smart home services in a changing landscape of devices and network protocols. The challenge to the scientific community is to provide robust tools and systems that are usable by ordinary people. Crowd source development offers an enticing tool for this approach. Our experience shows that the enabling technologies for EUD are now sufficiently mature as to support an open source community of geeks and hobbyists that can unleash the power of crowd sourcing for developing new systems and services. The challenge to this community is to make the technology usable by the masses without sacrificing control of smart home services or personal data.

Security, privacy and trustworthiness are essential to acceptance and acceptability of the smart home. While these are measurable technical qualities, ultimately their assurance requires ethical and legal safeguards. If companies and governments are allowed to freely exploit this new technology to track and monitor inhabitants, as they already have with the worldwide web, then smart home technologies will become a prison that goes beyond Orwell's vision of 1984. It is our responsibility to assure that this does not happen.

Acknowledgement. This work and ideas reported in this paper have been partially sponsored by the French Agence Nationale de la Recherche (ANR), program "Investissement d'Avenir" project reference ANR-11-EQPX-0002, Amiqual4Home.

Funding has also been received from the European program CATRENE project AppsGate (CA110) as well as EIT-ICTLabs Smart Energy Systems Activity 11831, Open SES Experience Labs for Prosumers and New Services. Special thanks to Pascal Estrallier and the DGRI Working group on Ambient Intelligence for support and encouragement.

References

1. Harper, R.: Inside the Smart Home. Springer, London (2003)
2. Odum, E.P., Odum, H.T., Andrews, J.: Fundamentals of Ecology. Saunders, Philadelphia (1971)

3. Young, G.L.: Human ecology as an interdisciplinary concept: a critical inquiry. Adv. Ecol. Res. **8**, 1–105 (1974)
4. Richards, E.H.: Sanitation in Daily Life. Forgotten Books, London (1907)
5. Abercrombie, M., Hickman, C.J., Johnson, M.L.: A Dictionary of Biology. Penguin Reference Books, London (1966)
6. Daily, G.C. (ed.): Nature's Services, Societal Dependence on Natural Ecosystems. Island Press, Washington, D.C. (1997)
7. Papazoglou, M.P., Georgakopoulos, D. (eds.): Special issue on service oriented computing. Commun. ACM CACM **46**(10), 25–28 (2003)
8. Brox, J.: Brilliant: The Evolution of Artificial Light. Houghton Mifflin Harcourt, New York (2010)
9. Bowden, S., Offer, A.: Household appliances and the use of time: the United States and Britain since the 1920s. Econ. Hist. Rev. **XLVII**(4), 725–748 (1994)
10. Fischer, C.: America Calling: A Social History of the Telephone to 1940. University of California Press, Berkeley (1992)
11. Damasio, A.: Descartes' Error: Emotion, Reason, and the Human Brain. Putnam Publishing, New York (1994)
12. Breazeal, C.: Designing Sociable Robots. MIT Press, Cambridge (2002)
13. Beaudouin-Lafon, M.: Designing interaction, not interfaces. In: Proceedings of Conference on Advanced Visual Interfaces, AVI 2004, Gallipoli, Italy, pp. 15–22. ACM Press, May 2004 (Invited keynote address)
14. Weiser, M.: The Computer for the 21st century, appeared in the scientific American. Special Issue on Communications, Computers, and Networks, September 1991
15. Ishii, H., Ullmer, B.: Tangible bits: towards seamless interfaces between people, bits and atoms. In: Proceedings of the ACM Conference on Computer Human Interaction, CHI 1997, March 1997
16. Gershenfeld, N.: When Things Start to Think. Henry Holt, New York (1999)
17. Rose, D.: Enchanted Objects: Design, Homan Desire and the Internet of Things. Scribner Press, Simon and Schuster, New York (2014)
18. Coutaz, J., Crowley, J.L.: Learning about end-user development for smart homes by eating our own dog food. In: Workshop on End-User Development for IOT Era, at CHI2015, Seoul (2015)
19. Argyros, A.A.: Tracking hands and hand-object interactions. In: BMVA meeting on Vision for Language and Manipulation, London, UK, 11 July 2014
20. Michel, D., Panagiotakis, C., Argyros, A.A.: Tracking the articulated motion of the human body based on two RGBD cameras. Mach. Vis. Appl. J. **26**(1), 1–14 (2014)
21. Bo, L., Lai, K., Ren, X., Fox, D.: Object recognition with hierarchical kernel descriptors. In: 2011 IEEE Conference on Computer Vision and Pattern Recognition (CVPR), pp. 1729–1736. IEEE (2011)
22. Lai, K., Bo, L., Ren, X., Fox, D.: RGB-D object recognition: features, algorithms, and a large scale benchmark. In: Fossati, A., Gall, J., Grabner, H., Ren, X., Konolige, K. (eds.) Consumer Depth Cameras for Computer Vision, pp. 167–192. Springer, London (2013)
23. Boehm, B., Brown, J.R., Kaspar, H., Lipow, M., MacLeod, G.J., Merritt, M.J.: Characteristics of Software Quality. North-Holland, New York (1978)
24. Dautriche, R., Lenoir, C., Demeure, A., Gérard, C., Coutaz, J.: End-user-development for smart homes: relevance and challenges. In: Proceedings of the Workshop EUD for Supporting Sustainability in Maker Communities, 4th International Symposium on End-user Development (IS-EUD), Eindhoven, Netherlands, p. 6 (2013)

25. Clarke, E.M., Emerson, A., Sifakis, J.: Model checking: algorithmic verification and debugging. Commun. ACM **52**(11), 74–84 (2009)
26. Coutaz, J., Calvary, G.: HCI and software engineering for user interface plasticity. In: Jacko, J.A. (ed.) The Human-Computer Handbook – Fundamentals, Evolving Technologies, and Emerging Applications, Ch. 52, 3rd edn., pp. 1195–1220. CRC Press Taylor and Francis Group, Boca Raton (2012)
27. Cockton, G.: A development framework for value-centred design. In: CHI 2005 Extended Abstracts on Human Factors in Computing Systems, pp. 1292–1295. ACM (2005)
28. Cockton, G.: Value-centred HCI. In: Proceedings of the third Nordic Conference on Human-Computer Interaction, pp. 149–160. ACM, October 2004
29. Orwell, G.: Nineteen Eighty-Four: A novel. Secker & Warburg, London (1949)

Modeling and Assessing Young Children Abilities and Development in Ambient Intelligence

Emmanouil Zidianakis[1], Danai Ioannidi[1], Margherita Antona[1(✉)],
and Constantine Stephanidis[1,2]

[1] Foundation for Research and Technology – Hellas (FORTH) - Institute
of Computer Science, N. Plastira 100, Vassilika Vouton,
700 13 Heraklion, Crete, Greece
{zidian, ioanidi, antona, cs}@ics.forth.gr
[2] Department of Computer Science, University of Crete,
Heraklion, Crete, Greece

Abstract. This paper presents a novel framework, called Bean, which aims to monitor, evaluate and enhance pre-school children's skills and abilities through playing in Ambient Intelligence environments. The framework includes: (i) a model of children development based on the ICF-CY model and the Denver - II assessment tool, aiming at early detection of children's potential developmental issues to be further investigated and addressed if necessary; (ii) a reasoning mechanism for the automated extraction of child development knowledge, based on interaction monitoring, targeted to model relevant aspects of child's developmental stage, maturity level and skills; (iii) content editing tools and reporting facilities for parents and therapists. The framework has been implemented in the context of an AmI environment for supporting children play in AmI, deploying a collection of augmented artifacts, as well as a collection of digital reproductions of popular games.

Keywords: Child play · Development · Ambient intelligence · Evaluation process and/or assessment

1 Introduction

Ambient Intelligence (AmI) applications aim to improve and enhance everyday living activities for a variety of target user groups, including non-traditional users of interactive technologies. However, the potential benefits and impact of AmI technologies for children and their parents is still to be investigated.

According to [6], children constitute a substantial segment of the market for Information and Communication Technology (ICT) products and services in Europe. A large number of products are available to young children that incorporate some aspect of ICT [31]. These include activity centers, musical keyboards, tape recorders, programmable and radio-controlled toys as well as everyday items such as remote controls, telephones, televisions and computers. This range of toys and devices is part of the move towards pervasive or ubiquitous computing in which technology blends

© Springer International Publishing Switzerland 2015
Kameas et al. (Eds.): AmI 2015, LNCS 9425, pp. 17–33, 2015.
DOI: 10.1007/978-3-319-26005-1_2

into the environment and is not necessarily visible. It is estimated that this market will be worth over €30B in a few years.

ICT has the potential to provide novel opportunities for children to develop and be creative, to develop generic learning skills and aptitudes and to practice their social skills [27]. Under this perspective, ICT can be seen as a new tool that could and should be incorporated into existing early-years practice in developmentally appropriate ways, supplementing, but not replacing, other important first-hand experiences and interactions and accompanied by quality adult input [33, 37]. By introducing state of the art ICT technologies, play can be expanded and enhanced. This is achieved, for example, when children use innovative equipment such as floor robots, smart artifacts, etc. ICT therefore, is seen as offering a range of potentially valuable pedagogic tools when properly utilized [7].

Ambient Intelligence (AmI) offers opportunities for supporting the needs of children and integrate ICT into children's everyday activities. By providing the appropriate modeling, monitoring and adaptation facilities, AmI environments can support day by day the development of young children through playing, and can help parents and experts follow and optimally facilitate this goal. This paper envisions an AmI framework which facilitates the automated extraction of knowledge regarding children's physical and cognitive skills, abilities and overall development based on interaction monitoring, so as to offer indications regarding the child's developmental stage, maturity level and skills. The framework has been design for children whose age of developmental stage corresponds to pre-school age. As a result, the provided technological infrastructure allows matching children's playing activities with their corresponding development stage, but also the detection of potential developmental issues to be further investigated and addressed if necessary. Parents are provided with general information about their child's play behavior. Finally, early childhood professionals are provided with extensive data in addition to the full interaction history for reasoning about whether the child is meeting certain developmental milestones. Child carers (parents and childhood professionals) are provided with information about child's playing behavior and about whether the child is meeting certain developmental milestones.

2 Related Work

2.1 Modelling User Abilities and Performance in Ambient Intelligence

User modelling (UM) has traditionally been concerned with techniques for modeling users and adapting interaction to their preferences, goals, and intentions, as well as to their cognitive and affective states. On the other hand, ubiquitous computing has produced approaches to recognizing and modeling the user's context, e.g., location, physical environment, and social environment. With the advent of smart and ubiquitous spaces, recent research efforts have focused on models that support intelligent environments to capture and represent information about users and contexts so as to enable the environment to adapt to both [20].

GUMO [17] is a general user model ontology for the uniform interpretation of distributed user models in intelligent semantic web enriched environments. The basic user dimensions represented in GUMO include ability and proficiency, personality, emotional state, physiological state, mental state, nutrition and facial expression. D-ME [10] is a multiagent architecture in which users and environments are represented by agents that negotiate tasks execution and generate results according to user in context features. User modelling in D-ME includes four main sections: IDENTITY (with identification data such as the user name, sex, id, password, and email), MIND (background knowledge, interests and know-how), BODY (disabilities or preferences in using a body part during interaction) and PERSONALITY (personality traits and habits). Agent-based user modelling in Ambient Intelligence is targeted to understanding human mental and physical processes and behaviour based on incomplete information provided by the environment in order to obtain appropriate agent reactions [3]. Models of human physiological and psychological states are formalized through a temporal logic and reasoning is performed through the derivation of agent beliefs.

Some user models have also been developed which focus on human functional limitations. For example, reference [5] discusses a model of older or disabled users leading to the creation of personas for design purposes. Reference [26] presents an open library of various categories of virtual user models, including VR models, covering a wide range of population groups and especially focusing on groups in risk of exclusion, e.g. older people and people with disability.

However, children as a dynamically evolving target user group have not been addressed in previous modelling efforts.

2.2 Software Assessment Tools

A range of software solutions have been developed to monitor potential developmental issues of children. Developmental skills can range from banging a toy on a table to displaying socially appropriate expressions [39]. A subset of these milestones are often used in screening diagnostics, and recent research suggests that the observation of object play interactions may help identify early indicators of certain developmental delays [1, 2]. Psychologists have created a coding scheme which quantifies the levels of sophistication displayed by infants while engaged in object play, as play is the most common therapeutic and educational intervention for children.

The Child's Play system [39] supports a subset of play activities, while automatically generating quantitative data from observations of children's behavior, based on the coding scheme of [2]. Measures include factors such as the frequency with which an object is played, the time spent attending between different objects, and the highest level of play sophistication reached by a child. Child's Play uses statistical pattern recognition techniques of sensor augmented toys and a mobile computing platform in order to receive data and identify play activities associated with developmental skills through the way in which children interact with objects [38, 39].

Plush Cube [2] is a system based on micro sensors which detects when a toy has been touched and how tightly it has been grasped, can be a considerably important tool for the professionals. CareLog helps occupational therapists collect better data for decision-making [16]. CareLog seeks to support teachers in a classroom in order to diagnose the causes of children's behavior by allowing retroactive video capture of events to help support systematic decision-making on the cause of the behavior.

Smart Pen has been developed as a tool that supports the therapy of developmental dyslexia, with particular regard to dysgraphia [9]. Smart Pen comprises a display monitor equipped with a high-sensitivity touchpad and specially designed writing tool equipped with pressure sensors. Smart Pen measures the pressure put on the surface of the display, eye-hand coordination and whether the pupil holds it properly or not. The application allows continuous monitoring of different parameters related to writing. All these parameters are stored in a database and can be easily reviewed by the therapist in order to observe the progress for each pupil.

KidCam is a prototype system designed to support the early detection of children with special needs [23]. It is a computer supported baby monitor that allows parents to collect pictures and videos of their child while also providing age-appropriate prompts for parents to enter developmental health-related information about their child. The basic functionality enables the recording of video, audio, and still pictures using either the front or the back camera, as well as reviewing multimedia data based on different annotations that are provided either during or after capture [22]. KidCam uses milestones from a standardized list applied in many pediatricians' offices across the United States, called the Ages and Stages Questionnaire [4].

LENA[1] (Language Environment Analysis) is a commercial system designed to help monitor language development in children, from new born to four years old. LENA uses digital signal processing to parse conversation into words. It monitors and measures linguistic progress by automatically monitoring child vocalizations, words spoken to the child, conversational turn taking, meaningful speech, and exposure to environmental language.

The emergence of AmI environments offer new opportunities in this research direction, as such environments encompass monitoring, modelling and reasoning facilities which can be exploited to the purpose of assessing children development in the context of usual everyday life activities such as playing, and provide a wealth of data on performance in different activities and task without necessarily formally testing each child.

3 Background

3.1 Play and Its Contribution to Child's Development

Child development is a progressive series of changes as the result of interactions between biological and environmental factors [32]. Development includes qualitative and quantitative changes, and is a product of intrinsic maturation and learning opportunities provided in the individual's environment [19]. The human developmental pattern is predictable, following specific phases and exhibiting specific characteristics. Children follow a similar developmental pattern with one stage leading to the next, even though there are individual differences in the rate and the manner that they follow the pattern [19].

---

[1] http://www.lenafoundation.org/.

Through play children learn, practice and improve skills, involve in social roles and experience emotions; therefore, play is a significant dimension of early learning [29]. According to Piaget, play stimulates interest, initiative, experimentation, discovery, and imagination of a child in order to enhance his capacity to learn [28].

Play "paves the way for learning", as it develops logical mathematical thinking, scientific reasoning, and cognitive problem solving [21]. In addition, it fosters creativity and flexibility in thinking, since there is no right or wrong way to do things [38]. During play, children construct knowledge by combining their ideas, impressions, and intuitions, experiences and opinions. They create theories about their world and share them with others. Due to the fact that play is self-directed, it leads to feelings of self-confidence and competence. As children play, they learn to solve problems, to get along with others and to develop the fine and gross motor skills needed to grow and learn.

Through play, children recreate roles and situations that reflect their sociocultural world, where they learn how to subordinate desires to social rules, cooperate with others willingly, and engage in socially appropriate behavior. Over time, these competencies are transferred to children's everyday behaviors [11]. Many forms of play that evolve over the course of early childhood, variously described as exploratory play, object play, construction play, physical play (sensorimotor play, rough-and-tumble play), dramatic play (solitary pretense), socio-dramatic play (pretense with peers, also called pretend play, fantasy play, make-believe, or symbolic play), games with rules (fixed, predetermined rules) and games with invented rules (rules that are modifiable by the players) [18]. Child's play develops in several stages from passive observation to cooperative purposeful activity [34]. For example, children of age 2–3 engage in symbolic and pretend play and begin to shift from parallel play to more interactive forms of play; between 3–5 years they engage in creative and group play, may begin to play simple board games. Associative play dominates by the 4th year of age as a child learns to share and take turns and is interested in friends; at 5–7 years the child enjoys games with rules, such as board games, plays well with others and enjoys social interaction and play to reach a common goal.

3.2 Knowledge Models and Assessment Tools

There is a great variety of evaluation methods and assessment tools used for identifying child's strengths, diagnosing developmental disabilities, determining eligibility for services, and making recommendations and offering resources where necessary. The work reported in this paper is based on the International Classification of Functioning, Disability and Health for Children and Youth (ICF-CY [40]) of the World Health Organization (WHO) as a universal modelling framework, and on Denver II [13], as a developmental screening test.

ICF-CY provides a common and universal language to facilitate the documentation and measurement of health and disability in children and youth. It is designed to record the characteristics of a child's development and the influence of its surrounding environment. ICF-CY can be used by providers, consumers and all those concerned with health, education, and well-being of children and youth [15]. ICF-CY can be used to document a single problem or a profile of limitations defining a child's difficulties related to health and functioning. ICF-CY provides an essential basis for the standardization of data concerning all aspects of human functioning and disability in the pediatric population by taking into account two relevant issues: (a) the dimensions of childhood disability which include health conditions, disorder, impairments, activity limitations as well as participation restrictions, and (b) the influence of the environment on the child's performance and functioning [30]. It is divided in two parts [30]: (a) Functioning and Disability, and (b) Contextual Factors. These parts are further subdivided into components. Functioning and Disability contains two components: Body Systems (Function and Structure) and Activities/Participation. Contextual Factors also contain two components (Environmental and Personal factors). Figure 1 shows these components and their corresponding functions [40].

Development tests are tools used by early childhood professionals to measure a child's developmental progress from infancy through adolescence. They may help to indicate early signs of a developmental problem and discriminate normal variations in development among children, depending on the age of the child. Such tools are designed according to the expected skills of children at a specific age. Types of development tests include infant development scales, sensory-motor tests, speech and hearing tests, preschool psycho-educational batteries, tests of play behavior, social skills and social acceptance tests [24]. There are many scales commonly used to evaluate and measure developmental skills, such as the Peabody Test [8], the Millani Comparetti scale [35], and the Denver Developmental Screening Test [12] which is the most widely used test for screening cognitive and behavioral problems for ages up to 6 years. The Denver Scale is not a tool of final diagnosis, but a quick method to process large numbers of children in order to identify those that should be further evaluated. It has been designed for use by the clinician, teacher, or other early childhood professional to monitor the development of infants and preschool-aged children. It enables the clinician to identify children whose development deviates significantly from that of other children warranting further investigation to determine if there exists a problem requiring treatment. In the work reported here, the Denver Scale II [13], a revision of the original one designed at the University of Colorado Medical Center, has been adopted. Denver II test uses both parent observation and direct observation for 125 included items in total. The scale reflects the percentage of a certain age group able to perform a certain task related to personal social, fine motor adaptive, language and gross motor skills.

In DENVER II, data is presented as age norms, similar to a growth curve. The more items a child fails to perform (passed by 90 % of his peers), the more likely it is that the child manifests a significant developmental deviation that warrants further evaluation [14].

4   The BEAN Framework

Against the background presented in the previous sections, this paper presents a novel framework, called Bean [41], which aims to monitor, evaluate and enhance children's skills and abilities through playing in AmI environments.

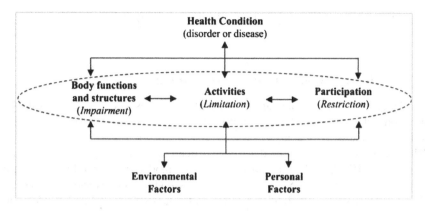

Fig. 1. ICF-CY

As a result, traditional games are turned into smart games that can be constantly adapted to the unique and continuously changing characteristics of each child, and at the same time the environment can act as assessment tool for early childhood professionals, providing relevant information about the activities occurred during playing. Moreover, parents can be informed at any time about children's behavior and performance during play. The system, apart from the initial knowledge about children's characteristics, continuously gathers and stores information about children's skills and abilities (i.e., interaction data) through the use of smart games in a predetermined protocol. The system analyzes this set of data and makes the results available back to the smart games for adaptation purposes, and exposes them to parents or early childhood professionals.

In more details, the framework includes:

- A model of children development based on the ICF-CY model and the Denver-II assessment tool, aiming at early detection of deviations in children's development that needs to be further investigated and addressed if necessary.
- A reasoning mechanism for the automated extraction of child development knowledge, based on interaction monitoring, targeted to model relevant aspects of child's developmental stage, maturity level and skills.
- Content editing tools and reporting facilities for parents and early childhood professionals.

The framework has been implemented in the context of an AmI environment deploying a collection of augmented artifacts, including an augmented children's table, a smart chair, a smart pen, augmented digital dices etc., as well as augmented common physical artifacts such as puzzle pieces, wooden identity cards, toys, etc. Such artifacts are capable of monitoring child play so as to provide the necessary data to the Bean framework to detect progress but also deviation from age-related expectations in playing skills and performance [43]. The ambient set up also offers a collection of digital reproductions of popular games such as puzzles, card games, labyrinths/mazes, (the tower game, the farm game, the mimesis game, etc.), designed with the involvement of

HCI experts and occupational therapists, which can be played on a smart table specifically designed for children [42].

4.1 Bean Model: A Knowledge-Based Data Model

A knowledge base was designed and implemented to act as a centralized repository of information relevant to children's profile and characteristics, smart games, data extracted from the activity analysis process, and interaction history.

The underlying entity data model is called Bean model (see Fig. 2). Adopting the structure of the ICF-CY, the top entity of the Bean model provides information (e.g., title) about each used ICF-CY component, such as body functions and activities.

The subset of skills and abilities selected as the target of the proposed monitoring and evaluation functionality was discussed and elaborated in collaboration with early childhood professionals. Such skills and abilities regard various ICF-CY codes of Activities and Participation) that a smart game may require. Each activity involves a number of body functions and this is reflected in the model through linking activities to the related body functions. Further properties stemming from ICF-CY are used to describe in more detail both activities and body functions. The Denver II scale is imported in the model in order to provide relevant information about expected child's capacity in selected activities. The entity representing expected capacity by age contains Denver II's scale data (i.e. age, capacity) that reflects the percentage of a certain age group able to perform the connected activity. Table 1 depicts a representative sample of the initial subset of activities and the involved body functions.

In the context of interaction monitoring, it is essential to model human tasks that a child may execute during play as reactions to system output.

Similarly, the Bean model describes system tasks regarding the employed communication functionality (both for input and output) between the user and the system (Table 2). Through the augmentation of everyday objects and the implementation of a novel sensory infrastructure [41], in the AmI environment a smart game is able to monitor and evaluate the play performance for selected required activities. These activities are categorized into general or specific according to the significance or impact they may have in child's play performance. Required activities are linked to: (a) the corresponding smart game, (b) the actual ICF-CY activity, (c) a subset of the activity's associated human tasks that may carry further description to define more accurately the user interactions during playing (with the corresponding smart game), and (d) a set of the employed system tasks required for the implementation of a certain smart game. A one-to-many relationship is established between required activities and a detailed description of a required activity's human tasks that may occur during playing a selected game. Similarly, a one-to-many relationship is established between required activities and system tasks.

The model also encodes the monitoring results during playing in a performance record. The latter is responsible to estimate the child's play performance in each required activity according to the current gameplay. In detail, the record contains an estimated score of child's play performance for a selected required activity within the

Table 1. Example of activities, expected capacity per age and body functions

ICF-CY Activities		Expected capacity				Involved body functions
		3y	4y	5y	6y	
Applying knowledge	**d1601**, Focusing attention to changes in the environment	25	50	75	100	**b1400** Sustaining attention
						b1401 Shifting attention
	d161, Directing attention	25	50	75	100	**b140** Attention functions
						b1400 Sustaining attention
						b1401 Shifting attention
						b1402 Dividing attention
						b1403 Sharing attention
	d130, Copying	25	50	75	100	**b147** Psychomotor functions
						b163 Basic cognitive functions
Basic learning	**d131**, Learning through actions with objects	25	50	50	100	**b760** Control of voluntary movement functions
						b1565 Visuospatial perception
						b163 Basic cognitive functions

Table 2. Modeled system tasks interfacing user for both input and output

1 Gesture/Posture recognition - (system input)	2. Presentation of still images – (system output)
3. Head pose estimation using – (system input)	4. Presentation of audio – (system output)
5. Face tracking – (system input)	6. Presentation of text – (system output)
7. Skeleton tracking – (system input)	8. Presentation of animation – (system output)
9. Speech recognition – (system input)	10. Presentation of video – (system output)
11. Physical object recognition – (system input)	12. Presentation of speech – (system output)

(Continued)

Table 2. (*Continued*)

13. Cursor recognition (Multitouch) - (system input)	14. Sign language - (system output)
15. Force pressure recognition at the interaction surface - (system input)	16. Braille; tactile writing system - (system output)
17. Force pressure recognition while sitting – (system input)	18. Other assistive devices for people with hearing, voice, speech, or language disorders
19. Force pressure recognition at the pen's tip – (system input)	20. Other assistive technologies for people with visual disorders
21. Motion sensing cube (e.g. dice) - (system input)	

range 0–100. Playing sessions are modeled as the time interval during which a child plays a specific game.

The basic user profile contains demographic user data as well as user roles in the system (such as child, parent, child development expert, administrator, etc.).

Children profiles are linked to: (a) sessions, (b) activity limitations, which refer to a list of activities in which the child has limitations, and (c) body functional limitations, which refer to a list of body functions in which the child faces (functionality) problems. Moreover, children profiles are linked to the respective parents' and professionals profiles. Finally, smart games are modeled and linked to a list of activities required for playing with a selected smart game and a list of sessions during which the game was played. The Bean Model is delivered with a software suite which provides content administration facilities and monitoring utilities suitable for use by early childhood professionals and parents.

4.2   Reasoning Mechanism

Child development monitoring is facilitated through a reasoning mechanism built upon the Entity Framework to access the Bean model. During play, the selected smart game is responsible to monitor and evaluate child's play performance and commit a representative score (range 0–100) to the reasoning mechanism. The latter monitors and assess child's maturity at the various levels of a selected smart game. In detail, it collects and analyzes the child's play performance commitments regarding specific and general activities required for the active game level and makes appropriate adaptation suggestions back to the smart game.

Activity analysis is based on the identification of the tasks which are involved during young children's play. Task monitoring (when applicable) may result into the measurement of the play performance and capacity which, in comparison with Denver II scale's expected scores, can drive to the extraction of useful indications about young children's development.

Play Performance is a measurement concept that describes what tasks a child performs while playing in a specific context and environment [41]. **Capacity**, on the other hand, indicates the highest probable level of functioning that a child may reach in the ICF-CY domain of Activities and Participation at a certain moment [41]. Capacity is measured in a standard environment, in order to reflect the environmentally adjusted ability of the individual. In summary, a capacity qualifier specifies what a child can do independent of context, i.e., in a standardized environment, whereas a performance qualifier specifies what a child does in a current environment, i.e., functional skills used in everyday life situations [25].

Data are collected from the first playing session of a game and repeatedly after some period of time, i.e., after one month or after a number of sessions. Through statistical analysis the reasoning mechanism extracts the current child's capacity in the execution of various activities and estimates the developmental rate based on the entire interaction history (i.e., play performance commitments). The analysis is conducted using time series forecasting methods (i.e., weighted moving average). The recorded data are imported to the time series in order to generate the developmental curve of the targeted specific activity of the currently active game level. In the weighted moving average model, every play performance value is weighted with a factor from a weighting group. Thus, recent data have greater influence. This approach was chosen because more recent play performance data are more representative and reliable than older data. Therefore, the reasoning mechanism is able to react more appropriately to a change in the play performance during playing. The accuracy of this method depends largely on the choice of the weighting factors which were determined with the help of early childhood professionals. The selected factors are $W_{15} = 15$, $W_{14} = 14 \ldots W_1 = 1$. The capacity of a required activity (AC) is the product of the following formula

$$AC = \frac{\sum_{t=1}^{n} W_t \times V_t}{\sum_{t=1}^{n} W_t}$$

where Wt is the weighting factor, Vt is the value of the play performance, n is the number of the weighting factors ($n = 15$) and AC is the average value representing the child's capacity to execute a required activity.

Based on the analysis' results, the reasoning mechanism is able to identify children whose play performance deviates significantly from the average of their age. Based on the result, a smart game can adapt to the child's evolving skills so as to choose the most appropriate level according to child's estimated abilities.

4.3 Reporting Facilities

Indications of the achieved maturity level and skills of the child are provided in reports to parents and early childhood professionals. These reports contain information about the child's capacity to execute the activities involved during game playing. Low capacity scores may be an indication of a functional difficulty that a child may have in a given developmental area. Capacity indicators are reported according to data collected at certain points in time, child's age, and degree of independent completion of the game or some specific tasks.

Two types of report are supported, a basic one for parents (see Fig. 3) and an extended one for early childhood professionals. Both types of report include child's profile characteristics such as impairments, system factors (information of the environmental factors in which the data has been collected), history of interaction (number of session, total number of sessions for the smart game, etc.), overall capacity according to age standards and the completion of the predefined levels (measured playing without help), level in game, explanation of the graphical representation specifying the level of difficulty encountered by the child in each task (no difficulty, slight/mild difficulty, moderate/medium difficulty, high/severe difficulty), and recommendations if the child reaches score values below age level.

The professional's report additionally contains information regarding child's performance in tasks or activities during a playing session. Performance data is collected throughout a session, and also contains information about the amount and the type of system guidance and the assistance that the child has been provided.

5 A Case Study: The Tower Game

Various smart games for pre-school children have been designed and developed to showcase, test and validate the Bean framework [41]. For example, the Tower Game [44] has been designed based on sound developmental theories and the definition of expected skills and tools [19, 32].

The Tower Game supports playing through tangible interaction with augmented artifacts. More specifically, the game allows children to learn, identify and compare six different colors on each side of a smart dice with those illustrated on the path of the game.

Some of the body functions involved in Tower Game are: (a) mental functions related to color discrimination and symbols representation of numbers, pictures and other visual stimuli, as well as to visual spatial perception and processing of acoustic

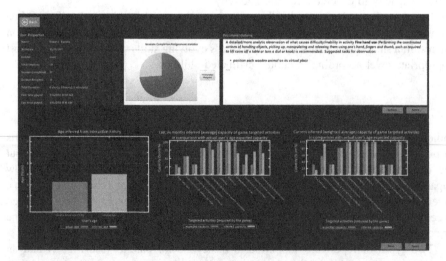

Fig. 2. Bean report for parents

stimuli, (b) mental functions involved in gaining knowledge about the use of objects and the organization and application of that knowledge in tasks, (c) mental functions to produce coordinated and targeted movements, (d) mental functions related to numeracy and writing, (e) higher level mental functions related to attention, thought processing, decision making, time management, space orientation, organization and planning functions, and (f) voice and speech functions. The performance skills of the game include: (a) remaining seated for a required period of time, (b) listening to spoken messages and responding properly, (c) responding to system instructions on time, (d) using various plain and smart objects necessary for playing the game, (e) locating and observing interactive virtual tiles of the maze and other pictures or visual elements, (f) handling objects in a coordinated fashion, (g) pointing an index finger onto virtual tiles in proper direction, (h) learning concepts such as colors and numbers, (i) learning to execute integrated sets of actions so as to follow rules and to sequence and coordinate movements, intentionally maintaining attention to specific actions or tasks for an appropriate length of time, (j) comprehending and responding to the messages conveyed by visual stimulus, drawings and pictures, and (k) ordering and counting.

The game is organized into four levels, each targeting a specific age range within 3–6 years old, following the performance expectations of child's play development. The difficulty of each level is adjusted according to developmental standards, while runtime adaptation is provided based on the child's estimated level of performance. In this way, the digital version of the game extends the age range supported by the original one.

The game is played using a smart dice, a smart custom-made pen and smart cards on a touch-sensitive surface small table specifically designed for pre-school children. In more details, the child rolls the colored dice and moves forward until he reaches the first tile of the same color. If the performed action is correct, he rolls the dice again and continues the previous procedure. If the dice roll is white, a card appears in a random position to which the young child should move. In case he reacts correctly, the card will be added to a staple of similar cards next to the display. The last tile of the path represents the entrance into the tower, however if the player rolls too high, he has to move backwards. The round is over when the rolling result is the exact color or number needed to enter the tower and simultaneously, the player has gathered all the cards. If the child enters at the tower while some cards are missing, he has to continue playing by rolling the dice again.

Fig. 3. Playing the tower game on bean table

Play performance in Tower Game is monitored and evaluated through the Bean framework, and appropriate adaptations are fed back to the game. In this way, the game can adapt to the child's evolving skills so as to choose the most appropriate level according to child's estimated abilities. For recording the play performance and player's abilities during interaction, predefined sets of activities for each level are used for elaborating the skills needed for to play the game efficiently.

A preliminary user-based evaluation of the framework has been conducted with the involvement of fourteen children, their parents, two occupational therapists, a psychologist and a special education teacher [41]. The evaluation mainly focused on the usability and playability of a number of games developed using the Bean framework, including the Tower Game, and was conducted though observation and picture cards for facilitating children in expressing their opinions. While the children were playing, parents and experts were observing from an observation room set-up in a remote location. In this observation space, a projector was projecting live video from the evaluation space, while a personal computer was showing information regarding the current play performance achieved by the child. The children were encouraged to play freely without any external interventions by adults. After each evaluation session, children, parents and early intervention professionals were required to fill in a posttest questionnaire developed separately for each user group. The experts completed their questionnaire after the completion of all the evaluation sessions. Despite the limited number of participants, interesting results were obtained which confirmed the validity of the Bean model and of the reasoning mechanism towards adequately capturing and following child development. In more details, for all children, the maturity levels detected by the system were consistent with the expectations of their parents and the judgment of the involved experts, while for two of them the system was able to correctly identify some skill immaturities potentially related to learning difficulties. A more extensive assessment of the framework on a larger scale is currently planned to further validate the validity of the results.

6 Conclusions and Future Work

Ambient Intelligence offer new opportunities to support young children development through play. To this end, this paper has presented a novel framework based on occupational therapy's expertise aiming at early detection of children's potential delays to be further investigated and diagnosed if necessary. The framework is composed of a model of children development based on the ICF-CY model and the Denver-II assessment tool, aiming at early detection of children's potential delays, a reasoning mechanism for the automated extraction of child development knowledge, based on interaction monitoring, as well as content editing tools and reporting facilities for parents and therapists. To the best of the authors' knowledge, the proposed framework is unique insofar it supports modeling and reasoning about children as users in Ambient Intelligence environments and embeds occupational therapy and child development knowledge for improving the playing experience of young children and supporting parents in following children's development. The framework has been implemented in the context of an AmI environment deploying a number of augmented physical artifacts, natural interaction techniques and a collection of purposefully designed digital reproductions of popular games.

Planned future work concerns the extensive assessment of the framework validity through testing with mixed group of children with and without diagnosed difficulties.

Acknowledgments. This work is supported by the FORTH-ICS internal RTD Programme 'Ambient Intelligence and Smart Environments'.

References

1. Adamson, L.B., Bakeman, R.: Viewing variations in language development: the communication play protocol. Augmentative Altern. Commun. **8**, 2–4 (1999) (Newsletter for ASHA Division 12)
2. Baranek, G.T., Barnett, C., Adams, E., Wolcott, N., Watson, L., Crais, E.: Object play in infants with autism: methodological issues in retrospective video analysis. Am. J. Occup. Ther. **59**(1), 20–30 (2005)
3. Bosse, T., Both, F., Gerritsen, C., Hoogendoorn, M., Treur, J.: Methods for model-based reasoning within agent-based ambient intelligence applications. Knowl. Based Syst. **27**, 190–210 (2012)
4. Bricker, D.D., Squires, J., Potter, L.W., Twombly, R.E.: Ages and Stages Questionnaires (ASQ): A Parent-Completed, Child-Monitoring System. Paul H. Brookes Publishing CO, Baltimore (1999)
5. Casas, R., Blasco Marín, R., Robinet, A., Delgado, A.R., Yarza, A.R., McGinn, J., Picking, R., Grout, V.: User modelling in ambient intelligence for elderly and disabled people. In: Miesenberger, K., Klaus, J., Zagler, W.L., Karshmer, A.I. (eds.) ICCHP 2008. LNCS, vol. 5105, pp. 114–122. Springer, Heidelberg (2008)
6. Clarke, A.M.: Young children and ICT-current issues in the provision of ICT technologies and services for young children. ETSI White Paper, No. 2 (2006)
7. Cooper, B., Brna, P.: Hidden curriculum, hidden feelings: emotions, relationships and learning with ICT and the whole child. Paper presented at the BERA conference, Exeter, September 2002
8. Costello, J., Ali, F.: Reliability and validity of peabody picture vocabulary test scores of disadvantaged preschool children. Psychol. Rep. **28**(3), 755–760 (1971)
9. Czyzewski, A., Odya, P., Grabkowska, A., Grabkowski, M., Kostek, B.: Smart Pen– New multimodal Computer Control Tool for Dyslexia Therapy. Gdansk University of Technology, Multimedia Systems Department, Poland (2010)
10. De Carolis, B., Pizzutilo, S., Palmisano, I.: D-Me: personal interaction in smart environments. In: Brusilovsky, P., Corbett, A.T., de Rosis, F. (eds.) UM 2003. LNCS, vol. 2702, pp. 388–392. Springer, Heidelberg (2003)
11. Fisher, K., Hirsh-Pasek, K., Golinkoff, R.M., Singer, D.G., Berk, L.: Playing around in school: implications for learning and educational policy. In: Pellegrini, A.D. (ed.) Oxford Handbook of the Development of Play. Oxford University Press, Oxford (2011)
12. Frankenburg, W.K., Dodds, J.B.: The denver developmental screening test. J. Pediatr. **71**(2), 181–191 (1967)
13. Frankenburg, W.K., Dodds, J., Archer, P., Shapiro, H., Bresnick, B.: The denver II: a major revision and restandardization of the denver developmental screening test. Pediatrics **89**(1), 91–97 (1992)

14. Frankenburg, W.K.: Developmental surveillance and screening of infants and young children. Pediatrics 109(109), 144–145 (2002)
15. Granlund, M., Eriksson, L., Ylven, R.: Utility of the international classification of functioning, disability and health participation dimension in assigning ICF codes to items for extant rating instruments. J. Rehabil. Med. 36(3), 130–137 (2004)
16. Hayes, G.R., Gardere, L.M., Abowd, G.D., Truong, K.N.: CareLog: a selective archiving tool for behavior management in schools. In: Conference on Human Factors in Computing Systems (CHI 2008), pp. 685–694. ACM Press, Florence, Italy (2008)
17. Heckmann, D., Schwartz, T., Brandherm, B., Schmitz, M., von Wilamowitz-Moellendorff, M.: Gumo – the general user model ontology. In: Ardissono, L., Brna, P., Mitrović, A. (eds.) UM 2005. LNCS (LNAI), vol. 3538, pp. 428–432. Springer, Heidelberg (2005)
18. Hewes, J.: Let the children play:nature's answer to early learning. Ph.D. Chair of the Early Childhood Education Program, Grant MacEwan College, Alberta, Canada (2006)
19. Hurlock, E.B.: Child Growth and Development. Tata McGraw-Hill Education, New Delhi (1978)
20. Jameson, A., Krüger, A.: Preface to the special issue on user modelling in ubiquitous computing. User Model. User-Adap. Interact. 15(3–4), 193–195 (2005)
21. Kalliala, M.: Play Culture in a Changing World. Open University Press, Berkshire (2006)
22. Kientz, J.A., Abowd, G.D.: KidCam: toward an effective technology for the capture of children's moments of interest. In: Tokuda, H., Beigl, M., Friday, A., Brush, A.J.B., Tobe, Y. (eds.) Pervasive 2009. LNCS, vol. 5538, pp. 115–132. Springer, Heidelberg (2009)
23. Kientz, J.A.: Decision support for caregivers through embedded capture and access. Ph.D. thesis, College of Computing, School of Interactive Computing, Georgia Institute of Technology, Atlanta, GA, USA (2008)
24. Knobloch, H., Pasamanick, B., Sherard, E.S.: A developmental screening inventory. Department of Pediatrics and Department of Psychiatry, Ohio State University College of Medicine, Columbus, Ohio (1966)
25. Msall, M.E., Msall, E.R.: Functional assessment in neurodevelopmental disorders. In: Accardo, P.J. (ed.) Capute and Accardo's Neurodevelopmental Disabilities in Infancy and Childhood, 3rd edn, pp. 419–443. Paul Brookes, Baltimore (2007)
26. Kaklanis, N., Moschonas, P., Moustakas, K., Tzovaras, D.: Virtual user models for the elderly and disabled for automatic simulated accessibility and ergonomy evaluation of designs. Univ. Access Inf. Soc. 12(4), 403–425 (2013)
27. O'Hara, M.: Young children, learning and ICT: a case study in the UK maintained sector. Technol. Pedagogy Educ. 17(1), 29–40 (2008)
28. Piaget, J.: Main Trends in Psychology. George Allen & Unwin, London (1973)
29. Reynolds, P.C.: Play, language and human evolution. In: Bruner, J.S., Jolly, A., Sylva, K. (eds.) Play: Its Role in Development and Evolution, pp. 621–635. Basic Books, New York (1976)
30. Riva, S., Antonietti, A.: The application of the ICF CY model in specific learning difficulties: a case study. Psychol. Lang. Commun. 14(2), 37–58 (2010)
31. Salah, A.A., Schouten, B.A., Göbel, S., Arnrich, B.: Playful interactions and serious games. J. Ambient Intell. Smart Environ. 6(3), 259–262 (2014)
32. Salkind, N.J.: An Introduction to Theories of Human Development. SAGE Publications Inc, California (2004)
33. Sarama, J.: Technology in early childhood mathematics: Building Blocks as an innovative technology-based curriculum. State University of New York, Buffalo (2003)
34. Mulligan, S.E.: Occupational Therapy Evaluation for Children. Lippincott Williams & Wilkins. Philadelphia, Pennsylvania, USA (2003)

35. Stuberg, W.A., White, P.J., Miedaner, J.A., Dehne, P.R.: Item reliability of the Milani-Comparetti motor development screening test. Phys. Ther. **69**(5), 328–335 (1989)
36. Sylva, K., Bruner, J.S., Genova, P.: The role of play in the problem-solving of children 3–5 years old. In: Bruner, J.S., Jolly, A., Sylva, K. (eds.) Play: Its Role in Development and Evolution, pp. 244–261. Basic Books, New York (1976)
37. Turbill, J.: A researcher goes to school: using technology in the kindergarten literacy curriculum. J. Early Child. Literacy **1**(3), 255–278 (2001)
38. Westeyn, T.L., Abowd, G.D., Starner, T.E., Johnson, J.M., Presti, P.W., Weaver, K.A.: Monitoring children's developmental progress using augmented toys and activity recognition. Pers. Ubiquit. Comput. **16**(2), 169–191 (2012)
39. Westeyn, T.L., Kientz, J.A., Starner, T.E., Abowd, G.D.: Designing Toys with Automatic Play Characterization for Supporting the Assessment of a Child's Development. College of Computing, Georgia Institute of Technology, Atlanta (2008)
40. World Health Organization: ICF CY the International Classification of Functioning, Disability and Health for Children and Adolescents. CH, WHO Ed, Geneva (2007)
41. Zidianakis, E.: Supporting young children in ambient intelligence environments. Ph.D. Thesis, University of Crete (2015)
42. Zidianakis, E., Antona, M., Paparoulis, G., Stephanidis, C.: An augmented interactive table supporting preschool children development through playing. In: The Proceedings of the 2012 AHFE International Conference (4th International Conference on Applied Human Factors and Ergonomics), San Francisco, California, USA, pp. 744–753, 21–25 July 2012. [CD-ROM]. USA Publishing (ISBN 978-0-9796435-5-2)
43. Zidianakis, E., Partarakis, N., Antona, M., Stephanidis, C.: Building a sensory infrastructure to support interaction and monitoring in ambient intelligence environments. In: Streitz, N., Markopoulos, P. (eds.) DAPI 2014. LNCS, vol. 8530, pp. 519–529. Springer, Heidelberg (2014)
44. Zidianakis, E., Zidianaki, I., Ioannidi, D., Partarakis, N., Antona, M., Paparoulis, G., Stephanidis, C.: Employing ambient intelligence technologies to adapt games to children's playing maturity. In: Antona, M., Stephanidis, C. (eds.) UAHCI 2015. LNCS, vol. 9177, pp. 577–589. Springer, Heidelberg (2015)

Augmented Home Inventories

Konstantinos Grivas[1,2(✉)] and Stelios Zerefos[2]

[1] Department of Architecture Engineering, University of Patras,
Rio University Campus, 26 500 Patras, Greece
kgrivas@upatras.gr
[2] Department of Applied Arts, Hellenic Open University (HOU),
Parodos Aristotelous 18, 26 335 Patras, Greece
zerefos@eap.gr

Abstract. Normally, households comprise of people and their material possessions, where persons exercise exclusive agency. The digital augmentation of
domestic environment transforms the constitution of households, populating them
with new types of entities, namely connected and 'smart' objects/devices and distributed services. These new "players" operating within the household, are complex in
nature, responsive, adaptive, blurring the given distinction between household
members and their stuff, and evading a simplified classification. We consider the
augmented home environment as an ecosystem which humans occupy among other
interacting entities or parties which are actively affiliated to other networks and
environments. Starting with the premise that a household inventory is one way to
formally describe and define the household, we examine the contents and structure
of traditional home inventories, and then elaborate on the potential evolution of the
augmented home inventories as new types of interacting entities are introduced.
Thus, we observe a shift from static and place-bound to dynamic classifications,
allowing for diverse groupings of home-stuff. We contemplate on the possibility of
integrating all parts of the household ecosystem into one unified classification and
ontological system. We, also, acknowledge that the exponential growth of IoT will
put increasing pressure for managing the huge volumes of data generated from
connected households, on which an effective, meaningful, and socially compatible
classification system is required. Finally, we highlight several challenges to the
augmented home inventory.

Keywords: Home inventory · Augmented home · Home ecosystem · Home
ontology · Classification of home entities · AmI environments

1 Introduction

What belongs to the augmented household?[1] The relatively fixed ownership and agency
over things (right of usage and exchange), and their accumulation under the same "roof"
(home property), by and large, defined what usually comprised the household in terms

---

[1] The term 'augmented household' in the present text does not refer to a household including an
extended family, kin and non-relatives members, but to a technologically augmented household.

© Springer International Publishing Switzerland 2015
Kameas et al. (Eds.): AmI 2015, LNCS 9425, pp. 34–47, 2015.
DOI: 10.1007/978-3-319-26005-1_3

of its inanimate members.[2] In one way or another, home possessions – from the space and edifice to utensils, minute memorabilia, or collections – constitute a tangible image of home. Yet, the kinds or categories of things comprising a household have changed significantly during the last two centuries due to fundamental changes in manufacturing, distribution and consumption of material goods of daily use, as well as reflecting significant advances in everyday technologies, electronics, devices etc., which mark the departure for a new experience of the domestic environment, at least in the developed world. The industrial revolution and the subsequent rise of extensive consumerism (19th and 20th centuries) were reflected into the flooding of households with hundreds of new mass-produced goods, domestic machines, and automated environments. Not only the constitution of the household stuff changed, but we also witnessed its transition from a system of symbolic yet embodied relations between domestic objects themselves and their owners, to an increasingly abstract and integrated system of functionality and sociality never fully experienced and apprehended in the practical level by the families [1]. The end of 20th century innovations on ubiquitous computing and ambient intelligence, starting nowadays to diffuse into everyday life, bring intelligent, hybrid and connected devices, as well as immaterial (digital) and dislocated (away from home) home possessions. The new kinds of home possessions pose several challenges for their identification, listing, categorization, and description. A reviewed approach towards home inventories (augmented home inventories) that incorporate recent transformations/transmutations of home-stuff and its organization will possibly provide hints for a modified view of *home* itself.

2   Home Inventories: A Brief History

One way to formally describe the material aspects of the household has been, traditionally, to compile its full inventory [2]. Before examining how digitally augmented home-stuff differs from any conventional (purely material domestic objects and machines), it is useful to run through a brief historical evolution of home inventories. Comparing examples of available household inventories from the 17th century onwards allow us to draw a few basic conclusions regarding the changes in the kinds of home possessions, as well as the evolution in the methods of their categorization. For this purpose we selected to compare three different household inventories sources from different periods.

The complete inventory of Vermeer household (1676) [3]. It contains only 120 individual objects grouped in only 10 different categories (artworks, furniture, carpets and tapestries, linen and bed sheets, clothing, etc.). Objects are listed one by one and grouped according to the room of the house they are placed/found/stored. A second distinction divides the objects between those that are bequeathed to Vermeer's wife and those bequeathed to her mother. A schematic table of this inventory would be the one presented in Table 1.

---

[2] Though sometimes animals and plants are included in household inventories, and in the - not so distant – past, humans like slaves and servants also belonged to the household.

Table 1. Schematic Table of J. Vermeer home inventory (1676)

	Owner A	Owner B
Room #01	Item#01, item#02, ... item#x	Item#x+1, item#x+2, ...
Room #02	Item#01, item#02, ... item#x	Item#x+1, item#x+2, ...
Room #ν	Item#01, item#02, ... item#x	Item#x+1, item#x+2, ...

- The lists and categories of objects compiled by researchers of "The Meaning of Things" (1981) [4]. The American homes that were studied contained up to 41 different categories of things, which can be grouped into at least 27 different basic categories (in some cases subcategories appear, for example *bed* is considered as a different category than furniture, but it is actually a sub-category of furniture). We have no detailed record of specific home inventories (we know that 1694 objects were recorded), but the survey recorded objects according their place (room), their category and their owner. (This survey does not list all objects in the houses studied. It records only those that have specific meaning for the inhabitants. Some objects categories might be missing, e.g. nobody mentions cleaning and washing equipment or tools). A schematic table reflecting those inventories would be the one presented in Table 2.

Table 2. Schematic Table of home inventory from "The Meaning of Things" research (1981)

	Category#01	Category#02	...	Category#ν
Room #01	Item#01, ... #x	Item#x+1, #x+2, ...	...	Item#x+x+1, #x+x+2, ...
Room #02	Item#01, ... #x	Item#x+1, #x+2, ...	...	Item#x+x+1, #x+x+2, ...
Room #ν	Item#01, ... #x	Item#x+1 #x+2, ...	...	Item#x+x+1, #x+x+2, ...

The list of objects included in the template from a contemporary home insurance company, randomly selected out of many available online today (2014) [5]. This contains up to 125 different kinds of home possessions which can be grouped into at least 44 distinct basic categories. In the above example, as in most others of the kind, home possessions are listed according to the room they belong (following a seemingly standard practice) but other attributes are also recorded such as purchase details, value, owner etc. More attributes can be introduced at will (especially in digital versions). So if the schematic table for this inventory may look like the previous one (Table 2), there are also complimentary ways to categorize household items attaching other related information about them as the ones presented in Table 3.

A first observation drawn from a comparison of the above home inventory examples is that the categories of home-stuff have changed and substantially increased as homes during the 20th century were gradually equipped with new kinds of products and appliances. This confirms a commonly shared belief that we live among more stuff and of a greater diversity than older generations did. Secondly, the listing of home stuff and their categorization follows a seemingly established rule: possessions are primarily identified

Table 3. Schematic list of items with related information attached

Item	Description	When/Where purchased	Make/Model
TV	27" Color	ABC Electronics, 1995	Panasonic, srl # 1234567
Rug	Antique Turkish 6' × 8'	Anniversary gift 1991	
Computer	Toshiba laptop	ABC Electronics, 2004	

by the room which they normally belong to, or placed/stored in (living room, kitchen, bedroom, basement, etc.), and secondly by their kind (clothing, tableware, etc.); a third categorization refers usually to the owner. Thirdly, as the diversity of household possessions increase, and the home inventory is furnished with more complicated objects (machines, devices and electronics), more information about those objects is considered useful to be included in the inventory, which do not just serve for an insurance cover claim, but help a good management and maintenance of the household stuff. This extra information makes it possible to categorize objects in alternative ways (e.g. size, value, date of acquisition, brand, warranty and maintenance details, etc.).

However, these are marginally meaningful categorizations, or at least unusual as an ordinary description of the constitution of the household, which is primarily based on a listing of rooms with their contents; the first clue (beyond its name) given about any of the home-stuff is its place within an orderly clustered environment. The basic premise to be highlighted here is that *home* and especially the *household*, remain, in the common experience, largely structured around the boundaries and enclosures set by architectural space, that is rooms and all sorts of storage furniture. This, in its turn, is telling enough for the space of house itself, which is viewed as a space where objects have a place to be stored or used in it, so one could rightly assume that home space serves as the classification system of home objects. All of the above home inventories are itemized lists of material home possessions. The persons of the household and information about them are not part of the inventory, or appear as implicit information (suggested by number of children rooms, maid's room, the dog-house, etc.). Other kinds of valuable possessions contained in the house, but without material presence or significance (e.g. documents and their content) are usually absent and not individually recorded, either because they usually lack commodity value, or because they are "packed" within larger groups of similar stuff (e.g. a folder with legal documents, a photo album).

3   New Household Items

How is the nature of the things that comprise the augmented household different than those found in existing homes? How this is reflected on the way one identifies, categorizes and refers to the augmented household things?

The case of digital files classification is especially indicative. The most common categorization of digital files follows the "container – object" structure, where the storage location of the file, described by the file *path,* is the most concrete instance. Yet, many alternative categorizations can apply and are indeed more useful, based on size, type, date, and many other attributes tagged onto digital files. The storing structure of digital files (path) is in its essence a topological replication based on levels of abstraction applied to populations of objects, much like the physical practice of sorting home objects described previously (e.g. house > room > wardrobe > drawer > object). However, the rigidity of the identification of a digital file through its path is rarely reflected in the ways this file:

a. exists; exact copies of the same file appear with different names in completely different locations,
b. evolves; the case of dynamic digital files where successive instances of the file are stored,
c. appears; there can be multiple appearances of the same file depending on the application it is opened,
d. is used; digital tasks usually involve simultaneous handling of files from completely different sources on the same display surface,
e. is shared; instances of the same file shared simultaneously in many different locations, and
f. is stored; chunks of the same file stored at different parts of the disk, in a piecemeal way.

Hence, it is the nature of digital files and of their uses that totally subverts a rigid, static and unique way of container – object type of classification. A digital object can participate simultaneously in as many groups and categories as needed, while the placement of physical objects within an ordered space[3] is exclusive of other simultaneous instances. Newer systems for classifying digital files such as *tagging* enable us to group and retrieve them in far more flexible and personalized way, identifying and naming categories as we like (folksonomy), and finally adapt and change far more easily than hierarchical classification systems [6]. The population of home with digitally connected devices and networks and the dissemination of IoT, which create intricate ties between material objects and data, bring forward the need to reflect on the possibility and purposefulness of a unified classification system.

In a short design experiment, named "House of Today", we created a hypothetical new inventory for a concept house, designed and built by Alison and Peter Smithson, "The House of the Future" [7], consisting of networked items and several applications that would cater for the everyday life of a couple of contemporary design and technology conscious urban inhabitants [8]. This hypothetical new inventory is superimposed to the existing household. The inventory is comprised entirely out of currently commercially available connected devices and applications. This proposed inventory caters domestic "needs" such as health care and monitoring, body caring, security and surveillance, connectivity and communication, recreation and leisure, management and advice on cooking or other domestic tasks, energy consumption monitoring, weather monitoring and overall environmental awareness.

---

[3] However chaotic, home spaces are always underpinned by a certain order.

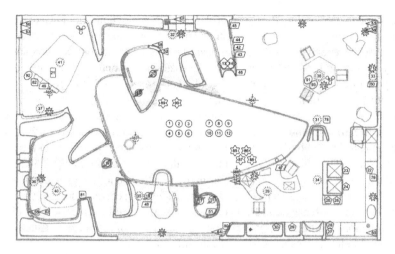

Fig. 1. "House of Today" plan view (based on the plan view of Smithsons' "House of the Future" with the new connected inventory.

The new inventory consists of 93 different devices, appliances, gadgets, applications, belonging into 15 basic categories, specifically: (1) wearables, (2) portables, (3) hubs, (4) bath, (5) sleep, (6) kitchen, (7) climate control, (8) electronics and media, (9) surveillance and security, (10) sensing, (11) lighting, (12) smart sockets, (13) robots, (14) plants, and (15) miscellaneous. As easily noted, these are categories formed with no single criterion; others refer to size and others to type, functionality, activity, task or location. So, some of those loosely formed categories have same type objects but dispersed location (e.g. lighting), and others have diverse devices in scale and functionality but accommodating a specific task or activity (e.g. cooking, surveillance, energy monitoring). Most of those things do find some specific and relatively permanent place inside home (e.g. thermostats, surveillance cameras, intelligent kitchen appliances, and other), but it seems insufficient to simply suggest a general categorization on rooms and their contents, simply because items like non-localized online applications, and portable or wearable devices as well as robots can roam around the house freely (Fig. 1: objects from 1 to 12 in the centre are actually "location-less" objects). More baffling is the fact that some of these new items have multiple functions/functionalities, and hybrid typologies, so one might fail to categorize them according to function or use (e.g. a smart toilet functions as toilet, but also as a health monitoring device; a smart showerhead sprinkles water as well as monitors water usage and waste, and showering behavior. So, one has to decide which is the primary function of an object, as opposed to its other secondary functions. Although traditional home items often had multiple usages, their primary function used for identification was not contested (e.g. a kitchen knife could be used also in gardening, but that wouldn't categorize it formally in the group of gardening tools). In the case of smart devices with ambiguous functionalities, having generic form and able to perform various tasks, the categorization is even more uncertain, depending on the activity they participate and open to manipulation by the inhabitants.

We found that compiling the inventory of the augmented household in a manner that is compatible with a casual and common understanding of the relations between things inside the house, ended feeling like a haphazard method. On the contrary, when we tried to apply a more consistent system of categorization and ontology, the process was puzzling and mystifying, with dubious results concerning our initial goal of compatibility with the structuring and experience of actual objects in place. Generally, we observed that we instinctively tend to categorize connected domestic devices, putting emphasis each time on their most prominent or meaningful for everyday life attribute. For example, *lights* emphasize on their function = to produce light, whatever technology they use to do it. The category *lighting* includes all devices that produce or control lights inside the house. *Portable devices* support many functions but their primary attribute is not function but size: they can be carried around. *Sensors* receive all sorts of stimuli and translating it into information. Their emphasis is not specific function (for different sensors function in different ways, translating different stimuli) but their functionality: their general help in translating stimuli into information. *Kitchen* or *bath devices* are mostly identified as such for mainly supporting in various ways specific activities: *cooking* and *bathing*, and at the same time because they clustered in or around the same area. *Robots* form a distinct category based on typological difference. And so on. All of the above devices share other functions, functionalities and many secondary attributes.

4   Emerging Home Entities and Societies

The augmentation of environment is transforming the constitution of households, adding new types of entities that belong to it, apart from connected objects/devices. In the traditional house people actively interact with each other and implicitly through the manipulation of inert things and space. The owners of the household have – and there is not sufficient evidence that this is challenged – the primary agency over the entire household. Although inert things and the environment do have implicit agency over the household, this is not active or purposeful. Augmenting technologies create composite objects and other types of entities that are active and responsive and have a high or low reasoning. They, also, create active and adapting societies of things. In an augmented home scenario – a case of an AmI environment – the privilege of explicit agency enjoyed by the inhabitants is distributed to a wider array of "parties", as decision making, even if it is at the lowest level, is exercised and shared by multiple agents.[4] This encourage us to consider the augmented home environment more in terms of an ecosystem[5] which humans, while being in charge, occupy among several other interacting entities or parties who form the home network participating, also, in other parallel networks on which the house is affiliated to. Other researches also align with similar approaches like the conceptualization of Ambient Ecologies (AE) which describes environments populated by smart, connected devices as identifiable clusters within the world wide web of things [9, 10].

---

[4] *Agents* here refer to the wide spectrum of responsive artifacts inside home.

[5] *Ecosystem* (definition): a system, or a group of interconnected elements, formed by the interaction of a community of organisms with their environment.

By speculating on the new types of things, entities and parties that constitute the augmented household, we ended up with a list of potential different types of entities. This list includes humans and other living organisms, software applications like AI agents or managers, hubs, nodes, complex devices, sensors, gadgets, to simple material objects and minute digital tags as well as digital files. An indicative list that is attempting to include most possible types of individual entities that comprise the augmented household is shown in Table 4.

Table 4. Indicative list of the types of augmented household entities, with a graphic suggestion of their population size.

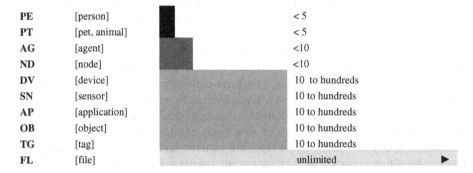

PE	[person]	< 5
PT	[pet, animal]	< 5
AG	[agent]	<10
ND	[node]	<10
DV	[device]	10 to hundreds
SN	[sensor]	10 to hundreds
AP	[application]	10 to hundreds
OB	[object]	10 to hundreds
TG	[tag]	10 to hundreds
FL	[file]	unlimited ▶

These entities are not expected to appear in equal populations within the house. Persons and pets rarely exceed the number of five members [11]. Similarly, it is unlikely that Agents, Nodes, Managers (devices) operating within a single household will exceed a limited number (less than 10). On the contrary, the populations of devices, sensors, applications, objects and tags may range from dozens to couple of hundreds, and finally, files (data/metadata) will easily gather in tremendous quantities.[6] The estimation of populations of each type is based on assumptions not grounded by research evidence at this point but reflects a common experience and logic. There can be of course diverse cases that do not conform to this logic. There is a pyramidal shape of the household entities, resembling an analogous distribution of members in natural ecosystems. As in the latter, higher class organisms or entities gather in lesser populations and the opposite. To question whether the above list of the types of augmented household entities and meta-entities is complete or not, misses the current point: the shift from a material/object/space-based static home order, to an interaction/connections/time/purpose-based dynamic home configuration (an ecosystem view) is clear. The dissemination of late technologies (bio/nano/AI-technologies) into everyday life is expected to produce newer types of home-stuff and more patterns for their interconnections. The apparent hierarchical vertical ordering of the entities

---

[6] In 2013 consumer generated data reached the volume of 2.9 trillion GB, and is anticipated to increase tenfold (X10) by the year 2020; that is roughly 380 Terabytes of data generated per person on the planet annually. With the current focus of IoT business on the domestic sector we may shortly see statistics concerning household generated data. Source: http://www.zdnet.com/article/the-internet-of-things-and-big-data-unlocking-the-power/.

(humans on top, tags and files at the bottom) is by no means a result of careful considera-tion, but only reflects a decreasing order of complexity, which may not align with the order of significance within the household.

Moreover, these individual parties can potentially team up together in order to form composite entities, small clusters or larger societies of same or different types of entities (e.g. PE + DV, DV + ND, OB + TG, PT + AG, DV + AP + ND, etc.). Yet, some of the combinations may have specific relevance to domestic life and could be identified as distinct types. Some of these may appear to be analogous to traditional parts of home (e.g. HOU [house] = the complete list of parties comprising the household joined together forms the house; the house can interact as an entity with other parties, or RM [room] = a portion of the house, not necessarily spatially defined, that supports a person or a set of activities, or has specific access rules or ownership; this can interact inde-pendently to house, or, FC [fence] = a virtual structure comprising of several parties – objects, devices, agents, etc. – that limits access or cuts off specific connections; example: 'energy waste fence', 'private data fence'). We can refer to them as *meta-entities*.[7] Endless possibilities for emerging meta-entities are opening up, but we cannot possibly speculate on which of those will achieve relevance and wider adoption.

It is exactly because of our speculation of the augmented home as an ecosystem, that issues concerning the classification of new home entities and societies arise. In an ecosystem mainly driven by interaction, the patterns and modes of interconnection between the different parties are the most essential attributes. It is possible then to decide on a classification of home stuff based on their connections. That means that clusters of things and entities, in general, will form not according to place (room) but according to connection or collaboration. The concept of Ambient Ecologies (AE) and Activity Spheres (AS) [9, 10] as well as the DomoML_env ontology prototype [12], are both attempts to investigate specific issues concerning ambient home ontologies (Fig. 2).

It is necessary to consider whether these new types of home entities – existing or hypothetical – listed above should be classified, hence referenced and related, under a unified classification system, analogous to the one providing detailed accounts about material home possessions – the home or household inventory.

We need to consider whether such a unified classification that contains all types of entities comprising the ecosystem of the household, from persons to data is meaningful. It seems that such an attempt draws similarities with older classifications of the worldly or heavenly things. In those, early classification systems, in medieval times, there were attempts to think of world as one container of a huge variety of beings and things (rocks, plants, animals, etc.) and present them in hierarchical order.

The clear division between objects (possessions) and subjects or agents (owners, inhabitants) that exists in a traditional home[8] is challenged. More or less active entities or combinations of them engage in higher or lower levels of decision taking around

---

[7] The distinction between home *entities* and *meta-entities* is analogous to the distinction between e.g. an individual ant and an ant-colony, or the distinction between a coral (already a colony) and a coral reef (a variety of organisms) in natural ecosystems.

[8] In all the text, the term 'traditional home' refers to the existing home in general, meaning 'not augmented home'.

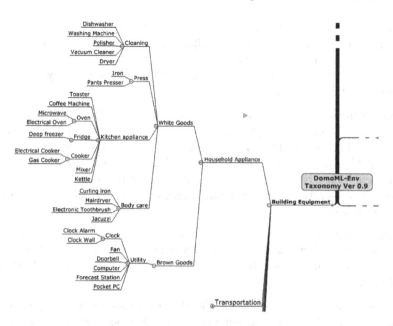

Fig. 2. Partial view of the ontology of DomoML-env, in Sommaruga, Lorenzo, Antonio Perri and Francesco Furfari, "DomoML-env: an ontology for Human Home Interaction", found at: http://ceur-ws.org/Vol-166/34.pdf

everyday domestic life. Communication between them, as well as the awareness of the situation at any given moment, requires a common exchange language and a possibility for mutual identification of the parties engaged. New types of home entities force us to think that we may need not only to expand the classification of home stuff [13] but also to reconsider its structure and, possibly, the formal or informal norms applied to naming, referring and describing home stuff.

A new type of home inventory or ontology might accommodate things that might not belong exclusively to the household, or things and assets that the household has access to and rights onto but are not integral. Perhaps, the revised "home inventory" is more like a dynamic record of the changing status of integral or peripheral home entities, and a continuous record of the transactions and exchanges.

It is always dangerous to delve into a system-oriented, logic-structured line of thought when dealing with this. A great amount of work that has been done during the past decades into intelligent environments and networks ontology is focusing on legibility and efficiency. We must not forget where this discussion started from. Home whatever that is, is more a personal and social construct. Computer language tends to objectify and quantify things. Everyday language is nuanced and informal.

5   Challenging the Home Inventory

The traditional household inventory was defined as a detailed, itemized list of material possessions, and recording of basic attributes and information about them, owned by a specific family or person, and housed/kept within in a specific place of residence. The augmented home concept poses several challenges to making home inventories that are operationally useful as well as meaningful as classification of home-stuff and other home entities. Concluding, there are several issues to be highlighted about augmented home possessions and their inventories:

Diversity of Home Possessions. While home inventories traditionally record material possessions (furniture, home appliances, objects, artwork, jewelry, etc.), it appears that the augmented home inventories may add to the lists items whose nature is different: immaterial (digital documents, information and files, media files, digital artifacts, personal settings and preferences), hybrid (physical objects with digital operations), or dynamic (digital agents,…), and composite entities created by societies of collaborating things and agents.

Suggestion. Categories need to expand to include many others, possibly bridging the distinction between living and inert members of the household. Description, also, of entities need to include more diversified information and links to related entities or related metadata.

Multiplied Possessions. It is anticipated that digital files such as videos, photographs, recordings and similar items containing memories about home and everyday life will increasingly belong to the category of "valued" multiple possessions. While material possessions can be also found in copies (12 identical plates) these are normally understood as a set, usually filed and stored together, or in groups (e.g. a set of plates, glasses, etc.) Digital files, on the other hand, may exist in several identical copies (back-ups for safety reasons), and could multiply infinitely. Copies are kept into different media (digital locations, e.g. different hard disks, even remote locations), and quite often each copy belonging to a different group, so listing a digital object should inform about all the locations and instances that the copies of this digital possession can be found at. A proper inventory should include these. *Suggestion*: inventories structured so that they show and link different instances of one entity.

Dynamic Home Possessions. While physical possessions are rather stable, digital possessions usually evolve through time, appearing in many different states. Digital entities (e.g. networks or societies of networked items) tend to change frequently. The home inventory itself (as a homely asset) is a good example. *Suggestion*: Inventories should become time specific, recording the constitution and state of the household at specific times or intervals. Differentiation between stable, continuously updated and non-present anymore items.

Meta-possessions. Analogous to metadata, meta-possessions are possessions about possessions. Statistics, Analyses, Visualizations, Mappings, and other types of digital files and digitally manufactured artifacts that are generated, usually automatically, by the combined use of other data and information could be equally classified as parts of the household, valued, and protected as such. *Suggestion*: The inventories should include meta-possessions in a way that provide meaningful and useful links between possessions and meta-possessions.

Dislocated Home Possessions. The assignment of specific place (e.g. room or cupboard) to household items is a basic rule for traditional home inventories. Yet the augmented home includes possessions and entities that are dislocated (e.g. intelligent agents that could operate externally to the house), or distributed (e.g. in many physical locations at the same time), or digitally located but physically distributed. *Suggestion*: in both the descriptive (lists, tables, records, etc.) as well as in the representational material (maps, visualizations) comprising the inventory, we might have virtual locations that are related in a comprehensive but distinct way to concrete physical locations.

Person-centric Possessions. The augmented home comprises of information and applications that are centered on specific persons, or generated by their actions and choices (environment settings, health status information and recordings). Logically, these meta-possessions are part of the augmented home inventory, but related and attached to specific persons and possibly regarded as private or sensitive information. *Suggestion*: Personal possessions might constitute a quasi-separate branch of the home inventory with specific protection and disclosure rules.

Prolific Data Files and Entities. The amassing material possessions has a certain natural limit (available physical space and expenditure resources), but this does not apply to immaterial possessions which can be gathering in tremendous pace and volume. The sheer amount of items to be recorded makes a complete view of the whole unobtainable. The updating of such an enormous list is equally compelling. Because of the tremendous number of digital possessions it is possible that in some instances we are more aware, and perhaps interested, of the general patterns of creating and storing digital possessions, than of the details of specific possessions. *Suggestion*: The augmented home inventory may provide intuitive search tools, using tags and keywords. It may also provide zoom-in and out views that expose the patterns of accumulation and categorization of home possessions, instead of the latter's particularities.

High Circulation and Sharing of Home Possessions. Material possessions rarely circulate in and out of the household; we lend home possessions, or share them less often than we give it away as exchange commodities or gifts. Digital possessions, on the other hand, tend to circulate in and out of the physical home much more freely and tend to be shared (e.g. torrent files), and it becomes difficult to monitor these transactions. *Suggestion*: Inventories should include mappings of the circulation and sharing of home possessions, with other households.

Ownership and Protection of Home Inventory Data. As it was mentioned earlier, possession, or more accurately ownership, of a household item, does not seem to be an absolute criterion for including or excluding the latter from the household inventory. At the same time, items belonging to traditional household inventories are usually protected (e.g. from theft or violation) by the house envelope or other device. Digital possessions are hard to safeguard and keep in private. What are the mechanisms for ensuring protection of this data? Are there degrees of ownership? *Suggestion*: Inventories of home possessions may portray the differentiated degrees of protection of home possessions, or otherwise the degrees of exclusive or shared ownership.

Activity and Usage Defined Inventories. Finally, traditional home inventories are often mere lists of material possessions, with an indication of their usual place inside home, for use, display or storage. This simple form of inventory is indifferent as to if, how, and when (or how frequently) these material possessions are being used. It is also quite straight forward to infer the activity one engages in when using certain objects. Moreover, material possessions occupy physical space so there is a limit to the sheer number of material possessions that can be accumulated in a household, while even unused and abandoned items do have a certain perceptible place that cannot be entirely forgotten. The population of home inventories with digital entities and possessions that can be dislocated or multiply present, can contribute to different activities, accumulate in far greater numbers than physical possessions, and can literally disappear and stay out of use in obscure digital paths challenges the meaningfulness of the old form of home inventories. *Suggestion*: Augmented home inventories can pursue different form of home-stuff categorization based on activities and usage. One can identify (or search) for a possession according to where or when, or how frequently it has been used, so the home-stuff categorization may emerge out of the usage and activities patterns of daily use, rather than being (pre) defined by the place of keeping or storage (e.g. objects within *my* room), or by a typological definition (e.g. kitchenware, tableware, books, etc.) In this case, forgotten and unused possessions can be treated and presented precisely as such, simplifying perhaps the perception of the totality of home possessions.

6   Conclusions

Augmenting, ambient technologies are gradually altering the constitution of the average household, as well as the nature of home possessions. The augmented household is a more flexible and diversified construct than the traditional one. We observe a transition from a structure mainly defined by rooms and their contents to a categorization structured around spheres of activities and ecologies that support them. The paper attempts to outline the basic transformations concerning new types of home possessions, emerging home entities and the challenges concerning the augmented home inventory itself. We anticipate that home inventories will have more operational value in the digitally augmented home. Dynamic classificatory systems of home entities and stuff that highlight patterns of connections, activities and usage, that also present the evolution of the household, will provide more transparent and eligible views and representations of home. This will enable inhabitants to participate actively in co-authoring their home ecosystems, as well as reflect critically. Finally, the issues briefly elaborated in this paper provide a conceptual framework through which to develop further more specific research topics.

References

1. Baudrillard, J.: The System of Objects. Verso, UK (2006)
2. Hoskins, L.: Reading the inventory: household goods, domestic cultures and difference in England and Wales, 1841–81. PhD Thesis, Queen Mary University of London (2011)

3. http://www.johannesvermeer.info/verm/house/h-a-invent-ENG.htm
4. Csikszentmihalyi, M., Rochberg-Halton, E.: The Meaning of Things: Domestic Symbols and the Self. Cambridge University Press, Cambridge (1981)
5. http://www.rmiia.org/homeowners/Walking_Through_Your_Policy/Home_Inventory.asp and https://www.knowyourstuff.org/iii/viewOnlyNoLogin.html?page=front_take
6. Smith, G.: Tagging: People-Powered Metadata for the Social Web. New Riders, Berkeley (2008)
7. Risselada, M., Van Den Dirk, H. (eds.): Alison and Peter Smithson - from the House of the Future to a House for Today. 010 publishers, Netherlands (2004)
8. Grivas, K., Stelios, Z.: The map as a tool for identifying pervasive interactions in today's home. In: Streitz, N., Markopoulos, P. (eds.) Distributed, Ambient, and Pervasive Interactions. Lecture Notes in Computer Science, vol. 9189, pp. 36–48. Springer, Heidelberg (2015)
9. Kameas, A.: Ambient ecologies and activity spheres. In: Charitos, D., Theona, I. et al. (eds.) Proceedings of Kameas, Achilles, "Ambient Ecologies and Activity Spheres", Proceedings of Hybrid City 2 International Conference 2013 (2013)
10. Seremeti, L., Achilles, K.: Ontology-based representation of activity spheres in ubiquitous computing spaces. In: Sobh, T. (ed.) Innovations and Advances in Computer Sciences and Engineering. Springer Science + Business Media B.V., Netherlands (2010)
11. https://www.census.gov/prod/cen2010/briefs/c2010br-14.pdf, or the Household Composition Statistics by Eurostat (2011). http://ec.europa.eu/eurostat/statistics-explained/index.php/Household_composition_statistics, or the 2012 US pet ownership statistics. https://www.avma.org/KB/Resources/Statistics/Pages/Market-research-statistics-US-pet-ownership.aspx
12. Sommaruga, L., Antonio P., Francesco F.: DomoML-env: an ontology for Human Home Interaction. In: Proceedings of WEWST 2011, 6th International Workshop on Enhanced Web Service Technologies (2011)
13. Miller, D.: Stuff. Polity, Cambridge (2010)

Ambient Intelligence from Senior Citizens' Perspectives: Understanding Privacy Concerns, Technology Acceptance, and Expectations

Florian Kirchbuchner[1]([⊠]), Tobias Grosse-Puppendahl[1], Matthias R. Hastall[2], Martin Distler[3], and Arjan Kuijper[3]

[1] Fraunhofer Institute for Computer Graphics Research IGD,
Fraunhoferstr. 5, 64283 Darmstadt, Germany
`florian.kirchbuchner@igd.fraunhofer.de`,
`tobias.grosse-puppendahl@igd-extern.fraunhofer.de`
[2] Faculty of Rehabilitation Sciences, TU Dortmund University,
Emil-Figge-Str. 50, 44227 Dortmund, Germany
`matthias.hastall@tu-dortmund.de`
[3] Faculty of Computer Science, Technische Universität Darmstadt,
Hochschulstr. 10, 64289 Darmstadt, Germany
`arjan.kuijper@gris.informatik.tu-darmstadt.de`

Abstract. Especially for seniors, Ambient Intelligence can provide assistance in daily living and emergency situations, for example by automatically recognizing critical situations. The use of such systems may involve trade-offs with regard to privacy, social stigmatization, and changes of the well-known living environment. This raises the question of how older adults perceive restrictions of privacy, accept technology, and which requirements are placed on Ambient Intelligent systems. In order to better understand the related concerns and expectations, we surveyed 60 senior citizens. The results show that experience with Ambient Intelligence increases technology acceptance and reduces fears regarding privacy violations and insufficient system reliability. While participants generally tolerate a monitoring of activities in their home, including bathrooms, they do not accept commercial service providers as data recipients. A comparison between four exemplary systems shows that camera-based solutions are perceived with much greater fears than wearable emergency solutions. Burglary detection was rated as similarly important assigned as health features, whereas living comfort features were considered less useful.

Keywords: Privacy concerns · Older adults · Perception of privacy · Technology acceptance

1 Introduction

Facing the demographic change in Europe, the number of elderly increases constantly [6,11]. This poses enormous challenges on care systems, relatives, and

Kameas et al. (Eds.): AmI 2015, LNCS 9425, pp. 48–59, 2015.
DOI: 10.1007/978-3-319-26005-1_4

institutional caregivers. The need to reduce costs in health care conflicts with the wishes of elderly individuals to maintain personal freedom and social participation as long as possible. Ambient Intelligence can partly act as a solution to this problem by supporting people who are in need of care. It can also support caregivers and institutions in their daily routines. Such systems may communicate emergency situations to caregivers, for example, when a person falls down. Besides, safety features such as burglary detection, or convenience features such as automatic light controls, are of interest for this target group. Ambient Intelligence strongly relies on analyzing data perceived from a person's living environment. Especially when using cameras, privacy concerns are wide-spread. Moreover, people often do not accept wearing new and unknown devices. The same applies to interventions within the environment, such as when sensor-augmented carpets are deployed to detect emergency situations like falls. To some extent, the reluctance to accept technological innovations is a result of "wrongly designed technologies that have been developed without thinking about the real needs and capabilities of the users" [4].

Our new study, therefore, aims to shed light on the target group's expectations and fears related to innovations of ambient intelligence. We were particularly interested to learn which features and systems are perceived as most or least important, and which trade-offs between functionality and privacy are deemed acceptable. These in-depth insights into the needs and worries of potential users in Germany do not only extend our knowledge about elderly individuals' perspectives on Ambient Intelligence, they also suggest areas for more effective system development and marketing.

2   Related Work

The primary purpose of Ambient Intelligence in elderly care is the unobtrusive monitoring of persons in their home environment to detect critical situations (e.g. falls) as well as relevant changes in individuals' behavior and sleeping patterns [12,13]. Convenience and safety features also play an important role. The implicit recognition of emergency situations is often accompanied by possibilities to communicate information explicitly, as applied in traditional wearable emergency button systems. Typical features comprise fall detection, intruder alarm, stove and oven safety control, as well as automatic lighting [9,10]. In these cases, the overall goal is to enhance the independence of residents and to improve the quality of life. Most older adults indeed believe that Ambient Intelligence features would increase their quality of life [13]. Specifically fall detection, intruder alerts, and stove and oven safety controls were perceived as useful [5,8,9]. Two types of systems for senior citizens can be distinguished: personal systems, with wearable devices, and infrastructure systems that use sensors embedded in the room or the house [3]. Most in-home monitoring systems are infrastructure systems, as elderly people often reject wearable devices for fears of being stigmatized as frail or in need of special assistance [9]. While designed to aid older adults in gaining independence and being able to age in their own places, in-home monitoring is often seen as "designed for the oldest", and, as a result, are rejected

[2,7,13]. Other factors related to the refusal of Ambient Intelligence technologies include the ease of use, ergonomics, stigmatization, visibility of devices, and fear of false alarms [7,9,17]. Previous studies often examined only individual aspects of technology acceptance, or approached this topic from the perspective of nurses and expert groups. In contrast, the current study examines the expectations of potential end users, viz. elderly individuals in Germany, and uses standardized measures to compare individuals' attitudes and worries towards six specific features and four system types in greater depth, particularly with regard to safety concerns.

3   Methods

3.1   Sample

Sixty older adults and senior citizens (70 % female; age: $M = 67.7$, $SD = 8.3$, $Min = 48$, $Max = 84$) were recruited during special events for the elderly in September 2014. The first event was an information day for senior citizens (*Darmstädter Seniorentage*), the second one was a public talk about patient directives and living will. Respondents had the option of completing the paper-and-pencil questionnaire either immediately or later at home by themselves. Personal assistance to fill out the questionnaire was offered. Three gift certificates were raffled off among all participants as an incentive for participation.

3.2   Questionnaire Design

The questionnaire started with a section that informed the respondents about the purpose of the study and the measures taken to ensure the participants' anonymity. It also provided a brief explanation of Ambient Intelligence systems for the elderly.

Overall Attitudes Towards Innovations in Ambient Intelligence. Previous experience with Ambient Intelligence technologies was measured using a simple dichotomic scale (0 = "no", 1 = "yes"). Questions about the importance of certain assistive technology features (seven items), acceptable limitations (four items), and fears associated with the use of home-based assistive technologies (eight items) were measured using a five-point Likert scale (endpoint descriptions: 0 = "do not agree at all", 4 = "fully agree").

Comparisons of Six Ambient Intelligence Features. Previous studies have shown that features like fall detection or intruder alerts are considered as particularly useful [5,8,9]. Based on these studies, we selected a set of six features for evaluation with our senior participants. Besides the previously mentioned features, we also included use-cases in energy saving and disease detection. The questionnaire section included a short descriptions of the six features selected: (1) detection of emergency situations such as falls or accidents; (2) fall prevention (e.g., through automated room light control); (3) disease (e.g., dementia) detection through behavior monitoring; (4) energy-saving functionality through intelligent home control (e.g., automated heating control, or automated power supply shut-off if the apartment is empty); (5) burglary detection; and (6) living comfort features (e.g., automated light and heating control, reminders for medication, supply of health-related information). It was noted for all six features that data processing occurred solely inside the apartments and that no information was transmitted to other parties except in cases of emergencies. For each functionality, respondents indicated the extent that they would accept the recording of, as well as the transmission of, recorded information (ten items) and their overall acceptance (three items) on a five-point Likert scale (endpoint descriptions: 0 = "do not agree at all", 4 = "fully agree").

Comparisons of Four Systems. Four different systems were presented in the next part of the questionnaire with a brief verbal description: (1) a wearable one-button emergency call system (calls the number of a predefined person if activated and can be worn on the wrist or on the neck); (2) a camera-based in-home emergency detection system (to detect falls or unusual behavior); (3) a sensor-based floor emergency detection system (also to detect falls or unusual behavior); and a (4) comprehensive emergency detection solution consisting of floor sensors and a wristband (to detect emergency situations such as falls, unusual behavior, and problematic health conditions such as fever). Especially the expectations towards data handling are an important aspect as previous studies have shown that many seniors do not fully understand the technical concepts and thus underestimate potential privacy risks [1,3]. It was again noted for all four systems that data processing occurred solely inside the apartments and that no information was transmitted to other parties except in cases of emergencies. For each system, respondents indicated how much they were concerned about certain features (four items), acceptance of data collection while being in the bedroom or bathroom (two items) and general acceptance (two items) on a five-point Likert scale (endpoint descriptions: 0 = "do not agree at all", 4 = "fully agree").

Socio-Demographic Information. Socio-demographic characteristics such as respondents' gender, age, and living conditions were collected in the last part of the questionnaire.

4 Results

The data collected was analyzed using IBM® SPSS® version 22. Two-sided t-tests were conducted to determine if mean differences between male and female respondents, or between experienced and inexperienced individuals, were statistically significant ($p < .05$). Sidak-corrected post-hoc comparisons were conducted to determine if the means for the six features or the four systems differ significantly from each other ($p < .05$).

4.1   Importance of Ambient Intelligence Features

Ease of use, particularly in case of emergency, emerged as the most important feature, and the safety of data as the second important priority (see Table 1 for details). Places three to five referred to the affordability of the system (low running and maintenance costs, energy-saving design, and affordability of the system). The lowest priority was given to a constant visibility of the system and a high number of features. No differences were found between senior citizens with and without previous experience with assistive technologies. Ease of use, however, was significantly more important for female than for male respondents.

Table 1. Importance of system features. A rating of 0 corresponds to "I do not agree at all", while 4 corresponds to "I fully agree". $N = 60$. Depicted are means and, in brackets, standard deviations. Means sharing the same upper-case letter (gender) or lower-case letter (experience level) differ significantly (two-sided t test, $p < .05$).

	Overall (N = 60)	Respondents' gender		Previous experience	
		Male (N = 18)	Female (N = 42)	yes (N = 7)	no (N = 51)
System is easy to use, especially in cases of emergency	3.48 (.85)	3.06[A] (.87)	3.67[A] (.79)	3.29 (.76)	3.63 (.63)
System processes its data exclusively inside my apartment, and information is only shared in cases of emergency	3.31 (1.05)	3.56 (.70)	3.20 (1.17)	3.67 (.82)	3.33 (.99)
System produces low running or maintenance costs	3.19 (.86)	2.94 (.75)	3.29 (.89)	3.00 (.82)	3.27 (.75)
System is energyQsaving	3.17 (.85)	3.11 (.68)	3.20 (.93)	3.33 (.82)	3.22 (.76)
System is inexpensive to purchase	3.05 (.94)	2.94 (.73)	3.10 (1.02)	3.00 (.89)	3.12 (.86)
System is constantly visible	2.24 (1.07)	1.94 (.94)	2.37 (1.11)	2.17 (.98)	2.31 (1.05)
System provides many features	2.10 (1.20)	2.00 (1.19)	2.15 (1.22)	2.33 (.52)	2.10 (1.24)

4.2   Acceptable System Limitations

The necessity to change one's habits was deemed least acceptable, followed by the functionality of the system to identify which and how many persons are currently in the apartment (see Table 2). Whether other people could notice the use of assistive technologies was considered as least problematic. No significant differences were found between male and female respondents or between senior citizens with experience in using assistive technologies and those with no experience.

Table 2. Acceptable system limitations. A rating of 0 corresponds to "I do not agree at all", while 4 corresponds to "I fully agree". $N = 59$. Depicted are means and, in brackets, standard deviations. Means sharing the same upper-case letter (gender) or lower-case letter (experience level) differ significantly (two-sided t test, $p < .05$).

	Overall (N = 60)	Respondents' gender		Previous experience	
		Male (N = 18)	Female (N = 42)	yes (N = 7)	no (N = 51)
Okay if other people can see that I am using assistive technology	2.24 (1.30)	2.00 (1.19)	2.34 (1.35)	2.67 (1.03)	2.25 (1.31)
Okay if system can identify how many people are currently in my apartment	1.83 (1.28)	1.39 (1.20)	2.02 (1.27)	2.00 (1.41)	1.86 (1.27)
Okay if system can identify which persons are currently in my apartment	1.57 (1.27)	1.22 (1.11)	1.71 (1.31)	1.00 (.82)	1.69 (1.30)
Okay if I have to change habits to meet system requirements	1.15 (1.11)	.94 (1.00)	1.24 (1.16)	1.17 (.75)	1.18 (1.16)

4.3   Fears Associated with the Use of Ambient Intelligence Technologies

The greatest fear associated with the use of Ambient Intelligence technologies was the concern that criminals might misuse the collected data, followed by the fear that the system would not be sufficiently reliable (see Table 3). Moderate levels of fears were related to the possible transmission of inaccurate data, the monitoring of social interactions, the continuous monitoring, and the transmission of information to the wrong persons. The lowest causes for concern were the possibility that using the system would be too demanding or that its use would lead to a loss of independence. While no significant differences were found between male and female senior citizens in this regard, inexperienced respondents reported greater levels of concern than experienced senior citizens in four cases (fears of an unreliable system, of transmitting inaccurate information, of social interactions being monitored, and of constantly being monitored). This also resulted in a significantly greater overall fear score for this group.

4.4   Detailed Feature Comparison

The comparison between different features indicates that safety functionalities (emergency detection and burglary detection) are perceived as considerably more useful than disease detection and living comfort features. Fall prevention and energy savings features fell in between (see Table 4 for details). Particularly for burglary detection extra costs are accepted, while the acceptance is much less for living comfort features and disease detection functionality. The comfort

Table 3. Fears and worries associated with system use. A rating of 0 corresponds to "I do not agree at all", while 4 corresponds to "I fully agree". $N = 60$. Depicted are means and, in brackets, standard deviations. Means sharing the same upper-case letter (gender) or lower-case letter (experience level) differ significantly (two-sided t test, $p < .05$).

	Overall (N = 60)	Respondents' gender		Previous experience	
		Male (N = 18)	Female (N = 42)	yes (N = 7)	no (N = 51)
Fear that criminals will misuse the data collected by the system	2.32 (1.25)	2.44 (1.25)	2.27 (1.27)	2.50 (1.38)	2.33 (1.23)
Fear that the system will not be sufficiently reliable operating	2.22 (1.10)	2.33 (.97)	2.17 (1.16)	1.29^d (.95)	2.38^d (1.03)
Fear that the system transmits inaccurate or wrong information (e.g., false alarms)	2.15 (1.20)	2.28 (1.07)	2.10 (1.26)	.67^c (.52)	2.35^c (1.11)
Fear of constantly being monitored	2.03 (1.16)	2.28 (1.18)	1.93 (1.16)	1.29^a (.76)	2.16^a (1.16)
Fears that social interactions are being monitored (e.g., visits from friends)	2.12 (1.26)	2.39 (1.29)	2.00 (1.24)	1.17^b (.41)	2.25^b (1.26)
Fear that the system transmits information to the wrong people	2.02 (1.31)	2.06 (1.39)	2.00 (1.29)	1.43 (1.13)	2.12 (1.31)
Fear that system use will be too demanding or straining for me	1.73 (1.27)	1.83 (1.29)	1.69 (1.28)	2.00 (1.29)	1.71 (1.27)
Fear to lose my independence when using the system	1.41 (1.19)	1.83 (1.42)	1.22 (1.04)	1.17 (.98)	1.43 (1.20)
Overall fear score (mean)	2.00 (.93)	2.18 (1.08)	1.92 (.86)	1.45^e (.35)	2.09^e (.92)

functionality is also rated as significantly less likely to be used than the burglary detection feature.

Interestingly, no differences emerged between these features for five items relating to the recording of information. The only difference in this regard is that respondents are more likely to accept the recording of information while being in the living room or in the kitchen if the system serves for emergency detection in contrast to living comfort features. Despite, several differences between features were found regarding the transmission of information to external recipients. This was considered least acceptable for energy-saving functionality, but very acceptable for emergency and fall prevention functionality.

Table 4. Acceptance and overall assessment of six system features. A rating of 0 corresponds to "I do not agree at all", while 4 corresponds to "I fully agree". $N = 58$. Depicted are means and, in brackets, standard deviations. Means sharing the same upper-case letter differ significantly (Sidak-corrected multiple comparison, $p < .05$).

I find it acceptable if ...	Emergency detection feature	Fall prevention feature	Disease detection feature	Energy saving feature	Burglary detection feature	Living comfort feature
... the system records information while I am in the living room or in the kitchen	2.90^E (1.01)	2.60 (1.21)	2.48 (1.24)	2.40 (1.38)	2.58 (1.35)	2.33^E (1.15)
... the system records information while I am in the bedroom	2.58 (1.32)	2.47 (1.31)	2.43 (1.31)	2.17 (1.48)	2.66 (1.31)	2.15 (1.31)
... the system records information while I am in bathroom	2.54 (1.34)	2.48 (1.35)	2.31 (1.37)	2:15 (1.43)	2.63 (1.31)	2.12 (1.26)
... the system records personal information such as my weight or my temperature	1.98^A (1.37)	1.53^A (1.44)	1.75 (1.40)	1.58 (1.55)	1.60 (1.42)	1.64 (1.33)
... the system records information about my behavior and my movement patterns	2.12 (1.38)	1.90 (1.49)	2.12 (1.46)	1.85 (1.46)	1.96 (1.47)	1.90 (1.29)
... the system records information about my sleeping habits	2.06 (1.34)	1.70 (1.48)	1.91 (1.48)	1.81 (1.54)	2.02 (1.50)	1.70 (1.31)
... the system transmits data to my primary care person	2.89^{ACDE} (1.09)	2.55^{AGHI} (1.23)	2.58^{JKL} (1.29)	1.83^{CGJ} (1.41)	1.94^{DHK} (1.43)	1.92^{EIL} (1.31)
... the system transmits data to family members	2.57^{BCDE} (1.32)	2.36^I (1.36)	2.21^B (1.46)	1.83^C (1.45)	2.11^D (1.40)	1.77^{EI} (1.37)
... the system transmits data to my doctor or to the police	2.47^{CE} (1.31)	2.36^{GI} (1.35)	2.25^L (1.43)	1.64^{CGM} (1.47)	2.77^{MO} (1.14)	1.72^{EILO} (1.32)
... the system transmits data to commercial service providers (e.g., electricity provider, insurance company)	.57 (1.01)	.57 (.93)	.57 (1.07)	.87 (1.16)	.75 (1.11)	.66 (1.02)
I perceive this feature as useful	3.13^{BE} (.94)	2.74 (1.16)	2.40^{BK} (1.28)	2.60 (1.28)	3.08^{KO} (1.02)	2.43^{EO} (1.15)
I would like to use a system with this functionality	2.43 (1.22)	2.28 (1.20)	2.23 (1.25)	2.26 (1.33)	2.51^O (1.20)	2.00^O (1.24)
I am willing to accept extra costs for this feature	1.98 (1.33)	1.78 (1.33)	1.75^K (1.37)	2.00 (1.34)	2.25^{KO} (1.32)	1.69^O (1.24)

4.5 Comparison of Four Ambient Intelligence System Types

The in-depth comparison between the four system configurations revealed that these systems were rated differently in all but one dimension (see Table 5 for details). The wearable one-button emergency call system consistently elicited the lowest levels of concern, was perceived as the most useful, and respondents

Table 5. Comparison of four assistive systems. A rating of 0 corresponds to "I do not agree at all", while 4 corresponds to "I fully agree". $N = 57$. Depicted are means and, in brackets, standard deviations. Means sharing the same upper-case letter differ significantly (Sidak-corrected multiple comparison, $p < .05$).

	Mobile one- button emergency call system	Behavior and emergency detection system	Indoor floor emergency detection system	Emergency detection solution
Overall fear score (mean)	1.20^{AC} (.86)	1.72^{AD} (.88)	1.44^{D} (.94)	1.58^{C} (1.03)
Fear of being constantly monitored	1.31^{A} (1.18)	2.49^{ADE} (1.22)	1.73^{D} (1.27)	1.75^{E} (1.38)
Fear of negative health effects through system use (e.g., due to electromagnetic radiation)	.89 (.99)	.89 (1.05)	1.04 (1.09)	1.18 (1.22)
Fear that personal information are spied out	1.40^{A} (1.26)	2.04^{AD} (1.39)	1.47^{D} (1.20)	1.65 (1.32)
Fear that the operation of the system is too difficult in emergency situations	1.18^{C} (1.09)	1.47 (1.23)	1.51 (1.20)	1.73^{C} (1.24)
I find it acceptable if the system records information while I am in the bedroom	2.85^{AC} (1.19)	1.39^{ADE} (1.42)	2.56^{DF} (1.21)	2.06^{CEF} (1.37)
I find it acceptable if the system records information while I am in the bathroom.	2.91^{AC} (1.19)	1.27^{ADE} (1.35)	2.62^{DF} (1.25)	1.95^{CEF} (1.28)
I find the system useful	3.46^{ABC} (.73)	1.91^{AD} (1.37)	2.67^{BDF} (1.23)	2.21^{CF} (1.36)
I can well imagine myself using this system.	3.34^{ABC} (.79)	1.73^{AD} (1.36)	2.54^{BDF} (1.13)	1.93^{CF} (1.28)

could also most likely imagine themselves using this system. The sensor-based indoor floor emergency detection system scored second on most dimensions. The camera-based behavior and emergency detection system, in contrast, was perceived as significantly more worrisome and less useful than the other two systems. The combined comprehensive emergency detection solution scored largely identical to the camera-based system, even though people reported lower levels of fear of constantly being monitored and indicated a higher acceptance of the system recording them while being in the bedroom or bathroom.

5   Discussion and Summary

To gain a better understand of how different features and system approaches are perceived by the target group, the current study explored older individuals' expectations and concerns related to different innovations in ambient intelligence.

5.1   Limitations

Several limitations affecting the generalizability and external validity of our findings should be noted. A convenience sample of elderly individuals was examined, in which females were overrepresented. Participants were recruited at information sessions for seniors and might thus be more interested and open-minded regarding technological innovations than the average person of their age group. Yet it could be argued that this group represents potential buyers relatively well. It is also unclear to which extent the findings can be generalized to individuals from other countries, as attitudes towards technology are likely to be influenced by cultural norms and expectations.

5.2   Main Findings

Overall, a relatively positive attitude towards ambient intelligence was observed. All six features, as well as all systems without behavior observation through cameras, were perceived as generally valuable. Respondents rated emergency detection and burglary detection as particularly useful and important, particularly in contrast to living comfort features. It is notable that senior citizens perceive burglary detection functionality as more useful than disease detection and living comfort features, and are willing to accept higher costs for it. Similar to the findings from previous studies [5,7,10], ease of use and affordability were elderly seniors' top priorities. This emphasizes the need for systems that are easy to use as well as easy to understand.

It is noteworthy that in the comparisons of the systems, the camera-based system is relatively poorly rated, although it is easy to use. Contrary to the abstract review of the requirements for Ambient Intelligence systems, privacy seems to be more important for respondents than ease of use. Yet, aspects of data protection and misuse of information did not appear to be important for them. Their privacy definitions seemed to focus more on aspects of system visibility to others and an avoidance of shame. The floor-based system received largely positive appraisal. Fear of electromagnetic radiation, which we expected to be an issue for elderly individuals, was not observed. Participants also did not consider it a general disadvantage that their behavior and motion patterns were recorded.

The relative positive attitude and openness to technical assistance systems are consistent with the findings from other studies [14,16]. At the same time, substantial worries regarding the type of recorded information and data safety were noted, as well as a low willingness to change daily habits. These results suggest that fears of technology were more pronounced among individuals with little or no previous experience with Ambient Intelligence, thus confirming the assumption that technological acceptance depends on each individual's experiences and previous contact with such technologies [15]. The fact that most respondents knew about the wearable mobile one-button emergency call system due to its high market penetration may partly explain the largely positive attitudes towards this system. While several studies [7–9, 17] expressed concern about older adults feeling stigmatized and labeled as too frail when using assistive technologies, such concerns could not be confirmed in our study.

The willingness to accept extra costs for certain features, however, was mediocre. Again, it is striking that the willingness to pay for security features is larger than for functionality related to health protection or living comfort enhancement. To some extent, this phenomenon might be specific for Germany, where costs of health care systems are expected to be fully covered by health insurance.

6 Summary

As our central scientific contribution, we present an extensive study on ambient intelligence with 60 German participants aged 65 or older. We analyze multiple factors including fears, desired features, and privacy trade-offs.

Our study shows that elderly persons in Germany have a relatively positive attitude towards Ambient Intelligence systems. It is conceivable that associated fears on privacy and reliability can be reduced significantly with technology pervasion. Nonetheless, usage of cameras or data exchanges with commercial service providers are generally not accepted.

References

1. Adams, A.: Users' perception of privacy in multimedia communication. In: CHI 1999, Extended Abstracts on Human Factors in Computing Systems, pp. 53–54. ACM (1999)
2. Aminzadeh, F., Edwards, N.: Exploring seniors' views on the use of assistive devices in fall prevention. Public Health Nurs. 15(4), 297–304 (1998)
3. Beckwith, R.: Designing for ubiquity: the perception of privacy. IEEE Pervasive Comput. 2(2), 40–46 (2003)
4. van den Broek, G., Cavallo, F., Wehrmann, C.: AALIANCE Ambient Assisted Living Roadmap, vol. 6. IOS press, Leiden (2010)
5. Chernbumroong, S., Atkins, A.S., Yu, H.: Perception of smart home technologies to assist elderly people. In: The Fourth International Conference on Software, Knowledge, Information Management and Applications (SKIMA 2010), pp. 90–97 (2010)
6. Christensen, K., Doblhammer, G., Rau, R., Vaupel, J.W.: Ageing populations: the challenges ahead. Lancet 374(9696), 1196–1208 (2009)
7. Coughlin, J.F., D'Ambrosio, L.A., Reimer, B., Pratt, M.R.: Older adult perceptions of smart home technologies: implications for research, policy & market innovations in healthcare. In: 29th Annual International Conference of the IEEE Engineering in Medicine and Biology Society, 2007, EMBS 2007, pp. 1810–1815. IEEE (2007)

8. Demiris, G., Hensel, B.K., Skubic, M., Rantz, M.: Senior residents perceived need of and preferences for smart home sensor technologies. Int. J. Technol. Assess. Health Care **24**(01), 120–124 (2008)
9. Demiris, G., Rantz, M.J., Aud, M.A., Marek, K.D., Tyrer, H.W., Skubic, M., Hussam, A.A.: Older adults' attitudes towards and perceptions of 'smart home' technologies: a pilot study. Inf. Health Soc. Care **29**(2), 87–94 (2004)
10. Edgcomb, A., Vahid, F.: Privacy perception and fall detection accuracy for in-home video assistive monitoring with privacy enhancements. ACM SIGHIT Rec. **2**(2), 6–15 (2012)
11. Giannakouris, K.: Ageing characterises the demographic perspectives of the european societies. Stat. Focus **72**, 2008 (2008)
12. Grosse-Puppendahl, T., Berlin, E., Borazio, M.: Enhancing accelerometer-based activity recognition with capacitive proximity sensing. In: Paternò, F., de Ruyter, B., Markopoulos, P., Santoro, C., van Loenen, E., Luyten, K. (eds.) AmI 2012. LNCS, vol. 7683, pp. 17–32. Springer, Heidelberg (2012)
13. Larizza, M.F., Zukerman, I., Bohnert, F., Busija, L., Bentley, S.A., Russell, R.A., Rees, G.: In-home monitoring of older adults with vision impairment: exploring patients', caregivers' and professionals' views. J. Am. Med. Inf. Assoc. **21**(1), 56–63 (2014)
14. Marcellini, F., Mollenkopf, H., Spazzafumo, L., Ruoppila, I.: Acceptance and use of technological solutions by the elderly in the outdoor environment: findings from a european survey. Zeitschrift Fur Gerontologie Und Geriatrie **33**(3), 169–177 (2000)
15. McCreadie, C., Tinker, A.: The acceptability of assistive technology to older people. Ageing Soc. **25**(01), 91–110 (2005)
16. Melenhorst, A.S., Rogers, W.A., Bouwhuis, D.G.: Older adults' motivated choice for technological innovation: evidence for benefit-driven selectivity. Psychol. Aging **21**(1), 190 (2006)
17. Noury, N., Fleury, A., Rumeau, P., Bourke, A., Laighin, G., Rialle, V., Lundy, J.: Fall detection-principles and methods. In: 29th Annual International Conference of the IEEE Engineering in Medicine and Biology Society, EMBS 2007, pp. 1663–1666. IEEE (2007)

Person Identification by Analyzing Door Accelerations in Time and Frequency Domain

Hristijan Gjoreski[1(✉)], Rok Piltaver[1,2], and Matjaž Gams[1,2]

[1] Jožef Stefan Institute, Ljubljana, Slovenia
{hristijan.gjoreski,rok.piltaver,matjaz.gams}@ijs.si
[2] Jožef Stefan International Postgraduate School, Ljubljana, Slovenia

Abstract. The paper describes an approach for recognizing a person entering a room using only door accelerations. The approach analyzes the acceleration signal in time and frequency domain. For each domain two types of methods were developed: (i) feature-based – use features to describe the acceleration and then uses classification method to identify the person; (ii) signal-based – use the acceleration signal as input and finds the most similar ones in order to identify the person. The four methods were evaluated on a dataset of 1005 entrances recorded by 12 people. The results show that the time-domain methods achieve significantly higher accuracy compared to the frequency-domain methods, with signal-based method achieving 86 % accuracy. Additionally, the four methods were combined and all 15 combinations were examined. The best performing combined method increased the accuracy to 90 %. The results confirm that it is possible to identify a person entering a room using the door's acceleration.

Keywords: Unobtrusive person identification · Door · Acceleration · Machine learning · Dynamic time warping

1 Introduction

Ambient intelligence (AmI) is a scientific field that refers to environments consisting of smart devices (sensors and actuators) that can sense and respond to the presence of people [1, 2]. An AmI system should work in a way that supports people's everyday life activities in an easy, natural way using information and intelligence that is hidden in the data provided by the sensors. In order to provide the appropriate assistance, the system has to recognize (identify) the user, i.e., to be aware of his/hers presence. This makes the process of person identification one of the most essential and basic building blocks and a key prerequisite for numerous tasks in AmI.

Person identification is a process through which a person is recognized using some information about him/her. This information can be biometrics (fingerprint, iris, voice, etc.), token-based (RFID), or using PIN codes. A disadvantage of these, existing identification methods (e.g., fingerprint, RFID, PIN), is that the identified person needs to perform an action (enter a password, perform a fingerprint scan) or carry an identification token (key or identification card).

This paper presents a novel, completely unobtrusive system for automatic person identification. Our approach identifies the person entering a room based on the

Kameas et al. (Eds.): AmI 2015, LNCS 9425, pp. 60–76, 2015.
DOI: 10.1007/978-3-319-26005-1_5

acceleration produced by the door movement. The main research hypotheses investigated in this paper are: whether each user has a unique way of entering, and whether the proposed methods enable accurate identification. In the experiments, the identification is performed using the acceleration signal recorded by an accelerometer fixed on a door. In particular, the acceleration signal is analyzed in time domain and frequency domain. For each domain two types of methods are tested: (i) feature-based – uses features to describe the acceleration and then uses classification method to identify the person; (ii) signal-based – uses the acceleration signal as input and find the most similar ones in order to identify the person. Additionally, we tested the combinations of the methods and exploited the performance of all 15 combinations.

The motivation for the work comes from the commonly observed phenomena that humans can recognize their friends and family members by their voice, silhouette, or even gait and other characteristic behavior. Furthermore, there are several known methods for person identification based on gait [3] and appearance [4] – both with considerable application limitations. Furthermore, body-worn accelerometers have been successfully applied to detect falls [5, 6], recognize person activity [7, 8], and estimate energy expenditure [9, 10], while accelerometers attached to door are used to recognize door malfunctions [11].

The paper is organized as follows. In the next section, the background of the study is presented: first by giving a brief description of the physics background and description of the acceleration signal, and then by presenting the relevant related work. In the next two Sects. 3 and 4, the methods for each of the domains are presented: feature-based and signal-based methods for the time and the frequency domain, respectively. Section 5 describes the experiments, first by describing the experimental dataset and then by giving the experimental results for each of the methods and their combination. Finally, the paper ends with a conclusion and directions for future work.

2 Background

2.1 Physics and Acceleration Signal Description

Several phases of door movement can be observed as the person enters (as shown in Fig. 1). The door is motionless before the entry, therefore minor deviations from the static values of accelerations in each direction are caused only by sensor noise and vibrations due to outside influences. When entering, the person first accelerates the door in order to open it, which is observed as an increase in angle of the door, angular velocity and acceleration. Then, the acceleration starts to decrease and becomes negative until the door stops at the maximum angle. The door can remain in this state for a period of time or just an instance. Then the person accelerates the door in the opposite direction (closing), angular velocity becomes negative and the angle starts to decrease. Before the door angle returns to zero (door closed) the person decreases the angular velocity. If the door is not slowed down enough (door is slammed), a period of damped oscillation lasting up to about a second is observed after closing the door. Examples are shown in Fig. 1.

The described physical phenomena can be measured using various sensors such as accelerometer, gyroscope, magnetometer, and door-opening angle sensor.

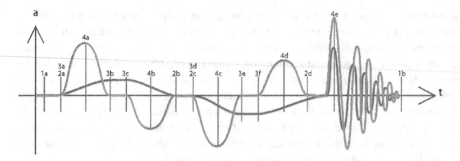

Fig. 1. The 14 phases of the acceleration signal. The x axis shows the time (t) and the y axis shows the acceleration α (e.g., 4a) and the velocity ω (e.g., 3b, 3c).

The accelerometer was chosen for the experiment because of availability, installation simplicity, past experiences, successful applications, and extensive related work. A 3-axis accelerometer was attached to the door so that one of its axis was aligned with the direction of gravitation, resulting in measurement of gravitation acceleration a_g. The second axis was parallel and the third perpendicular to the door-plane, resulting in measurements of the radial a_r and tangential accelerations a_t respectfully. The gravitation acceleration depends only on the geographical position of the door and remains constant during the entry unless the axis become misaligned with direction of gravity, e.g., when the door is slammed hard and starts oscillating. Radial acceleration $a_r = \omega^2 R$ depends on the angular velocity ω and the distance of the accelerometer from the axis of door rotation R. Tangential acceleration $a_t = \alpha R$ depends on the angular acceleration α and R (Fig. 2).

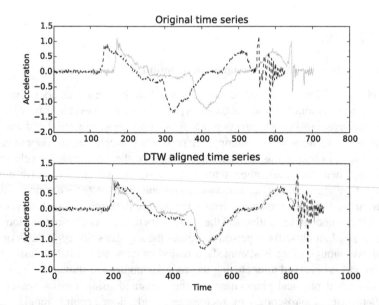

Fig. 2. An example of recorded and DTW aligned acceleration during two entries.

2.2   Related Work

There are various approaches to identify a person entering a room, home, or building. The person is usually recognized or authenticated using a sensor placed near the entrance, which may be: a fingerprint scanner, a camera-based face recognition, RFID reader, a PIN pad, or similar. The following paragraphs describe these approaches and explain how they compare to ours.

Fingerprint scanners are one of the most commonly used and well-established identification sensors [12]. With the recent developments in sensor technology, fingerprint scanners are also being used in the high-end smartphones for various security related functions, such as unlocking the phone and authenticating financial transactions [13]. The scanner analyses the person's fingerprint, i.e. the pattern of the ridges and furrows on the surface of the fingerprint, to identify the person. The reason for the success of fingerprint scanners is that each individual has a unique fingerprint, which enables high identification accuracy. Similarly, hand scanners identify the person using a print of the whole hand instead of a single finger. However, there are several limitations for successful identification with a fingerprint or hand scanner: a complete scan with a reliable quality is needed; moisture, sweat and partial scans significantly impair the identification accuracy; and finally, it is obtrusive for the identified person because one has to make an action in order to be identified: take of a glove, wipe out the finger/hand, put the hand on the scanner.

The recent advancements in machine vision enable camera-based approaches for identification of people [14]. This approach analyzes an image of a person's face in order to perform face recognition by matching it to known face images saved in a database. Even though this approach can perform without bothering the person, the cameras are not widely accepted due to the intrusion of the person's privacy. Similarly as fingerprint scanners, camera-based face recognition performs poorly with partial face images, and strongly depends on the environment and the light conditions.

Token-based identification is also commonly used. It became attractive with the development of the RFID and Near-Field Communication (NFC) technology [15]. Typically, each user is issued the respective token — for example, an RFID card — that contains data indicating the user's identity. This approach is practical for multi-site large-scale installations of access-control systems having many access points and users. Even though token-based identification is quite effective and commonly used in practice, it is obtrusive because it requires additional effort from the user upon each entry. Furthermore, it is not as secure as the approaches discussed above, because the user may lose the identification token and any other person having the token can access the facility. A solution to this problem is the use of PIN instead of a card. However, this approach is still considered obtrusive. First, the person has to remember the PIN, which is problematic because users have to remember multiple PINs (credit cards, web-passwords). Second, it has the same drawback as the fingerprint scanner: it requires an additional effort from the user to enter the PIN. Third, it can be stolen.

The main advantage of our approach is that we use a simple, small and inexpensive accelerometer sensor attached to the door. Therefore, the sensing is completely unobtrusive, except the fact that the system needs certain number of recording to be recorded by the people to be recognized before it is applied in practice. To the best of our knowledge, our work is the first attempt to identify a person using door accelerations.

3 Time Domain Identification

This section presents the methods that are analyzing the door acceleration data in time domain, i.e., as provided by the accelerometer. An example of the acceleration signal in time domain is given in Fig. 1. Two classification methods were implemented:

- *Feature-based* method. The method first extracts dozens of domain-specific features from the signal, combines them in a feature vector, which is passed to a pre-trained classification model to recognize the person.
- *Signal-based* method. The method takes the signal as input, compares it to the already known signals (training data) and finds the most similar ones. The signal is classified according to the class values of the most similar signals.

3.1 Feature-Based Identification

The first method, *TD-Feature*, analyzes the acceleration signal in time domain using domain specific features. That is, the method first uses the raw acceleration data to extract various domain-specific features, then the most relevant features are selected, and finally the person is identified by a previously trained ML classification model.

The identification starts with the feature extraction from the acceleration signal. The method analyzes the acceleration signal for each opening and closing of the door. In order to calculate the features, three parameters are considered: radial acceleration α, angular velocity ω, and the angle by which the door is opened φ. These parameters are analyzed in 14 phases as illustrated in Fig. 1:

- 1a–b: the start and end of entrance
- 2a–d: door opens, door stops, door closes
- 3a–f: acceleration changes between negative, zero and positive
- 4a–e: acceleration maximums and minimums in each level-3 subsection

Besides the duration of each phase, the following features are extracted for each phase and for each parameter (α, ω, φ), resulting in the total of 266 features:

- extreme value of the parameter in the particular phase;
- linear interpolation of the slope of the parameter in the particular phase;
- standard deviation of the parameter in the particular phase; and
- area under the curve (integral) of the parameter in the particular phase.

Because door moves with a single degree of freedom, some of these features are redundant (highly correlated) and some are irrelevant. In order to find and remove the irrelevant and the most correlated (redundant) features, a correlation matrix for all of the features was first calculated and then the most correlated features were removed [16]. This procedure reduced the number of feature from 266 to 97. After removing the most correlated features, the WrapperSubsetEval (WSE) algorithm [17] was applied, which further reduced the number of features to 36.

Once the features were extracted and selected, the feature vector was fed into a classification model. The model is trained to identify the person that enters the room according to the feature vector extracted from the acceleration signal. The person's name is used as the class label (the value to be predicted). Four classification algorithms were considered when constructing the model: Decision Tree j48 [18], Random Forest [19], k-NN [20], and Support Vector Machine (SVM) [21]. We used the implementation provided in WEKA-ML tool [23]. The results of each algorithm are given in Sect. 5.1.

3.2 Signal-Based Identification

The second method, i.e., *TD-Signal*, used to identify people entering through the door is based on comparison of the signals (accelerations) in time domain. The method applies dynamic time warping (DTW) to the time-series to calculate their similarity and then uses k-nearest neighbors method to identify the person.

Dynamic time warping [22] was successfully applied in many areas such as speech recognition [24], handwriting recognition [25], gesture recognition [26], time-series clustering [27], etc. The DTW algorithm applies non-linear stretching (in the time dimension) to the compared time-series in order to find the optimal match. Figure 2 shows two original time-series (top) and the optimal match between them (bottom) computed using DTW. The optimally time-stretched time series are then used to calculate the dissimilarity of the two time series, i.e. DTW distance.

A naïve DTW algorithm has O(nm) time and space complexity where n and m are the lengths of the two compared time series. However, more efficient algorithms such as FastDTW [28] and SparseDTW [29] exist.

The DTW distances between the door-acceleration time-series recorded during the entry and the labeled acceleration time-series of previous entries (labels correspond to persons) are used to identify the person that entered the door using the k-nearest neighbors method. Therefore time complexity of this method is O(N) where N is the number of labeled time-series (i.e. the size of the training set). The time complexity can be reduced by decreasing the number of labeled instances: instead of all the labeled instances only a few entries representing each user are kept.

The labels of the most similar previous entries are finally used to identify the person who entered the door. Two variants of the k-nearest neighbors method were compared. The first is to identify the person entering the door as the most frequent label among the k most similar previous entries — majority voting. The second variant is to use weighted voting, which considers the more similar entries as more relevant. It does so by assigning them higher voting weight compared to the less similar entries. The weight of the vote $w = 1/d$ for each of the k most similar entries is inversely proportional to its DTW distance d from the identified time series. The label with the highest sum of the votes is the predicted identity of the person who entered. If several labels have an equal sum of votes (in case of weighted voting) or frequency (in case of majority voting), a random label among them is returned as the predicted identity.

4   Frequency Domain Identification

This section presents the person identification process that is based on the analysis of the door acceleration data in frequency domain, i.e., the time-domain signal is transformed in frequency domain using Fast Fourier Transform [30]. Figure 3 shows an example of door acceleration during an entrance in time (top-left) and frequency domains (bottom-left).

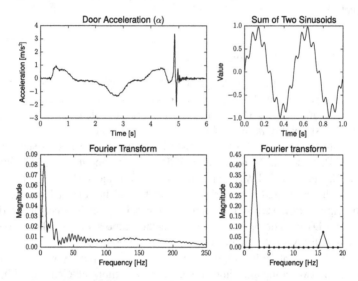

Fig. 3. Door acceleration signal (left) and sum of two sinusoids (right) in time (top) and frequency domain (bottom).

The Fourier transform decomposes a function — in our case the sampled angular acceleration of the door — into the composing frequencies. For example, the transform of the signal shown in the top-right graph in Fig. 3, given by equation $f(t) = 0.85\sin(t\alpha) + 0.15\sin(8t\alpha)$, is shown in bottom-right graph in Fig. 3. It clearly shows the two frequencies (2 and 8 × 2 Hz) and their relative amplitudes. Since the acceleration signal is discrete in both time and value, discrete Fourier transform was applied. Similar to the time-domain methods, two methods were developed: feature-based and signal-based methods.

4.1   Feature-Based Identification

This section presents the feature-based method that uses the acceleration signal in frequency domain, i.e., *FD-Feature method*. In order find and calculate the most relevant features, we first computed the average Fourier transform – an example for four persons is shown in Fig. 4. The visualization shows that the maximum average magnitude is between 6 and 8 Hz; that a local minimum is between 12 and 18 Hz, and the local maximum is between 19 and 22 Hz. Magnitudes of higher frequencies are considerably lower and local extremes are less distinct. Analysis of the graphs resulted in the definition of the initial set of features: magnitudes of several frequencies below 30 Hz, sums of magnitudes for windows of 10 sequential frequencies below 100 Hz, and sums of magnitudes for larger frequency windows of up to 800 Hz.

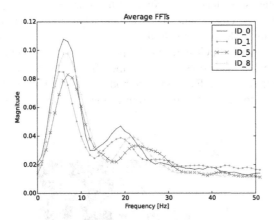

Fig. 4. Average Fourier transform of door acceleration for four persons.

The initial set of features was further analyzed using attribute ranking measures, such as ReliefF, Information Gain and Gini Ratio. Additionally, the features were analyzed using the Orange toolkit [31]. For pairs with considerable negative interaction, the feature with the lower feature quality rank was removed from the feature set. For positive interaction and for features with high quality rank, a similar feature was added to the set of features. The interactive process for selecting the feature set was stopped when the accuracy of classification models stopped increasing.

Once the final feature vector was defined, the traditional ML classification process was applied. That is, the selected frequency domain features were extracted and composed into a feature vector, which was fed into a training algorithm that produced a classification model. Similarly to the TD-Feature method, the same four classification algorithms were used: Decision Tree j48 [18], Random Forest [19], k-NN [20], and Support Vector Machine (SVM) [21].

4.2 Signal-Based Identification

The second method developed for the frequency domain, *FD-Signal method*, is similar to the TD-Signal method except that distance between door entrances is computed in frequency domain and not in time domain. To identify the person, first the time window of door acceleration containing the entire door opening event is extracted. Second, the fast Fourier transform of the window is computed. To compute the distance between the identified door entry and a labeled door entry, Manhattan distance, i.e. the sum of absolute differences in magnitude for each frequency, is used. The distance is to each labeled door entry is computed and the labels of the most similar entries are used to identify the person who entered the door. Similar to the TD-Signal method, the majority voting and weighted voting for 1 to 10 most similar entries (i.e. neighbors in the k-nn algorithm) was used. In addition, the maximal frequency was used to compute the Manhattan distance between FFT of two entries.

Figure 5 shows the Manhattan distances between the average FFTs for each person. It shows that there are five clusters of people with similar entries: people with IDs 4, 5 and 7 belong to the first cluster, and IDs 3, 2, and 11 to the second cluster, which is quite similar to the first. The person with ID 1 is the only one in the third cluster; IDs 6, 10, and 8 belong to the fourth cluster. Finally, people with IDs 9 and 0, which are very different from the rest of the people, belong to the fifth cluster. Observing this relations was the first indication that the FT-Signal method can be used to identify people when entering through the door. The full evaluation of the method is given in Sect. 5.2.

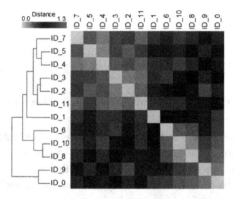

Fig. 5. Distance between average entrance of each person according to the distance between the average FFT transforms of acceleration signals and hierarchical clustering of persons.

5 Experiments

The experiments were performed on a dataset recorded in an office. The office door was equipped with a 3-axis accelerometer fixed near the door handle. Total of 12 people (aged 21 to 87) were asked to enter and leave the office multiple times. A total of 1007 entries were recorder. In order to obtain unbiased recordings, the volunteers did not know that the goal was to record the movement of the door. Instead, they were asked to perform the following task: remember a password with a dozen of characters written on a paper in the office and then to re-write the password on a paper outside the office. During the recordings, an experiment supervisor labeled each entry using a smartphone, which synchronized with the acceleration data. The supervisor marked the start and the end of each recording, and labelled each entry with the person's name.

The evaluation of the methods was performed using leave-one-out cross-validation technique. That means each example was evaluated using the rest of the examples as a training set. This way, in each case the training data contained examples of the tested person, which is acceptable for our application because the system is supposed to recognize people which are already present in the database of recordings.

In the next two subsections the results achieved for the time domain and the frequency domain are presented. In the last Subsect. 5.3, the methods for both domains are combined and the results for all of the combinations are presented.

5.1   Time Domain

Figure 6 shows the results for the time domain feature based method – TD-Feature. The accuracy achieved for each of the four classification algorithms is presented: Decision Tree j48, Random Forest, k-NN, and Support Vector Machine (SVM). The results show that the SVM is the best performing achieving 84.6 % accuracy. We additionally checked the difference in accuracy using paired T-test with p-value of 0.05. The statistical tests showed that j48 achieves significantly lower accuracy compared to the other three methods, and that the difference between the SVM, k-NN and Random Forest is not significant.

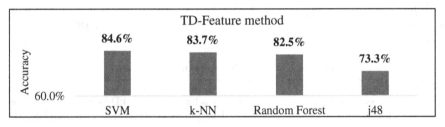

Fig. 6. The classification performance (accuracy) achieved for the TD-Feature based method using four classification algorithms: Decision Tree j48, Random Forest, k-NN, and Support Vector Machine.

Figure 7 shows the identification accuracy of the TD-Signal method for various number of nearest neighbors. The identification accuracy of weighted voting approach was computed using 1 to 10 most similar entries. Using the single most similar entry results in 84.8 % identification accuracy. For higher k the identification accuracy generally increases until it reaches its maximum of 86.3 % at $k = 8$ and then starts decreasing. The differences in accuracy between different numbers of k are not significant.

5.2   Frequency Domain

Figure 8 shows the results for the FD-Feature method. The accuracy achieved for each of the four classification algorithms is presented: Decision Tree j48, Random Forest,

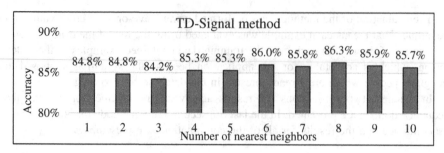

Fig. 7. The accuracy achieved with the TD-Signal method using different number of nearest neighbors.

k-NN, and SVM. The results show that the SVM performs the best, achieving 70.5 % accuracy. Similar to the TF-Feature method, the statistical tests showed that j48 achieves significantly lower accuracy compared to the other three algorithms, and that the difference between the SVM, k-NN and Random Forest is not significant.

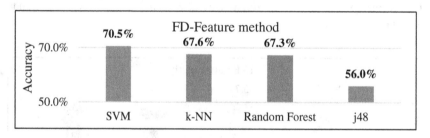

Fig. 8. The classification performance (accuracy) achieved for the FD-Feature based method using four classification algorithms: Decision Tree j48, Random Forest, k-NN, and Support Vector Machine.

Figure 9 shows the accuracy of the FD-Signal method for various number of nearest neighbors (k) and different maximal frequencies. The accuracy for the weighted and majority voting approaches was computed using 1 to 10 most similar entries. Weighted voting performed better in each case compared to the majority voting. If k is too low, the method is sensitive to noise and outliers. If k is too high, the method blurs the boundary between classes (identities). The number of nearest neighbors where the maximum identification accuracy is reached depends on the maximal frequency used for comparison. The accuracy in general also depends on the maximal frequency. Similar as with the number of nearest neighbors, the accuracy increases with increasing frequency cut-off until it reaches the maximum at 50 Hz and then starts decreasing. If the maximal frequency used for comparison is too low, the method loses too much information and performs poorly. If it is too high, it gives more emphasis to high frequencies that do not enable distinguishing between identities of the entering persons.

The highest identification accuracy of 68.72 % was achieved with 5 nearest neighbors, weighted voting and frequency cut-off at 50 Hz.

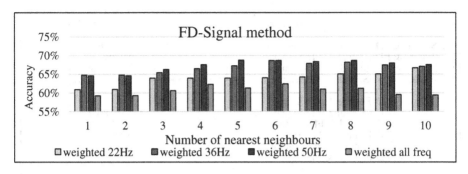

Fig. 9. The accuracy achieved with the FD-Signal method using different number of nearest neighbors and different frequencies.

5.3 Combining the Time and Frequency Domain Methods

Figure 10 summarizes the accuracy achieved by the best performing algorithm for each of the four methods: TD-Feature, TD-Signal, FD-Feature, and FD-Signal. It shows that the TD-Signal method performs the best, achieving 86.3 %. The statistical tests showed that this difference is not significant when the TD-Signal is compared to the TD-Feature and that it is significant compared to the other two. These results show that the representation of the acceleration data in time domain (as originally provided by the accelerometer) provides richer information about the person's signature of opening and closing a door.

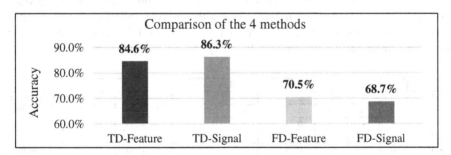

Fig. 10. Comparison of the accuracy achieved by the four methods: TD-Feature, TD-Signal, FD-Feature, and FD-Signal.

In the next step, we combined the four methods and exploited the 15 combinations, which are shown in Fig. 11. The combination was achieved by combining the prediction outputs of each method. For each test instance, each method provides an array of prediction probabilities for each class value (for each person). This probabilities are summed for each of the combination methods and the class value (person) that has the biggest sum is chosen as the final one.

The results show that when the TD-Feature and TF-Signal are combined, the accuracy increases to 89.5 %, which is significantly better compared to each of the

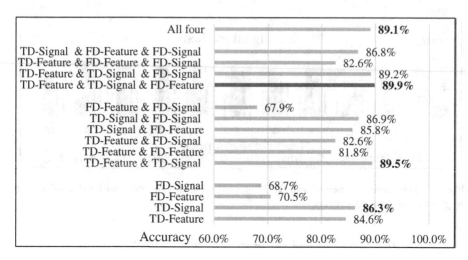

Fig. 11. The accuracy achieved by combining the best performing algorithms for each of the 4 methods.

methods used individually, i.e., 84.6 % and 86.3 % respectively. The highest accuracy of 89.9 % is achieved when the three methods are combined: TD-Feature, TF-Signal and FD-Feature.

Figure 12 shows the confusion matrix for the best performing combination, the combination of the three methods: TD-Feature, TF-Signal and FD-Feature, which achieved 89.9 % accuracy. It also lists the recall and precision values for each person. The confusion matrix shows that person 10 has the lowest recall (43.1 %) and is often incorrectly identified as person 11. Similarly person pairs 4–5 and 6–8 have similar entries and are mutually misidentified. By analyzing per-person results (recall) one can

	ID	0	1	2	3	4	5	6	7	8	9	10	11	Recall
						Predicted Class (Person)								
	0	79	0	0	0	0	0	0	0	0	4	0	0	95.2%
	1	0	50	0	0	0	0	0	0	0	0	0	0	100.0%
	2	0	0	49	0	0	0	0	0	0	0	0	0	100.0%
	3	0	0	0	47	0	0	1	0	0	0	0	0	97.9%
True Class (Person)	4	0	0	0	0	80	16	1	2	0	2	0	0	79.2%
	5	0	0	0	1	7	90	0	3	0	4	0	0	85.7%
	6	0	0	0	0	0	0	80	0	13	1	0	0	85.1%
	7	0	0	0	0	2	4	0	32	0	1	0	0	82.1%
	8	0	0	0	0	0	0	10	0	61	0	0	0	85.9%
	9	1	0	0	0	0	0	0	0	0	208	0	0	99.5%
	10	0	0	0	0	0	0	0	0	0	0	22	29	43.1%
	11	0	0	0	0	0	0	0	0	0	0	0	105	100.0%
Precision		98.8%	100.0%	100.0%	97.9%	89.9%	81.8%	87.0%	86.5%	82.4%	94.5%	100.0%	78.4%	Accuracy: 89.9%

Fig. 12. The confusion matrix for the best performing combination of three methods: TD-Feature, TF-Signal and FD-Feature. Recall and precision are given for each person as well as overall accuracy.

note that for half of the people, i.e., 6, the recall is above 95 %, which is a promising result, given that the recognition is performed using only the door acceleration.

These results show that there is a considerable difference in identification accuracy for different people and that some people have similar ways of opening and closing the door, which in some cases makes the identification difficult.

6   Conclusions

The paper presented a novel unobtrusive approach to identify a person entering a room (e.g., home or office) using the acceleration produced by the door movement. To the best of our knowledge, our work is the first attempt to identify a person using door accelerations, and was also patented at the Slovenian national patent office [32]. Please note that the unobtrusiveness is regarding that the user does not have to wear any additional sensors or to perform any action to identify himself. However, our system still requires the user to pre-record certain number of entries.

The paper described four methods that recognize the person by analyzing the door acceleration data in time and frequency domain. For each domain we tested two types of methods: (i) feature-based – use features to describe the acceleration and then uses classification method to identify the person; (ii) signal-based – use the acceleration signal as input and find the most similar labeled entries in order to identify the person. The four methods were evaluated on a dataset of 1005 entrances recorded by 12 people. The results show that signal-based method that analyzes the signal in time domain performs best, achieving 86 % accuracy. The comparison of the four methods (see Fig. 10) shows that the methods that exploit the acceleration represented in time-domain perform significantly better compared to the methods that exploit the frequency domain. Therefore, one can conclude that the representation of the acceleration data in time domain (as originally provided by the accelerometer) provides richer information about the person's signature of opening and closing a door. Additionally, we combined the outputs of the four methods and examined all 15 combinations. Even by using simple technique for combination, i.e., weighted voting, the accuracy significantly increased up to 89.9 %. By analyzing per-person results (recall) one can note that for half of the people, i.e., 6, the recall is above 95 %, which is a promising result, given that the recognition is performed using only the door acceleration. These results confirm that it is possible to identify a person with a system that is completely unobtrusive — no additional action such as scanning a fingerprint is required.

Some may argue that the identification accuracy is not high enough for a secure access-control applications, where almost perfect system is required. However, the proposed approach is novel and the results are promising for application when slightly lower accuracy is not problematic. Moreover, the approach is completely unobtrusive to the user and can therefore be used as an assistive technology or a smart-home sensor in offices and homes with limited number of people to enable smart-home automation personalization. After all, the goal of our system is not to substitute other reliable identification systems (e.g., fingerprint scanners), but to be used as an assistive technology (assist in daily tasks) and enable smart-home personalization in applications with a limited number of people (e.g., in a home or an office) by making the identification more comfortable, i.e. not requiring users to perform additional action. Therefore, a reasonable decrease in identification accuracy is tolerated in return for the increase in comfort of identification procedure.

One of the limitations of this study is that the data was recorded in a controlled lab scenario. Real-life poses challenges that are not addressed in this study, e.g., people sometimes enter in pairs or enter in a specific way, e.g., when carrying a heavy object. These issues need further attention before practical applications are considered.

For future work, we first plan to improve the identification accuracy by using more advanced combining approaches, such as meta-learning, Stacking [33], and Bayesian approach [34]. Another significant improvement should be achieved by classifying only members of a typical family or co-workers in an office. Our preliminary experiments show promising results [35]. We also plan to improve the computational performance of the DTW implementation by comparing the identified entrance signal only with the most representative labeled entries of each person instead of comparing with the entire database of examples. This can be done by clustering the entry signals of each person and using only the cluster centroids or by calculating an average entry signal to represent each person. Finally, we plan to test the methods on data recorded in real-life, e.g., by installing the system in an office and monitoring the office's entries and exits.

Acknowledgements. The authors would like to thank Tadej Vodopivec for recording the dataset and coding the initial version of software for data pre-processing and feature extraction. The authors would also like to thank mag. Borut Grošičar, for the discussions about the physics analysis of the door acceleration signal.

References

1. Aarts, E.: Ambient intelligence: a multimedia perspective. IEEE Multimedia **11**(1), 12–19 (2004)
2. Cook, D.J., Augusto, J.C., Jakkula, V.R.: Ambient intelligence: technologies, applications, and opportunities. Pervasive Mobile Comput. **5**(4), 277–298 (2009)
3. Bashir, K., Xiang, T., Gong, S.: Gait recognition without subject cooperation. Pattern Recogn. Lett. **31**, 2052–2060 (2010)
4. Wang, L., Tan, T., Ning, H., Hu, W.: Silhouette analysis-based gait recognition for human identification. IEEE Trans. Pattern Anal. Mach. Intell. **25**(12), 1505–1518 (2003)
5. Gjoreski, H., Gams, M., Luštrek, M.: Context-based fall detection and activity recognition using inertial and location sensors. J. Ambient Intell. Smart Environ. **6**(4), 419–433 (2014)
6. Li, Q., Stankovic, J., Hanson, M., Barth, A.T., Lach, J., Zhou, G.: Accurate, fast fall detection using gyroscopes and accelerometer-derived posture information. In: Proceedings of Sixth International Workshop on Wearable and Implantable Body Sensor Networks, pp. 138–143 (2009)
7. Gjoreski, H., Kozina, S., Gams, M., Luštrek, M., Álvarez-García, J.A., Hong, J.H., Ramos, J., Dey, A.K., Bocca, M., Patwari, N.: Competitive live evaluation of activity-recognition systems. IEEE Pervasive Comput. **14**(1), 70–77 (2015)

8. Gjoreski, H., Kozina, S., Luštrek, M., Gams, M.: Using multiple contexts to distinguish standing from sitting with a single accelerometer. In: European Conference on Artificial Intelligence (ECAI) (2014)
9. Vyas, N., Farringdon, J., Andre, D., Stivoric, J.: Machine learning and sensor fusion for estimating continuous energy expenditure. In: Proceedings of 23rd Conference on Innovative Applications of Artificial Intelligence, IAAI, 2011, pp. 1613–1620, San Francisco, CA, USA (2011)
10. Gjoreski, H., Kaluža, B., Gams, M., Milić, R., Luštrek, M.: Context-based ensemble method for human energy expenditure estimation. Applied Soft Computing, (2015) (in press)
11. Patent application, door monitoring system, patent no. WO 2011011282 A2
12. Hong, L., Wan, Y., Jain, A.: Fingerprint image enhancement: algorithm and performance evaluation. IEEE Trans. J. Pattern Anal. Mach. Intell. 20(8), 777–789 (1998)
13. Apple pay. https://www.apple.com/apple–pay/
14. Turk, M.A., Pentland, A.P.: Face recognition using eigenfaces. In: IEEE Computer Society Conference on Computer Vision and Pattern Recognition, Proceedings CVPR 1991, pp. 586–591, 3–6 June 1991
15. Juels, A.: RFID security and privacy: a research survey. IEEE J. Sel. Areas Commun. 24(2), 381–394 (2006)
16. Piltaver, R., Gjoreski, H., Gams, M.: Person identification using door accelerations. In: AITAmI 2015 Workshop, IJCAI (2015)
17. Kohavi, R., George, H.: Wrappers for feature subset selection. Artif. Intell. 97(1–2), 273–324 (1997)
18. Quinlan, R.: C4.5: Programs for Machine Learning. Morgan Kaufmann Publishers, San Mateo (1993)
19. Breiman, L.: Random forests. Mach. Learn. 45(1), 5–32 (2001)
20. Aha, D., Kibler, D.: Instance-based learning algorithms. Mach. Learn. 6, 37–66 (1991)
21. Platt, J.: Fast training of support vector machines using sequential minimal optimization. In: Schoelkopf, B., Burges, C., Smola, A. (eds.) Advances in Kernel Methods — Support Vector Learning. MIT Press, Cambridge (1998)
22. Bellman, R., Kalaba, R.: On adaptive control processes. IRE Trans. Autom. Control 4(2), 1–9 (1959)
23. Hall, M., Frank, E., Holmes, G., Pfahringer, B., Reutemann, P., Witten, I.H.: The WEKA data mining software: an update. SIGKDD Explor. 11(1), 10–18 (2009)
24. Sakoe, H., Chiba, S.: Dynamic programming algorithm optimization for spoken word recognition. IEEE Trans. Acoust. Speech Signal Process. 26(1), 43–49 (1978)
25. Tappert, C.C., Suen, C.Y., Wakahara, T.: The state of the art in online handwriting recognition. IEEE Trans. Pattern Anal. Mach. Intell. 12(8), 787–808 (1990)
26. Kuzmanic, A., Zanchi, V.: Hand shape classification using dtw and lcss as similarity measures for vision-based gesture recognition system. In: The International Conference on "Computer as a Tool" EUROCON, pp. 264–269 (2007)
27. Liao, T.W.: Clustering of time series data—a survey. Pattern Recogn. 38(11), 1857–1874 (2005)
28. Salvador, S., Chan, P.: FastDTW: toward accurate dynamic time warping in linear time and space. In: KDD Workshop on Mining Temporal and Sequential Data, pp. 70–80 (2004)
29. Al-Naymat, G., Chawla, S., Taheri, J.: SparseDTW: a novel approach to speed up dynamic time warping (2012)
30. Cooley, J.W., Tukey, J.W.: An algorithm for the machine calculation of complex Fourier series. Math. Comput. 19, 297–301 (1965)
31. Jakulin, A.: Machine learning based on attribute interactions. Ph.D. dissertation (2005)

32. Gams, M., Piltaver, R., Gjoreski, H.: Postopek identifikacije osebe, ki vstopa v prostor, patent P-201300281, Slovenian Intellectual Property Office, filed, 19 September 2013
33. Wolpert, D.: Stacked generalization. Neural Networks 5(2), 241–259 (1992)
34. Bailer-Jones, A.L.C., Smith, K.: Combining probabilities. Gaia (GAIA-C8-TN-MPIA-CBJ-053). In: Data Processing and Analysis Consortium (DPAC), issue 2 (2011)
35. Piltaver, R., Vodopivec, T., Gams, M.: Identifikacija oseb ob vstopu skozi vrata z uporabo pospeškomera in strojnega učenja. In: Proceedings of 16th International Multiconference Information Society, vol. A, pp. 90–93 (2013)

Design Factors for Flexible Capacitive Sensors in Ambient Intelligence

Silvia Rus[1(✉)], Meltem Sahbaz[3], Andreas Braun[1], and Arjan Kuijper[1,2]

[1] Fraunhofer IGD, Fraunhoferstr. 5, 64283 Darmstadt, Germany
{silvia.rus,andreas.braun,arjan.kuijper}@igd.fraunhofer.de
[2] Technische Universität Darmstadt, Hochschulstr. 10, 64289 Darmstadt, Germany
arjan.kuijper@gris.tu-darmstadt.de
[3] Hochschule Furtwangen, Robert-Gerwig-Platz 1,
78120 Furtwangen im, Schwarzwald, Germany
meltem.sahbaz@hs-furtwangen.de

Abstract. Capacitive sensors in both touch and proximity varieties are becoming more common in many industrial and research applications. Each sensor requires one or more electrodes to create an electric field and measure changes thereof. The design and layout of those electrodes is crucial when designing applications and systems. It can influence range, detectable objects, or refresh rate. In the last years, new measurement systems and materials, as well as advances in rapid prototyping technologies have vastly increased the potential range of applications using flexible capacitive sensors. This paper contributes an extensive set of capacitive sensing measurements with different electrode materials and layouts for two measurement modes - self-capacitance and mutual capacitance. The evaluation of the measurement results reveals how well-suited certain materials are for different applications. We evaluate the characteristics of those materials for capacitive sensing and enable application designers to choose the appropriate material for their application.

Keywords: Capacitive sensing · Conductive materials · eTextiles

1 Introduction

In the last years more and more applications using Capacitive Sensing have been developed. Rapid prototyping tool-kits like the OpenCapSense Board [1] and the CapToolKit [2] have enabled us to rapidly try out different electrode setups. However, mainly copper electrodes or copper wires have been used like in [3,4] or [5]. In [3] the lying position in the bed is detected by placing copper electrodes under the mattress while in [4] and [5] copper electrodes and copper wires are used on a flexible surface to detect the lying position. These and other developments show that capacitive sensing has found its way in the application field of wearables and smart textiles. For this, actual developments have shown the need to use more flexible materials like the iSkin in [6] where a flexible, customizable touch sensor is applied to the skin enabling on-body interaction.

© Springer International Publishing Switzerland 2015
Kameas et al. (Eds.): AmI 2015, LNCS 9425, pp. 77–92, 2015.
DOI: 10.1007/978-3-319-26005-1_6

This is possible due to the layering of thin, flexible silicone, an organic polymer. Here the material has been chosen due to its transparency, elasticity and biocompatibility. We observe that new application domains need new materials with different properties. These need to be explored for the field of capacitive sensing.

The goal of this paper is to evaluate how well suited different electrode materials are for building applications using capacitive sensing. Our main contribution are extensive measurements for five different materials using different setups. We provide measurements in self and mutual capacitance mode and in two different electrode sizes. The evaluation of the results will show a comparison of the characteristics of the different materials and reveal suitable application domains.

2   Related Work

Recently capacitive sensing with different materials has been used as technology for different materials. For example in [7] they use clothing as input/control device. For this capacitive electrodes are built out of conductive textile and can be integrated in various clothing or in furniture. Also using conductive textiles the authors of [8] prevent falls or control a head worn device using different touch areas of the belt [9]. Conductive paint is used in [10] to paint interdigital capacitive sensors on regular textile in order to detect specific movements of the arm by integrating the painted sensor into clothing. The multitude of applications show how new materials find their way into capacitive sensing. However, most of them use a special electrode design and only cover capacitive touch. They don't evaluate the spatial resolution and the interaction range which is possible. In [4] they propose a circular electrode design composed of a guard ring and an electrodes. The authors evaluate the influence of electrode area, shielding and of the gap between guard ring and electrode on the capacitance. However, they did not evaluate the spatial resolution like it has been done in [1] where different electrode materials like foil of polyethylene terephthalate (PET) coated with indium tin oxide (ITO) or PEDOT:PSS, conductive polymer are compared to different sizes of copper electrodes for distances up to 40 cm. Braun et al. [11] evaluate capacitive proximity sensors in smart environments. They focus on practical guidelines, gained in the design of various prototypes, but do not provide measurements of flexible materials or different measurement modes.

3   Evaluating Flexible Capacitive Sensors

In this section we give an overview over the application domains of flexible capacitive sensors. Table 1 reflects a selection of applications grouped into application domains. The four identified application domains are smart appliances in clothing, on body and physiological property measurement in clothing and in furniture. In the third column of the table the materials which were used to accomplish the applications are listed. Mostly conductive thread and conductive fabric are used, especially in smart appliances on clothing and in furniture.

Table 1. Overview of application domains for Flexible Capacitive Sensors

Name	Description	Electrode material, Measurement mode
Smart Appliances in clothing		
Inviz [7]	Gesture recognition system for paralysis patients that uses flexible textile-based capacitive sensor arrays for movement detection	Conductive fabric, self capacitance
Interactive Belt [9]	Wearable input device controlling head-worn displays	Aluminium rivet, capacitive touch
Touch input on clothes [12]	Generic platform for attaching different capacitive sensors in phone bag, helmet, gloves and apron	Conductive foil, conductive thread, wire, self capacitance
Pinstripe [13]	Provide input by pinching a part of clothing between thumb and another finger	Conductive thread, self capacitance
Smart Appliances in clothing, physiological monitoring		
Fall prevention [8]	Textile capacitive sensor array-based system built into clothing that can reliably capture spatio-temporal gait attributes in a home setting	Conductive fabric, self capacitance
Activity monitoring [10]	Easy to paint sensor directly on the clothes detecting large amplitude movements	Conductive paint, mutual capacitance
Smart Appliances in furniture, physiologial monitoring		
ECG-monitor [14]	Obtain electrocardiographic potential through thin cloth between the measuring electrodes and the skin of a subject's dorsal surface	Conductive fabric, self capacitance
SmartBedsheet [5]	Bedsheet detecting the bed posture	6x8 wire electrodes, mutual capacitance
SmartSkin [15]	Surface tracks the position of the user's hands on and above	Copper wires mesh, mutual capacitance
Sketching Touch Sensors: stretchable wristband [16]	Rapid prototyping of touch sensitive objects of arbitrary shape	Conductive thread, conductive ink, self capacitance, time domain reflectometry (TDR)
On-body Smart Appliances		
iSkin [6]	Skin-worn sensors for touch input on the body	Silicone-based organic polymer filled with carbon black particles (cPDMS), mutual capacitance
Hairware [17, 18]	Seamless artificial hair extensions where touching triggers devices	Metalized hair extensions, capacitive touch

For the on-body interaction new, special materials have been developed, to fit to the requirements of not harming the human body. Nearly all these applications are developed for capacitive touch interaction. Mostly the applications built into furniture exploit the biggest advantage of capacitive sensing of being unobtrusively mountable.

The measurement modes used is predominantly self capacitance, while applications which need to cover a larger surface like [5,15] and hence need more measurement nodes explore the advantage of mutual capacitance of having multiple measurement nodes.

The applications from Table 1 have been developed by trying out new materials and electrode layouts. The gathered experiences will guide the further development. However, a more quantitative approach might reveal qualities of the materials which will help developers to optimize the choice for the used materials for their application.

4   Electrode Material Evaluation

In this section, we present our measurement setup and the materials used for the quantitative evaluation. Five electrode materials have been chosen, all of which appear in the third column of Table 1, which reflects the used electrode materials for flexible capacitive sensor applications. Conductive thread, conductive fabric and conductive paint are evaluated together with the classic copper electrode. More on the evaluated materials can be found in Sect. 4.2.

4.1   Measurement Setup

Figure 1 shows the measurement setup. A copper electrode of the same size of 10×16 cm as the evaluated electrode materials is used to measure the capacitance at different distances. The chosen size is approximately the size of a hand palm. This should simulate a hand getting closer to the electrode. Due to the fact that when we interact with our hand we are coupled to ground, this electrode is in the different measurements loosely grounded and connected to the ground. Depending on the size of the electrode the sensing distance can vary. Capacitive sensing distances up to 50 cm are achievable with acceptable electrode sizes. Hence, we have effectuated measurements up to distances of 50 cm. When measuring the self capacitance a single electrode is needed. This electrode is connected to a sensor which sends the sensed signal to an OpenCapSense evaluation board [1]. Through a serial connection a MATLAB script is collecting the data. For measuring the mutual capacitance, multiple sending and receiving electrodes are used. The sending electrodes send out a signal generated by the sending OpenCapSense board, while the two receiver electrodes are connected to two sensors, which are connected to the receiving OpenCapSense board. From there the values are transmitted to the MATLAB script.

Fig. 1. Measurement setup: adjustable distance of copper electrode to different electrode materials

Fig. 2. Electrode materials samples of same size used in self capacitance measurement mode: (from left to right) copper electrode, conductive paint, conductive thread, conductive fabric, conductive paint on fabric

4.2 Electrode Materials

We evaluated the electrodes using self and mutual capacitance measurement mode. For each setup we used five different materials for the measurements. These materials are: copper electrode and wires, conductive paint, conductive paint on fabric, conductive fabric and conductive thread. In Figs. 2 and 3 the used

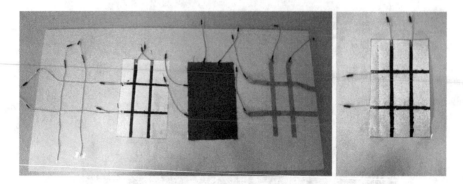

Fig. 3. Electrode material samples of same size used in mutual capacitance measurement mode:(from left to right) copper wires, conductive paint, conductive thread, conductive fabric, conductive paint on fabric

electrodes are shown in the different measurement modes. For self capacitance measurements only one electrode is used to measure the capacitance. Therefor, we choose electrodes of the same size of 10×16 cm. Next to the copper electrode one can see in Fig. 2 the black conductive paint, which we applied on paper and contacted using copper tape. To the right of the conductive paint, conductive thread is sewn into a green piece of fabric. The conductive thread is sewn in narrow s-lines with spacing of about 0.5 cm. Conductive thread is contacted by knotting the thread to the connector. The forth electrode material sample is conductive fabric which is contacted using conductive thread which is sewn to the connector. The last electrode also shows conductive paint like in the second sample but this time the used substrate is fabric. It is contacted using copper tape. For the mutual capacitance measurement mode one sending and one receiving electrode are needed. We use two sending and two receiving electrodes which are placed as a two times two grid. Instead of the copper electrode, wires are used. These are already isolated and can simply cross each other. For the other electrode setups 0.5 cm thick stripes of conductive paint and fabric have been used. After the horizontal electrodes have been placed, the crossing points were isolated using tape. Then the vertical electrodes have been added. In the case of conductive thread the fabric itself is used as isolation at the two crossing points by sewing the receivers and the senders on top and on the bottom of the fabric. The contacting methods are the same as described measuring the self capacitance.

5 Results

In the following Sects. 5.1 and 5.2 the measurement results are presented. We have effectuated three kinds of measurements, for both self and mutual capacitance measurement modes.

First, we have used the measurement setup described in Sect. 4.1 for distances of up to 50 cm. From 1–30 cm we measured in steps of 1 cm while from

30–50 cm we measured in steps of 2.5 cm. During these measurements the electrode simulating the hand was loosely coupled to the ground through the environment. Second, we connected the human hand simulating electrode to ground and measured the sensed value for distances up to 30 cm. This time we measured up to 15 cm in steps of 1 cm while from 15–30 cm we measured in steps of 2.5 cm. Additionally, we evaluated how the materials react to touch. For this the moving electrode has been placed on the different electrode materials with an isolating layer in-between. The touch measurement has been evaluated once without weight and once with a weight of 0.5 kg, to reflect the behaviour of pressing a button. The resulting diagrams are presented in the following for the two capacitive measurement modes.

5.1 Self Capacitance Measurements

Figure 4 shows the mean and standard deviation for distances of 1–50 cm. One can observe that the standard deviation is approximately small. Also one can infer the deviations due to noise which lead to unusual drops and spikes in the signal. The influence of noise is especially visible if one compares the curve of the electrode from conductive paint on fabric to the other materials. The influence of the environment through the noise which is sensed because of the loose coupling to the ground can be observed even better in Fig. 5. In this Figure the moving electrode is grounded and yields a much smoother and constant signal throughout all electrode materials with very small standard deviations. For direct comparison we normalized the curves and show them in the bottom right graph of Figs. 4 and 5.

Figure 6 shows a closer view at the first 5 cm. This includes the capacitive touch measurement. The first measurement is the one where pressing on a capacitive electrode is shown while the second value only shows light touch. They are shown together with the normalized values for distances up to 5 cm.

The results of self capacitance measurements for distances up to 30 cm with the electrode size, half of the one before, now 10×8, are shown in Fig. 7. They depict a very similar course as the whole electrode size.

5.2 Mutual Capacitance Measurements

Unlike the self capacitance the mutual capacitance measurements for two sender and two receiver electrodes yield four sensing nodes. Because we are using a single moving electrode centered over the four sensor nodes, these behave approximately the same. Figure 8 shows the normalized values of the sender and receiver pair (1,1) while Fig. 9 shows the mean and standard deviation of each of them. We observe the very big standard deviation, which shows once again the influence of the noise (parasitic capacitance) of the environment when the electrode is coupled loosely to the ground. Grounding the moving electrode reveals the right graph from Figs. 8 and 10. One can see that all materials show a smooth curve. At first, the measurements for the conductive paint electrode was very different from the graph of the conductive paint electrode on fabric. This lead to

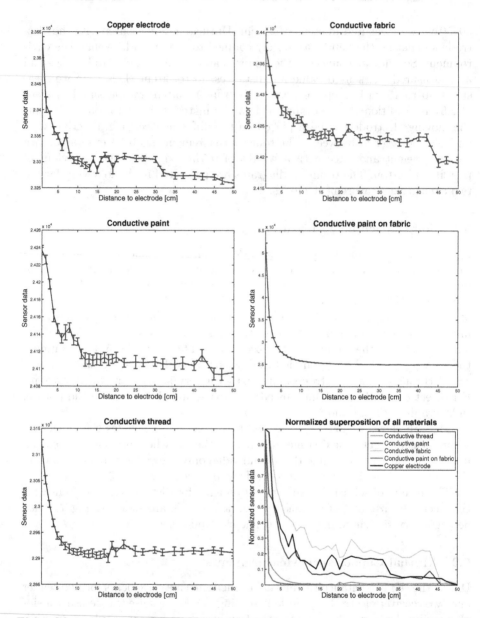

Fig. 4. Mean and standard deviation of self capacitance measurements, loosely coupled to ground at distances of 1–50 cm; normalized view of all electrode materials (bottom right)

the assumption, that the measurements were heavily noise prone. After repeating the measurements the conductive paint on fabric and the conductive paint both showed nice characteristics. For mutual capacitance the capacitance change measured is very small, only at the crossing of the sender and receiver electrode.

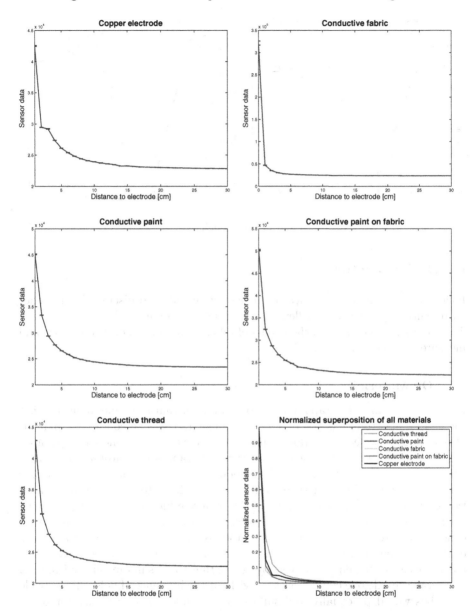

Fig. 5. Mean and standard deviation of self capacitance measurements, grounded, distances of 1–30 cm; normalized view of all electrode materials (bottom right)

The noise can increase so much that the change in capacitance generated by the moving electrode can be to small and overruled by noise.

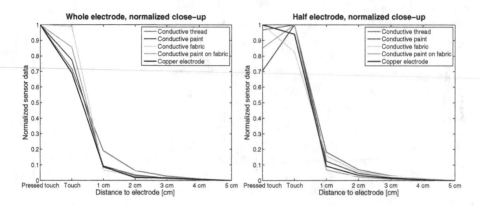

Fig. 6. Capacitive touch and pressed touch close-up 1–5 cm, grounded

6   Design Factors

Following our quantitative measurements, we are able to discuss the influence on potential applications for flexible capacitive sensors in Ambient Intelligence. This discussion builds upon the results of different materials, electrode sizes, and measurement modes.

6.1   On Materials

From the bottom right graph of Fig. 5 one can infer that even due to much noise, the copper electrode has the best measurement range. The conductive paint is also quite good with a good range until 12 cm. However, the conductive paint on fabric shows a different course with measurement ranges until around 5 cm. However, when grounding the moving electrode the measurement ranges get closer together. In mutual capacitance mode, it is very hard to infer a recommendation on which electrodes to use due to the strong influence of the noise for some electrode materials. However, from the right graph of Fig. 8 one can infer that conductive thread, copper wire and conductive paint on fabric have a similar course. For conductive fabric the measurements would need to be repeated to make a clear statement. However, by comparing the results in self and mutual capacitance mode one could infer that without the influence of noise all electrode materials would be equally well suitable for flexible capacitive sensor applications.

6.2   On Size

The self-capacitance mode allows for changing the electrode size. We repeated the grounded measurements for distances of 1–30 cm with half the size of the previous electrode. The comparing Figures are the bottom right graphs of Figs. 7 and 5. Both are very similar. If one looks more closely one can see that the bigger electrode has better spacial resolution but similar range as the smaller electrode.

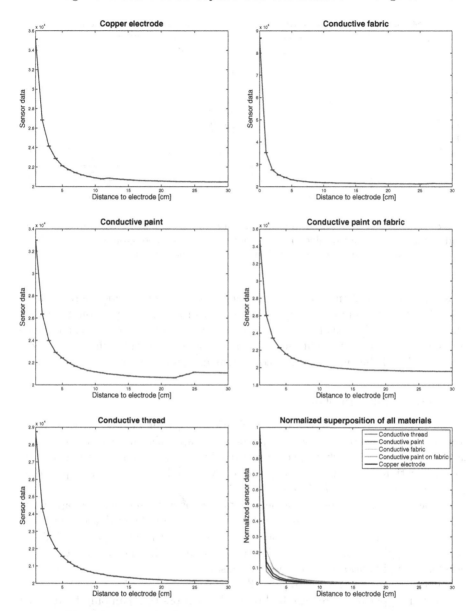

Fig. 7. Mean and standard deviation of half electrode, self capacitance measurements, grounded at distances of 1–30 cm

6.3   On Modes

From the top and middle graphs of Fig. 4 we can see that in self capacitance mode the measured capacitance is still high enough in comparison to the capacitive noise, so that it is possible to distinguish a change in capacitance. Figure 8

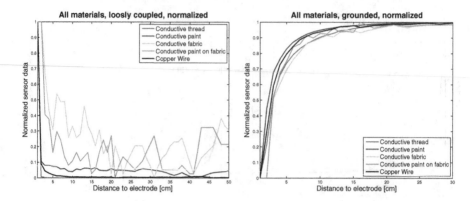

Fig. 8. Superposed normalized mutual capacitance measurements with different electrode materials, sender-receiver pair (1,1) for loosly coupled grounded electrode at distances 1–50 cm and for grounded electrode at distances 1–30 cm

shows the equivalent measurements in mutual capacitance mode. Here we have seen that the environmental capacitive noise can make it impossible to distinguish the signal. This leads us to the recommendation to prefer self capacitance measurement mode over mutual capacitance mode, especially when robustness is required and the environmental conditions are prone to a lot of change.

6.4   Designing Applications

As outlined in Sect. 3 there are 4 application areas for flexible sensors. If we would like to use capacitive sensors in those domains, the choice of material and layout is crucial. By asking five simple questions associated to design factors, the application designer can choose the optimal combination for their purpose.

What sensing range do I need?

Depending on the specific layout, flexible capacitive sensors are capable of detecting touch or proximity to a distance of 10 cm for the evaluated electrode size. Several competing technologies possess only touch detection capabilities. Accordingly, if a proximity detection is required in the specific use case, the designer can give priority to capacitive sensors.

What level of flexibility is required?

Certain applications require highly flexible sensors that can only be realized using some technologies. For other sensors it limits the design options. For example high levels of bending can influence the conductivity of some materials. This limits the choice for applications using capacitive sensors.

Are capacitive sensors the right choice for my application?

The vast variety of materials, shapes, and modes to choose from, make capacitive sensors a powerful choice for applications. However, in many use cases this is not required or suitable. Capacitive sensors can only detect conductive objects and the presence of those. If we need information about other characteristics, such as color, other sensors are required.

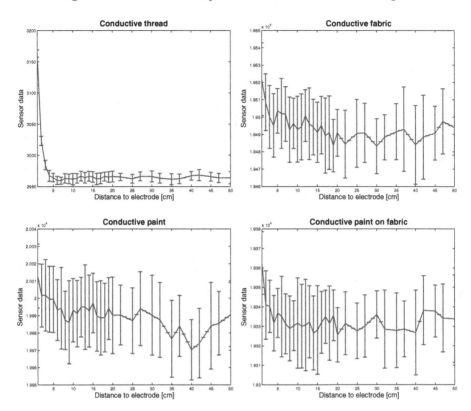

Fig. 9. Mutual capacitance measurements with different electrode materials of sender 1 and receiver 1 at distance 1–50 cm

What is the best sensor material?

Giving a definite answer on this is impossible, as the material and use case have to be chosen in accordance. Some instances may require specific properties, such as transparency. Our measurements have shown that all materials are good candidates for a large number of different use cases, as they equally combines high detection range and resolution.

How many sensors are needed?

This factor entirely depends on the use case. If we want to precisely measure the location of a small object, numerous small electrodes connected to sensors are required, e.g. small conductive thread patches that detect the presence of a finger for explicit interaction scenarios. For physiological measurements the size has to be adapted to the measured object. Detecting the breathing rate may require a large thread electrode near to the chest.

Which layout and measurement mode should I choose?

The most notable advantage of shunt mode is the reduced number of required sensors in grid layouts. This mutual capacitance measurement is often chosen in touch screens. If we require similar levels of precision, using a grid and reduced

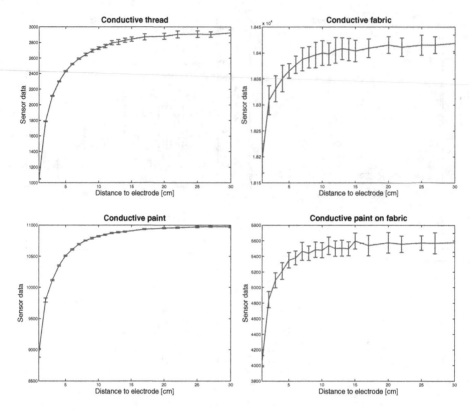

Fig. 10. Mutual capacitance measurements with different electrode materials of sender 1 and receiver 1 at distance 1–30 cm

number of sensors may be beneficial. For heterogeneous setups, using loading mode systems may be advantageous, since they do not require two electrodes in proximity.

7   Conclusion and Outlook

In this paper we presented a quantitative approach for choosing electrode materials. We identified criteria which enable developers of flexible capacitive sensing applications to choose the convenient electrode material for their application. We compared self and mutual capacitance mode and got to the conclusion, that for applications which need to be robust and are surrounded by changing environmental properties it is advisable to choose the self capacitance mode over the mutual capacitance mode. This is because the parasitic capacitance is at some point so high that the small change in capacitance in mutual capacitance mode is not detectable anymore in comparison to the fluctuations in the noise. However, by comparing the results in self and mutual capacitance mode of the different electrode materials we infer that without the influence of noise all electrode materials would be equally well suitable for flexible capacitive sensor applications. Finally, in the last section we presented some guideline questions to help developers choose the suitable layout for their application. Further, one could extend the evaluation criteria by effectuating measurements with different electrode layouts and shapes. Due to the fact that the measurements might be error prone to ambient noise, a system to detect these situations would be helpful. Additionally, it would be of interest to evaluate the characteristics of different materials while bending them.

References

1. Grosse-Puppendahl, T., Berghoefer, Y., Braun, A., Wimmer, R., Kuijper, A.: OpenCapSense: a rapid prototyping toolkit for pervasive interaction using capacitive sensing. In: IEEE International Conference on Pervasive Computing and Communications (2013)
2. Wimmer, R., Kranz, M., Boring, S., Schmidt, A.: A capacitive sensing toolkit for pervasive activity detection and recognition. In: Fifth Annual IEEE International Conference on Pervasive Computing and Communications (PerCom 2007), pp. 171–180 (2007)
3. Djakow, M., Braun, A., Marinc, A.: MoviBed - sleep analysis using capacitive sensors. In: Stephanidis, C., Antona, M. (eds.) UAHCI 2014, Part IV. LNCS, vol. 8516, pp. 171–181. Springer, Heidelberg (2014)
4. Chang, W.-Y., Chen, C.-C., Yang, C.-L.: The applications of projected capacitive array sensing in healthcare. In: 2014 IEEE International Symposium on Bioelectronics and Bioinformatics (IEEE ISBB 2014), pp. 1–4. IEEE, April 2014
5. Rus, S., Grosse-Puppendahl, T., Kuijper, A.: Recognition of Bed Postures Using Mutual Capacitance Sensing. In: Aarts, E., et al. (eds.) AmI 2014. LNCS, vol. 8850, pp. 51–66. Springer, Heidelberg (2014)
6. Weigel, M., Lu, T., Bailly, G., Oulasvirta, A., Majidi, C., Steimle, J.: Iskin: flexible, stretchable and visually customizable on-body touch sensors for mobile computing. In: Proceedings of the 33rd Annual ACM Conference on Human Factors in Computing Systems, CHI 2015, pp. 2991–3000. ACM, New York, NY, USA (2015)
7. Singh, G., Nelson, A., Robucci, R., Patel, C., Banerjee, N.: Inviz: low-power personalized gesture recognition using wearable textile capacitive sensor arrays. In: 2015 IEEE International Conference on Pervasive Computing and Communications (PerCom), March 2015
8. Baldwin, R., Bobovych, S., Robucci, R., Patel, C., Banerjee, N.: Gait analysis for fall prediction using hierarchical textile-based capacitive sensor arrays. In: Proceedings of the 2015 Design, Automation & Test in Europe Conference & Exhibition, DATE 2015, pp. 1293–1298. EDA Consortium, San Jose, CA, USA (2015)
9. Dobbelstein, D., Hock, P., Rukzio, E.: Belt: an unobtrusive touch input device for head-worn displays. In: Proceedings of the 33rd Annual ACM Conference on Human Factors in Computing Systems, CHI 2015, pp. 2135–2138. ACM, New York, NY, USA (2015)
10. Teodorescu, H.-N.: Textile-, conductive paint-based wearable devices for physical activity monitoring. In: E-Health and Bioengineering Conference (EHB), pp. 1–4. IEEE (2013)
11. Braun, A., Wichert, R., Kuijper, A., Fellner, D.W.: Capacitive proximity sensing in smart environments. J. Ambient Intell. Smart Environ. 7(4), 1–28 (2015)

12. Holleis, P., Schmidt, A., Paasovaara, S., Puikkonen, A., Häkkilä, J.: Evaluating capacitive touch input on clothes. In: Proceedings of the 10th International Conference on Human Computer Interaction with Mobile Devices and Services, Mobile-HCI 2008, pp. 81–90. ACM, New York, NY, USA (2008)
13. Karrer, T., Wittenhagen, M., Lichtschlag, L., Heller, F., Borchers, J.: Pinstripe: eyes-free continuous input on interactive clothing. In: Proceedings of the SIGCHI Conference on Human Factors in Computing Systems, CHI 2011, pp. 1313–1322. ACM, New York, NY, USA (2011)
14. Ueno, A., Akabane, Y., Kato, T., Hoshino, H., Kataoka, S., Ishiyama, Y.: Capacitive sensing of electrocardiographic potential through cloth from the dorsal surface of the body in a supine position: A preliminary study. IEEE Trans. Biomed. Eng. **54**(4), 759–766 (2007)
15. Rekimoto, J.: SmartSkin: an infrastructure for freehand manipulation on interactive surfaces. In: Proceedings of the SIGCHI Conference on Human (2002)
16. Wimmer, R., Baudisch, P.: Modular and deformable touch-sensitive surfaces based on time domain reflectometry. In: Proceedings of the 24th Annual ACM Symposium on User Interface Software and Technology - UIST 2011, (1), p. 517 (2011)
17. Vega, K., Cunha, M., Fuks, H.: Hairware: conductive hair extensions as a capacitive touch input device. In: Proceedings of the 20th International Conference on Intelligent User Interfaces Companion, IUI Companion 2015, pp. 89–92. ACM, New York, NY, USA (2015)
18. Vega, K., Cunha, M., Fuks, H.: Hairware: the conscious use of unconscious auto-contact behaviors. In: Proceedings of the 20th International Conference on Intelligent User Interfaces, IUI 2015, pp. 78–86. ACM, New York, NY, USA (2015)

Knowledge vs. Support

Approaching a Benchmark for Privacy in AmI

Jasper van de Ven[(⊠)] and Frank Dylla

Cognitive Systems Group, University of Bremen, Bremen, Germany
{vandeven,dylla}@informatik.uni-bremen.de

Abstract. Privacy is recognized as one of the key factors regarding the acceptance of *ambient intelligence* (AmI). However, privacy is neglected in many projects. We address a formal representation of AmI allowing to model systems including privacy expectations and assumptions. In order to be able to compare systems, either existing or theoretically defined, we develop a benchmark framework that is based on this formal representation. We demonstrate the applicability of our approach with a system implementing two different privacy settings.

1 Introduction

The increasing miniaturization and embedded presence of technology and artificial intelligence in our everyday life has made the vision of *ambient intelligence* (AmI) a reality. AmI can provide support like personalized and automated control of environments, e.g., control lights and heaters according to preferences or situational context, present desired information, or provide communication possibilities, e.g., [1–3]. Privacy has been recognized as one of the key acceptance factors, but is mostly dealt with using an ad-hoc approach, postponed, or even neglected at all. The reasons for this practice include that a generally accepted understanding and formalization of privacy with a focus on systems is missing.

To address this gap, we compare different concepts of privacy provided in literature, e.g., from the research fields of AmI, Smart Environments, Pervasive, and Ubiquitous Computing (Sect. 2.1). This review lead to the observation that a formal representation is beneficial, as it allows to logically analyze an AmI. As a foundation we build o a general model of AmI (Sect. 2.2) and apply general purpose abstractions from the field of Qualitative Spatio-Temporal Representation and Reasoning (QSTR) (Sect. 2.3). Due to its mathematical properties this combination allows for reasoning about a system on an abstract logical level.

Firstly, we demonstrate how such a representation allows for including privacy expectations and assumptions (Sect. 3). Secondly, it allows us to provide formal methods to evaluate given systems regarding specific scenarios (Sect. 4). For this, we present a first approach to a benchmark framework for privacy in ambient intelligence (based on our understanding of the concept of privacy). To this end, an abstract design for general systems and a set of scenarios, including pre processed sensor readings, reasoning rules, action rules, and privacy policies

© Springer International Publishing Switzerland 2015
Kameas et al. (Eds.): AmI 2015, LNCS 9425, pp. 93–108, 2015.
DOI: 10.1007/978-3-319-26005-1_7

are addressed. We propose a measure relating available knowledge, supportive actions, privacy violations, and required computation time. The applicability of the measure is evaluated on the basis of the results of a prototypical system with two different privacy affordance implementations.

2   Related Work

In order to embed our work we start with an overview of general privacy concepts and their adaptations in AmI (Sect. 2.1) and address a general model of AmI (which we adopt in the rest of the paper (Sect. 2.2). As we build our system on qualitative abstractions, we give an introduction to a general qualitative formalization framework (Sect. 2.3).

2.1   Concepts of Privacy

We provide a brief overview of dominating conceptualizations and related work in the general research fields of AmI, Smart Environments, Awareness Systems, as well as Pervasive and Ubiquitous Computing regarding privacy. In this context, we do not differentiate between the fields, but focus on the notions and application of privacy concepts and methods. As a result of the literature review, we do not believe that a general and unifying definition of the privacy concept is possible.

The question of why it is hard to define privacy is partly answered by the statement that "privacy issues are fundamentally not technical" [4]. That is, they are highly dependent on the concerned individual, its situational, and cultural background [5], i.e., user expectations also called privacy assumptions [6]. In the context of the above mentioned research fields the literature mainly focuses on four perspectives on privacy:

- *Information Privacy* (e.g., [7,8]) addresses the accessibility of (personal) information by other entities. That is, understanding the concept as an abstract data-protection or access-control problem, i.e., assumed theoretic access rights.
- *Personal Privacy* (e.g., [9]) follows the concept of information privacy, but also includes aspects of information security as being in the main focus privacy.
- *Territorial Privacy* (e.g., [10–12]) addresses the perceptibility of information by other entities. That is, understanding the concept as a spatio-temporal problem. For example, if we close the door to the room we are in, someone outside should not be able to see us (assuming the door is opaque).
- *Location Privacy* (e.g., [4,13]) addresses the availability of information regarding the (current) location of an individual. This concept originated due to the increasing number of mobile devices and availability of location-based services.

All these notions agree on two aspects: (1) privacy is addressing the availability of information and (2) privacy is generally user-centric. That is, users have expectations and assumptions about other entities having and using information concerning them. These expectations and assumptions are mostly defined by privacy policies, e.g., [14].

Regarding the application of privacy protecting or enhancing methods in AmI, van de Ven and Dylla [15] found that these are not sufficiently addressed in most existing (communication targeting) systems developed in the field of AmI. Only one (ATRACO/iSpace [16]) out of 17 investigated systems provides a definition of how the general concept of privacy was understood.

Another aspect of privacy implementations is their comparability, i.e., the existence of an applicable measure. This seems to be a rather unattended research aspect. A general overview of the problem of measuring privacy is addressed, for example, by [5,7,8,14]. Coney et al. [17] propose a measure based on stochastic and conditional independence of additional information from a known fact. That is, measuring the "amount of privacy loss". A similar approach is to compare results generated by a system to results provided beforehand (often referred to as *gold standard*), e.g., [15]. In addition, Lopez et al. [14] propose to create a *social pressure measure* to enforce the application of privacy enabling or enhancing methods.

For the remainder of this paper, we adopt a notion of privacy similar to the concept of territorial privacy. However, we do not restrict to perceptibility of physical and virtual worlds, but also allow non physically extended space, e.g., the memory of an individual or cloud storage. This allows us to understand the concept of informational privacy in a spatio-temporal context and the concept of privacy in general as the existence and availability of information. The specific definitions of expected or assumed existence and availability of information is formalized through privacy policies for specific contexts. That is, a provided privacy policy defines rules expressing which information is allowed to exist when, where (or to whom), and under which situational context. Furthermore, we adopt the concept of *privacy as a service* (introduced by van de Ven and Dylla [15]), i.e., not taking the user-centric perspective, but seeing privacy as a service a system wants to offer.

2.2 General Model of Ambient Intelligence

From the users' perspective an ambient intelligence is often a black-box, i.e., a system receiving input through embedded sensors and somehow generating output in form of actions. Following Augusto's [18] definition of ambient intelligence research, we see the focus on the artificial intelligence aspect and not on the development and deployment of devices. Regarding the process of deriving output, i.e., deciding which action of the system at hand to execute, most ambient intelligence depends on the ability to perceive and interpret context information. Thus, if an applied ambient intelligence is based on computational reasoning, a respective formal representation of the world is required. This can be viewed as the problem of describing a spatio-temporal scene (e.g., [19,20]) or processes (e.g., [21]) and related contextual information, e.g., presence of individuals or objects, activity, and social information. We address the fundamentals behind these spatio-temporal representations in more detail in Sect. 2.3.

We adopt the general architecture for ambient intelligence introduced in [15,22]. The authors provide a full set of logical formulas describing a system

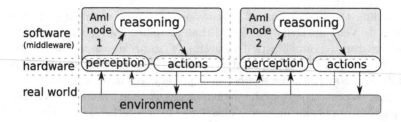

Fig. 1. General model of AmI

and describe system functionality in detail. Figure 1 depicts the architecture and indicates, how physical world, hardware, and software can be connected to create an ambient intelligence.

That is, a system perceives the environment and stores the gained information. Next, reasoning methods are applied to infer further knowledge and decide what to do. Finally, actions are executed to achieve the decided upon goal. Together, these three steps form the *reasoning cycle* of an AmI, i.e., the artificial intelligence aspect. This architecture allows to create a system consisting of a single device (also called *node* or *peer*) or multiple devices that exchange information. The exchange of information can in general be modeled by means of perceptions and actions of individual devices. Therefore, we are able to restrict our presentation to single device systems, although results carry over to multidevice systems directly.

2.3   Qualitative Framework for Environmental Modelling

Our work is based on Qualitative Spatio-Temporal Representation and Reasoning (QSTR) and an integration thereof with modal logic operators.

In order to tell an AmI to follow the needs of users, e.g., privacy, these needs must be formalized. By means of qualitative descriptions one can focus on distinctions between objects that make an important and relevant difference with respect to a given task [23]. Therefore, we need to capture such distinctions about objects in the real world, also considered as commonsense knowledge, with a limited set of symbols, i.e., without numerical values [24]. These distinctions are captured by *relations*, which summarize indistinguishable cases into a single symbol, e.g., whether two regions are **overlapping** or **disconnected**. In the field of QSTR the underlying physical structure of space can be exploited for performing well defined reasoning. A set of relations together with operations on them is called a *qualitative calculus*.

Qualitative calculi are based on partition schemes of the underlying domain. The set of all possible relations between two spatial entities (or n in case of n-nary calculi) is categorized into a set of atomic relationships called *base relations* ($\mathcal{BR}$) which either represent themselves meaningful relations for the task at hand or which allow these relations to be obtained by means of union of base relations. Since relations are ordinary sets, set-theoretic operations are applicable to

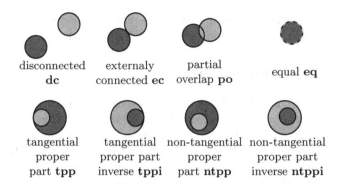

disconnected   externaly   partial
dc   connected **ec** overlap **po**   equal **eq**

tangential   tangential   non-tangential non-tangential
proper   proper part proper   proper part
part **tpp**   inverse **tppi** part **ntpp**   inverse **ntppi**

Fig. 2. The eight base relations of RCC-8.

qualitative relations. For the purpose of this paper it is sufficient that a qualitative calculus allows us to model binary relations between spatial entities using unions of base relations. Since base relations are defined by a partition scheme, they are naturally disjoint and thus conjunction would be useless. The most widely considered knowledge representation for qualitative calculi is constraint-based. Given a set of variables $X = \{x_1, \ldots, x_n\}$ and a set of base relations $\mathcal{BR} = \{b_1, \ldots, b_m\}$, a knowledge base consists of constraints $(x_i \{b_{i_1}, \ldots, b_{i_k}\} x_j)$ which say that spatial entities x_i and x_j are in relation $b_{i_1} \cup \ldots \cup b_{i_k}$. Qualitative spatial reasoning then provides us with (calculi-specific) algorithms to decide whether a constraint-satisfaction problem (CSP) consisting of such constraints is satisfiable or not [25]. This kind of reasoning also allows to derive new constraints that follow from a given set of constraints.

We exemplify the idea of a qualitative calculus with the *Region Connection Calculus* (RCC-8) [26]. Topological distinctions are inherently qualitative in nature and also represent one of the most general and cognitively adequate ways for the representation of spatial information [27]. RCC-8 is based on a binary *connection* relation $C(a, b)$ denoting that region a is connected to region b. Exploiting the connectivity of regions eight base relations are defined (see Fig. 2).

For representing dynamics in our AmI we require temporal sequence knowledge, i.e., in which order states occur. For this, we adopt the approach taken in [28] to model social conventions. The authors apply the modal logic LTL (Linear Temporal Logic) [29] in order to connect states by means of modal operators like *next* or *always*. The integration is implemented by encoding qualitative spatial relations in terms of propositional symbols and extending the semantics to also include a spatial semantic such that only spatially consistent states are considered. The building blocks of this logic, called QLTL, are (a) a set of spatial symbols, which are possibly of different sorts representing entities in the environment, e.g., the nodes n_i, (b) a set of functional symbols, e.g., to address the sensor space of a node $range(n_1)$, (c) a set of qualitative relation symbols, e.g., RCC-8, and (d) a set of general proposition symbols to represent non spatial knowledge, e.g., whether the environment is *populated*. Thereupon, they define the set of propositions allowed and how formulae are structured.

3   Formalizing Ambient Intelligence

In order to compare and investigate different systems with respect to provided privacy, we introduce a formal representation of AmI. For this, we adopt the QLTL approach in order to provide a formal representation of the situational context of an AmI and how this context evolved to its current state. To simplify the understanding of the structure we refine the components of QLTL, specifically the functional symbols. Thus, the ingredients for our formal representation are:

- $\mathcal{O}$ is a set of symbols for physical and immaterial object
- $\mathcal{Q_S}$ is a set of symbols for qualitative spatial functions (qualitative spatial features of an object, e.g., region or orientation)
- $\mathcal{Q_A}$ is a set of symbols for activity functions (activities of an object)
- $\mathcal{A_S}$ is a set of symbols for sensor perceptions
- $\mathcal{A_I}$ is a set of symbols for actions (actuator changes by the AmI)
- $\mathcal{A_R}$ is a set of symbols for reasoning rules
- $\mathcal{A_A}$ is a set of symbols for action rules
- $\mathcal{R}$ is a set of symbols for qualitative relations
- $\mathcal{G}$ is a set of symbols for further propositions

The set of all possible propositions $\mathcal{P}$ (Eq. 1) is the combined set of objects, the activities specific objects are conducting, current sensor perceptions and actuator uses, and spatial relations[1] between objects.

$$\mathcal{P} = \mathcal{O} \cup \mathcal{G} \cup \{a(o)|a \in \mathcal{Q_A}, o \in \mathcal{O}\} \cup$$
$$\{p(o)|p \in \mathcal{A_S}, o \in \mathcal{O}\} \cup \{i(o)|i \in \mathcal{A_I}, o \in \mathcal{O}\} \tag{1}$$
$$\{r(x,y)|r \in \mathcal{R}, x,y \in \{s(o)|s \in \mathcal{Q_S}, o \in \mathcal{O}\}\}$$

We consider a *state* as a (partial) snapshot of currently holding propositions recursively defined by:

- p is a state for every $p \in \mathcal{P}$
- if ϕ is a state, so is $\neg\phi$
- if ϕ, ψ are states, so is $\phi \otimes \psi$ with $\otimes \in \{\wedge, \vee\}$

A *situation description* also includes temporal relations between contained states. Thus, if ϕ is a state, then $M\phi$ with $M \in \{\circ[t_i, t_j], \diamond[t_i, t_j]\}$ is a situation description. The time points t_i and t_j define the existence and duration of an interval in which the related state holds. We assume linear time, i.e., it holds that $\forall t_i, t_j : t_0 \leq t_i \leq t_j < t_\infty$. The semantics of the modal operations M connect states sequentially to situation descriptions:

---

[1] Currently, we define only the set of binary relations, due to readability and simplicity. However, this can be changed to any arity of relation without influence on the remaining representation specification.

- $\circ[t_i, t_j]\phi$ (during): $\forall t_x$: ϕ holds at t_x with $i \leq x \leq j$ (i.e., $t_0 \leq t_i \leq t_x \leq t_j$)
- $\diamond[t_i, t_j]\phi$ (within): $\exists t_x$: ϕ holds at t_x with $i \leq x \leq j$ (i.e., $t_0 \leq t_i \leq t_x \leq t_j$)

Based on this formalism for situation descriptions, we formalize an AmI through its knowledge base. The knowledge base is understood as the internal representation of the world, as perceived by the system, i.e., a set of descriptions of perceived situations connected by specific internal actions of the system. Thus, if $\delta_1, \delta_2, \ldots \delta_n$ are situation descriptions, then $\delta_1 \oplus_1 \delta_2 \oplus_2 \cdots \oplus_{n-1} \delta_n$ with $\oplus_i \in \mathcal{A}_\mathcal{S} \cup \mathcal{A}_\mathcal{I} \cup \mathcal{A}_\mathcal{R} \cup \mathcal{A}_\mathcal{A} \cup \{\odot[t_i, t_j]\}$ is a knowledge base description, i.e., a description of the respective AmI and its situational context. The semantics of $\odot[t_i, t_j]$ explicate inertia between the two connected situation descriptions, i.e., all contained propositions that hold at t_i also hold at t_j (with $t_0 \leq t_i < t_j$). For reasons of simplicity, we restrict the use of the modal operator M regarding situation descriptions that are part of a knowledge base to only allow $\circ[t_i, t_j]$ to prevent ambiguous interpretations of a given knowledge base.[2]

Regarding the rules represented in the sets $\mathcal{A}_\mathcal{R}$ and $\mathcal{A}_\mathcal{A}$, each symbol represents an event-condition-action (ECA) rule (e.g., [3,30]) to trigger actions or infer additional knowledge based on a knowledge base provided. These are rules firing on a specified event if a specified condition holds to execute the specified action. For the defined representation, each rule consist of a trigger part T, which is a disjunction of conjunctions of situation descriptions, and an action part C, which is a conjunction of the form $\circ[t_{i_a}, t_{j_a}]P_a \wedge \cdots \wedge \circ[t_{i_b}, t_{j_b}]P_b \wedge c_1 \wedge \cdots \wedge c_n$ with $n \in \mathbb{N}, \forall P_z \in \mathcal{P}, \forall c_y \in \mathcal{A}_\mathcal{I}, \forall t_{i_x}, t_{j_x} : t_0 \leq t_{i_x} \leq t_{j_x}$. That is, the action part can either introduce new knowledge, e.g. $\circ[t_{i_a}, t_{j_a}]P_a$, or tell the system to use one of its actuators, e.g., c_1. An exemplary rule checking existence of the proposition P_1 at time 3 as well as P_2 within the temporal interval [1, 3] and if fired issues P_3 to be holding at time 3 is $\circ[3,3]P_1 \wedge \diamond[1,3]P_2 \longrightarrow \circ[3,3]P_3$. The according generic rule to check at arbitrary time point t_x would be $\circ[t_x, t_x]P_1 \wedge \diamond[t_{x-2}, t_x]P_2 \longrightarrow \circ[t_x, t_x]P_3$. To check the trigger of a rule regarding the knowledge base provided, methods from the field of logics can be applied, e.g., model-checking [31].

However, we acknowledge that these kind of rules allow to define 'broken' systems, i.e., create loops and by that possibly leading to deadlock situations. The reason to allow this is, that we want to have a very general model of AmI, even if their respective rule sets contain mistakes or are badly designed.

As a last step, we add another set of rules $\mathcal{A}_\mathcal{P}$ representing a privacy policy, defining the privacy assumptions, i.e., privacy violations and allowances. Thus, by applying these rules to a given knowledge base, we can determine, if the defined policy is meet by ensuring activation or inactivity of the provided rules.

4   Approaching a Benchmark

In order to create a measure for comparing different AmI implementations regarding privacy, we adopted the privacy balance measure introduced in [15]

---

[2] In general, usage of $\diamond[t_i, t_j]$ is possible, but would lead to multiple interpretations of a single knowledge base.

and developed a general benchmark framework around it. The privacy balance measure indicates how much knowledge is available to a system in relation to theoretically possibly available knowledge. The same is provided for triggered actions, i.e., support provided, and privacy violations detected. At this point, we assume a sound and complete violation detection method, i.e., it will always detect a privacy violation if one exists.

To approach a benchmark framework, we start with an existing AmI laboratory. The formal representation introduced is applied to generate a (simplified) description of the system. This formal representation provides the basis for the *scenarios* used in our benchmark. A scenario is a description of an environment, i.e., sensors, actuators, and applied privacy policy. Furthermore, a set of sensing event sequences is provided. Each sequence is to be evaluated individually against a provided set of perfect results, called *gold standard*. We assume a sequential execution of the investigated AmI, synchronized on sensor events and reasoning cycles. We acknowledge, that this is not strictly true in real-world applications, but it provides the possibility to also investigate systems which are not online-processing capable. However, this approach indicates whether an evaluated system would be able to handle a provided scenario in real-time as the execution time is part of the data collected.

In contrast to the privacy balance originally proposed in [15], we only gather data at the end of a reasoning cycle to simplify data collection[3]. That is, we collect the number of privacy violations only at the end of a reasoning cycle (*violations*). This value is complemented with the number of actuator instructions (*support*), the number of facts in the knowledge base (*knowledge*), the computing time in seconds per individual reasoning cycle, and the computing time for an entire scenario to be processed.

4.1   The Spatial Interaction Lab

Using the model of AmI introduced in Sect. 2.2 as a basis and building on the privacy functionality introduced in [15], we implemented a prototypical system using the *Spatial Interaction Lab* (SIL) environment [22,32]. SIL consists of 18 12″, single core touchscreen computers with visual and audio sensors embedded in an office floor environment replacing regular doorplates. Figure 3 gives an impression of the environment together with an overall layout. Additionally, it provides an impression of what some of the visual sensors perceive. Figure 4 depicts the architecture of the plug-in based middleware of SIL. It is implemented in C++ in combination with Qt. The middleware provides general communication infrastructure and its functionality is extensible through plug-ins, e.g., sensor data abstraction, visual output generation, or a reasoning engine.

In order to evaluate our approach we developed required plug-ins. Among them a privacy affording reasoning engine and a people detector. Furthermore, we implemented a plug-in to provide simulated sensor data in order to create

---

[3] In [15] data is collected at three different locations in the reasoning cycle. In general, we assume subsequent adaption of existing systems unfeasible.

Fig. 3. Impression of the SIL environment

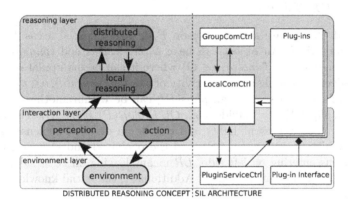

Fig. 4. The SIL middleware

reusable scenarios for testing functionality, e.g., different privacy affordances, of our system.

4.2 Example Scenario Description

We now present an example scenario description and corresponding sensing event sequences. The environment of the hypothetical scenario is depicted in Fig. 5. The AmI is supposed to control the lights in the environment based on the position of a person. That is, the light closest to the person, as well as the lights next to it, are to be turned on. Additionally, the proposition *POPULATED* is to be set to true, indicating that the floor is populated. The formal description is provided through the sets:

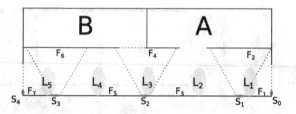

Fig. 5. The restroom scenario environment

- $\mathcal{O} = \{P, F_1, F_2, F_3, F_4, F_5, F_6, F_7, A, B\}$
- $\mathcal{A}_{\mathcal{S}} = \{S_0E, S_0L, S_4E, S_4L, S_1ER, S_1EL, S_1LR, S_1LL, S_2ER, S_2EL, \\ S_2EF, S_2LR, S_2LL, S_2LF, S_3ER, S_3EL, S_3LR, S_3LL\}$
- $\mathcal{A}_{\mathcal{I}} = \{L_1, L_2, L_3, L_4, L_5\}$
- $\mathcal{Q}_{\mathcal{S}} = \{phys(X), func(X)\}$
- $\mathcal{Q}_{\mathcal{A}} = \{waits(X)\}$
- $\mathcal{R} = \{IN(X,Y), OUT(X,Y)\}$
- $\mathcal{G} = \{POPULATED\}$

The involved objects are a single person P, abstract spatial areas $F_1, \ldots, F_7$, and two rooms A, B. An object can have a physical extend $(phys(o), o \in \mathcal{O})$ and a functional space $(func(o), o \in \mathcal{O})$ where it can be manipulated. Furthermore, an object can indulge in the activity of waiting $(waits(o), o \in \mathcal{O})$. Regarding spatial relations, a space, e.g., $phys(P)$, can be within another space, e.g., $IN(phys(P), phys(A))$, or outside, e.g., $OUT(phys(P), phys(A))$. The actuator symbols $L_1, \ldots, L_5$ represent lights and can be on or off. The sensor symbols denote the emitting sensor, e.g., S_2, and the perceived and abstracted action, e.g., EL means entering on left side, LR means leaving on right side, and EF means entering in fornt of the sensor. Additionally, the initial knowledge base is assumed to be

$$KB = \{ \circ [t_0, t_0]F_1 \wedge \circ[t_0, t_0]F_2 \wedge \circ[t_0, t_0]F_3 \wedge \circ[t_0, t_0]F_4 \wedge$$
$$\circ [t_0, t_0]F_5 \wedge \circ[t_0, t_0]F_6 \wedge \circ[t_0, t_0]F_7 \wedge \circ[t_0, t_0]A \wedge \circ[t_0, t_0]B\} \quad (2)$$

The applied privacy policy states, that the system is not allowed to know, when an individual is inside room A or B. The system can detect an individual entering room B by sensor S_2 explicitly. In contrast, no sensor is given to detect an individual entering room A. Therefore, the system will deduce this fact implicitly if an individual stays in area $F3$ longer than 2000 milliseconds.[4] Table 1 provides six different sensor event sequences (C1-C6) for the scenario.

4.3   The Gold Standard

Overall, we generated six scenarios (C1-C6) for a hypothetical but perfect AmI in the sense of privacy awareness affordance (Table 1). Therefore, we provide

---

[4] We randomly decided to use this duration and also assume a maximal duration of 1000 milliseconds between reasoning cycles.

Table 1. Scenario and gold standards

time	sensor	actuator	knowledge	support	violations	sensor	actuator	knowledge	support	violations	sensor	actuator	knowledge	support	violations
		C1					C2					C3			
+0	S_0E	L_1,L_2	14	2	0	S_0E	L_1,L_2	14	2	0	S_0E	L_1,L_2	14	2	0
+1000	S_1ER	L_1,L_2	28	0	0	S_1ER	L_1,L_2	28	0	0	S_1ER	L_1,L_2	28	0	0
+2000	S_1LL	L_1,L_2,L_3	43	1	0	S_1LL	L_1,L_2,L_3	43	1	0	S_1LL	L_1,L_2,L_3	43	1	0
+3000		L_1,L_2,L_3	57	0	0		L_1,L_2,L_3	57	0	0		L_1,L_2,L_3	57	0	0
+4000	S_2ER	L_2,L_3,L_4	72	2	0		L_1,L_2,L_3	71	0	1	S_2ER	L_2,L_3,L_4	72	2	0
+5000	S_2LL	L_3,L_4,L_5	87	2	0		L_1,L_2,L_3	85	0	1	S_2LF	L_2,L_3,L_4	87	0	1
+6000	S_3ER	L_4,L_5	101	1	0		L_1,L_2,L_3	99	0	1		L_2,L_3,L_4	101	0	1
+7000	S_3LL	L_4,L_5	115	0	0		L_1,L_2,L_3	113	0	1		L_2,L_3,L_4	115	0	1
+8000	S_4L		125	2	0		L_1,L_2,L_3	127	0	1		L_2,L_3,L_4	129	0	1
		C4					C5					C6			
+0	S_0E	L_1,L_2	14	2	0	S_0E	L_1,L_2	14	2	0	S_0E	L_1,L_2	14	2	0
+1000	S_1ER	L_1,L_2	28	0	0	S_1ER	L_1,L_2	28	0	0	S_1ER	L_1,L_2	28	0	0
+2000	S_1LL	L_1,L_2,L_3	43	1	0	S_1LL	L_1,L_2,L_3	43	1	0	S_1LL	L_1,L_2,L_3	43	1	0
+3000		L_1,L_2,L_3	57	0	0		L_1,L_2,L_3	57	0	0		L_1,L_2,L_3	57	0	0
+4000		L_1,L_2,L_3	71	0	1	S_2ER	L_2,L_3,L_4	72	2	0		L_1,L_2,L_3	71	0	1
+5000		L_1,L_2,L_3	85	0	1	S_2LF	L_2,L_3,L_4	87	0	1		L_1,L_2,L_3	85	0	1
+6000		L_1,L_2,L_3	99	0	1		L_2,L_3,L_4	101	0	1	S_2ER	L_2,L_3,L_4	100	2	0
+7000		L_1,L_2,L_3	113	0	1		L_2,L_3,L_4	115	0	1	S_2LF	L_2,L_3,L_4	115	0	1
+8000	S_2ER	L_2,L_3,L_4	128	2	0		L_2,L_3,L_4	129	0	1		L_2,L_3,L_4	129	0	1
+9000	S_2LL	L_3,L_4,L_5	143	2	0	S_2EF	L_2,L_3,L_4	144	0	0		L_2,L_3,L_4	143	0	1
+10000	S_3ER	L_4,L_5	157	1	0	S_2LL	L_3,L_4,L_5	159	2	0		L_2,L_3,L_4	157	0	1
+11000	S_3LL	L_4,L_5	171	0	0	S_3ER	L_4,L_5	173	1	0	S_2EF	L_2,L_3,L_4	172	0	0
+12000	S_4L		181	2	0	S_3LL	L_4,L_5	187	0	0	S_2LL	L_3,L_4,L_5	187	2	0
+13000	—	—	—	—	—	S_4L		197	2	0	S_3ER	L_4,L_5	201	1	0
+14000	—	—	—	—	—	—	—	—	—	—	S_3LL	L_4,L_5	215	0	0
+15000	—	—	—	—	—	—	—	—	—	—	S_4L		225	2	0

perfect results for each reasoning cycle, i.e., the gold standard. For each reasoning cycle we provide sensor readings as defined in A_S (sensor), expected actuator activations as defined in A_I (actuator), size of the knowledge base (knowledge), number of triggered action rules as defined in A_A, and number of privacy rules triggered as defined in A_P (violations). The results were created by means of the formal definition of the AmI and its functionality.

With the proposed benchmark framework for ambient intelligence it can be evaluated how close an investigated system is able to reach the provided gold standard. Figure 6 depicts the connection between the scenario, gold standard, AmI, and results evaluated. It has to be noted, that the AmI has to offer the possibility to record the required data. Regarding the conducted actions, this is most likely no problem as one could monitor the actuators of the system. However, information about available knowledge, privacy violations, and computation time have to be logged by the investigated system.

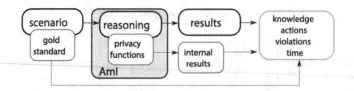

Fig. 6. Measuring Privacy in AmI

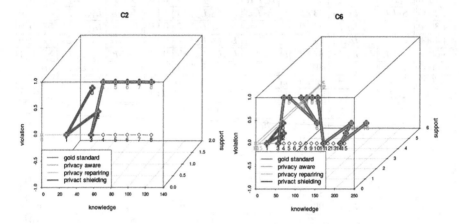

Fig. 7. Exemplary results using knowledge erasing strategy

4.4 Evaluation of Prototypical Systems

We implemented two prototypical reasoning systems with privacy affordances following the architecture introduced in [15] and addressed in Sect. 2.2. These two systems only differ in the utilized *resolve*-strategy: (1) *clear knowledge base* and (2) *remove only triggering knowledge*. Clearing the knowledge base means that all knowledge contained in the knowledge base is removed, regardless whether it is part of a privacy violation or not. By removing only knowledge related to the trigger condition of a rule from the privacy policy, we also provide a method that tries to preserve knowledge.

We evaluated both systems in the scenario and collected all data regarding knowledge base size, support, privacy violations, and computation time. However, the computation time should only be regarded as a general indicator as it is unreliable, i.e., we did not use an actual *real-time* system environment, and highly depend on the hardware[5].

In order to provide a visual interpretation of collected data, we present the results in a colored 3D-graph by creating tuples containing the knowledge base size, support, and violation count for each reasoning cycle (as introduced in [15]). That is, whenever displaying a graph presenting a result also a graph presenting the gold standard should be provided for comparison. In addition, we separately

---

[5] We applied a computer featuring an Intel Core i7-2600 CPU and 16 GB memory.

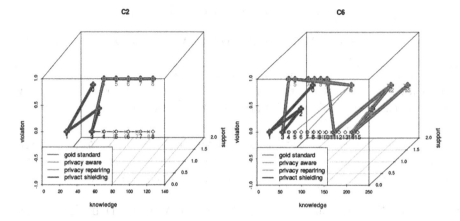

Fig. 8. Exemplary results using knowledge preserving strategy

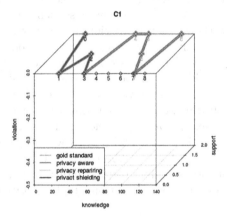

Fig. 9. Exemplary results without privacy violations

provide results regarding the mean, minimal, and maximal computation time per reasoning cycle. Furthermore, the total computation time needed to process all reasoning cycles. The results yielded by our prototypical system implementing the strategy of erasing the entire knowledge base to solve a privacy violation are presented in Fig. 7 and Table 2 for the scenario C2 and C6. These were also evaluated using the strategy to only remove knowledge directly indicating a privacy violation (C2 and C6 in Fig. 8). The results show, that the privacy aware system matches the gold standard derived using the formal representation, indicating sound functionality of the applied detection method. That is, the graph representing the information count at the end of the reasoning cycle exactly matches the graph representing the gold standard. Also, the results show that resolving privacy violations by erasing the entire knowledge base prevents a system to provide support. However, removing only information directly triggering privacy violation rules does not. Furthermore, our results show that applying

Table 2. Exemplary computational time results in seconds

	MEAN	MAX	MIN	TOTAL	MEAN	MAX	MIN	TOTAL
	C2e				C2p			
privacy aware	0.1721	0.348	0.028	1.549	0.1224	0.308	0.017	1.102
privacy repairing	0.0447	0.112	0.002	0.402	0.1582	0.298	0.031	1.424
privacy shielding	144.2193	447.217	0.102	1297.974	150.6969	475.325	0.111	1356.272
	C6e				C6p			
privacy aware	0.2813	0.658	0.016	4.501	0.4638	1.116	0.028	7.421
privacy repairing	0.0312	0.113	0.002	0.499	0.4169	1.031	0.03	6.671
privacy shielding	79.7898	446.501	0.103	1276.637	79.6798	444.506	0.104	1274.877

privacy shielding affordance proposed by van de Ven and Dylla [15] quickly leads to the prevention of any support. The reason is, that all information that might lead to a privacy violation in relation with possible future perceptions is ignored and as soon as the knowledge base reaches a certain size, this is almost always the case. For example, the sensor event sequence C1e depicted in Fig. 9 represents a scenario without any privacy violations occurring. However, the privacy shielding method quickly prevents any support and only applies the inertia action to its knowledge base. This also explains the small minimal computation time for this methods, as it stops as soon as it finds a possible future violation. Regarding the required computation time, our prototype was able to solve the provided scenarios with a maximal computation time of under one second for all privacy affordances, except privacy shielding. These results do not provide any evidence regarding real-time capabilities, as we only evaluated the system on a rather small knowledge base (≈ 200 entries). However, the computation time results for the privacy shielding method indicate that this method is not suitable for real-time approaches (at least our implementation is not).

5   Summary and Future Work

In this paper, we presented a benchmark framework regarding the balance between knowledge, support, and privacy for AmI, based on gold standards. The gold standards were generated based on a formal representation of a perfect AmI and describe desired scenarios and assumed sensor event sequences. We introduced one scenario environment together with six respective sensor event sequences as a first collection to investigate systems. Furthermore, we implemented and evaluated two prototypical systems with differing privacy resolution strategies, gaining promising results. With presenting a corner stone for specific measures, we hope to foster the comparison of existing as well as future AmI systems.

However, this approach still addresses privacy as being a technical problem at its core and not as the socio-technical problem it is (see [4]). Thus, a social measure as an acceptance indicator and social pressure to comply with general standards should be researched.

Next steps will be to also include the projection of privacy violations into the proposed benchmark framework and to provide further and larger scenarios and sensor event sequences. Furthermore, other algorithms and methods for privacy detection, resolution, projection and shielding functionality have to be researched. For example, possibilities to exploit findings from the field of qualitative spatio-temporal reasoning to describe, combine, and evaluate privacy policies and general situation descriptions within AmI seem promising to us. That is, exploiting further properties of the formal representation we introduced. This also directly addresses research regarding the scalability of our approach.

Acknowledgement. We acknowledge German Research Foundation (DFG) funding for project SOCIAL (FR 806/15-1). We thank the four anonymous reviewers for their thoughtful and constructive comments.

References

1. Dewan, P., Ehrlich, K., Greenberg, S., Johnson, C., Prakash, A., Dourish, P., Ellis, C., Ishii, H., Mackay, W.E., Roseman, M.: Computer Supported Co-operative Work. Wiley, New york (1999)
2. Harrison, S.: Media Space 20 + Years of Mediated Life. Computer Supported Cooperative Work. Springer, London (2009)
3. Sadri, F.: Ambient intelligence: A survey. ACM Computing Surveys (CSUR) **43**(4), 36 (2011)
4. Göorlach, A., Heinemann, A., Terpstra, W.W.: Survey on location privacy in pervasive computing. In: Robinson, P., Vogt, H., Wagealla, W. (eds.) Privacy, Security and Trust within the Context of Pervasive Computing. The International Series in Engineering and Computer Science, vol. 780, pp. 23–34. Springer, US (2005)
5. Nissenbaum, H.: Privacy as contextual integrity. Wash. Law Rev. **79**(1), 119–158 (2004)
6. Schaub, F., Könings, B., Weber, M.: Context-adaptive privacy: leveraging context awareness to support privacy decision making. IEEE Pervasive Comput. **14**(1), 34–43 (2015)
7. Solove, D.J.: Understanding Privacy. Harvard University Press, Cambridge (2008)
8. Raab, C.D., Bennett, C.J.: Taking the measure of privacy: can data protection be evaluated? Int. Rev. Adm. Sci. **62**(4), 535–556 (1996)
9. Langheinrich, M.: A privacy awareness system for ubiquitous computing environments. In: Borriello, G., Holmquist, L.E. (eds.) UbiComp 2002. LNCS, vol. 2498, pp. 237–245. Springer, Heidelberg (2002)
10. Konings, B., Schaub, F.: Territorial privacy in ubiquitous computing. In: Proceedings of WONS, pp. 104–108. IEEE (2011)
11. Könings, B., Schaub, F., Weber, M., Kargl, F.: Towards territorial privacy in smart environments. In: AAAI Spring Symposium Series (2010)
12. Könings, B., Schaub, F., Weber, M.: Who, how, and why? enhancing privacy awareness in ubiquitous computing. In: Proceedings of PERCOM Workshop, pp. 364–367 (2013)
13. Wernke, M., Skvortsov, P., Dürr, F., Rothermel, K.: A classification of location privacy attacks and approaches. Pers. Ubiquit. Comput. **18**(1), 163–175 (2014)

14. Lopez, M., Pedraza, J., Carbo, J., Molina, J.M.: Ambient intelligence: applications and privacy policies. In: Corchado, J.M., et al. (eds.) PAAMS 2014. CCIS, vol. 430, pp. 191–201. Springer, Heidelberg (2014)
15. van de Ven, J., Dylla, F.: Privacy classification for ambient intelligence. Proc. Am. 1, 328–343 (2014)
16. Könings, B., Wiedersheim, B., Weber, M.: Privacy management and control in ATRACO. Proc. Am. 1, 51–60 (2010)
17. Coney, L., Hall, J.L., Vora, P.L., Wagner, D.: Towards a privacy measurement criterion for voting systems. In: Proceedings of DGO, Digital Government Society of North America, pp. 287–288 (2005)
18. Augusto, J.: Ambient intelligence: the confluence of ubiquitous/pervasive computing and artificial intelligence. In: Schuster, A.J. (ed.) Intelligent Computing Everywhere, pp. 213–234. Springer, London (2007)
19. Dylla, F., Bhatt, M.: Qualitative spatial scene modeling for ambient intelligence environments. In: Xiong, C.-H., Liu, H., Huang, Y., Xiong, Y.L. (eds.) ICIRA 2008, Part I. LNCS (LNAI), vol. 5314, pp. 716–725. Springer, Heidelberg (2008)
20. Falomir, Z., Museros, L., Gonzalez-Abril, L., Escrig, M.T., Ortega, J.A.: A model for the qualitative description of images based on visual and spatial features. Comput. Vis. Image Underst. 116(6), 698–714 (2012)
21. Kreutzmann, A., Colonius, I., Frommberger, L., Dylla, F., Freksa, C., Wolter, D.: On process recognition by logical inference. In: Lilienthal, A.J., Duckett, T. (eds.) Proceedings of ECMR, pp. 7–12 (2011)
22. van de Ven, J., Schmid, F., Hesselmann, T., Boll, S.: A framework for communication and interaction in spatially distributed social groups. In: Proceedings of SISSI Workshop, pp. 73–82. Copenhagen, Denmark (2010)
23. Kuipers, B.: Qualitative Reasoning: Modeling and Simulation with Incomplete Knowledge. MIT Press, Cambridge (1994)
24. Cohn, A.G., Hazarika, S.M.: Qualitative spatial representation and reasoning: an overview. Fundamenta Informaticae 46(1–2), 1–29 (2001)
25. Renz, J., Nebel, B.: Qualitative spatial reasoning using constraint calculi. In: Handbook of Spatial Logics, pp. 161–215 (2007)
26. Cohn, A.G., Bennett, B., Gooday, J.M., Gotts, N.: RCC: a calculus for region based qualitative spatial reasoning. GeoInformatica 1, 275–316 (1997)
27. Renz, J., Rauh, R., Knauff, M.: Towards cognitive adequacy of topological spatial relations. In: Habel, C., Brauer, W., Freksa, C., Wender, K.F. (eds.) Spatial Cognition 2000. LNCS (LNAI), vol. 1849, pp. 184–197. Springer, Heidelberg (2000)
28. Dylla, F., Kreutzmann, A., Wolter, D.: A qualitative representation of social conventions for application in robotics. In: AAAI Spring Symposium Series (2014)
29. Pnueli, A.: The temporal logic of programs. In: Proceedings of FOCS, pp. 46–57 (1977)
30. Augusto, J.C., Nugent, C.D.: The use of temporal reasoning and management of complex events in smart homes. In: Proceedings of ECAI, vol. 16, p. 778 (2004)
31. Schnoebelen, P.: The complexity of temporal logic model checking. Adv. Modal Logic 4(393–436), 35 (2002)
32. van de Ven, J., Dylla, F.: The spatial interaction laboratory - a distributed middleware and qualitative representation for ambient intelligence. In: Proceedings of STAm I AAAI Workshop (2013)

Lighten Up! — An Ambient Light Progress Bar Using Individually Controllable LEDs

Heiko Müller[1]([✉]), Anastasia Kazakova[2], Wilko Heuten[1], and Susanne Boll[2]

[1] OFFIS - Institute for Information Technology, Oldenburg, Germany
{heiko.muller,wilko.heuten}@offis.de
[2] University of Oldenburg, Oldenburg, Germany
{anastasia.kazakova,susanne.boll}@uni-oldenburg.de

Abstract. Ambient light displays can be used to convey information to office workers in the periphery of their attention without cluttering their computer monitor or distracting users from their primary task. In this paper we report on a user study evaluating *"Lighten Up"*, an ambient light display to give information about secondary task progress over time. We explored the design space with 42 light patterns. We chose two for a study comparing *Lighten Up* against a state-of-the-art on-screen progress bar. Our results suggest that users prefer *Lighten Up* over the on-screen display, if the ambient light display uses a stepwise increase in illumination. Increasing brightness in steps gives users a sense of rhythm and helps them keep track of the progress from the corner of their eye.

1 Introduction

Working on the computer, people need to monitor the progress of various tasks. New software is downloaded from the internet, programs are being installed on the computer, complex calculations need to be finished before continuing work on a given problem. While these tasks are in progress, people continue working on their computers and check on the tasks from time to time. This usually involves finding the window containing the progress information and bringing it to the front of the screen. However, focussing on progress information may hide the current task thus making its resumption more difficult.

We suggest taking the progress information off the screen completely. We introduce *Lighten Up*, an ambient light display designed to update the user on the progress of a task in the periphery of the user's attention. While the person focuses on the current task, she can perceive the progress of the secondary task without having to change focus.

To gain insights into the design space of individually controllable LEDs for display of progress information over time, we first created 42 light patterns and tested for suitability, acceptability, and perceived duration. We then took two promising candidate patterns and evaluated them against a state-of-the-art on-screen progress bar.

In this paper, we report on the design process leading to *Lighten Up* (see Figs. 1 and 2) and on the user study in which we evaluated two promising pattern

© Springer International Publishing Switzerland 2015
Kameas et al. (Eds.): AmI 2015, LNCS 9425, pp. 109–124, 2015.
DOI: 10.1007/978-3-319-26005-1_8

Fig. 1. Study setup of second study showing both *Lighten Up* and on-screen progress bar together with game used as primary task

candidates against a state-of-the-art on-screen progress bar. Our results suggest that users prefer *Lighten Up* over the on-screen display, if the ambient light display uses a stepwise increase in illumination. Increasing brightness in steps gives users a sense of rhythm and helps them keep track of the progress from the corner of their eye.

2 Related Work

When trying to display progress information in the periphery of a person's attention, we need to look at related work from two areas of HCI. One is the area of ambient information display, the other is the area of continuously informing users on the progress of a task.

The concept of "calm technology" was first introduced by Weiser and Brown [19]. Ishii et al. [9] gave a more multi-modal approach to ambient information displays in their ambientROOM.

Stress from waiting periods has been addressed by e.g. Moraveji and Soesanto [14]. They present design heuristics to help create stress-less user interfaces. Also, there is a large scope of work on interruptions and task resumptions, e.g. [1,4,5,12]. Our approach aims to minimize interruptions and keep the user in the loop without distracting his focus away from the primary task. Ambient light displays addressing the peripheral vision of a human being seems is a well-suited modality as perceptional resources differ between focused and peripheral vision according to Wickens and Leibowitz et al. [10,20]. Matthews et al. presented a concept of various attentional and notification levels for ambient information displays [13]. *Lighten Up* is meant to operate on the "make aware" level.

Likkanen and Gomez provide guidelines for system development when designing for user experience with consideration for "subjectively experienced time" [11]. One of the suggestions is to turn waiting time into occupied time. Further they suggest informing a person about the wait time quickly and accurately.

By taking the information off the screen and putting it into the periphery, we expect to be able to better inform a user on the progress of a task. Being available off-screen all the time, the user will not have to search for the information among the various things displayed on the monitor. In addition, the display area, i.e. the illuminated parts of the wall, will provide a larger display of the information.

Progress information can be displayed using various modalities. The auditory channel has been explored by Crease and Brewster [3] as well as Peres [17]. Vibrotactile progress bars were presented by Brewster and King [2]. Harrison et al. report on the design of on-screen progress bars [6]. They found that the type of pattern used for displaying progress greatly affects the perceived duration of the progress.

Using ambient light to convey information on upcoming events and meetings in the office environment, Müller et al. introduced Ambient Timer [15]. Their ambient light display used uniformly controlled LEDs to create a homogeneous light pattern. Focussing on displaying the progress of time rather than the advent of a meeting, Ostendorp et al. presented the Ambient Progress Bar [16], also using uniformly controlled LEDs to present the progress information.

What is missing is a study on how patterns created from individually controlled LEDs can be used to convey progress information in the periphery of a person's attention. In this paper, we report on two studies used first to explore the design space for light patterns from individually controlled LEDs and second to evaluate pattern candidates against a state-of-the-art on-screen progress bar.

3   Lighten Up

Lighten Up is a four-sided frame equipped with individually controllable LEDs (see Fig. 2). It is mounted to the back of a computer monitor. To function properly, the system must either be placed against a reflective surface, e.g. an office wall, or requires another reflective frame to make the light emitted by the LEDs visible to the user.

We used four pre-cut segments of an Adafruit Neopixel Digital RGB LED strip with 60 LEDs per meter. These four segments were mounted to the frame and soldered together. For our prototype we were able to mount a total of 86

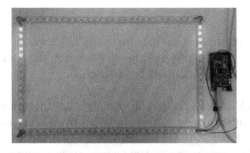

Fig. 2. Lighten Up apparatus with individually controlled LEDs.

LEDs to the frame. We used an Arduino micro-controller to control the LEDs. All patterns were implemented in the Arduino code and selected via a serial connection from a computer.

4   Exploring the Design Space

Our first approach to the design space of ambient light displays for progress information was to try and determine which light patterns were suitable for this type of information. After initial tests, we decided not to use patterns that would be shown both horizontally and vertically, or performing a circular display. All patterns used in the following were either working in the horizontal or vertical dimension.

We designed four basic light behaviours. These behaviours were designed both with either increasing brightness (turning the LEDs on) and decreasing brightness (turning the LEDs off). In the following description, we only use the term increase:

Gradual Illumination. The illumination intensity of the first LED was increased in steps of 1/10th from 0 to 100 % before starting on the next LED, creating a smooth and gradual illumination increase (see Fig. 3).

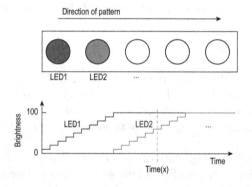

Fig. 3. Gradual Illumination pattern at Time(x). Sketch of the LED-stripe at the top, graph of the brightness of involved LEDs at the bottom.

Stepwise Illumination. In this pattern, each LED was turned on from 0 to 100 % brightness in a single step, then followed by the next LED. There was no gradual increase in illumination (see Fig. 4).

Ladder Fill. All LEDs turn on and off one after another until the last LED in line is reached and stays on. This is followed by another round in which the second to last LED also stays on, and so on (see Fig. 5). This pattern was adopted from the way many slot-machines cycle through the various prize levels when trying to attract people.

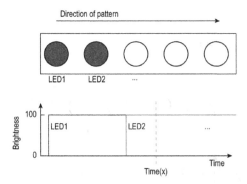

Fig. 4. Stepwise Illumination pattern at Time(x). Sketch of the LED-stripe at the top, graph of the brightness of involved LEDs at the bottom.

Blinking. The first LED turns on, turns off, turns on again. The second LED turns on, both LEDs turn off, turn on again. The third LED turns on, all three LEDs turn off, turn on again, and so on (see Fig. 6). This pattern is similar to the Stepwise Illumination pattern with added blinking of the LEDs.

The timing of the individual control of the LEDs is dependent on the number of LEDs available and the overall pattern duration defined in the Arduino micro-controller for patterns "Gradual Illumination", "Stepwise Illumination" and "Ladder Fill". For the "Blinking" pattern, the blinking part was set to be 200ms on and 200ms off, regardless of overall duration which was, of course, constrained by a minimal threshold. At the end of the progress display, all LEDs were switched off.

Each of the behaviours could be displayed in one of five directions (see Table 1). If the direction was horizontal, both the top and the bottom LED-stripe on the frame were used in parallel. If the direction was vertical, both the left and the right LED-stripe were used in parallel (see Fig. 7).

Table 1. Directions for display of patterns

Dimension	Direction
Horizontal	Centered (H_C)
	Left-Right (H_{LR})
	Right Left (H_{RL})
Vertical	Bottom-Up (V_{BU})
	Top-Down (V_{TD})

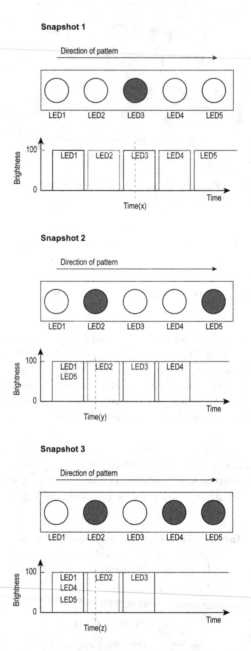

Fig. 5. Ladder-Fill pattern at Time(x) (Snapshot 1), Time(y) (Snapshot 2), and Time(z) (Snapshot 3). Sketch of the LED-stripe at the top, graph of the brightness of involved LEDs at the bottom.

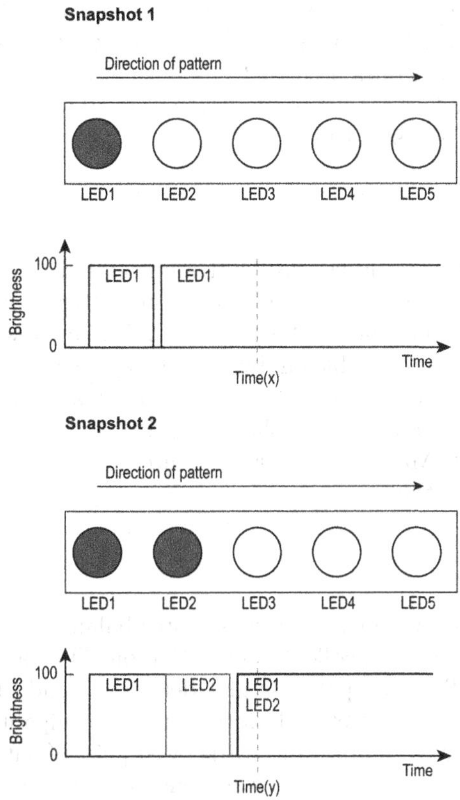

Snapshot 1

Direction of pattern

| LED1 | LED2 | LED3 | LED4 | LED5 |

Brightness

100

LED1   LED1

0

Time(x)

Time

Snapshot 2

Direction of pattern

| LED1 | LED2 | LED3 | LED4 | LED5 |

Brightness

100

LED1   LED2   LED1
                LED2

0

Time(y)

Time

Fig. 6. Blinking pattern at Time(x) (Snapshot 1), and a later Time(y) (Snapshot 2). Sketch of the LED-stripe at the top, graph of the brightness of involved LEDs at the bottom.

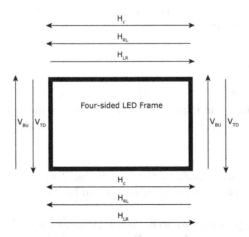

Fig. 7. Directions for light patterns

To complete our set of patterns, we added two patterns where all LEDs were controlled in a uniform fashion, one with increasing and one with decreasing brightness, similar to the ones used by Ostendorp et al. [16].

Overall we used a $4 * 5 * 2 + 2$ combination of patterns for a total number of 42 patterns for our first user study.

4.1 Methodology

Our first approach to the design space of ambient light displays for progress information was to try and determine which light patterns were suitable for the display of this type of information. We wanted to determine which patterns were easy to follow, had a recognizable ending and were thought to be acceptable by our participants. Similar to the work by Harrison et al. [6], we wanted to find out, if the type of pattern influenced the perception of duration (Perceived Time Ratio [PTR], see [8]). Maybe some patterns are better suited to "cut waiting time short" [11] than others.

4.2 Design

We conducted a study in which we used counter-balanced selections of 20 patterns for each participant. To collect information on PTR, acceptance, and participant ability to follow the progress and detect the end of the progress, we showed each pattern and collected data from the participants. To gain further insight into PTR in direct comparisons, we showed pairs of patterns and collected answers from the participant after each presentation of a pair.

4.3 Apparatus

For this study, we used the previously described *Lighten Up* prototype mounted to a 22" monitor which was placed against a matt white office wall. We controlled environmental light at 400 lux.

4.4 Participants

We conducted our study with 12 participants (4f, 8m) aged between 16 and 38 ($M = 28.4$, $SD = 5.7$). Participants did not receive any monetary compensation.

4.5 Procedure

We introduced our participants to the aim of the study and had them sign an informed consent before proceeding with the study. The whole study lasted for about one hour.

In a first round, participants were shown 20 randomly selected patterns out of the 42 in a random order. Each pattern had a random duration between 15 and 45 s. We asked participants to estimate the duration of the display of each pattern and collected further qualitative data in a questionnaire. Participants were asked to rank on a five-point Likert scale how much they liked the pattern, how well they were able to follow the progress, and whether they could easily detect the end of the pattern. For each of these questions, participants were able to provide further thoughts and opinions.

In a second round we presented pairs of randomly selected patterns with a duration of 30 s each. The participants were unaware that all patterns were of the same duration. After showing a pair of patterns we asked them to tell us if one of the patterns had a shorter duration and which one it was or if they thought they were of equal duration. In addition, we asked them which of the patterns they preferred or if they did not have any preference toward any of the patterns.

4.6   Results

Overall results suggest that participants liked patterns in the horizontal dimension better ($Avg = 2.93$) than the ones in the vertical dimension ($Avg = 3.35$). While there is no clear preference in the horizontal dimension, it is clear for the vertical dimension that patterns with LEDs turning off are least liked by the participants ($Avg = 3.74$).

Regarding the perceptibility of the progress horizontal patterns turning LEDs off score the best average result ($Avg = 2.35$) while vertical patterns turning LEDs off are least suited for progress perception ($Avg = 3.32$).

When asked to rate the ability to see the end of the progress, participants rated horizontal patterns turning LEDs on best ($Avg = 2.07$) and vertical patterns turning LEDs off worst ($Avg = 3.11$). This may be due to the orienting reflex [18] which might get triggered when the LEDs switch off altogether.

When comparing patterns by type (i.e. Gradual, Step, Ladder, Blink, combining results for both turning LEDs on and off, and for all five directions), the stepping patterns were liked best ($Avg = 2.71$), followed by gradual changes ($Avg = 2.93$), ladder-fill patterns ($Avg = 3.44$) and blinking patterns ($Avg = 3.45$). Progress was easiest to follow using stepping patterns ($Avg = 2.42$), followed by blinking patterns ($Avg = 2.51$), gradual changes ($Avg = 2.63$) and ladder-fill patterns ($Avg = 3.05$). Concerning the ability to recognize the end of the pattern, gradual patterns scored best overall ($Avg = 2.30$), followed by step changes ($Avg = 2.35$), blinking patterns ($Avg = 2.59$) and ladder-fills ($Avg = 2.68$).

All patterns tested by us had a $PTR > 1$. There was no difference in the average perceived time ratio when comparing pattern groups or dimensions. This suggests that ambient light displays seem to be suitable to reduce the perceived time of a waiting period. Best PTR (in terms of coming closest to the actual time passed) was scored by the V_{BU} blinking pattern switching LEDs off (.845). Worst overall PTR came from the V_{TD} ladder fill pattern switching LEDs off (.473).

Due to the small number of participants and individual ratings for each of the patterns, we did not test for significance.

4.7   Conclusion

We learned from our first study of ambient light displays that horizontal patterns were preferred over vertical ones. Patterns turning LEDs on made it easier to detect the end of progress. No pattern had a Perceived Time Ratio greater than one.

For the next study, we chose the two patterns with the best median scores on progress perceptibility. These were:

$H_{rl}StepOn$ A horizontal pattern turning LEDs on stepwise from right to left.
$H_{lr}GradualOff$ A horizontal pattern turning LEDs gradually off from left to right.

Both patterns received good ratings concerning detectability of the end of the pattern with $(Med(H_{rl}StepOn) = 1.5)$ and $(Med(H_{lr}GradualOff) = 2.0)$. Perceived time ratio for $H_{rl}StepOn$ was slightly better (.565) than for $H_{lr}GradualOff$ (.510).

5   Evaluating Against the State-of-the-Art

In the second study, we wanted to gain insights into how *Lighten Up* would perform compared to a state-of-the-art on-screen progress bar.

5.1   Methodology

We created a visually demanding primary task to keep participants focused. We chose a game that required the participants to look closely but that did not put them under any time/reaction time pressure. For this we used the browser game "Brick Brake"[1]. While in our first study we used only short durations of up to 45 s, we now extended the time frame to about 5–6 min. Our hypotheses were that:

H1: People will be better able to keep track of the progress of time when using the ambient light display.

H2: People will be better able to recognize the end of the progress when using the ambient light display.

H3: People will experience less workload on the primary task when using the ambient light display.

H4: People will prefer ambient light displays over state-of-the-art on-screen displays.

5.2   Design

We conducted a within-group study, in which each participant was subjected to three conditions:

---
[1] http://www.netzwelt.de/forum/arcade/game.1319/.

1. Showing an on-screen progress bar. The progress bar was placed at the bottom of the screen in a way that it was always visible to the participant.
2. Using *Lighten Up* in $H_{rl}StepOn$ mode.
3. Using *Lighten Up* in $H_{lr}GradualOff$ mode.

Each condition lasted between 4:30 min and 6:45 min. Both order of conditions and durations were counter-balanced to avoid learning and fatiguing effects. We noted the score the participants achieved in the game during each condition. During each condition, we asked participants four times to estimate the progress shown, after 30 %, 50 %, 70 % and 90 % of progress duration. After each condition, we asked participants to fill out a NASA-TLX form (using the raw NASA-TLX without weighting [7]) as well as answer a few questions regarding the condition, either on a five-point Likert scale or as a free-text answer.

Our independent variables were the condition and the duration of the condition.

Dependent variables were:

- The score of the game in each condition
- NASA-TLX rating
- The subjective ratings of the participants.

5.3 Apparatus

We used the same apparatus as we did in the study exploring the design space. We placed *Lighten Up* behind a 22" monitor, on which we ran the primary task as well as the on-screen progress bar in the baseline condition. We used the browser game "Brick Break" as our primary task. Environmental lighting was controlled for all participants.

5.4 Participants

We conducted our study with 13 participants (3f, 10m) between 16 and 47 years old. Participants did not receive any monetary compensation.

5.5 Procedure

First we introduced the participants to the scope of the study. Once all questions were answered and the informed consent was signed, we started with a training round of the "Brick Break" game. When participants felt familiar with the game, we started with the study. Overall we conducted three rounds of playing the game while observing a progress bar as secondary task. The order of progress bars was randomized to avoid learning or fatiguing effects. The duration of each round varied between 4:30 min and 6:45 min. During each round, we asked participants four times how much time they thought had passed already: after 30 %, 50 %, 70 % and 90 % of the total time. After each round, we asked participants to complete a NASA-TLX questionnaire as well as rate a few statements concerning the progress bar shown on a 5-point Likert scale.

6 Results

In the following, we will report our results separated into quantitative and qualitative results. Unless reported differently, we used repeated measures one-way ANOVA and Tukey HSD to test our data for significant effects.

6.1 Quantitative Results

While the overall average score was about 20 % higher in both *Lighten Up* conditions compared to the baseline, we could not detect significance in the data.

Comparing the estimates of the time passed, we did not find any significant differences between the baseline ($M = 2.85$, $SD = 3.74$) and either of the experimental conditions. However, there was a significant difference between $H_{rl}StepOn$ ($M = -.74$, $SD = 12.69$) and $H_{lr}GradualOff$ ($M = 6.38$, $SD = 11.85$), $p < .01$, with the PTR in the $H_{rl}StepOn$ condition being greater 1, while in $H_{lr}GradualOff$ being less than 1.

For the NASA-TLX, we recorded a significant effect between the two *Lighten Up* conditions only. $H_{lr}GradualOff$ produced a significantly higher workload ($M = 38.97$, $SD = 10.06$) than $H_{rl}StepOn$ ($M = 28.85$, $SD = 10.02$), $p < .05$. This is in line with our preliminary results from the first study. There was no significance between the *Lighten Up* conditions and the baseline ($M = 32.37$, $SD = 13.84$).

Even though we did not ask our participants to look for the end of progress, eight participants stopped performing the primary task in condition $H_{rl}StepOn$ stating that they had seen that the progress was over. Four participants noticed the end of the progress in the baseline condition, none noted the end in the $H_{lr}GradualOff$ condition.

6.2 Qualitative Results

In the following section we report the results of our inquiries on how the users felt while using the system. When asked about how they liked the pattern shown in each condition, there was a significant effect between the baseline ($M = 3.5$, $SD = .58$) and $H_{rl}StepOn$ ($M = 2.08$, $SD = 1.08$), $p < .01$. There was no significant effect between the two *Lighten Up* conditions, nor between the baseline and $H_{lr}GradualOff$ ($M = 2.58$, $SD = 1.31$).

Regarding the ability to follow the progress of the pattern, there were no significant differences between the baseline ($M = 1.92$, $SD = 1.31$) and the two *Lighten Up* conditions $H_{rl}StepOn$ ($M = 2.17$, $SD = 1.27$) and $H_{lr}GradualOff$ ($M = 2.58$, $SD = .90$).

Concerning the ability to detect the end of the overall progress displayed by the progress bars, participants rated $H_{rl}StepOn$ ($M = 1.33$, $SD = 0.65$) significantly better than the baseline ($M = 2.58$, $SD = 1.62$) and $H_{lr}GradualOff$ ($M = 2.67$, $SD = 1.37$), both $p < .05$.

We asked our participants to rank the three conditions. In this ranking $H_{rl}StepOn$ came first (6x first, 6x second, 1x third place), followed by the baseline (6x first, 4x second, 3x third place) and $H_{lr}GradualOff$ (1x first, 3x second, 9x third place), see Fig. 8. While this is a narrow margin for the $H_{rl}StepOn$ pattern, the results for $H_{lr}GradualOff$ clearly show that not all ambient light display patterns are suitable for the task.

6.3 Comments and Observations

Regarding baseline and *Lighten Up* there were two basic observations. First, participants were immediately familiar with the baseline - as expected. Second, eleven participants stated that displaying information in the periphery helped them focus on the primary task, as the information quickly blended in with the environment but was still visible from the corner of the eye. Further it was seen as an advantage that *Lighten Up* did not use up screen real estate, even though one participant wished for a system that used the $H_{rl}StepOn$ pattern on-screen.

When asked about a ranking of systems, participants noted for $H_{rl}StepOn$ that on the one hand having the light go from right to left was counter-intuitive as it was against the participants' direction of reading. On the other hand, they stated that this counter-intuitiveness along with the stepwise illumination gave the ambient light display enough saliency to help them follow the progress of the secondary task.

Those participants who ranked the baseline display first mentioned the easiness of interpreting the on-screen progress bar as it was familiar to them. Further, they felt that the reading was more accurate on-screen than when using *Lighten Up*.

Further comments on *Lighten Up* were that four participants liked the fact that was visible from "anywhere in an office". Others mentioned that such a system could be used by-standers to give feedback to the user (e.g. "you have been doing this task for too long now", when imagining a timer function). Four participants mentioned that they liked the lack of detailed information, as they deemed exact information on the progress of the task as unimportant.

Regarding acceptability, eleven participants could imagine using *Lighten Up* for their daily work.

6.4 Discussion

In our second study, we evaluated two *Lighten Up* patterns against a state-of-the-art on-screen progress bar. Qualitative results suggest that participants were significantly better able to detect the end of the progress shown by *Lighten Up* in the $H_{rl}StepOn$ condition. Further, participants preferred $H_{rl}StepOn$ over the baseline. Quantitative results show no significant differences in incurred workload. However, there was a significant effect between the two *Lighten Up* patterns in this study concerning the perceived time ratio.

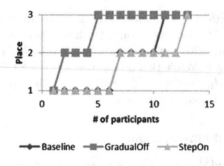

Fig. 8. User ranking of patterns

With regard to our hypotheses, we can say that while H1 and H3 have to be rejected according to our data, H2 and H4 can be supported, when selecting a suitable light pattern for *Lighten Up*.

However, we need to further differentiate the results in our discussion. While both *Lighten Up* patterns were ranked similarly with respect to the participants' ability to follow the progress of time in the first study, the results of the second study suggest that $H_{rl}StepOn$ scores better results than $H_{lr}GradualOff$. For example, there was a significantly larger error in the estimation of the progress in the second study in $H_{lr}GradualOff$. Further, participants stated that the end of the progress was significantly better recognizable in the $H_{rl}StepOn$ condition. This was also supported by our observations.

While there was no significant difference in the experienced workload between the baseline the ambient light display conditions, we would like to point out that we designed the baseline in a way that the progress bar was always visible on screen. This may not be the default situation in a real-life scenario but we did not want the participants to have a much more complex process of obtaining information in the baseline condition.

During our first study, all patterns tested showed a perceived time ratio less than one. However, when we extended the time frame in the second study, participants thought that less time had passed in the $H_{rl}StepOn$ condition than the pattern really showed. While we did merely ask for an estimate of the percentage of time passed and not for, we find this result remarkable.

One limitation to our study is that we were only able to cover a small portion of the design space of individually controllable LEDs for the display of the temporal progress of tasks. Further, more significant results may have been obtained from a larger participant group and a more complex baseline.

7   Conclusions

In this paper we presented *Lighten Up*, an ambient light display to show the temporal progress of a task in the periphery of a user's attention. We reported two studies: one investigating the design space of light patterns for the use of individually controllable LEDs for progress display, and one comparing two pattern candidates against a state-of-the-art on-screen progress bar. Our results suggest that *Lighten Up* is preferred over the state-of-the-art when used in the $H_{rl}StepOn$ condition.

Participants in our study liked the way *Lighten Up* moves information off the screen and into the periphery of attention. However, there is the need for a certain amount of saliency in the light pattern to make the progress information easy to follow. A pattern with increasing brightness help participants to detect the end of the progress when all LEDs are switched off. This may be due to the orienting reflex which is, of course, not triggered by a pattern that continuously decreases the brightness of the LEDs.

Our contribution lies in systematically evaluating the parameter brightness for displaying progress information over time with individually controllable LEDs. We created and tested four light pattern groups containing two modes (i.e. switching LEDs on and off) and five directions of display. We showed that patterns in the horizontal direction achieve better results than vertical patterns. We identified a pattern that was preferred over the state-of-the-art by participants. Participants identified features of ambient light displays (i.e. working in the periphery of attention, and not taking up screen real estate) as beneficial and desirable.

Future work will extend both the exploration of the design space toward other basic parameters such as colour or saturation as well as compare ambient light displays using uniformly controlled LEDs with those using individually controlled LEDs.

References

1. Adamczyk, P.D., Bailey, B.P.: If not now, when?: the effects of interruption at different moments within task execution. In: Proceedings of CHI 2004, CHI 2004, pp. 271–278. ACM, New York, NY, USA (2004). http://doi.acm.org/10.1145/985692. 985727
2. Brewster, S.A., King, A.: The design and evaluation of a vibrotactile progress bar. In: Proceedings of the First Joint Eurohaptics Conference and Symposium on Haptic Interfaces for Virtual Environment and Teleoperator Systems, WHC 2005, pp. 499–500 (2005)
3. Crease, M., Brewster, S.A.: Making progress with sounds-the design and evaluation of an audio progress bar. In: Proceedings of ICAD 1998 (1998)
4. Czerwinski, M., Horvitz, E., Wilhite, S.: A diary study of task switching and interruptions. In: Proceedings of CHI 2004, CHI 2004, pp. 175–182. ACM, New York, NY, USA (2004). http://doi.acm.org/10.1145/985692.985715
5. Fogarty, J., Hudson, S.E., Atkeson, C.G., Avrahami, D., Forlizzi, J., Kiesler, S., Lee, J.C., Yang, J.: Predicting human interruptibility with sensors. ACM Trans. Comput. Hum. Interact. **12**(1), 119–146 (2005)
6. Harrison, C., Yeo, Z., Hudson, S.E.: Faster progress bars: manipulating perceived duration with visual augmentations. In: Proceedings of the SIGCHI Conference on Human Factors in Computing Systems, CHI 2010, pp. 1545–1548 (2010)

7. Hart, S.: Nasa-task load index (NASA-TLX); 20 years later. Proc. Hum. Factors Ergon. Soc. Annu. Meet. **50**, 904–908 (2006)
8. Hertzum, M., Holmegaard, K.D.: Perceived time as a measure of mental workload: effects of time constraints and task success. Int. J. Hum. Comput. Inter. **29**(1), 26–39 (2013). http://dx.doi.org/10.1080/10447318.2012.676538
9. Ishii, H., Wisneski, C., Brave, S., Dahley, A., Gorbet, M., Ulmer, B., Yarin, P.: Ambientroom: integrating ambient media with architectural space. In: Proceedings of CHI 1998 (1998)
10. Leibowitz, H.W., Shupert, C.L., Post, R.B.: The two modes of visual processing: implications for spatial orientation. In: Peripheral Vision Horizon Display (PVHD) (1984)
11. Liikkanen, L.A., Gómez, P.G.: Designing interactive systems for the experience of time. In: Proceedings of the 6th International Conference on Designing Pleasurable Products and Interfaces, DPPI 2013, pp. 146–155 (2013)
12. Mark, G., Gonzalez, V.M., Harris, J.: No task left behind?: examining the nature of fragmented work. In: Proceedings of CHI 2005, CHI 2005, ACM, New York, NY, USA (2005)
13. Matthews, T., Dey, A.K., Mankoff, J., Carter, S., Rattenbury, T.: A toolkit for managing user attention in peripheral displays. In: Proceedings of UIST (2004). http://doi.acm.org/10.1145/1029632.1029676
14. Moraveji, N., Soesanto, C.: Towards stress-less user interfaces: 10 design heuristics based on the psychophysiology of stress. In: CHI 2012 Extended Abstracts on Human Factors in Computing Systems, CHI EA 2012, pp. 1643–1648 (2012)
15. Müller, H., Kazakova, A., Pielot, M., Heuten, W., Boll, S.: Ambient timer – unobtrusively reminding users of upcoming tasks with ambient light. In: Winckler, M. (ed.) INTERACT 2013, Part I. LNCS, vol. 8117, pp. 211–228. Springer, Heidelberg (2013)
16. Ostendorp, M.C., Harre, A., Jacob, S., Mller, H., Heuten, W., Boll, S.: Ambient progress bar - relaxed and efficient work in waiting periods. In: Mensch & Computer 2013: Interaktive Vielfalt, pp. 221–229 (2013)
17. Peres, S., Kortum, P., Stallmann, K.: Auditory progress bars: preference, performance and aesthetics. In: Proceedings of the International Conference on Auditory Display (ICAD2007) (2007)
18. Sokolov, E.: Higher nervous functions: the orienting reflex. Annu. Revs. Physiol. **25**, 545–580 (1963)
19. Weiser, M., Brown, J.S.: Designing calm technology. Powergrid Journal **1**, 75–85 (1996)
20. Wickens, C.D.: Multiple resources and mental workload. Human Factors: The Journal of the Human Factors and Ergonomics Society (2008)

Use of Self-Reporting Questionnaires to Evaluate Augmented Paper Maps for Group Navigation

Andreas Komninos[1(✉)], Jeries Besharat[2], and John Garofalakis[2]

[1] University of Strathclyde, Glasgow, UK
andreas.komninos@strath.ac.uk
[2] RACTI, University of Patras, Rio, Patras, Greece
{besarat,garofala}@ceid.upatras.gr

Abstract. One popular and widely use of augmented reality based application, is the projection of points of interests on top of the phones' camera view. In this paper we discuss the implementation of an AR application that acts as a magic lens over printed maps, overlaying POIs and routes. This method expands the information space available to members of groups during navigation, partially mitigating the issue of several group members trying to share a small screen device. Our work complements existing literature by focusing on the navigation tasks and by using self-reporting questionnaires to measure affective state and user experience. We evaluate this system with groups of real tourists in a preliminary field trial and report our findings.

Keywords: Augmented reality · Group navigation · Mobile maps · Tourism · Augmented maps

1 Introduction

Many location based mobile applications today allow users to discover the location of Points of Interest (POIs) in a city. Teevan et al. [20] found that the most common reason of searching for a POI on a mobile device was to get directions to that POI. Typically, map exploration and navigation with mobile devices are done using the small screen space available. While navigation applications for single users are well developed and manage to empower users sufficiently, in many situations users do not navigate alone, but as part of a group. In such cases, the convergence of multiple users over a single small-screen device is problematic, as the information display area is too small to be viewed by all members of the group. Hence, collaborative navigation, where multiple users can offer their interpretation of instructions or make decisions on routes to take, is difficult when using mobile devices. In this paper we describe an alternative approach for group navigation, based on the augmentation of a physical paper map. We believe that such a hybrid system can be shared more easily within a group. Our prototype, which is called HoloPlane, shows POIs collected from the Foursquare API. HoloPlane uses real-time and historical data from social networking services (as in, e.g. [7]), to display

© Springer International Publishing Switzerland 2015
Kameas et al. (Eds.): AmI 2015, LNCS 9425, pp. 125–137, 2015.
DOI: 10.1007/978-3-319-26005-1_9

these POIs in a manner that allows users to understand their popularity under the current temporal context. Users can see their own location on the map as a virtual marker and can select POIs to navigate to. Routes are displayed as a set of virtual lines, aligned with the street structure on the printed map. Our paper presents results from a preliminary field evaluation study on the prototype's use during group navigation tasks, using a validated questionnaire approach to evaluation that has not been employed in related research in the past.

2   Related Work

Traditionally, paper maps have played major roles in conveying spatial information and guiding people around in space. However, this standard experience could be enhanced and improved, as it is shown that augmented paper maps could be used to develop interactive paper maps that will provide added values services for tourists [13]. Stroila et al. [17] demonstrated an AR navigation application, which allows users to interact with transit maps in public transit locations and vehicles.

In [12] the acceptance and usability of an AR system that provides pedestrian navigation through a combination of mobile devices and public displays are studied, but with focus on single users and not collaborative use, as does most literature on this subject. The effectiveness of navigating to POIs with an AR browser and a 2D digital map interface is studied in [5]. It is found that although the use of AR with a digital map did not offer any advantages to performance, users preferred this mode strongly as it doesn't lock users into one type of interaction.

Other research has identified a range of issues concerning the use of AR and magic lens interaction. One is the dual-view problem in magic lens viewing [4], where users have to shift their attention between the mobile screen (magic lens) and the background augmented object. This causes difficulty in matching the mobile view with the background, as the mobile view appears at a different zoom level than the background object, hence posing cognitive difficulties to the user. A further issue arising from natural use of the mobile device, is the angular difference in the user's view of the background object and the device (e.g. the background object might be perpendicular to the ground as in the case of a fixed poster, while the mobile screen might be tilted in varying degrees, for example when the user holds the device up high to bring a tall part of the background object into view). A further issue concerns the size of the augmented object, in this case the background map.

In [6] it has been found that static peephole interfaces for maps are better than magic lenses, when the area of the map to be explored is small. As the size of the map increases, the differences even out and in fact, the magic lens interface becomes better to use in larger maps. The researchers obtained their findings using physical map sizes that are considerably larger than the typical handheld map (the smallest map used was 1.38 m × 0.76 m), making these findings applicable to large maps, of the kind that would be placed on a wall as a poster, or on a public display.

Finally, in [17], researchers find that item density can have an effect on how much time users spend looking at the background object, compared to the magic lens view.

It was found that for low item density situations, users tended to focus more on the background object, confirming a previous experiment [16] where users focused more on the magic lens view, above a certain item density threshold.

In [3] the problems faced by tourists during holidays are outlined. The most common problems in an unfamiliar place, are what to do and when. The researchers explore how tourists solve their problems by relying on sharing the visit with other tourists (79 % of leisure visits involve groups of two or more) and how they worked as a group by using digital technologies. The leisure activity seemed to be less important than the fact the tourists spent significant time with others. As a result, technologies that are woven into this sociality are likely to be used in preference to those that are not.

Reilly et al. [15] examined how groups of two share a single device during a collaborative indoor way finding activity. They developed two basic interfaces (one that combines map and textual descriptions and a textual interface that numbers the route description) in order to conduct the experiment. Their analysis on the results showed that the application's interface impacts the strategy users followed to complete the tasks. They found that some pairs heavily favored specific navigation strategies or sharing styles. This emphasizes the importance of group dynamic on the use of spatial applications.

A set of requirements for mobile indoor navigation systems that support collaborative path finding tasks is presented in [2]. The researchers observed and analyzed the actions participants performed such as walking, pointing, looking etc. and found that the pointing action, as a communication purpose, occurs much more in groups. Furthermore, the number of people involved in a group does complicate the process of completing the task. 76.4 % of the participants stated that positioning and navigation signs helped them to find their target locations. There is very little relevant literature that discusses group navigation aspects using AR.

In [11], researchers augmented a map with POIs (but not navigation instructions) using a device as a magic lens as part of a pervasive game. They found that augmented maps offer advantages to groups as a collaboration tool, since groups that used them found it easier to establish common ground than groups of users who used only a digital map. Further work in [10] included use of multiple devices on the same map, which found that up to 2 devices are usable without causing issues. It was also shown that the ability to cluster and collaborate over the physical map enhanced the "feelgood" factor between group members. Neither [10] nor [11] seem to consider the dual-view problem, item density or map size for their effect on the usability of the AR maps. A significant shortfall of studies like [10, 11] lies in the fact that only qualitative data was obtained by the researchers, in the form of interviews, coupled with their own direct observation. As pointed out in [1], these methods suffer from potential subjectivity bias and also from the researchers' own bias. This observation is highlighted again in [14], where it is found that the user's own context (i.e. whether they see themselves as a future user of the system under evaluation) can place a strong influence on the reported assessment of a system's usability. Hence, the findings in [10, 11] provide a good insight into the usability of AR maps for collaborative use, but have to be considered as incomplete. As can be seen, the use of AR maps is an on-going subject of research with many unanswered questions, in both the cases of single users and collaborative use. Our main focus is, for this paper, to add to the small body of literature on user experience during AR-assisted group navigation, taking a different approach to evaluation (i.e. using self-reporting questionnaires that have been validated for effectiveness, to assess affective state and user experience). This element is entirely missing from existing literature, where results are largely based on direct observation and interviews.

3   HoloPlane Interface

Our prototype (HoloPlane) is built using the Qualcomm Vuforia SDK and Unity for Android. For the experiment described in this paper, our users were not asked to interact with the prototype features, except from viewing the route between the POIs that were pre-selected for them by the researchers. However, in the next section we provide an overview of how the prototype works, in order to demonstrate the full potential of our idea. The interface has been designed using several iterations of expert-based usability methods but the full UI design has not been tested with users for usability – this remains the subject of further work. Here we are primarily concerned with the concept of showing routes on an augmented paper map interface.

The printed map does not require special markings to be recognized by the device, as it is a recognition target in itself. When the application detects the map, it connects to our server and fetches the required POI information. This is overlaid on the map image along with a marker that shows the user's location. Once a user selects a POI to navigate to, the application downloads guidance instructions from the Google Directions API and renders route segments as virtual lines on the map. The application does not need to remain connected for its operation from this point onwards. The main interface of the application consists of five buttons that are placed on the top area of the screen and one informative panel on the bottom area of the screen. With this layout, we developed a service that conveys a range of contextual information to the user in a multi-layered view. The graphical elements in brackets are shown in Fig. 1 (top). Layer 1: This layer is responsible for overlaying the POI information retrieved from our server. The POIs are presented as 3D that show, on all their surfaces, an icon that indicates the category the POI belongs to (1). The POIs are colour-coded to indicate whether they are popular or not, depending on the current time and day. The navigation route (if selected) is also shown (2), using virtual lines, aligned with the street structure on the map. The user's position, which is determined using the devices' GPS sensor, is also displayed as an arrow (3). Layer 2: This layer has all the UI control and is split in two sections, the top UI control bar (Fig. 1 middle) and the bottom navigation panel (Fig. 1 bottom). In the UI control bar, button (4) shows a list view with the names of all the POIs currently on the device screen. Users can select a POI from that list to identify it on the map. The application then "scales up" the POI cube briefly, to help the user identify it. This helps users to find POIs by name and to select POIs in cases when they appear too small (device far from the map) or when many POIs are clustered together. Button (5) shows a popup panel, which allows the user to filter the POIs by category. Buttons (6) and (7) allow control over the temporal context colour-coding, by allowing users to display popularity information for specified days of the week and times (hours) of the day, selectable through drop down lists. Button (8) refreshes the information each time a user selects different values from the drop down buttons. Finally, button (9) is used to find the location of the user if the application did not succeed in finding it automatically. The navigation panel in the bottom of the screen (10) provides navigation details to the user, such as the name of the destination, the estimated time to arrival and the remaining walking distance.

Fig. 1. The HoloPlane AR Interface working with a paper map (top), detailed view of the top bar UI controls (middle) and navigation panel (bottom)

4   Evaluation

Experiment Design. Our participants were 23 undergraduate engineering students from various disciplines (14 male, 9 female), from 17 European countries, who were visiting the city of Patras for a summer school. Their ages ranged between 18 and 26 years old and none had previous experience with mobile AR applications. All participants mentioned familiarity with navigation applications, with 40 % stating frequent use and 17 % indicated always using just a mobile application while visiting a new place. We found a low preference for fixed city maps (e.g. wall-mounted) and paper maps (22 % in both cases) compared to mobile navigation apps. To establish thus a baseline that would be representative of our participants' usual behaviour, we chose to compare our prototype to the most preferable navigation aid for our participants, i.e. a mobile navigation app and not a paper map. Hence we selected the familiar navigation tool installed on all Android devices, i.e. Google Maps (GM). For the field experiment we provided participants with four devices of equivalent capabilities in terms of processor speed and screen size (LG Nexus 4 and Nexus 5 and Samsung S3 and S4), which all ran our application with good performance. In order to test our prototype in navigation tasks, we established two routes of equal complexity in terms of turns and walking distance (Fig. 2), requiring approximately 10 min of walking time from a person familiar with the area. We let participants split themselves into 8 groups, allowing friends to work together to better simulate real tourist groups – the first four groups completed the first route using the HoloPlane AR prototype and proceeded to GM navigation for the second route. This order was reversed for the remaining four groups. Each team was accompanied by a researcher who knew the routes and was able to provide help if the team did not succeed to find the destination. Finally, in each team, one user volunteered to control the device and map (where used), while the other two participants were termed as "companions" and were instructed to ask for control of the device and map, if they so desired. This setup is representative of situations where one person assumes the navigator's role, typically because they own the device. As stated previously, HoloPlane is designed to be used with any simple printed map. For our experiment, we provided participants with a colour printed map from the Google Maps website that shows the experiment area at a scale of roughly 1: 18055 (zoom level 16). This is the smallest scale at which Google shows names for all streets and not just major ones. Furthermore, this scale allows the map to depict as wide an area as possible, maintaining label readability for the users. We selected an A4 print size, to represent a typical situation for users who might have printed a map at home before travelling, or during their stay (e.g. at Internet café), as few users would typically have access to a large format printer such as A3 or larger.

Data Collection. We collected GPS positioning data for each team. The researchers, who accompanied each team, also noted the number of times participants stopped to consult the application and make a route choice during navigation. At the end of each navigation task we asked each participant to complete a NASA TLX questionnaire, so that we could obtain their subjective workload impression. We also asked them to complete two validated questionnaires for each system: a Brief Mood Introspection Scale (BMIS) [9] in order to measure mood and a User Experience Questionnaire (UEQ) [8] for their overall experience.

Results. This section reports our observations based on the quantitative and qualitative results. The tests reported in this section were chosen according to the outcomes of normality tests on all our variables.

Quantitative Measures. In Fig. 2, we show the participants' walking behaviour during navigation, which is visualized through a heatmap-based depiction of GPS traces. We report this data as recorded by the device GPS without statistical significance analysis, since the number of teams was too small to provide an adequate sample size for statistical significance.

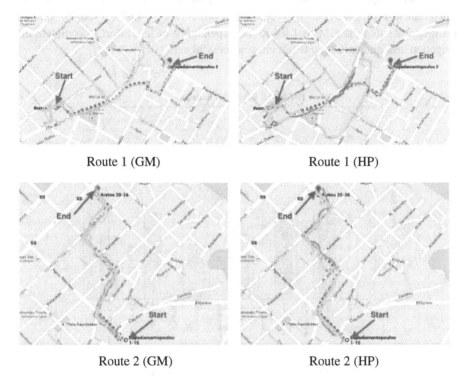

Route 1 (GM)   Route 1 (HP)

Route 2 (GM)   Route 2 (HP)

Fig. 2. Participant Routes and heatmapped GPS traces. The red segments show where participant speed was less than 1 km/h

Overall teams took less time to navigate with GM ($m_{gm} = 896.96$ s, $sd_{gm} = 295.93$ s, $m_{hp} = 1093.93$ s, $sd_{hp} = 319.10$ s). However with GM they made more stops to consult the tool ($m_{gm} = 8.75$, $sd_{gm} = 9.77$, $m_{hp} = 7.88$, $sd_{hp} = 3.41$). We measured the length of pauses they made during navigation, i.e. periods longer than 5 s where the speed was less than 1 km/h. There were fewer such periods with GM ($m_{gm} = 10.86$, $sd_{gm} = 3.31$, $m_{hp} = 17.86$, $sd_{hp} = 7.22$) which lasted also less time ($m_{gm} = 273.88$, $d_{gm} = 241.19$, $m_{hp} = 316.87$, $sd_{hp} = 178.0$). Finally, in terms of distance covered, this was less with GM ($m_{gm} = 690.80$ m, $sd_{gm} = 81.01$ m, $m_{hp} = 842.79$ m, $sd_{hp} = 192.8$ m).

Participant Workload Assessment. At the end of each navigation task, we issued each participant with a NASA-TLX questionnaire to obtain their subjective ratings of their experience with each navigation tool. The overall results are summarized in Fig. 3. Overall it can be seen that GM was rated better than our prototype (a lower score is better), with the exception of physical effort. The latter is expected, as the routes were carefully chosen to present equal levels of walking difficulty and length. Concerning the remaining five variables, a statistical significance in the difference of means was only found for effort to complete the task, using a paired-sample T-test ($m_{gm} = 7.61$, $sd_{gm} = 4.878$, $m_{hp} = 10$, $sd_{hp} = 3.357$, $p < 0.05$) and performance, using a Wilcoxon signed rank test ($m_{gm} = 3.43$, $sd_{gm} = 3.287$, $m_{hp} = 6.26$, $sd_{hp} = 4.826$, $p < 0.05$). Overall thus it appears that the GM tool led to the expenditure of less effort to complete the navigation task and participants felt more successful using it.

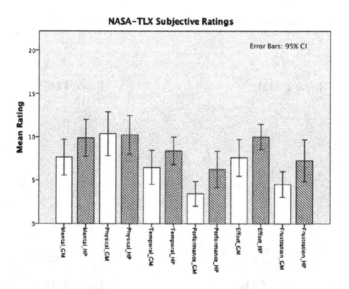

Fig. 3. Subjective workload assessment

Participant Affective State. Using the BMIS questionnaire at the end of each task, we asked participants to give us insight to their affective state during the tasks. This questionnaire contains 16 adjectives describing affective state. Before letting the participants answer the questionnaire, we explained in detail each adjective, in order to be sure that they fully understood the choices and their meaning. The analysis of the user responses was made on the Calm - Arousal and Unpleasant - Pleasant axes, and is depicted below in Fig. 4. It can be generally seen that the participants' experience was rated positively in terms of pleasantness and that participants felt averagely aroused during the navigation tasks.

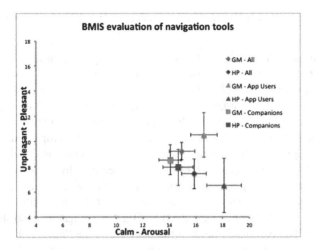

Fig. 4. Affective state during navigation tool use

Further analysis reveals that when considering all users, no statistically significant differences using Wilcoxon signed rank tests for the two navigation tools, on either the Unpleasant-Pleasant ($m_{gm} = 9.22$, $sd_{gm} = 4.69$, $m_{hp} = 7.44$, $sd_{hp} = 5.67$) or the Calm-Arousal axis ($m_{gm} = 14.96$, $sd_{gm} = 3.28$, $m_{hp} = 15.87$, $sd_{hp} = 4.38$). We went further by breaking up the users according to their roles (app users and companions) and analyzing the respective data. We did not find any statistically significant differences using Wilcoxon signed rank tests in either axis for any of these user categories. Given the previously found statistically significant difference in performance, we conclude that while the participants believe they fared worse with the HoloPlane prototype, nevertheless, their experience was just as pleasant as with GM.

Participant User Experience. At the end of each navigation task, we asked each participant to complete the User Experience Questionnaire, in order to obtain a measure of their assessment of each navigation tool. The questionnaire generally assumes a positive appraisal on each dimension if the mean exceeds 0.8, or a negative appraisal if the mean is less than 0.8. Analysis with Wilcoxon signed rank tests reveals that statistically significant differences appear only in the dimensions of perceived *Efficiency* ($m_{gm} = 1.978$, $sd_{gm} = 0.170$, $m_{hp} = 0.578$, $sd_{hp} = 0.875$, $p < 0.01$), *Dependability* ($m_{gm} = 1.674$, $sd_{gm} = 0.82$, $m_{hp} = 0.924$, $sd_{hp} = 0.89$, $p < 0.05$), *Stimulation* ($m_{gm} = 0.728$, $sd_{gm} = 1.047$, $m_{hp} = 1.467$, $sd_{hp} = 0.728$, $p < 0.01$) and *Novelty* ($m_{gm} = -0.63$, $sd_{gm} = 1.297$, $m_{hp} = 1.609$, $sd_{hp} = 0.856$, $p < 0.01$). These outcomes for the *Stimulation, Efficiency* and *Dependability* are in line with the outcomes from our previous questionnaires. The observed difference in *Stimulation* measures is somewhat unexpectedly in disagreement with the parity observed in the Arousal-Calm axis earlier. However, a more careful inspection of the wording of the UEQ adjectives used to measure on the positive scale for this axis, uncovers that these imply a level of *engagement*, instead of measuring affective state (*valuable, exciting, interesting, motivating*). Finally, there is clear indication here that our participants considered HoloPlane to present significant novelty.

Other Observations. When observing participant bodily configuration, we noticed a more relaxed approach with the AR tool, compared to "squeezing in" to view the device instructions when using GM, an observation also made in [11]. In Fig. 5, we show several examples of use of the HoloPlane prototype. In these, the shared use of the hybrid working space is evident in several collaboration examples: In the first (Fig. 5a), the "navigator" has control of both the paper map and the device. Companions are gathered around the map, paying attention to the printed surface which is clearly visible and intelligible to all, while the screen of the device is used only by the navigator. His role here is to communicate what he sees on the device, to the companions, so that a shared understanding can be achieved. Communication is verbal, since both the navigator's hands are occupied. In the second example (Fig. 5b), the "navigator" controls the device, while one of the companions is holding the map. Here, the "navigator" is seen to be pointing on the map, in order to communicate to the companions his knowledge in a more comprehensible manner. This mode of communication is more direct and helps companions understand more easily what the navigator sees. Finally, in Fig. 5c, we note that the communication of spatial awareness is initiated by the companion, who is holding the paper map and at the same time pointing to a location on it. At the same time, the navigator is trying to understand the companion's communication and match it to what is represented on the device screen. This example shows that the hybrid system allows for more active participation in the navigation task by all group members.

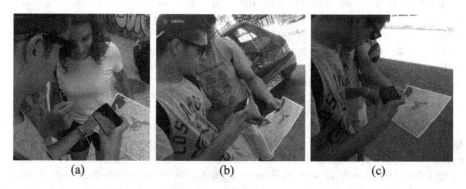

(a)   (b)   (c)

Fig. 5. Group behaviour during use of the Holoplane hybrid interface

The next figure (Fig. 6) shows some instances of the navigation task, during use of the Google Maps interface. Here it is easy to observe that the planning task is made much more difficult for all users, since the screen real-estate is quite small and participants have to gather tightly to see what is displayed. Not all participants are able to point to the screen in order to communicate their understanding, hence limiting their ability to make a contribution to the planning (Fig. 6a). During transit to established waypoints, the companions often resigned to being simple followers (Fig. 6b). Here, the companion on the right is talking to the navigator, since they were able to plan the route together previously, leaving the female companion unable to contribute to the planning. The female companion, adopts a passive mode since she did not participate in the planning stage, and is seen to be walking just ahead of the group, keeping an ear out for the navigator's next instruction. This is evident also in Fig. 6c, where the female companion is simply looking around. The navigator is ahead of the group on his own, trying to determine the group's whereabouts, while the male companion is trying to visually match the surrounding location to the printout of the navigation target given to the group.

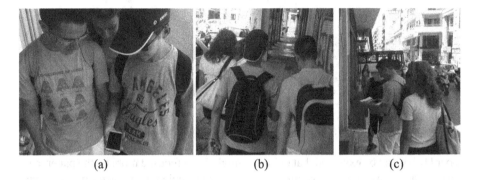

(a)   (b)   (c)

Fig. 6. Group behaviour during use of the Google Maps interface

5   Discussion and Future Work

Our evaluation was based on the use of validated questionnaires whose use is not wide-spread in the field of mobile HCI. This approach contrasts previous research in [10, 11] whose findings are based on the analysis of qualitative interviews. Yet, our preliminary evaluation did not find any significant performance advantages of augmenting a paper map for navigation, a result that is completely in line with [10, 11]. This outcome provides indication that the questionnaire-based approach has merit and can be used effectively in the place of qualitative interviews, where the danger of researcher bias in the analysis of results is significant. Another similarity with [11] is that when observing participant bodily configuration, we noticed a more relaxed approach with the AR tool, compared to "squeezing in" to view the device instructions when using GM (Figs. 5 and 7).

The reason why no advantages were observed with the AR interface may relate to the size of the augmented paper map. We selected a relatively small printed area (A4) to represent a typical situation of users printing their own maps. Perhaps a larger shared map might make the magic lens interface more usable, as suggested by [6], although there, maps were fixed on to a wall surface, where as in our scenario users have to be able to conveniently hold the map. Hence, while providing a larger printed map might make its augmentation more usable, it might detract from its key benefit (i.e. portability and manipulability). A further consideration for performance is item density: In our situation, the item density was very low and included just two POIs and the route.

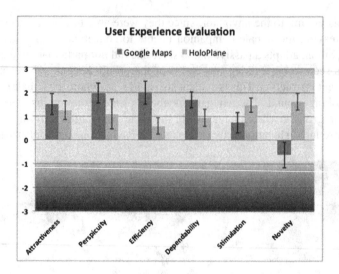

Fig. 7. User experience during navigation tool use

As per [16], it can be expected that our users might have focused more on the paper map than the magic lens, hence preventing the system from achieving its performance potential. Further tests with different item densities (e.g. routes with multiple waypoints) would be needed to verify any effects.

As indicated by the Stimulation axis in the UEQ, our participants felt more engaged as group members with the HP system than GM, where a single user takes on the role of the navigator and collaboration is hindered, as the small screen limits the information space. The reported level of engagement might be an effect of the high perceived novelty of the system, since both axes (Stimulation and Novelty) relate to hedonic quality perception. However, the UEQ Novelty axis has been found not to correlate with the Stimulation axis in other research [18]. As a side effect of increased engagement with the navigation task, the acquisition of spatial knowledge for all users might be improved for users as per [21], but further tests would be needed.

It is encouraging that participants found the AR tool just as attractive as the standard navigation tools. The issues of mental workload and efficiency appraisals can be attributed to the novelty and unfamiliarity of our application to users.

To this end, we are hoping to conduct further, more extensive trials to eliminate familiarity factors from the results. Furthermore, given that augmented maps can be used as a collaboration tool, our future research will also encompass the use of our AR tool with public displays of maps.

References

1. Adams, A., Cox, A.L.: Questionnaires, indepth interviews and focus groups. In: Cairns, P., Cox, A.L. (eds.) Research Methods for Human Computer Interaction, pp. 17–34. Cambridge University Press, Cambridge (2008)

2. Bouwer, A., Nack, F., Evers, V.: Towards support for collaborative navigation in complex indoor environments. In: Proceedings of CSCW 2011, pp. 601–604 (2011)
3. Brown, B., Chalmers, M.: Tourism and mobile technology. In: Proceedings of ECSCW 2003, pp. 335–354 (2003)
4. Čopič Pucihar, K., Coulton, P., Alexander, J.: The use of surrounding visual context in handheld AR: device vs. user perspective rendering. In: Proceedings of CHI 2014, pp. 197–206 (2014)
5. Dünser, A., Billinghurst, M., Wen, J., Lehtinen, V., Nurminen, A.: Exploring the use of handheld AR for outdoor navigation. Comput. Graph. **36**(8), 1084–1095 (2012)
6. Grubert, J., Pahud, M., Grasset, R., Schmalstieg, D., Seichter, H.: The utility of Magic Lens interfaces on handheld devices for touristic map navigation. Pervasive Mobile Comput. **18**, 88103 (2014)
7. Komninos, A., Stefanis, V., Plessas, A., Besharat, J.: Cloud-based capture and sharing of urban dynamics using scarce check-in data. IEEE Pervasive Comput. **12**(4), 20–28 (2013)
8. Laugwitz, B., Held, T., Schrepp, M.: Construction and evaluation of a user experience questionnaire. In: Holzinger, A. (ed.) USAB 2008. LNCS, vol. 5298, pp. 63–76. Springer, Heidelberg (2008)
9. Mayer, J.D., Gaschke, Y.N.: The experience and meta-experience of mood. J. Pers. Soc. Psychol. **55**, 102–111 (1988)
10. Morrison, A., Mulloni, A., Lemmelä, S., Oulasvirta, A., Jacucci, G., Peltonen, P., Regenbrecht, H.: Collaborative use of mobile augmented reality with paper maps. Comput. Graph. **35**(4), 789–799 (2011)
11. Morrison, A., Oulasvirta, A., Peltonen, P., Lemmela, S., Jacucci, G., Reitmayr, G., Juustila, A.: Like bees around the hive: a comparative study of a mobile augmented reality map. In: Proceedings of CHI 2009, pp. 1889–1898 (2009)
12. Müller, J., Jentsch, M., Kray, C., Krüger, A.: Exploring factors that influence the combined use of mobile devices and public displays for pedestrian navigation. In: Proceedings of NordiCHI 2008, pp. 308–317 (2008)
13. Norrie, M., Signer, B.: Overlaying paper maps with digital information services for tourists. In: Proceedings of ICTT 2005, pp. 23–33 (2005)
14. Raita, E.: User interviews revisited: identifying user positions and system interpretations. In Proceedings of NordiCHI 2012, pp. 675–682 (2012)
15. Reilly, D., Mackay, B., Watters, C., Inkpen, K.: Planners, navigators, and pragmatists: collaborative wayfinding using a single mobile phone. Pers. Ubiquit. Comput. **13**(4), 321–329 (2009)
16. Rohs, M., Schöning, J., Raubal, M., Essl, G., Krüger, A.: Map navigation with mobile devices: virtual versus physical movement with and without visual context. In: Proceedings of ICMI 2007, pp. 146–153 (2007)
17. Stroila, M., Mays, J., Gale, B., Bach, J.: Augmented transit maps. In: Proceedings of WACV 2011, pp. 485–490 (2011)

The Interactive-Token Approach to Board Games

Simone Mora[1(✉)], Ines Di Loreto[2], and Monica Divitini[1]

[1] Department of Information and Computer Science,
NTNU, Trondheim, Norway
{simone.mora,monica.divitini}@idi.ntnu.no
[2] TechCICO, ICD-Université de technologie de Troyes, Troyes, France
ines.di_loreto@utt.fr

Abstract. Recent advances in interactive surfaces and Tangible User Interfaces created a new interest in digital board games, aiming at mixing the benefits of traditional board games with the interactivity of video games. Within this strand of research, we propose a new approach centered on the concepts of tokens, constraints, spatial expressions and interaction events. While mainstream solutions implement game interaction using interactive surfaces, our approach relies on physical manipulation of interactive objects on conventional surfaces. We illustrate the proposed approach by describing the design and development of a game for training of emergency workers. Building on feedbacks from user evaluation and our experience with the development, we outline design opportunities and challenges of the approach.

Keywords: Tangible user interface · Digital board game · Interactive objects

1 Introduction

Playing board games is an engaging social experience characterized by two levels of interaction: between the players themselves (e.g. discussing strategies), and mediated by physical artifacts representing information and actions (roll a dice, draw a card). Such rich experience is facilitated by the social and physical affordances of the principal elements in common to any board game: board and game pieces. While sitting around a board affords for face-to-face and gestural communication and cooperation, game pieces allow for tangible interaction and physical feedbacks.

Starting from the 80 s, computer versions of popular board games came to the market, like *Chess* and *Risk* for the commodore and Atari platforms, offering a full virtualization of board and game pieces. Keyboard and point-and-click interaction replaced physical actions around the board. Even if some of these games offered a multiplayer mode, this did not facilitate face-to-face interaction (rather a shoulder-to-shoulder interaction) [1] and simultaneous actions. With the evolution of computers fully virtualized digital board games gained higher-definition graphic and sound. Still, the lack of tangible interactions impacts on the game experience, because the manipulation of digital and of physical media are fundamentally different [2]. Moreover, the social experience is different as a computer or a console are acting as a mediator [3].

Kameas et al. (Eds.): AmI 2015, LNCS 9425, pp. 138–154, 2015.
DOI: 10.1007/978-3-319-26005-1_10

Taking advantage of advances in interactive surfaces and Tangible User Interfaces (TUIs), several works aim at introducing interactivity in board games while preserving their traditional social and physical affordances. This is achieved by replacing the game cardboard with a touchscreen computer (e.g. iPad, tabletops). The screen becomes an interactive board capable of graphical and auditory stimuli and reacting to touch-inputs and manipulation of objects tagged with fiducial markers. Although this approach has become mainstream, it confines interactivity to a touchscreen area, posing a tradeoff between size of the touchscreen (the interactive space) and cost.

In this paper we introduce a novel approach to the digitalization of board games inspired by the Token+Constraint paradigm [4]. Rather than focusing on interactive surfaces, we focus on transforming game pieces into interactive tokens, preserving the board as passive element. The actions players can perform on game pieces are defined by the physical and visual constraints provided by the board and game rules, as it is with traditional board games.

In order to prove its validity, we applied our approach to the augmentation of *Don't Panic* (DP) [5], an existing board game to train emergency workers on panic management. Starting from a cardboard prototype, we re-designed *Don't Panic* around interactive tokens and we built a working prototype leveraging digital manufacturing techniques. This game was chosen because it implements elements that are generic to board games, like *pawns* and *cards*, and it has a complex but limited set of rules to illustrate our approach in a concise way.

The paper is structured as follows. We first review the state of the art of current digital board games implemented with interactive surfaces. Our design approach is then presented and grounded in existing conceptual frameworks. Next we describe its application to *Don't Panic* and the related evaluation. Finally, we draw lessons learnt in form of design opportunities and challenges.

2   State of the Art

In this section we present research on digital board games with elements of physical interaction. The research presented hereafter can be set in the broader field of pervasive gaming, which aims at bringing physical and social interaction back to computer games [6]. Within this research we identify two main themes: games using (i) stationary interactive surfaces, and (ii) mobile interactive surfaces.

2.1   Stationary Interactive Surfaces

Computer-augmented tabletops have recently been proposed as an ideal platform for digital board game development [7], able to mix some of the advantages of low-tech board games with the benefits of video games [8]. Indeed, sitting around a technology-augmented tabletop allows users to be closer to the digital information and at the same time it enhances collaboration and communication among the users [9], re-introducing the user experience of face-to-face gaming and simultaneous actions. Tabletops can be augmented with technology to play games using different forms of augmented reality, as in [10, 11]. In particular, with the introduction of projectors and touchscreens, a number of works have used tabletop computers like Diamon-Touch [12] and Reactable [13] as platforms for digital board games development. Several examples are available in literature, including e.g. games to foster learning [14] and entertainment [15]; for a review see [7]. Whilst the direct manipulation of virtual objects supported by vision-based systems and touch-screens makes these games more similar to analog board games, the resulting social experience is still different from the three-dimension sensory feedbacks experienced by playing with dices, pawns and cards. For example, physical objects allow for peripheral interaction during the game and permit passive players (in turn-based games) to manipulate game pieces as long as they don't break the rules [16].

To address these limitations, game designers have started combining the touch-based interaction of tabletop computers with interactions through physical objects placed on the screen surface as means for controlling virtual game elements. In this way conventional objects can become game pieces (i.e. pawns, cards) by attaching active or passive tags recognizable by the tabletop computer. Several works have introduced physical objects in tabletop board games. For example, in *Weathergods* [15] players use different physical artefacts as players' avatars and to perform actions in the game. In *False Prophets* [17], *KnightMage* [1] and the STARS edition of *Monopoly* [1] tangible objects act as characters in the game. In *IncrediTable* [18] players can modify the game board with smart-pens and combine physical and virtual objects to solve puzzles. In order to facilitate the implementation of tabletop-based tangible games toolkits are available, for example [19].

The two main drawbacks of tabletops computers are mobility (they are bulky and heavy) and costs, limiting their widespread use for gaming. Low-cost alternatives, e.g. [20], are under development, but not yet available outside research labs.

2.2 Mobile Interactive Surfaces

Considering the limitations of stationary interactive surfaces, a complementary strand of research focused on the use of smaller but more affordable touch-screen devices, i.e. smartphones and tablets. Several technology solutions can be used to make the touchscreens of smartphones and tablets able to identify and track physical objects, for example using active [21] or passive [22] tags. Recently, various game companies have commercialized physical pawns for playing board games on tablets, e.g. *iPieces* [23]. These solutions attempt to recreate a tabletop-like setting using tablet hardware, but the small screen (compared to a traditional paper board) can deteriorate the gaming experience due to information occlusion and overloading. A recent trend in game development for tablets tries to overcome these issues by exploiting the emerging research in Around-Device Interaction (ADI) [24]. This approach allows to expand the area of play outside the device's screen for example using magnetic accessories [25] or employing an hybrid, partially interactive board as in the Hasbro *zAPPed Monopoly* edition [26]. In the latter, the original Monopoly board is augmented with digital contents produced by an iPad; some interactions are low-tech, e.g. moving the pawns on the board, others are mediated by technology, e.g. buying a property. Notably, in this implementation the digital and physical representations of the state of the game are disconnected. Finally, *Disney Infinity* [27] and *Activision's Skylanders* [28] make use of RFID-enabled platforms and collectible figurines to store players' profiles and unlock videogame features.

Mobile interactive surfaces are a good approach for playing digital board games in highly mobile contexts; yet due to screen and hands occlusion issues they often fail in delivering the complete social experience of traditional games.

3   The Interactive-Token Approach to Board Games

As detailed in the state of the art the dominant paradigm for designing digital board games consists in adding active or passive objects on top of interactive surfaces. These objects complement and facilitate interaction with the interactive surface by offering affordances proper of the physical world for controlling virtual artefacts and controls (buttons, menus).

We propose a different approach: the game pieces are the means to bring interactivity and not the board per se. Hereafter we will use the term interactive token to refer to game pieces with added interactivity.

Distributing interactivity across multiple components opens for a wider space of possibility and a higher degree of flexibility in shaping the game experience. For example, game pieces can influence the state of a game not only when they sit on the interactive surface, but also when they are manipulated over and around it. In this way, the board is mainly used to stage the game and set a context for the use of the pieces, as in traditional board games. Also, the interactive area of the board is less limited by size, which also determines the portability of the game (and costs).

3.1   Shifting Perspective

Our investigation aims at augmenting the two intrinsic roles commonly found in board games: *control* and *representation*. For example: pawns serve as a visual representation of players, shared items (e.g. houses in Monopoly) as a representation of a resource count. The action of rolling a dice or drawing a card acts as a control for a (random) variable, allowing the game to evolve from a representational state to another. Each game piece can serve one role (as in Monopoly), or both (as in Chess). Pieces usually represent players and resources via iconic or symbolic artifacts; moreover the spatial configuration of game pieces on the board provides the players with a shared awareness of the state of the game.

In interactive-surface implementations of board games, technology is usually employed to virtualize pieces' representations by means of computer graphic and sound. The player's physical interactions with game pieces are often substituted with traditional GUI metaphors. For example, the actions of rolling a dice or drawing a card are implemented in touchscreen gestures like pushing a button or pinching a virtual dice.

In our approach the role of technology is twofold. On one side it brings interactivity by augmenting, not virtualizing, pieces' material representations; on the other side sensor technology is used to capture players' tangible interaction with control pieces aiming at preserving their traditional physical affordances. For example, an accelerometer embedded in a dice can sense the result of a dice throw, and update a digital variable in a way that is transparent to the player.

Interactivity is a consequence of players' interaction with control pieces and regulated by game rules. Interactivity can be provided, e.g. by means of small LEDs or LCD displays embedded onto pieces to convey graphic and video contents, or through auditory or haptic feedbacks. Game pieces might still preserve their traditional aspect, having a tangible representation that complements an intangible or ephemeral representation provided by technology. As matter of fact pieces in board games are used to convey both static and dynamic information: for example, players' identity and role don't change throughout the game and are often represented by a set of distinguishing pawns (or tokens), while resources or score associated to each player vary and they are usually represented by a number of shared artifacts (e.g. houses and hotels in Monopoly). In our approach designers can define the trade off between the two representations as a balance by static information to be provided by the tangible representation and dynamic information provided by intangible ones. For example, in a revisited version of Monopoly tokens might preserve their physical semblances to identify players but might embed an intangible representation of the number of property owned by the player (e.g. in digits, icons or symbols on a LCD display).

3.2 Architectural View of Interactive-Token Board Games

From an architectural point of view (Fig. 1), a digital *model* of game variables and rules (stored in a computer game engine) mirrors the spatial configuration of physical game token on the board. Each token has a *tangible representation* (i.e. shape, color) that identifies the piece and defines its affordances; in addition, it might have an *intangible representation* (graphic, auditory), controlled by the digital model, that is updated anytime the manipulation of a piece with control power pushes a change in the model. The interaction with pieces is based on a double loop [29].

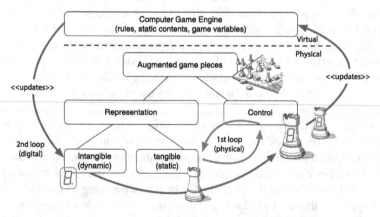

Fig. 1. Double interaction loop in interactive board games

A first interaction loop consists in the passive haptic and visual feedback the player perceives when manipulating pieces on the board, this loop is in common with traditional board games. A second loop adds interactivity by means of graphical and auditory feedbacks conveyed via the tokens' intangible representation. This loop requires technology for sensing tokens' manipulations as well as providing visual/audio feedbacks (Fig. 1). Our approach is conservative towards traditional game mechanics. Technology is used for augmenting players' interactions with the pieces rather than reinventing them. The set of valid interactions with game pieces is defined by the affordances of pieces and by game rules. To formalize these rules we build on two theories: the Token+Constrain framework [4], providing a powerful descriptive language, and the MCRit (Model-Control-Representation intangible and tangible) [30], proposed by Ulmer and Ishii, addressing issues of representation and control in TUI.

3.3   Theory Grounding

The Token+Constraint framework defined by Ullmer et al. [4] defines *Tokens* as discrete physical objects that represent digital information and *Constraints* as either mechanical or visual confining regions that are mapped to digital operations. By the interaction phases of association and manipulation of tokens within a system of constraints it is possible to map physical actions to a set of computational operations; for example, the presence or absence of a token in a constrained area could be easily digitalized in binary information.

Besides the T+C paradigm focus on the use of tokens and constraints as means to trigger digital operations, physical artefacts are also characterized by their physical appearance. Indeed, the "seamless integration of control and representation" [30] is a distinctive characteristic of TUIs over traditional GUIs, where control and representation are decoupled in input (e.g. keyboard, mouse) and output (e.g. screen, printer) devices. Aiming at going beyond the traditional MVC (Model-View-Controller) paradigm, in [30] Ulmer and Ishii propose an interaction model for TUIs called MCRit, Model-Control-Representation (intangible and tangible). They redefined the view concept of graphical interfaces as a balance between a physical (the token's shapes and affordances) and an intangible representation (e.g. computer graphics and sounds). This approach allows for blending the flexibility offered by graphical elements of GUIs with the natural manipulation offered by TUIs.

The presented interaction paradigms can be integrated to drive the design of digital board games. The Token+Constraint approach provides conceptual tools for building tangible user interfaces that leverage interaction with physical game pieces for controlling digital representation of game elements, hence preserving the affordances of board games. The MCRit paradigm allows for adding interactivity by augmenting, not replacing or virtualizing, the physical representation of game pieces with an intangible representation of digital information.

3.4   Key Design Constructs

Aiming at extending the T+C paradigm, we define a game, which is composed by *game dynamics* (the sum of game logic and rules), as a sequence of player-initiated *interaction events* that modify *spatial configurations* of *tokens* with respect to board *constraints* and other tokens. Sequences of interaction events describe players' interaction during the game and allow a game to evolve thru states. In the following we describe how we extended T+C to address the design of interactive board games.

Tokens are technology-augmented artifacts capable of triggering digital operations that can activate game dynamics. Tokens may be capable of sensing information (e.g. proximity with other tokens) and displaying computer graphic and sound. Some tokens are personal, embodiment of the players on the board, while others are public and can be handed around during the game. Tokens conceptualize all the tangible pieces traditionally used in board games. They range from elements of chance (e.g. an augmented dice in backgammon or RFID-enabled cards in monopoly) to game pieces, e.g. a pawns augmented with an LCD displaying the player's rank in the game.

Constraints are physical or visual confining regions in the board space. The association or dissociation of a token within a constraint can be mapped to digital operations to activate game dynamic. Constrained regions are determined by a perimeter that could be visual or physical; the structure of the perimeter might permit a certain degree of freedom for the token (e.g. allowing for translation or rotation). Examples of constraints are checks for Chess pieces and territories in Risk.

Interaction events are player-triggered manipulations of tokens, recognizable with sensor technology, that modify the (digital and physical) state of a game. We identified three types of events:

- *solo-token event (T)* - the manipulation of a single token over or on the board. For example, the action of rolling a dice or drawing a card
- *token-constraint event (T-C)* - the operation of building transient token-constraint associations by adding or removing *tokens* to a constrained region of the board. T-C events can have different consequences depending on game rules: in *Risk*, moving army pieces beyond a territory line is an attack action; in *Mancala* solitaire game the marble can only fit in an empty space and implies to eat another marble
- *token-token event (T-T)* - the operation of building transient token-token adjacency-relationships, achieved by moving tokens on the board. For example, moving a token next to another token to unlock special powers, or to exchange a resource between two players. For example, creating a king in the *Draughts* game requires that the player puts a game piece on top of another.

Spatial Configurations are static relationships of *tokens* both with respect to *constraints* and to other tokens. They limit the space of interaction of players to a set of valid Token-Constraint and Token-Token relationship defined by a grammar of game-specific rules. For example, certain tokens can be associated only to selected constraints, relationship of proximity among tokens can be meaningful or not. Spatial configurations are used to validate players' *interaction events* against game rules, narrowing the set of actions that are valid for activating game rules.

Sequence of valid interaction events activate specific game dynamics, thus allowing the game to evolve from a state to another and triggering a change in intangible representation produced by tokens. For example, we can model the act of capturing a piece in chess as a sequence of interaction events that modify proximity between two chess tokens within checkers constraints.

4 Applying the Interactive-Token Approach

In this section we illustrate the approach by describing how it has been used to design interactive tokens, board constraints and interaction events for augmenting a serious board game called Don't Panic (DP) [5]. The game shares similarity with many board games like the use of *pawns* to represent players, *items* to trigger game mechanics, and *cards* as elements of chance. This effort allowed us to evaluate the feasibility of the approach.

4.1 Don't Panic Game Dynamics and Rules

Don't Panic is a collaborative game inspired by Pandemic [31]. Four players start the game as member of a panic management team that must work together to manage panicking crowds, in turn-based actions. A map representing a city is displayed on the game board and the territory is divided in *sectors*. Each sector contains a number of people (PO) characterized by a panic level (PL). During the game panicking events (e.g. fires, explosions), randomly triggered by *card* drawing, increase PLs in determinate sectors. In addition, the panic increases at regular intervals. Each player is represented on the board space by a *pawn token* and gets a limited number of actions with the goal to lower the panic level in the city. Using the "calm!" and "move!" tokens a player can either reduce the panic in a specific sector or move panicked people to an adjacent sector (with lower PL). Information *cards* distributed in each turn can lower the panic in multiple sectors, for example the action "TV-broadcast" reduces the PL in all the sectors. Players collectively win the game when the PL in all sectors is zero. For a full description of game rules see [5].

4.2 Design of Tokens, and Board Constraints

Don't Panic, in its augmented version, is composed by a cardboard and a set of tokens. In the following we describe the objects and their meaning as game pieces.

The Board (Fig. 2-a) – is a cardboard that visualizes a map portraying a territory divided in nodes, sector and paths. Nodes are edges between sectors and are connected by paths, as in closed cyclic graphs. Nodes feature physical constraints and no degree of freedom for the hosted tokens; sectors and paths provide visual constraints allowing tokens' translation and rotation, within the perimeter.

The Card Deck (Fig. 2-c) – dynamically print information cards. Each card has a textual description of how it affects the game and a barcode that links the card to its digital representation. The top surface of the card deck can read the barcode on the card and trigger actions in the game (Fig. 2-d). Therefore cards don't affect game dynamics immediately after they are produced; they can be kept or exchanged by players, until when they are activated by the card deck.

Pawn Tokens (Fig. 2-b) – embody the players' presence on a node, each player interact with a personal pawn during a game. Pawns can be dragged from node to node, as long as a path directly connects the two. Each pawn provides static and dynamic information via a LCD display. The static information shows icons linking to a specific player.

The dynamic representation visualizes the number of people present in sectors adjacent to each of the four pawn's sides and their panic level (symbolized with colors). This information is contextually updated according with a pawn's location, since different nodes face different sectors. Besides their representational functions pawn also have a control role: in order to activate nested actions with other tokens the player has to reach the relevant node.

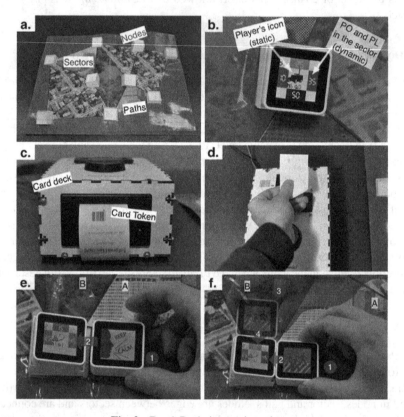

Fig. 2. Don´t Panic interactive tokens

The Calm! token (Fig. 2-e) – represents the action of going on the field and calming people talking to them, thus reducing the PL in a specific sector. The top display shows a numeric representation of how effective the action of calming people is, given the player's role in the active turn. When it is activated by proximity towards a pawn's side, it provides visual and auditory feedbacks.

The Move! token (Fig. 2-f) – simulates moving people between sectors, in this way the people who are moved acquire the panic level of the recipient sector. The top display shows the number of people that can be moved, given the player's role in the active turn. It also provides visual and auditory feedbacks.

4.3 Design of Spatial Configurations

After designing tokens and constraints, we defined valid token-constraint and token-token configurations and interaction events (Table 1). Token-constraint relationships are defined by univocal, transient associations created by the add/remove interaction event. Token-token relationships are defined by adjacency achieved via the move interaction event. The types of constraint limit the interaction events that tokens can afford. For example, physically confined tokens can only afford the *add/remove* (association with constraint) event, while visually constrained ones leave the player free to manipulate the token, e.g. to build proximity relationships with other tokens.

Table 1. Valid spatial configurations and interaction events

Token	Allowed constraint	Allowed proximity with other token
Pawn	Nodes (physical)	Adjacency to Calm! and Move!
Calm!, Move!	Sectors (visual)	Adjacency to Pawn
Cards	Card Deck (visual)	None

4.4 Mapping Valid Interaction Events to Game Dynamics

Table 2 presents the mapping between *Don't Panic!* game dynamics and sequences of interaction events validated against spatial configurations (Table 1). Each sequence of interaction events results in a new physical configuration of tokens on board and in a update of the digital representation of tokens in the game engine. It also produces a change in tokens' intangible representations (graphic and audio).

Table 2. Mapping game dynamics to Interaction Events

Game dynamic	Interaction event (Type)	Digital feedbacks
Move from node A to node B	1-Remove pawn from node A (T-C)	Panic and people display update
	2-Add pawn to node B (T-C)	
Calm down people in sector A (Fig. 2-e)	1-Add the Calm! tool to sector A (T-C)	Panic display update, auditory feedback
	2-Move the Calm! tool towards a pawn's side facing sector A (T-T)	
Move people between sectors A and B (Fig. 2-f)	1-Add the Move! tool to sector A (T-C)	People display update, auditory feedback
	2-Move the Move! tool towards the pawn's side facing the sector A (T-T)	
	1. Repeat step 1,2 in sector B	
Calm down people in multiple sector	1-Approach a card towards the card deck top surface (T-C)	Panic displays updated, auditory feedback

5   Technologies and Tools for Implementation

Don't Panic has been implemented in a fully functional prototype. We designed the hardware and the software with the help of several commercial and open source toolkits. The system we implemented, a loosely coupled modular architecture, is composed by a game engine and a set of token handlers. The game engine implements game rules and stores a digital representation of game variables (e.g. PO and PL levels); token handlers bridge players' physical interaction with game pieces with their digital representations. Modules exchange information over an event-based messaging system over the socketIO protocol. As an example, when the player associates a pawn to a node, the relative location of the node to the board surface is acquired by sensors on the pawn, encoded in a JSON message and sent to the game engine. The engine updates the digital representation of the game state and messages back the pawn the list of sector adjacent to the node and relative PO and PL variables; the pawn uses the data to update information on the LCD display (Fig. 2-b).

5.1   The Game Engine

The game engine has been implemented in javascript using the node.js framework. Besides activating game rules the game engine also acts as a server for handling communication with token handlers; moreover it exposes an HTML-based interface for remotely administrating game sessions and customizing game rules. The game engine runs on a raspberry pi, which is configured as WiFi hotspot to handle TCP/IP connections with TUI clients and with remote clients for game administration. The game engine also produces auditory feedbacks and music.

5.2   Tokens Handlers

Pawns, Calm! and Move! tokens have been implemented using the 1st generation of the Sifteo cubes [32]. Each cube is capable of sensing accelerations, proximity with other cubes on any of its four sides, and to display graphics on the top surface. The cubes' behavior is wirelessly controlled. Sifteos cubes didn't provide any API for sensing cubes' location relative to visual constrains on a 2D board space; in order to make the cubes recognize discrete locations on a board (required to use the cubes as pawns reacting to nodes constraints) we exploited in an unconventional way the data from the 3-axis accelerometer embedded in each of them. We designed sockets for the cubes each of them featuring a combination of unique horizontal tilt angles over two axes; the aggregated value of tilts angles is used as a fingerprint for the socket. We 3D-printed and embedded the sockets into the board as nodes constraints (Fig. 2-a) and we coded the relation between sockets fingerprints and nodes' location. In this way when a player associates a pawn to a socket, the cube senses the surface tilt over 2 axes using the accelerometer, the aggregated valued is matched against socket fingerprints and thus the position of the pawn on the board is updated in in the game engine. As a current limitation, after each interaction with a cube the player has to push the upper side of the cube to confirm the action.

The card deck is crafted in form of a wooden box that encloses a thermal printer, a CCD barcode scanner and a raspberry pi (which also runs the game engine). The card deck allows for printing and recognizing cards during a game. A card manager module developed in Python allows for information exchange with the game engine. Although both game engine and card manager are deployed to the same hardware (raspberry pi) they are loosely coupled, allowing flexibility for future development. Each printed card displays text, graphic and a distinct barcode that is used to link the physical card to its intangible representation stored in the game engine. When the action of drawing of a random card is activated by a game rule, the game engine notifies the card handler to print text and a unique barcode onto the card. When a player plays a card by waving it towards the barcode reader, the engine is notified and it triggers an update in the set of variables and thus in the representation of panic levels on the pawns' display. The card deck area also features a push button and a LCD display, in the current implementation these devices are used to pass the turn and to display status information.

6   Evaluation

The *Don't Panic* prototype (Fig. 3) was tested with 16 players aged 20–59, 6 were female. The goal was to explore (i) how the traditional social affordances of board games are preserved; (ii) how players understand tokens interactivity; and (iii) to reflect on design opportunities and challenges presented by our approach. The evaluation of *Don 't Panic* game dynamics is beyond the scope of this paper.

Fig. 3. The Don't Panic prototype tested during evaluation

Each evaluation session was composed by 4 participants in a controlled environment. After a game walkthrough, players were asked to play for 30 min, then to fill in usability

(SEQ) questionnaires. In addition, sessions were observed and video recorded with the consent of the participants. A qualitative and quantitative analysis was done by two researchers on the collected data (2-h video footage and questionnaires) following [33].

Utterances analysis shows that 65 % of statements concerned *game strategies*. Only 18 % (most of them in the firsts minutes of the game) concerned game management tasks (e.g. rules), demonstrating a steep learning curve. The remaining 17 % of utterances concerned the use of token interfaces, often about usability issues, also noticed by the observers. Some group used a lot of verbal interaction (202 in 30 min) while others kept verbal utterances very low (52 in 30 min).

Regarding *physical manipulations of tokens*, the usability of the system was rated very high (M = 4, SD = 0.9 in a 5-steps likert scale) by the under 40, and 3 (SD = 1.5) by older players. Despite these results we observed some usability issues. Metaphors used for representing panic level and people per sector were difficult to learn. Moreover, several players had problems in reading and manipulating tokens when associated to nodes with high tilt angles.

The interactivity brought by technology was highly appreciated by the players (M = 4, SD = 0.8). When asked about how interactive tokens fostered gameplay, players answered that they were helpful as (i) memory helpers "*[tokens' LCD display] let rules be clearer and there is no need to remember them*", (ii) facilitators for social interaction "*[tokens] add more interaction with people and make it easier to remember actions*". Moreover, the 87 % of the players agreed that the usage of the objects made the game engaging.

Finally, when asked (open question) to compare *Don't Panic* with respect to a traditional board game experience, players considered it as "*less repetitive, quicker, more reactive*"; amusing and more interesting because of the interactive tokens: "*...[Interactive] objects add to the realism of the game*".

7 Discussion

Our evaluation highlights that the introduction of technology didn't alter the traditional social affordances of board games. Even if the interactive tokens were richer in terms of actions and feedbacks than traditional game pieces, this choice didn't disrupt the flow of actions in the game. Regarding physical interaction, game dynamics were successful implemented through sequences of interaction events. In the following we reflect on our experience highlighting design challenges and opportunities.

Blending Strengths from the Physical and Digital Domain. The blend of elements taken from the digital and analog worlds introduced new design opportunities that, in our experience, resulted in added interactivity and fun for the players. For example, by adopting a card printer, we were able to mix the power from the digital domain, to sort and select a huge number of choices, yet preserving the physicality of tangible interaction with cards, their flexibility of manipulation and extended visibility. We observed that game cards printed "on the fly" brought elements of excitement and surprise due to the players hanging on while a card gets (slowly) printed. Furthermore, information on card can be designed to be highly contextual with the status of the game, or random, or tailored to role of active player or the level in the game. The physicality of cards also allows for playful interaction not conventionally available in traditional board gaming: card can be annotated, kept by the players for future reference or tossed.

Unconstrained Interactivity. Besides analog affordances of board gaming, in our approach videogames interactivity (e.g. 3D-graphic, audio), useful to convey rich information and creating ambiance, can be still exploited by designers to a certain degree. Interactivity, rather than being confined on a single surface, becomes mobile being distributed across an ecology of tokens. This opens for two new design opportunities. First, the role of computer graphic representations provided by tokens' LCDs can serve both as a private and public display. For example, a token can provide secret information when it is sheltered in a player's hand, yet becoming a display of public information when it sits on a board constraint. Tokens can be scattered around the board to provide dynamic information over static regions of space; also they can be positioned side by side for extending display surface. This opportunity could be further exploited for designing games that make use of single-player interaction with tokens when they are off the board, and multiplayer interaction once they are back within board edges.

Balancing Tangible and Intangible Representations. The design of tangible and intangible representations is critical to avoid usability issues. For example, in *Don't Panic* a single token (Fig. 2-b) captures information about the player (role and number of actions left) and information about the state of the game (distribution of people and panic levels). Although providing a quick awareness of the game status, in our experience this design has been perceived as overloading and confusing. This issue opens for a wider design challenge: how to find the right balance between the information encoded in tangible representations and information represented in dynamic intangible ones (e.g. on small embedded displays). Furthermore, it is important to pay attention to the symbolic and iconic representations to adopt. For example, we used a discrete color-coded scale to symbolize ranges of values (panic levels). Being the information only updated when a threshold is reached, most of the players experienced this design choice as a frustrating lack of feedback from the system. Though this is a general HCI problem, it takes a different connotation when using a TUI approach which poses stricter limitations compared to GUIs to the design space [29]. The design choices for tokens' intangible representations can be influenced by a specific technology, by the physical affordances of the token, or to add a fun factor.

Lack of Technology Toolbox. During implementation we were challenged by the current lack of technology tools to assist designers in the development of digital board games based on interactive tokens. In order to build tokens that afford for the interaction events required in *Don't Panic*, we had to use multiple hardware platforms, different coding languages and to hack the Sifteo platform. Although this modus operandi was coherent with the goal of rapid-prototyping *a token-based game* to validate our approach, it poses limitations to the generalization of our approach and high entry-barriers for designers. The lack of a technology toolkit might create barriers to the implementation of a planned sequence of interaction events. For example, the use of Sifteos as tokens in *Don't Panic* required adding a final step, pushing the upper surface of the cube to signal the operation was terminated, when moving the token between nodes; thus creating a breakdown in the user experience.

8 Conclusions and Future Work

In this paper we present the interactive-token approach to the design of digital board games. The proposed approach provides a change in perspective from mainstream works in interactive board games, which are centring design on interactive surfaces. Our approach relies instead on physical manipulation of interactive objects on conventional surfaces, with the aim to preserve the physical and social affordances that are the basis for the success of traditional board games.

The main contribution of this paper is in the extension of the Token+Constraint interaction approach [4], providing *constructs* that can be used by designer to augment board games with interactivity in accordance with the game rules. These constructs are intended as a way to describe games, supporting the transition to implementation.

The approach proposed in the paper has successfully supported the design of *Don't Panic* in terms of tokens, constraints, and interaction events. Results from the evaluation reveal that the social affordances of traditional board game are preserved and the addition of computer interactivity is well accepted. The design and implementation of the game served as evaluation of the feasibility of the approach and allowed us to identify a set of challenges and opportunities that can be useful to other designers.

As part of our future work, we aim to generalize the approach. Starting with the experience discussed in this paper, we aim at formalising a design process for the creation of interactive-token board games; and to provide a toolkit supporting game designers in the implementation of hardware and software for system of tokens and constraints.

Acknowledgments. We thank the students who helped with the development of our prototype and the volunteers who joined our user studies, in particular Mr. Gianni Della Valle for helping with the organization of the evaluation studies.

References

1. Magerkurth, C., Memisoglu, M., Engelke, T., Streitz, N.: Towards the next generation of tabletop gaming experiences. In: Proceedings of Graphics Interface 2004, pp. 73–80 (2004)
2. Terrenghi, L., Kirk, D., Sellen, A., Izadi, S.: Affordances for manipulation of physical versus digital media on interactive surfaces. In: Proceedings of CHI 2007, pp. 1157–1166 (2007)
3. Magerkurth, C., Engelke, T., Memisoglu, M.: Augmenting the virtual domain with physical and social elements: towards a paradigm shift in computer entertainment technology. In: Proceedings of ACE 2004 (2004)
4. Ullmer, B., Ishii, H., Jacob, R.J.K.: Token+constraint systems for tangible interaction with digital information. ACM Trans. Comput.-Hum. Interact. (TOCHI) **12**, 81–118 (2005)

5. Di Loreto, I., Mora, S., Divitini, M.: Don't panic: enhancing soft skills for civil protection workers. In: Ma, M., Oliveira, M.F., Hauge, J.B., Duin, H., Thoben, K.-D. (eds.) SGDA 2012. LNCS, vol. 7528, pp. 1–12. Springer, Heidelberg (2012)
6. Magerkurth, C., Cheok, A.D., Mandryk, R.L., Nilsen, T.: Pervasive games: bringing computer entertainment back to the real world. ACM Comput. Entertainment **3**, 4 (2005)
7. Haller, M., Forlines, C., Koeffel, C., Leitner, J., Shen, C.: Tabletop games: platforms, experimental games and design recommendations. In: Art and Technology of Entertainment Computing and Communication, pp. 271–297 (2010)
8. Bakker, S., Vorstenbosch, D., Van Den Hoven, E., Hollemans, G., Bergman, T.: Tangible interaction in tabletop games. In: Proceedings of ACE 2007, pp. 163–170 (2007)
9. Rogers, Y., Rodden, T.: Configuring spaces and surfaces to support collaborative interactions. In: O'Hara, K., Perry, M., Churchill, E., Russell, D. (eds.) Public and Situated Displays, pp. 45–79. Springer, Netherlands, Dordrecht (2003)
10. Barakonyi, I., Weilguny, M., Psik, T., Schmalstieg, D.: MonkeyBridge. In: Proceedings of ACE 2005, pp. 172–175 (2005)
11. Cooper, N., Keatley, A., Dahlquist, M., Mann, S., Slay, H., Zucco, J., Smith, R., Thomas, B.H.: Augmented reality chinese checkers. In: Proceedings of ACE 2004, pp. 117–126 (2004)
12. Dietz, P., Leigh, D.: DiamondTouch: a multi-user touch technology. In: Proceedings of UIST 2001, pp. 219–226 (2001)
13. Jordà, S.: The reactable: tangible and tabletop music performance. In: Proceedings of CHI EA 2010, pp. 2989–2994 (2010)
14. Horn, M., Atrash Leong, Z., Block, F., Diamond, J., Evans, E.M., Phillips, B., Shen, C.: Of BATs and APEs: an interactive tabletop game for natural history museums. In: Proceedings of CHI 2012, pp. 2059–2068 (2012)
15. Bakker, S., Vorstenbosch, D., Van Den Hoven, E., Hollemans, G., Bergman, T.: Weathergods. In: Proceedings of TEI 2007, pp. 151–152 (2007)
16. Krzywinski, A., Chen, W., Røsjø, E.: Digital board games: peripheral activity eludes ennui. Proc. of ITS **2011**, 280–281 (2011)
17. Mandryk, R.L., Maranan, D.S.: False prophets: exploring hybrid board/video games. In: Proceedings of CHI EA 2002, pp. 640–641 (2002)
18. Leitner, J., Haller, M., Yun, K., Woo, W., Sugimoto, M., Inami, M., Cheok, A.D., Been-Lirn, H.D.: Physical interfaces for tabletop games. ACM Comput. Entertainment (CIE) **7**, 61 (2009)
19. Marco, J., Baldassarri, S., Cerezo, E.: ToyVision: a toolkit to support the creation of innovative board-games with tangible interaction. In: Proceedings of TEI 2013 (2013)
20. Wolfe, C., Smith, J.D., Graham, T.C.: A low-cost infrastructure for tabletop games. In: Proceedings of FuturePlay 2008, pp. 145–151 (2008)
21. Yu, N.-H., et al.: TUIC: enabling tangible interaction on capacitive multi-touch displays. In: Proceedings of CHI 2011, pp. 2995–3004 (2011)
22. Burnett, D., Coulton, P., Lewis, A.: Providing both physical and perceived affordances using physical games pieces on touch based tablets. In: Proceedings of IE 2012 (2012)
23. iPieces. http://www.jumbo.eu/ipieces/
24. Butler, A., Izadi, S., Hodges, S.: SideSight. In: Proceedings of UIST 2008, pp. 201–204 (2008)
25. Bianchi, A., Oakley, I.: Designing tangible magnetic appcessories. In: Proceedings of TEI 2013, pp. 255–258 (2013)
26. Hasbro Monopoly zAPPed Edition. http://www.hasbro.com/monopoly/
27. Disney Infinity. https://infinity.disney.com/
28. Activision Skylanders. http://www.skylanders.com/
29. Ishii, H.: Tangible bits: beyond pixels. In: Proceedings of TEI 2008 (2008)

30. Ullmer, B., Ishii, H.: Emerging frameworks for tangible user interfaces. IBM Syst. J. **39**, 915–931 (2000)
31. Pandemic Board Game. http://zmangames.com
32. Merrill, D., Sun, E., Kalanithi, J.: Sifteo cubes. In: Proceedings of CHI EA 2012, pp. 1015–1018 (2012)
33. Bødker, S.: Applying activity theory to video analysis: how to make sense of video data in human-computer interaction. Massachusetts Institute of Technology, USA (1995)

Why Should I Use This? Identifying Incentives for Using AAL Technologies

Christina Jaschinski[1,2(⊠)] and Somaya Ben Allouch[1]

[1] Saxion University of Applied Sciences, Enschede, The Netherlands
{c.jaschinski,s.benallouch}@saxion.nl
[2] University of Twente, Enschede, The Netherlands

Abstract. Ambient Assisted Living (AAL) technologies have the potential to target the challenges of our aging population. However, little is known about what motivates older adults to adopt these new technologies. Most research in this area relies on single cases with a specific AAL application and a limited number of users. To fill this gap, a content analyses of 35 AAL reports was conducted. The aim was to provide a comprehensive overview of potential incentives for using AAL technologies. The data was coded using the Social Cognitive Theory (SCT). In total 13 incentives could be identified, which were grouped into six categories: (1) social incentives, (2) health and safety incentives, (3) activity incentives, (4) novel sensory incentives, (5) status incentives and (6) self-reactive incentives. Within these categories 'social connectedness' and 'health and safety' were the most important incentives. These results provide a comprehensive and theoretically grounded understanding of what motivates older adults to adopt AAL technologies.

Keywords: Ambient Assisted Living (AAL) · Older adults · Technology adoption · Social cognitive theory

1 Introduction

Demographic projections state that by 2050, for the first time in history, the share of older persons (≥60 years) in our population will match the share of younger persons (≤14 years). In the more industrialized regions, such as the EU or the United States, the older population has already outnumbered the younger population [1]. This demographic shift entails major challenges for our society and the healthcare system including more people who suffer from chronic diseases, increasing healthcare costs, a shortage of caregivers and a higher demand on family caregivers [1, 2].

1.1 AAL Technologies

A new generation of assistive technologies, known as 'Ambient Assisted Living' (AAL) technologies, could meet these challenges by facilitating active, healthy and independent aging in place [3]. This is also in the interest of the older adults who prefer to age in their own trusted home environment [4]. AAL technologies are developed in line

© Springer International Publishing Switzerland 2015
Kameas et al. (Eds.): AmI 2015, LNCS 9425, pp. 155–170, 2015.
DOI: 10.1007/978-3-319-26005-1_11

with the ambient intelligence paradigm which aims to create digital environments which are unobtrusive, adaptive and responsive to human needs [2, 5, 6]. AAL is an umbrella term for a variety of innovative technologies including smart homes, robotics and ambient, mobile and wearable sensors. Different algorithms and computational techniques such as activity recognition, context modeling, location identification, planning and anomaly detection enable these technologies to monitor and improve the well-being of older adults [2]. While some AAL technologies focus on the older adults' physical well-being, by monitoring vital signs and activity patterns [7], providing reminders [8] and detecting falls [9]; other AAL technologies target the older adults' emotional well-being, by facilitating communication and interaction with peers and family members [10, 11].

AAL technologies have the potential to facilitate independent and healthy aging and therefore offer a promising solution to the challenges of our aging population. However, many of these technologies are still in the development phase and it is unclear if older adults are ready to adopt and use these technologies. Moreover, compared to younger age groups, older adults are a highly heterogeneous target group in terms of technology experience, activity level, level of social involvement and physical and mental well-being [12, 13]. This translates into highly diverse needs and preferences, making it challenging for developers to design a technology which appeals to the target user.

1.2   Theories of User Acceptance and AAL Technologies

To successfully develop AAL technologies for the older adults we need to understand which factors drive the acceptance process of these technologies. Some of the most influential models to explain the adoption and use of new technologies stem from information systems research (e.g., Technology Acceptance Model (TAM) [13, 14]; Unified Theory of Acceptance and Use of Technology (UTAUT) [15]) and media use research (e.g., Uses and Gratifications Approach (U&G) [16, 17] and Social Cognitive Theory (SCT) [18]). Although these models have their own focus, they all incorporate the expectancy-value principle [19] which has its origin in social psychology e.g., [20]. In essence, expectancy-value theories suggest that future behavior is based on the expected outcomes of the behavior (expectancy or belief) and the affect, positive or negative, attributed to these expected outcomes (evaluation) [21]. Thus, the expected outcomes of using a technology seems to be an important predictor of technology adoption.

Drawing the attention to TAM and UTAUT, both are very influential and widely applied models for investigating the adoption of new technologies. However, in TAM and UTAUT expected outcomes are constructed rather one-dimensional in terms of 'perceived usefulness' and 'performance expectancy' respectively. Originally created in an organizational context, these constructs mainly reflect the instrumental value of a technology. A similar notion was made by Benbasat and Barki [22], who stated with regard to TAM that "study after study has reiterated the importance of PU (Perceived Usefulness), with very little research effort going into investigating what actually makes a system useful" [p. 212]. In our view, TAM and UTAUT are therefore not entirely appropriate to explain the expected outcomes of AAL technologies. Those technologies consist of a wide array of different applications and can entail besides instrumental values also intrinsic values for the target group. Therefore, we turn to a different approach: Social Cognitive Theory (SCT) that acknowledges the multi-dimensional nature of expected outcomes.

1.3   Social Cognitive Theory

Social Cognitive Theory [23] stems from the field of psychology and is an extension to social learning theory. SCT depicts human behavior as reciprocal causation of behavior, cognition and other personal factors and environmental influences. According to SCT a large part of human behavior is purposive and regulated by forethought. Individuals use their forethought to plan actions, set goals and anticipate potential consequences. This means that people anticipate the outcome of their actions and adapt their behavior to achieve desired consequences. Beliefs about the expected outcomes can be either grounded in one's own direct experience or through observing others (observational learning). Thus, one's current beliefs about the expected outcomes of a certain behavior are an important motivator for implementing this behavior [23, 24]. Translating these principles to the context of the current study, the expected outcomes of AAL technology use, will be a leading factor in the older adults' adoption of these technologies.

In contrast to TAM and UTAUT, SCT depicts expected outcomes as a multidimensional construct which are organized around six basic types of behavioral incentives: social (e.g., social interaction), activity (e.g., feel entertained), novel sensory (e.g., obtain new information), status (e.g., get respect from others), self-reactive (e.g., relieve boredom), and monetary (e.g., monetary benefits) [23, pp. 232–240, 25]. These incentives were initially theoretically constructed but have been validated to study the use of innovations such as the internet [25, 26] and social media [27]. However, these studies put the focus on media use, which let us assume that not all of these incentives are equally relevant with regard to AAL technologies. For example, other incentives such as self-preservation incentives are very likely to be important in the context of AAL technologies. Nevertheless, SCT is a broad theory of human behavior that was successfully applied to understand different types of behavioral processes. Therefore, we regard SCT as an adequate approach to get an insight in what could motivate older adults to adopt and use AAL technologies.

The current research uses SCT as theoretical approach to identify potential incentives for using AAL technologies as perceived by the older adults. Thereby, we also allow for additional incentives to surface from the data. Understanding which incentives older adults expect from the use of AAL technologies, can help developers in designing AAL technologies which appeal to the needs and wishes of the user, which in turn aids the likelihood of future adoption.

2   Method

To identify which incentives older adults perceive as important for the use of AAL technologies, we conducted a content analyses of published reports from projects funded by the Ambient Assistant Living Joint Programme (AAL JP).

2.1   AAL Joint Programme

The Ambient Assistant Living Joint Programme (AAL JP) is a funding activity, cofinanced by the European Commission, that aims to promote active and healthy aging in Europe through the use of innovative information and communication technology (ICT). Their goal is to foster result-oriented research projects that deliver concrete solutions for independent aging. In doing so, AAL JP seeks to strengthen the European market for Ambient Assisted Living products and services, and in the long term, reduce costs regarding health and social care [3]. So far six calls with 155 projects have been launched.

2.2   Sample

In June 2014 the AAL JP launched a website containing all public deliverables from their funded projects [28]. During the same month the website was accessed and all uploaded documents were screened, applying the inclusion and exclusion criteria displayed in Table 1. To be included in the sample, deliverables had to contain results of the user-requirement analyses or the pilot testing with older adults directly involved in the testing of the AAL application. In the first round we included 64 documents from 22 projects based on their online availability and title. After scanning the full-text another 28 documents were removed from the selection, leaving us with a selection of 35 document from 17 different AAL projects. This means that in the final sample some projects yielded multiple reports.

Table 1. Inclusion and exclusion criteria

Inclusion Criteria	Exclusion Criteria
Deliverables documenting the results of the user-requirement analyses and the pilot testing	Deliverables that contant no original results (e.g., methodological decription, state of art)
Older adult end-users were involved in the testing of the requirements and the AAL application	Deliverables that neglected user acceptance factors (e.g., only technical requirements)
Online availability	Doubles

2.3   Data Extraction and Coding

To get an overview of the nature of the selected AAL deliverables we extracted data about the project name, call, number of extracted documents, technology category, technology objective, target user characteristics, test countries and the used methodology from the full-text reports (Appendix A), prior to in-depth coding. To identify potential incentives for using AAL technologies we used a mixed-method approach in coding the full–text reports, with some of our codes developed a-priori, using the knowledge from the social cognitive theory (deductive), and other codes emerging from the data (inductive) [29]. During the coding procedure, we especially focused on the sections describing the user's feedback and evaluation of the tested AAL application. Hereby, we included explicit statements from the involved end-users but also inferred statements from the researchers. We applied a comparative method approach, comparing new codes to previous assigned codes to ensure that codes remain valid [30]. After several rounds of coding, remaining inconsistencies were discussed between two researchers until consensus was reached.

3   Results

3.1   General Characteristics of the Analyzed Projects

With one exception, all of the analyzed project documents originated from the first and second AAL call. This was mainly due to the low online availability of documents originating from later calls. The AAL technologies in these projects were diverse in nature, with eight social networks, three daily life support systems, two communication systems, two robots, and two game applications. The technology objectives defined by the project members were also diverse. Social inclusion was mentioned in most projects as an objective (n = 12), followed by stimulate leisure activities (n = 9), support with activities of daily living (n = 5), safety (n = 5), health and care monitoring (n = 4), information (n = 3), self-confidence (n = 2), physical fitness (n = 2) and improve intergenerational relations (n = 1). User studies were conducted in 13 different European countries with Germany and Spain being represented most often (n = 6). The applied methods were very diverse, including observational methods, surveys, interviews, focus groups and pilot studies in laboratory and natural settings. The age of the older adults included as subjects in these projects ranged from 47 to 96 years. Most subjects still lived independently with some of them receiving care. Some of the analyzed projects specifically focused on subjects with cognitive impairments. The ICT experience among the subject varied from little to solid ICT experience.

3.2   Incentives for Using AAL Technologies

After thoroughly coding the data, 13 incentives could be identified which were then clustered according to the categories identified by SCT. As expected, a new category related to self-preservation emerged, which we labeled 'health and safety incentives'. However, our data did not show support for outcome expectations in terms of 'monetary incentives'. In fact, we noticed that in the majority of the analyzed projects older adults were afraid that the potential technology could be expensive and unaffordable to them, suggesting that money is rather a disincentive in the context of AAL technologies. Table 2 shows the number of assigned quotes per code as well as the number of source projects in which the codes appear.

Table 2. Number of assigned quotes and source projects per code

Codes	Assigned quotes (n)	Source projects (n)
Social incentives		
Social connectedness	351	16
Involvement	28	8
Health and safety incentives		
Health and safety	103	15
Support with dailly activities	111	12
Connect to care network	8	5
Activity incentives		
Leisure and personal interests	110	13
Enjoyment	51	9
Novel sensory incentives		
Education	44	11
Information	49	9
Status incentives		
Self-expression/self-worth	58	10
Independence	9	4
Status	6	2
Self-reactive incentives		
Relieve boredom	3	2

3.3   Social Incentives

Social Connectedness. The most prevalent incentive for future use of AAL technologies which surfaced from the data is 'social connectedness', with a total quote count of n = 351 and appearance in 16 of the 17 analyzed projects. Social connectedness can be understood in terms of connecting, communicating and interacting with other individuals. These can be either existing connections such as friends and family, or new contacts developed with the help of the AAL technology. For example, during the initial user-requirement assessment of the 3rD-LIFE social network several older adults, who were asked about desired features for 3rD-LIFE, stated that they would appreciate the opportunity to meet new people and talk to them [31]. AAL technologies were also viewed as a valuable tool to combat loneliness. As one older adult indicated after watching a facilitator using the EasyReach social network: "Today, in general elderly people are alone. The system could be a key point for them. It could help elderly people to socialize" [32, p. 34]. In the Domeo project which developed an assistive robot, the technology itself was seen as a possible form of companionship [33]. In sum, older adults recognized that AAL technologies could be an instrument to socialize, feel closer to friends and family and combat loneliness.

Involvement. A second incentive in this category is 'involvement'. Several projects showed that AAL technologies were seen as a way to stay connected and involved with society and making new technologies accessible for older adults, who feel more and more excluded through the increasing digitalization of our world. One older adult described the EasyReach social network as a "window to the world" [32, p. 34]. Another participant stated "EasyReach is another chance for us, elderly people. It is an innovation and for the first time we are part of it. I could feel part of the network of today" [32, p. 24]. Similar expectations were expressed by older adults in the FoSIBLE project, that developed a TV-based communication system: "I think that it is to make the computer available to all" [34, p. 15]. 'Involvement' as an incentive was somewhat less prevalent, with a total quote count of n = 28, divided among eight projects.

3.4   Health and Safety Incentives

Health and Safety. Besides 'social connectedness', 'health and safety' is the second most important incentive associated with the potential use of AAL technologies. The total quote count was n = 103, with appearance in 15 of the 17 projects. Older adults perceived that AAL technologies could benefit their physical and mental health, for example by finding health-related information or providing games which train their abilities. For instance, in the 3rD-LIFE project older adults said they would like the social network to include videogames with exercises for motor coordination and rehabilitation to maintain their functionality [31]. Another aspect was the increased feeling of safety if AAL technologies would be present in their homes. In the pilot phase of the HOPE system the majority of the end-users who tested this daily life support system that includes different functionalities for monitoring, fall detection and communication in their homes, agreed that it had increased their feeling of safety and security [35].

Support with Daily Activities. Another highly important incentive which was identified from the data is 'support with daily activities'. The older adults recognized that AAL technologies had the potential to support them in their daily life for example with memory and reminder functions or administrative tasks. For example, in the Domeo project, reminders were regarded as a highly important feature for the tested assistive robot [33]. AAL technologies were also viewed as a tool for people that were physically limited as becomes clear by this statement of an older adult in the FoSIBLE project, that developed a TV-based communication system: "It will be very useful for people with reduced mobility" [34, p. 19]. The total quote count was n = 111, extracted from 12 documents.

Connect to Care Network. The final incentive which fits this category is 'connect to care network'. Older adults recognized that AAL technologies could be useful to easily connect with their caregivers. For instance, in the EasyReach project, that developed a social network application, one older adult said: "It would be helpful to connect EasyReach to networks of home care" [32, p. 36]. Moreover, older adults from different projects stated that AAL technologies could provide some peace of mind to family caregivers. However, this incentive was less prevalent, with a total citation count of n = 8, divided among only five projects.

3.5   Activity Incentives

Leisure and Personal Interests. The incentive 'leisure and personal interests' was mentioned in 13 projects with a total quote count of n = 110. The fact that AAL technologies could stimulate leisure activities, was highly appreciated by older adults. They were very keen on the idea of personal interest forums or games they could play with other seniors via AAL technologies. For instance, when prioritizing different features of the SeniorEngage social network application, the most popular feature mentioned by the focus group participants was interest groups for hobbies or professions [36].

Enjoyment. Another incentive in this category is the feeling of 'enjoyment'. The first interaction with AAL technology prototypes was often perceived as interesting, fun and entertaining, which in turn motivated future use. For example, one older adult from the Connected Vitality project said after testing the video communication feature of the system in the home: "we really, really enjoyed it" [37, p. 15]. The total quote count was n = 51, divided among nine projects.

3.6   Novel Sensory Incentives

Education. Common stereotypes suggest that older adults have neither the ability, nor the motivation to learn new things. However, our data suggest otherwise. 'Education' was another frequently mentioned incentive for the potential use of AAL technologies, with a total citation count of n = 44, divided among 11 projects. Older adults were excited about potential educational features of AAL technologies which would allow them to acquire new knowledge and skills. For instance, in the 3rD-LIFE project participants found educational applications like lectures, courses or e-learning very attractive potential features for this social network application [31]. Older adults also indicated that they would like to expand their knowledge through the exchange with others, for example in an online discussion group which could be facilitated via AAL technologies.

Information. Another incentive in this category is 'information'. Older adults believed that AAL technologies could provide them with information of their interest such as news, weather or events in their neighborhood. In the SeniorEngage project, the tested social network application was perceived as a platform where older adults could find information and activities at a glance [36, p. 32]. This incentive was mentioned in more than half of the projects with a total quote count of n = 51.

3.7   Status Incentives

Self-expression and Self-worth. The first and most important incentive in this category is 'self-expression and self-worth'. This incentive was identified in 10 projects with a total quote count of n = 58. Older adults perceived AAL technologies as a potential platform for self-expression, where they could share their values, opinions, experience and knowledge with others, for instance through a discussion group feature. The researchers of the FoSIBLE project concluded that for many participants the motivation to use the groups feature of the TV-based communication system is to display and share their knowledge with others [38]. This in turn gives them the feeling of being capable, being needed and being meaningful to society.

Independence. Surprisingly 'independence' was only mentioned in 4 of the 17 projects as an incentive for the use of AAL technologies, with a total quote count of n = 9. This could be explained by the fact that independence is also implied by other incentives such as 'health and safety' and 'support with daily activities'. Therefore, we still assume that 'independence' is an important incentive for the use of AAL technologies.

Status. The final incentive in this category is 'status'. Some older adults were keen on using AAL technologies in order to earn respect of others, especially there family members as become clear by this statement of an older adult from the FoSIBLE project: "It is also about my grandchildren. I want to impress them, to make them proud perhaps" [34, p. 20]. However, 'status' was only mentioned in two of the projects with a total quote count of n = 6. Thus, we can conclude that status is not an important incentive for older adults to use AAL technologies.

3.8 Self-reactive Incentives

Relieve Boredom. The least prevalent incentive was 'relieve boredom' as it was only mentioned in 2 of the 17 projects with a total quote count of n = 3. Thus, using AAL technology just to pass time is not a major incentive for older adults.

4 Conclusion and Discussions

In this study we conducted a content analyses of 35 AAL project reports extracted from 17 projects to identify potential incentives for older adults to adopt and use AAL technologies. SCT was used as a theoretical approach to identify and group the incentives emerging from the data. However, we also allowed for new categories to surface from the data. In total 13 incentives could be identified, which we grouped into six categories: (1) social incentives, (2) health and safety incentives, (3) activity incentives, (4) novel sensory incentives, (5) status incentives and self-reactive incentives. Except for health and safety incentives (additional category) and monetary incentives (missing category) these categories are identical to the incentive categories used in the SCT. This suggest that expected outcomes indeed should be considered as a multi-dimensional construct rather than as a one-dimensional construct.

Moreover, these results show that the majority of the incentive categories identified by SCT are also applicable in the context of AAL technologies. However, Bandura's original approach [23] does not include a category for self-preservation incentives.

Yet, our results showed that in many of the analyzed project health and safety were important incentives to use AAL technologies. Therefore, this was added as a new category. Bandura's later work applied SCT in the context of health promotion [39]. Within the context of health behavior one of the three essential outcome expectation categories is 'physical' which is defined as "pleasant sensory experiences and physical pleasures in the positive forms, and aversive sensory experiences, pain and physical discomfort in the negative forms" [39, p. 627]. This supports our decision to add "health and safety" as an self-preservation incentive category for AAL technologies. Monetary incentives were not supported by the data, but we assume that monetary matters rather form a disincentive. Earlier case studies of AAL technologies support this assumption, as older adults were often afraid that the tested AAL application is unaffordable to them [e.g., 40, 41]. This is interesting, as the vision of AAL technologies is to reduce the costs of health and social care [42]. However, there seems to be a discrepancy between how AAL is envisioned by the policy makers and how it is perceived by the older adults. Policy makers should therefore carefully think about the financing models and ensure that those technologies are affordable for all seniors.

Looking more specifically at the incentives within a category, thereby taking into account the number of different projects in which a code occurs as well as the total quote count, 'social connectedness' and 'health and safety' are the most important incentives in the context of AAL technologies. This implies that older adults are likely to use AAL technologies when they perceive that those technologies can help them to connect with others or when they benefit their health and safety. This is in line with previous case studies of AAL technologies, that also found that "health and safety" [e.g., 43, 44] and "social connectedness" [45, 46] are important incentives of AAL technologies. Other important incentives for the use of AAL technologies include 'support with activities of daily living'; 'leisure and personal interest'; 'education' and 'self-expression and self-worth'. In contrast, 'relieve boredom' and 'status' were the least important incentives. This suggest that older adults are not likely to use AAL technologies just to pass their time or to get respect from other individuals. Surprisingly, the data showed that 'independence' was also one of the least important incentives for the use of AAL technologies. We assume that this can be explained by the fact that the other incentives such as 'health and safety' or 'support with daily activities' also imply independence and the incentive 'independence' can therefore be viewed as an umbrella term for these other incentives. Following this argumentation we still think that 'independence' is a highly important incentive for AAL technologies.

The previously described results should not be interpreted without taking into account several limitations. First, our documents were sampled from a single research framework which is EU based. Therefore, generalizability is somewhat limited by the research focus and the geographical scope. Second, the sample was affected by the online availability of the documents which were mostly sampled from the first and second call, so important data sources might have been missed. Third, we did not have access to the original transcripts of end-users' evaluations. Therefore, the available data already went through a filtering process which in turn could have affected our results.

Future research should take into account more AAL projects from a broader geographical scope, various research frameworks and more recent calls, in order to verify our results and give an outlook on the future trends and direction of the AAL community. Second, while this research describes several potential incentives for the use of AAL technologies, we cannot make valid predictions about their explanatory power. Thus, future work should apply advanced statistical method to operationalize these incentives and verify their power in explaining AAL technology adoption and use. Third, in this research we specifically focused on potential incentives for using AAL technologies. However, previous research [47, 48] also identified several barriers or disincentives which are likely to play a role in the decision to use AAL technologies. Other potentially relevant factors include personal factors (e.g., technology experience, health status). Future research should distinguish between different types of older adults in terms of health status and technology experience and investigate how their perception of potential AAL incentives might differ.

Despite its limitations, this study provides a comprehensive and theoretically grounded overview of incentives which are likely to motivate older adults to use AAL technologies. Our findings can be used as a starting point by other researchers to further investigate the explanatory power of these incentives and help them to build an empirical model which can predict AAL technology adoption. Developers, policy makers and health care professional can use our insights to further shape the vision of AAL and help them to design technologies which appeal to the need and wishes of the older adults.

Acknowledgements. Part of this research is supported by the AAL Joint Program under contract number AAL-2012-5-187.

Appendix A: General Characteristics of the Analyzed Projects

Project Name	Call	Documents [Reference no.]	Technology Category	Technology Objective[1] (as stated by the consortium)	Test User Characteristics	Test Countries	Applied Method	Identified Incentives (based on the results of the current study)
3rD-LIFE	2	[31]	social network	a, b	60-75 years living independently no specific cognitive/physical impairment ICT experience	Austria Spain	survey interviews focus groups	Social Connectedness Involvement Health and Safety Support with Daily Activities Leisure and Personal Interests Education Information Self-Expression/Self-worth
Alias	2	[49,50,51,52]	robot	a, b, c, d ,e,	54-84 years **Group 1:** living independently no specific cognitive/physical impairment ICT experience **Group 2:** living in nursing homes cognitive/physical impairment little ICT experience	Germany	survey interviews workshop pilot test in lab setting with pre-scripted use scenarios pilot test at care facilty with pre-scripted use scenarios	Social Connectedness Health and Safety Support with Daily Activities Leisure and Personal Interests Enjoyment Independence

[1] a = social inclusion, b = leisure, c = health care & monitoring, d = safety, e = support with daily activities, f = information , g = fitness, h = self-confidence, i = improve intergenerational relations

Project Name	Call	Documents [Reference no.]	Technology Category	Technology Objective[1] (as stated by the consortium)	Test User Characteristics	Test Countries	Applied Method	Identified Incentives (based on the results of the current study)
CCE	1	[53,54]	daily life support system	c, d, e	69-78 years living independently or with family member mild cognitive impairment ICT experience and little ICT experience	Germany UK Hungary	observation survey interviews pilot test in lab setting with pre-scripted use scenarios	Social Connectedness Health and Safety Support with Dailly Activities
Connected Vitality	2	[37][55,56,57]	communication system	a, b	55-89 years living independently physical limitations/in need of care ICT experience	Spain Netherlands Sweden	survey interviews workshops pilot test in older adult's homes diary with prompts for tasks	Social Connectedness Connect to Care Network Leisure and Personal Interests Enjoyment Education Information Self-Expression/Self- worth
Domeo	1	[33]	robot	c, d, e	77-85 years mild cognitive impairment	Austria Hungary France	focus groups	Social Connectedness Health and Safety Support with Dailly Activities Leisure and Personal Interests Information
E2C-Express to connect	2	[58,59]	game	a, b	50-80+ years	Finland Sweden	pilot test	Social Connectedness Involvement Health and Safety Support with Dailly Activities Connect to Care Network Leisure and Personal Interests Enjoyment Education Self-Expression/Self- worth Relieve Boredom

Project Name	Call	Documents [Reference no.]	Technology Category	Technology Objective[1] (as stated by the consortium)	Test User Characteristics	Test Countries	Applied Method	Identified Incentives (based on the results of the current study)
EasyReach	2	[32]	social network	a, f	55-80 years	Italy Germany	pilot test in lab setting with pre-scripted use scenarios demonstrated by a facilitator use experience was accessed with focus groups, interviews and a survey	Social Connectedness Involvement Health and Safety Support with Dailly Activities Connect to Care Network Leisure and Personal Interests Enjoyment Education Information Self-Expression/Self- worth Relieve Boredom
Elisa	2	[60,61]	social network	a, b	55-75 years ICT experience and little ICT experience	Greece Hungary	focus groups pilot test in lab setting with pre-scripted use scenarios	Social Connectedness Health and Safety Support with Dailly Activities Leisure and Personal Interests Education Information
Elder-Spaces	2	[62,63]	social network	a, b	55+ years little ICT experience	Greece Spain	survey workshops pilot test	Social Connectedness Health and Safety Leisure and Personal Interests Education Self-Expression/Self- worth
FoSIBLE	2	[34][38][64,65,66,67]	communication (and entertainment) system	a, b	50-96 living experience no severe physical/cognitive impairment ICT experience and little ICT experience	Germany France Austria	observation survey interviews focus groups workshops pilot test in lab setting with pre-scripted use scenarios pilot test in older adult's homes with prompts for tasks diary	Social Connectedness Involvement Health and Safety Support with Dailly Activities Leisure and Personal Interests Enjoyment Education Information Self-Expression/Self- worth Independence Status

Project Name	Call	Documents [Reference no.]	Technology Category	Technology Objective[1] (as stated by the consortium)	Test User Characteristics	Test Countries	Applied Method	Identified Incentives (based on the results of the current study)
Go-myLife	2	[68]	social network	a, f	majority 61-65 years ICT experience and little ICT experience	Austria UK	focus groups workshops	Social Connectedness Involvement Health and Safety Support with Dailly Activities Connect to Care Network Leisure and Personal Interests Enjoyment Education Information Self-Expression/Self- worth Independence
HOPE	1	[35]	daily life support system	c, d, e	cognitive impairment living independently, with family member or in nursing home	Italy Spain Greece	survey pilot test in nursing home	Social Connectedness Health and Safety Support with Dailly Activities Independence
JoinIn	2	[69]	game	a, b, g	not available	Germany Hungary Ireland	observation survey interview focus groups workshops	Social Connectedness Involvement Health and Safety Leisure and Personal Interests Enjoyment Education Self-Expression/Self- worth
MyGuardian	4	[70]	daily life support system	d,e	60-83 years living independently with help of caregivers cognitive impairment little ICT experience	Netherlands, France Spain	probe interview	Health and Safety Support with Dailly Activities Connect to Care Network

Project Name	Call	Documents [Reference no.]	Technology Category	Technology Objective¹ (as stated by the consortium)	Test User Characteristics	Test Countries	Applied Method	Identified Incentives (based on the results of the current study)
SeniorEngage	2	[36][71,72]	social network	h	55+	Finnland a Austria	focus groups pilot test in lab setting with pre-scripted use scenarios	Social Connectedness Involvement Support with Dailly Activities Leisure and Personal Interests Enjoyment Education Information Self-Expression/Self- worth Status
TAO	2	[73,74]	social network	a,b,f, h, i	not available	Switzerland Germany Netherlands	survey interview focus groups workshops pilot test in lab setting with pre-scripted use scenarios	Social Connectedness Involvement Health and Safety Leisure and Personal Interests Enjoyment Education Information Self-Expression/Self- worth
TraiNutri	2	[75]	social network	a,g	47-63 years ICT experience and little ICT experience	Greece Spain Switzerland	survey pilot test in natural setting diary	Social Connectedness Health and Safety

References

1. United Nations: DESA: World Population Ageing: 1950–2050. United Nations Publications, New York (2002)
2. Rashidi, P., Mihailidis, A.: A survey on ambient-assisted living tools for older adults. IEEE J. Biomed. Health Inform. **17**, 579–590 (2013)
3. Ambient Assisted Living Association. http://www.aal-europe.eu/about
4. Eckert, J.K., Morgan, L.A., Swamy, N.: Preferences for receipt of care among community-dwelling adults. J. Aging Soc. Policy **16**, 49–65 (2004)
5. Aarts, E., Marzano, S.: The New Everyday: Views on Ambient Intelligence. 010 Publications, Rotterdam (2003)
6. Kleinberger, T., Becker, M., Ras, E., Holzinger, A., Müller, P.: Ambient intelligence in assisted living: enable elderly people to handle future interfaces. In: Stephanidis, C. (ed.) UAHCI 2007 (Part II). LNCS, vol. 4555, pp. 103–112. Springer, Heidelberg (2007)
7. Choudhury, T., et al.: The mobile sensing platform: an embedded activity recognition system. Pervasive Comput. **7**, 32–41 (2008)
8. Pollack, M.E., et al.: Autominder: an intelligent cognitive orthotic system for people with memory impairment. Robot. Auton. Syst. **44**, 273–282 (2003)
9. Chen, J., Kwong, K., Chang, D., Luk, J., Bajcsy, R.: Wearable sensors for reliable fall detection. In: Proceedings of the 27th IEEE Conference on Engineering in Medicine and Biology, pp. 3551–3554. IEEE Press, New York (2005)
10. Rowan, J., Mynatt, E.D.: Digital family portrait field trial: support for aging in place. In: Proceedings of the SIGCHI Conference on Human Factors in Computing Systems. ACM, New York (2005)
11. Gamberini, L., Raya, M.A., Barresi, G., Fabregat, M., Ibanez, F., Prontu, L.: Cognition, technology and games for the elderly: an introduction to ELDERGAMES Project. PsychNology J. **4**, 285–308 (2006)
12. Moschis, G.P.: Marketing to older adults: an updated overview of present knowledge and practice. J Consum. Mark. **20**, 516–525 (2003)
13. Davis, F.D.: A Technology Acceptance Model for Empirically Testing New End-User Information Systems: Theory and Results (Doctoral dissertation). MIT, Cambridge, MA (1986)
14. Davis, F.D.: Perceived usefulness, perceived ease of use, and user acceptance of information technology. MIS Q. **13**, 319–340 (1989)
15. Venkatesh, V., Morris, M.G., Davis, G.B., Davis, F.D.: User acceptance of information technology: toward a unified view. MIS Q. **27**, 425–478 (2003)

16. Blumlerand, J., Katz, E.: The Uses of Mass Communications. Sage Publications, Beverly Hills, CA (1974)
17. Palmgreen, P., Rayburn, J.D.: An expectancy-value approach to media gratifications. In: Rosengren, K.E., Palmgreen, P., Wenner, L.A. (eds.) Media Gratification Research: Current Perspectives, pp. 61–72. Sage Publications, Beverly Hills, CA (1985)
18. Bandura, A.: Social Foundations of Thought and Action: a Social Cognitive Theory. Prentice Hall, Englewood Cliffs, NJ (1986)
19. Peters, O.: Social Psychological Determinants of Mobile Communication Technology Use and Adoption: a Comparison of Three Models to Explain and Predict Mobile Communication Technology Behavior (Doctoral dissertation). University of Twente, The Netherlands (2007)
20. Fishbein, M.: Attitude and the prediction of behaviour. In: Fishbein, M. (ed.) Readings in Attitude Theory and Measurement. Wiley, New York (1967)
21. Palmgreen, P.: Uses and gratifications: a theoretical perspective. In: Bostrom, R.N. (ed.) Communication Yearbook, vol. 8, pp. 61–72. Sage Publications, Beverly Hills, CA (1984)
22. Benbasat, I., Barki, H.: Quo vadis TAM? J. Assoc. Inf. Syst. **8**, 219–222 (2007)
23. Bandura, A.: Social Foundations of Thought and Action: a Social Cognitive Theory. Prentice Hall, Englewood Cliffs, NJ (1986)
24. Bandura, A.: Social cognitive theory. In: Vasta, R. (ed.) Annals of Child Development. vol. 6, Six Theories of Child Development, pp. 1–60. JAI Press, Greenwich, CT (1989)
25. LaRose, R., Eastin, M.S.: A social cognitive theory of internet uses and gratifications: toward a new model of media attendance. J. Broadcast. Electron. Media **48**, 358–377 (2004)
26. LaRose, R., Mastro, D., Eastin, M.S.: Understanding internet usage a social-cognitive approach to uses and gratifications. Soc. Sci. Comput. Rev. **19**, 395–413 (2001)
27. Khang, H., Han, E., Ki, E.: Exploring influential social cognitive determinants of social media use. Comput. Hum. Behav. **36**, 48–55 (2014)
28. Ambient Assited Living Association. http://deliverables.aal-europe.eu/
29. Ryan, G.W., Bernard, H.R.: Techniques to identify themes. Field Methods **15**, 85–109 (2003)
30. Strauss, A., Corbin, J.: The Basics of Qualitative Research: Techniques and Procedures for Developing Grounded Theory. Sage Publications, Thousand Oaks, CA (1998)
31. 3rD-LIFE Consortium: Report of User Requirements and User Definition of the System. http://deliverables.aal-europe.eu/
32. EasyReach Consortium: Report of the Pilot Results. http://deliverables.aal-europe.eu/
33. Domeo Consortium: Interviews Results Report. http://deliverables.aal-europe.eu/
34. FoSIBLE Consortium: Psychological Impacts of the System Usage. http://deliverables.aal-europe.eu/
35. HOPE Consortium: Assessment and Evaluation Report. http://deliverables.aal-europe.eu/
36. Senior Engange Consortium: Senior's Participation and Roles. http://deliverables.aal-europe.eu/
37. Connected Vitality Consortium: A document with results of the Dutch field test at Sensire - PresenceDisplays (month 27). http://deliverables.aal-europe.eu/
38. FoSIBLE Consortium: Redesigned Use Cases. http://deliverables.aal-europe.eu/
39. Bandura, A.: Health promotion from the perspective of social cognitive theory. Psychol. Health **13**, 623–649 (1998)
40. Sixsmith, A.J.: An evaluation of an intelligent home monitoring system. J. Telemed. Telecare **6**, 63–72 (2000)
41. Steele, R., Lo, A., Secombe, C., Wong, Y.K.: Elderly persons' perception and acceptance of using wireless sensor networks to assist healthcare. Int. J. Med. Inform. **78**, 788–801 (2009)
42. Ambient Assited Living Association. http://www.aal-europe.eu/about/objectives/

43. Wild, K., Boise, L., Lundell, J., Foucek, A.: Unobtrusive in-home monitoring of cognitive and physical health: reactions and perceptions of older adults. J. Appl. Gerontol. **27**, 181–200 (2008)

44. Van Hoof, J., Kort, H.S.M., Rutten, P.G.S., Duijnstee, M.S.H.: Ageing-in-place with the use of ambient intelligence technology: perspectives of older users. Int. J. Med. Inform. **80**, 310–331 (2011)

45. Huber, L.L., et al.: How in-home technologies mediate caregiving relationships in later life. Int. J. Hum.-Comput. Int. **29**, 441–455 (2013)

46. Beer, J.M., Takayama, L.: Mobile remote presence systems for older adults: acceptance, benefits, and concerns. In: Proceedings of the 6th International Conference on Human-Robot Interaction, HRI 2011, pp. 19–26. ACM, New York (2011)

47. Jaschinski, C., Ben Allouch, S.: An extended view on benefits and barriers of ambient assisted living solutions. Int. J. Adv. Life Sci. **7**, 40–53 (2015)

48. Peek, S.T., Wouters, E.J., van Hoof, J., Luijkx, K.G., Boeije, H.R., Vrijhoef, H.J.: Factors influencing acceptance of technology for aging in place: a systematic review. Int. J. Med. Inform. **83**, 235–248 (2014)

49. ALIAS Consortium: Requirements list regarding the needs and preferences of the user groups. http://deliverables.aal-europe.eu/

50. ALIAS Consortium: Analysis of pilot's first test-run. http://deliverables.aal-europe.eu/

51. ALIAS Consortium: Analysis of pilot's second test-run with qualitative advice on how to improve specific functions/usability of the robot. http://deliverables.aal-europe.eu/

52. ALIAS Consortium: Final report on the requirements list. http://deliverables.aal-europe.eu/

53. CCE Consortium: Guidance Document Summarising User Requirements and Potential Barriers. http://deliverables.aal-europe.eu/

54. CCE Consortium: Summary of pilot results. http://deliverables.aal-europe.eu/

55. Connected Vitality Consortium: A document with the results of the Spanish field test. http://deliverables.aal-europe.eu/

56. Connected Vitality Consortium: A document with the results of the Dutch field test at Sensire. http://deliverables.aal-europe.eu/

57. Connected Vitality Consortium: A document with the results of the Swedish field test. http://deliverables.aal-europe.eu/

58. Express to Connect Consortium: Impact Assessment: Final field tests. http://deliverables.aal-europe.eu/

59. Express to Connect Consortium: Impact Evaluation: Summary of all the studies. http://deliverables.aal-europe.eu/

60. Elisa Consortium: End User Requirements. http://deliverables.aal-europe.eu/

61. Elisa Consortium: Usability study (III). Usability test results according to SIMPLIT methodology. http://deliverables.aal-europe.eu/

62. Elder-Spaces Consortium: End-User Requirements. http://deliverables.aal-europe.eu/

63. Elder-Spaces Consortium: Report on user trials. http://deliverables.aal-europe.eu/

64. FoSIBLE Consortium: Report on user requirements as with respect to the addressed applications. http://deliverables.aal-europe.eu/

65. FoSIBLE Consortium: Report on inHaus lab evaluation results. http://deliverables.aal-europe.eu/

66. FoSIBLE Consortium: Report on usability tests. http://deliverables.aal-europe.eu/

67. FoSIBLE Consortium: Test Results (in the form of problems to be solved in update packs). http://deliverables.aal-europe.eu/

68. Go-myLife Consortium: Synthesis Report on target group analysis and user needs and requirements. http://deliverables.aal-europe.eu/

69. Join-In Consortium: Report on User Requirement Analysis. http://deliverables.aal-europe.eu/

70. MyGuardian Consortium: User Requirements Report. http://deliverables.aal-europe.eu/
71. SeniorEngange Consortium: Usability and Ergonomics Report. http://deliverables.aal-europe.eu/
72. SeniorEngange Consortium: E-Participation for senior citizens best practices. http://deliverables.aal-europe.eu/
73. TAO Consortium: Overall research project final report. http://deliverables.aal-europe.eu/
74. TAO Consortium: Exploratory Studies: Beginning Users 60 plus & Volunteers. http://deliverables.aal-europe.eu/
75. TraiNutri Consortium: Test user report of Usability and Acceptance. http://deliverables.aal-europe.eu/

The SOCIAL Project
Approaching Spontaneous Communication in Distributed Work Groups

Jasper van de Ven[1][(✉)], Dimitra Anastasiou[2], Frank Dylla[1], Susanne Boll[2], and Christian Freksa[1]

[1] Cognitive Systems Group, University of Bremen, Bremen, Germany
{vandeven,dylla,freksa}@informatik.uni-bremen.de
[2] University of Oldenburg, Oldenburg, Germany
dimitra.anastasiou@uni-oldenburg.de,
Susanne.Boll@informatik.uni-oldenburg.de

Abstract. The aim of the project SOCIAL is to explore possibilities to facilitate spontaneous and informal communication in spatially distributed groups by exploiting ambient intelligence and smart environments. Spontaneous and informal communication has a strong impact on the productivity, social identity, and wellbeing of work groups. The spatial distance between peers plays a key role in successfully establishing and maintaining such communication. In co-located teams, spontaneous communication occurs daily: People occasionally meet on office floors, at the coffee corner, or have lunch together. Today, due to globalization we often encounter distributed work settings that impede spontaneous communication between co-workers, as teams are distributed over branch offices located in different cities and countries. We propose to approach this problem by (1) detecting situations with the potential for spontaneous informal communication, (2) representing and raising awareness for these situations appropriately, and (3) enabling users to engage seamlessly in spontaneous communication spanning spatially separated locations. In this paper we focus on the second aspect. A pilot study is described with results on combining various interaction modalities in order to raise awareness for communication. In addition, we describe a formal representation for ambient intelligence incorporating situational context and the system itself.

1 Introduction

Positive effects attributed to frequent spontaneous communication include seamless progress and coordination of work [1], a reduction in work-based conflicts [2], and more efficient collaborative learning [3]. In contrast, a lack of such communication is known to cause "difficulty in forming close collaborations, dealing flexibly with one another, and expanding the breadth of [...] relationships" [1], which can lead to further difficulties, such as a less successful transfer of complex knowledge between peers [4].

© Springer International Publishing Switzerland 2015
Kameas et al. (Eds.): AmI 2015, LNCS 9425, pp. 171–186, 2015.
DOI: 10.1007/978-3-319-26005-1_12

The spatial separation between peers plays a key role in successfully establishing and maintaining spontaneous communication. In co-located teams, spontaneous communication occurs daily: People occasionally meet on office floors, at the coffee corner, or have lunch together. However, today we often encounter distributed work settings that impede spontaneous communication between coworkers, as teams are distributed over branch offices located in different cities and countries.

Due to our need to stay connected with our peers, we use a multitude of methods to bridge such distances, including telephone, email, video-conferencing, and social networks. Nevertheless, the asynchronous (e.g., email, social networks) or synchronous (e.g., telephone, video-conference) nature of these methods fail to mimic the complexity of spontaneous interpersonal communication. When we are spatially separated, we cannot perceive implicit cues indicating the availability of our remote peers to communicate, such as the presence of a co-worker on the office floor. Furthermore, we typically cannot easily assess whether and when it is appropriate to engage in communication. For example, we would typically not call someone if we knew he/she is in a meeting or having lunch. As we usually have insufficient knowledge of the remote situation, we need to rely on other, possibly more formal and asynchronous channels for communication, such as email. In combination, these factors substantially reduce our opportunities to engage in spontaneous communication with remote peers.

We propose to approach this problem by exploiting capabilities of distributed smart environments and ambient intelligence focused on awareness and communication. The idea is to address three main tasks: (1) *detect situations* with the potential for spontaneous communication spanning multiple spatially distributed locations, (2) *present detected situations* appropriately to the users concerned, i.e., provide awareness without being obtrusive, and (3) *enable users* to engage seamlessly in spontaneous communication in a convenient way.

In this paper we introduce the project SOCIAL and motivate the approach. Especially, we present first insights of how to create respective awareness. That is, we describe an initial user study testing and evaluating social awareness signals. Furthermore, we present a formal representation for ambient intelligence allowing to describe the situational context and involved system.

2   Related Work

As the project SOCIAL addresses interdisciplinary research, we present related fields and projects. Comprising a brief overview of the sociological and psychological background (Sect. 2.1), as well as an introduction of implicit and explicit communication (Sect. 2.2). We conclude this section with a small survey of ambient intelligence and related projects, that focus on communication and awareness (Sect. 2.3).

2.1   Sociological and Psychological Background

Researchers in sociology and psychology have extensively studied the influence of spatial separation on the characteristics and behavior of work groups.

Kraut et al. [5] stated that when the distance between work places increases to about 30 m or more, the amount of contact declines. Kiesler and Cummings [1] provide a survey of related work ranging from the middle of the 20th century to the beginning of the 21th century. They emphasize the relevance of (spatial) proximity for successful teamwork, which causes "emotional, cognitive, and behavioral changes that affect the work process for the better" [1]. Furthermore, they found that in distributed settings the frequency of daily contact as well as informal, i.e., spontaneous, communication decreased dramatically. They identified several negative effects resulting from this, including a drastic reduction of voluntary collaboration.

In addition, Kiesler and Cummings describe two effects of proximity in teams: First, co-location enables people to perceive the presence of peers, which lays the foundation for interaction among them. Second, it enables people to communicate with peers casually to exchange information. Today's work settings often prevent the geographical proximity of co-workers. To transfer the beneficial effects of proximity to a spatially distributed setting, we need to develop appropriate methods that detect and represent the presence of remote co-workers and provide methods to engage seamlessly in communication on demand in a dynamic spatial environment with multiple (interchanging) locations. In this context, we need to differentiate between two aspects of communication: implicit and explicit communication.

2.2   Implicit and Explicit Communication

Implicit communication can be understood in the notion of the first axiom of communication formulated by Watzlawick et al.: "one cannot *not* communicate" [6]. Even if we do not explicitly communicate, our behavior, e.g., body language, tone of voice, and facial expression, provide information that becomes communication when perceived by another person. Vinciarelli et al. [7] describes these aspects as *behavioral cues* emitted by humans. Furthermore, using social intelligence, we can interpret *social signals* from these cues, such as disagreement, fear, or joy. In the context of computing systems, Schmidt and Gellersen refer to these aspects as implicit input, "which is not primarily targeted towards interaction with computers, but is interpreted by computers as input" [8], *translated from German*.

In contrast to implicit communication, people are typically more aware of explicit means of communication, which we use on a daily basis to stay in contact with our peers. Explicit communication typically refers to specific information we communicate via speech or text, e.g., face-to-face talks, phone calls, or emails. The latter examples show the important role of explicit communication to stay connected to remote peers. Kiesler and Cummings [1] point out that explicit means of communication can indeed effectively support social communication between distributed peers.

With SOCIAL, we aim for interaction methods that permit seamless transition between implicit and explicit communication. This aspect, while playing a key role for effective social communication, is still an emerging field that has not been comprehensively studied. In this context, we point out the work of Streitz et al., who used a concept of three zones around an ambient interactive display for transition from implicit to explicit interaction [9]. In the notion of proxemic interaction, they infer a user's readiness for interaction based on his/her distance, i.e., users could only establish explicit interaction when in reaching distance of the display. Vogel and Balakrishnan revisited this approach, integrating the position and movement of the body into the recognition of interaction zones. They also suggested design principles and interaction techniques for different phases of implicit and explicit interaction of a human with a computer interface displaying information [10].

2.3   Ambient Intelligence and Related Projects

With the increasing miniaturization and integration of pervasive and ubiquitous devices in our everyday world, smart environments become a reality. In buildings technology is applied to provide supportive, ecofriendly, and security increasing functionality. Examples are motion detector activated lights or heating systems controlled by computers based on time and temperature sensors. Mark Weiser presented an early vision of the direction this research could take: "Ubiquitous computing has as its goal the nonintrusive availability of computers throughout the physical environment, virtually, if not effectively, invisible to the user." [11] Building on this vision and technological development the term *ambient intelligence* (AmI) appeared in Europe around the year 2000: "The concept of Ambient Intelligence (AmI) provides a vision of the Information Society where the emphasis is on greater user-friendliness, more efficient services support, user-empowerment, and support for human interactions. People are surrounded by intelligent intuitive interfaces that are embedded in all kinds of objects and an environment that is capable of recognizing and responding to the presence of different individuals in a seamless, unobtrusive and often invisible way" [12].

Thus, AmI also includes a variety of other disciplines, e.g., computer networks, sensor and actuator technology, artificial intelligence (AI), human-computer interaction (HCI), and computer supported cooperative work (CSCW), awareness systems, social sciences, or architectural science. Possible scenarios for the application are similarly diverse [13–15], e.g., smart homes and work places, patient or student monitoring and assistance, assistance for navigation and search tasks, or support of interaction and communication.

An early approach, around the 1980s, to provide interaction and communication possibilities to separated individuals by exploiting technologically equipped environments are so-called *Media Spaces*. A comprehensive survey of the projects, findings, and results is provided in [16].

A further important branch of related research deals with *awareness systems* [17]. This research addresses an individual's awareness of others, objects, or how to provide awareness for specific contexts. Thus, the goal is to gather or provide information updates about an individual's context, including events and situations. Gutwin and Greenberg defined workspace awareness as "the collection of up-to-the-moment knowledge a person uses to capture another's interaction with the workspace" [18].

In over 30 years of research, the fields of media spaces and awareness systems have provided a number of projects demonstrating the usefulness of mediated communication and awareness in public and private settings. Possibilities to increase productivity, to support wellbeing, and to decrease costs (e.g. [19–21]) have been addressed by investigating systems for synchronous and asynchronous communication as well as systems mediating awareness on a more abstract level.

An example of a project focusing on communication in the early 90s is RAVE (Ravencroft Audio Video Environment) [22,23] at EuroPARC. RAVE aimed at allowing interpersonal communication and awareness by connecting places in their laboratory building. The system consisted of audio-video nodes with a camera, monitor, microphone, and speakers placed in all rooms. These nodes were directly accessible, controllable, and modifiable by all users. RAVE was designed to support interactions. It works by providing means for informal encounter as well as formal cooperative tasks. These tools were mainly continuous longterm connections between two places and ad-hoc video-conference sessions. A further example is Telemurals [24] (2004), a system connecting two university dormitories through an abstracted audio-video stream. The project used cameras, microphones, and projectors installed in two seperate locations. The level of detail of the transmitted audio and video data was determined by the activity level at the respective sites. A low level of detail corresponded to low activity at the remote site. A less public and more personal project developed in 2010 is Family Window [20], which aimed at connecting and maintaining awareness between distant family members and close friends. It was designed to connect two locations through mobile communication units. The authors used two mobile displays providing a continuous audio-video connection and also supported small text or image messages.

An example focusing on awareness is the early Xerox PARC and EuroPARC project Portholes [25] (1992). To create interpersonal awareness, *Portholes* provided regularly updated images of remote sites. Another example is the ASTRA project [26] (2006) that aimed at providing awareness through asynchronous communication between family members. ASTRA was designed for a heterogeneous communication environment. This included the use of stationary and mobile computers and personal mobile devices, in order not to be dependent on specific locations.

3   The Big Picture of SOCIAL

In this section, the general approach taken in the project SOCIAL is introduced by presenting and discussing a first scenario. Furthermore, we describe how we intend to facilitate spontaneous communication in spatially distributed environments using ambient intelligence.

The initial question was how a spontaneous encounter and evolving communication, i.e., a serendipitous meeting at a coffee dispenser, could be realized in spatially distributed environments. Additionally, the locations to be connected should be dynamically changeable, preventing the use of static connections.

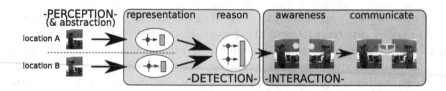

Fig. 1. Automated process to initiate spontaneous distributed communication

We decided to start with a scenario of a situation with potential for spontaneous communication in a co-located environment and transform it to a comparable spatially distributed version. The spatially distributed scenario not only requires a comparable situational context to the co-located scenario, but also methods for automated detection of the situation and for enabling a communication channel.

The *co-located coffee encounter scenario* features two individuals Alice and Bob located in the same office floor environment. Initially, Alice is in her office and fancies a coffee. She leaves her office to go to the coffee dispenser and have a cup. At the same time, Bob is already waiting for his cup of coffee to be prepared at the coffee dispenser. When Alice arrives, she greets Bob and the two start to talk to one another.

In order to transform this scenario into a comparable spatially distributed version, i.e., *distributed coffee encounter scenario*, it is assumed that Alice and Bob are located in two spatially separated office floor environments. Again, Alice is in her office and fancies a coffee. She leaves her office to go to the coffee dispenser and have a cup. At the same time in a branch office, Bob is waiting for his cup of coffee to be prepared at his local coffee dispenser. When Alice arrives at her local coffee dispenser, Bob is still waiting for his cup of coffee. An ambient intelligence installed at both locations perceives that Alice and Bob are both waiting at the coffee dispensers of the respective offices. The ambient intelligence initiates an unobtrusive transition from awareness to interpersonal communication. First, creating awareness of the fact that a colleague is also waiting at a coffee dispenser and then creating a direct communication channel for the two to talk with one another.

Based on this distributed scenario, we propose an automated three-step process to enable spatially distributed situations providing possibilities for spontaneous communication. This process is depicted in Fig. 1 and features the following steps:

- *perception* of the current situational context of all environments, i.e., obtaining raw sensor data and providing semantically meaningful symbolic abstractions,
- *detection* of a suitable spatially distributed situation, and
- *interaction* is made possible in an appropriate and unobtrusive manner.

We restrict our research on the perception step to the use of-the-shelf products. Thus, we will use existing and available libraries, e.g., OpenCV[1] (computer

---

[1] http://opencv.org/ (visited: 03/19/2015).

vision), RAVL[2] (recognition and vision), Shark[3] (machine learning), and SIL [27] (laboratory environment). However, our focus within the SOCIAL project is on the detection and interaction steps.

4   Detection of Situations

The detection step addresses the identification of (spatially distributed) situations with potential for spontaneous communication, i.e., representation and reasoning about the situational context. This requires a formal language to describe specific situations of interest, available knowledge, e.g., abstracted perceptions of situation context, and the behavior of the system, e.g., reasoning and action rules. In addition, an appropriate method to process available knowledge to identify existing situations is required.

Regarding the formal representation language, we apply methods from the field of qualitative spatio-temporal representation and reasoning (QSTR), e.g., [28,29]. The applicability of these methods to the field of AmI is, for example, shown by Hois et al. [30]. QSTR deals with relations between spatio-temporal entities of a domain, i.e., representations that explicate spatial or temporal aspects relevant for a given task, while neglecting others. Furthermore, QSTR also provides a range of formalizations, i.e., calculi, for aspects like topology (e.g., RCC-8 [31]) or position (e.g. OPRA [32]). These calculi also include methods for reasoning, e.g., checking consistency of a given scenario or explicating implicit knowledge, e.g., [28].

Especially, we adapt a representation formalism provided in [33] for representing and reasoning with qualitative spatial information in combination with propositional modal-logic. The resulting formalism includes a collection of symbol sets representing the objects, functions regarding spatial features and activities of objects, spatio-temporal relations between objects, possible sensors perceptions and actuator actions, and how different states of the ambient intelligence connect regarding time and processed operations. Our formal representation is now introduced in a bottom-up way, starting with its ingredients and closing with an example.

- $\mathcal{O}$ is a set of symbols for physical and immaterial object
- $\mathcal{Q}_\mathcal{S}$ is a set of symbols for qualitative spatial functions (qualitative spatial features of an object, e.g., region or orientation)
- $\mathcal{Q}_\mathcal{A}$ is a set of symbols for activity functions (activities of an object)
- $\mathcal{A}_\mathcal{S}$ is a set of symbols for sensor perceptions
- $\mathcal{A}_\mathcal{I}$ is a set of symbols for actions (actuator changes by the AmI)
- $\mathcal{A}_\mathcal{R}$ is a set of symbols for reasoning rules
- $\mathcal{A}_\mathcal{A}$ is a set of symbols for action rules
- $\mathcal{R}$ is a set of symbols for qualitative relations
- $\mathcal{G}$ is a set of symbols for further propositions

---

[2] http://ravl.sourceforge.net/ (visited: 03/19/2015).
[3] http://shark-project.sourceforge.net/ (visited: 03/19/2015).

The set of all possible propositions $\mathcal{P}$ (Eq. 1) is the combined set of objects, the activities specific objects are conducting, current sensor perceptions and actuator uses, and spatial relations[4] between objects.

$$\mathcal{P} = \mathcal{O} \cup \mathcal{G} \cup \{a(o)|a \in \mathcal{Q}_\mathcal{A}, o \in \mathcal{O}\}\cup$$
$$\{p(o)|p \in \mathcal{A}_\mathcal{S}, o \in \mathcal{O}\} \cup \{i(o)|i \in \mathcal{A}_\mathcal{I}, o \in \mathcal{O}\} \tag{1}$$
$$\{r(x,y)|r \in \mathcal{R}, x, y \in \{s(o)|s \in \mathcal{Q}_\mathcal{S}, o \in \mathcal{O}\}\}$$

We consider a *state* as a (partial) snapshot of currently holding propositions recursively defined by:

- p is a state for every $p \in \mathcal{P}$
- if ϕ is a state, so is $\neg\phi$
- if ϕ, ψ are states, so is $\phi \otimes \psi$ with $\otimes \in \{\wedge, \vee\}$

A *situation description* also includes temporal relations between contained states. Thus, if ϕ is a state, then $M\phi$ with $M \in \{\circ[t_i, t_j], \diamond[t_i, t_j]\}$ is a situation description. The time points t_i and t_j define the existence and duration of an interval in which the related state holds. We assume linear time, i.e., it holds that $\forall t_i, t_j : t_0 \leq t_i \leq t_j < t_\infty$. The semantics of the modal operations M connect states sequentially to situation descriptions:

- $\circ[t_i, t_j]\phi$ (during): $\forall t_x : \phi$ holds at t_x with $i \leq x \leq j$ (i.e., $t_0 \leq t_i \leq t_x \leq t_j$)
- $\diamond[t_i, t_j]\phi$ (within): $\exists t_x : \phi$ holds at t_x with $i \leq x \leq j$ (i.e., $t_0 \leq t_i \leq t_x \leq t_j$)

Based on this formalism for situation descriptions, we formalize an AmI through its knowledge base. The knowledge base is understood as the internal representation of the world, as perceived by the system, i.e., a set of descriptions of perceived situations connected by specific internal actions of the system. Thus, if $\delta_1, \delta_2, \ldots \delta_n$ are situation descriptions, then $\delta_1 \oplus_1 \delta_2 \oplus_2 \cdots \oplus_{n-1} \delta_n$ with $\oplus_i \in \mathcal{A}_\mathcal{S} \cup \mathcal{A}_\mathcal{I} \cup \mathcal{A}_\mathcal{R} \cup \mathcal{A}_\mathcal{A} \cup \{\odot[t_i, t_j]\}$ is a knowledge base description, i.e., a description of the respective AmI and its situational context. The semantics of $\odot[t_i, t_j]$ explicate inertia between the two connected situation descriptions, i.e., all contained propositions that hold at t_i also hold at t_j (with $t_0 \leq t_i < t_j$). For reasons of simplicity, we restrict the use of the modal operator M regarding situation descriptions that are part of a knowledge base to only allow $\circ[t_i, t_j]$ to prevent ambiguous interpretations of a given knowledge base.[5]

Regarding the rules given in the sets $\mathcal{A}_\mathcal{R}$ and $\mathcal{A}_\mathcal{A}$, each symbol represents an event-condition-action (ECA) rule (e.g., [34,35]) to trigger actions or infer additional knowledge based on a knowledge base provided. These are rules firing on a specified event if a specified condition holds to execute the specified action. For the defined representation, each rule consist of a trigger part T, which is a disjunction of conjunctions of situation descriptions, and an action part C, which

---

[4] We define only the set of binary relations, due to understandability. However, this can be changed to any arity of relation without influence on the remaining specification.

[5] In general, usage of $\diamond[t_i, t_j]$ is possible, but would lead to multiple interpretations of a single knowledge base.

is a conjunction of the form $\circ[t_{i_a}, t_{j_a}]P_a \wedge \cdots \wedge \circ[t_{i_b}, t_{j_b}]P_b \wedge c_1 \wedge \cdots \wedge c_n$ with $n \in \mathbb{N}, \forall P_z \in \mathcal{P}, \forall c_y \in \mathcal{A}_\mathcal{I}, \forall t_{i_x}, t_{j_x} : t_0 \leq t_{i_x} \leq t_{j_x}$. That is, the action part can either introduce new knowledge, e.g. $\circ[t_{i_a}, t_{j_a}]P_a$, or tell the system to use one of its actuators, e.g., c_1. An exemplary rule checking existence of the proposition P_1 at time 3 as well as P_2 within the temporal interval $[1, 3]$ and if fired issues P_3 to be holding at time 3 is $\circ[3, 3]P_1 \wedge \diamond[1, 3]P_2 \rightarrow \circ[3, 3]P_3$. The according generic rule to check at arbitrary time point t_x would be $\circ[t_x, t_x]P_1 \wedge \diamond[t_{x-2}, t_x]P_2 \rightarrow \circ[t_x, t_x]P_3$. To check the trigger of a rule regarding the knowledge base provided, methods from the field of logics can be applied, e.g., model-checking [36].

For example, the scenarios from Sect. 3 can be defined as follows:

- $\mathcal{O} = \{person_1, person_2, coffee_1, coffee_2, videophone\}$
- $\mathcal{Q_S} = \{phys(X), func(X)\}$
- $\mathcal{Q_A} = \{waits(X)\}$
- $\mathcal{R} = \{IN(X, Y), OUT(X, Y)\}$

With the spatial functions $phys(X)$ denoting the physical space of some object X, $func(X)$ denoting the functional space of some object X; the object activity function $waits(X)$ denoting that some object X is currently waiting on something; the (spatial) relations $IN(X, Y)$ denoting that some space X is within some space Y, and $OUT(X, Y)$ denoting that some space X is not within some space Y.

Then Eq. 2 provides an exemplary formalization of the context in the co-located coffee encounter scenario directly before the communication starts. That is, Alice $(person_1)$ and Bob $(person_2)$ are waiting for their coffee at the coffee dispenser $(coffee_1)$.

$$\circ[t_n, t_n]person_1 \wedge \circ[t_n, t_n]IN(phys(person_1), func(coffee_1)) \wedge$$
$$\circ[t_n, t_n]person_2 \wedge \circ[t_n, t_n]IN(phys(person_2), func(coffee_1)) \wedge \qquad (2)$$
$$\circ[t_n, t_n]waits(person_1) \wedge \circ[t_n, t_n]waits(person_2)$$

The same context in the distributed coffee encounter scenario can for example by described by Eq. 3.

$$\circ[t_n, t_n]person_1 \wedge \circ[t_n, t_n]IN(phys(person_1), func(coffee_1)) \wedge$$
$$\circ[t_n, t_n]person_2 \wedge \circ[t_n, t_n]IN(phys(person_2), func(coffee_2)) \wedge$$
$$\circ[t_n, t_n]OUT(phys(coffee_1), physf(coffee_2)) \wedge \circ[t_n, t_n]videophone \wedge$$
$$\circ[t_n, t_n]waiting(person_1) \wedge \circ[t_n, t_n]waiting(person_2) \wedge \qquad (3)$$
$$\circ[t_n, t_n]IN(phys(videophone), func(coffee_1)) \wedge$$
$$\circ[t_n, t_n]IN(phys(videophone), func(coffee_2)) \wedge$$
$$\circ[t_n, t_n]IN(phys(person_1), func(videophone)) \wedge$$
$$\circ[t_n, t_n]IN(phys(person_2), func(videophone))$$

By using one of these formalizations as trigger, we can define action rules to initiate the interaction step.[6]

---

[6] Currently only brute-force model-checking is applied, however, we intend to investigate the use of existing computational reasoners to address scalability.

5   A Pilot Study on Awareness

In SOCIAL, the interaction step follows the detection step (see Fig. 1). We sub-categorize the interaction step into two phases: (i) awareness and (ii) communication. In this Section we describe a pilot study that focuses on awareness, and provide some initial results about which awareness signals are more appropriate to support informal communication at distant workplaces. The goal of our pilot study was to explore how participants would react to close and peripheral signals. Moreover, we made a distinction between simple visual and auditory signals in order to evaluate the general preference of the users. Last but not least, the transition from one state (awareness) to the other (communication) was tested in order to evaluate the whole interaction step. Müller et al. [37] presented six examples of ambient light information displays, which address humans' perception abilities to gain cues from the periphery instead of attracting the user's visual focus. Our system differentiates from [37], as it is an awareness system and not an information display system; however, both explore the "peripherality" sof the system and perception through visual cues. Regarding sound, Kainulainen et al. [38] presented guidelines regarding six common auditory techniques: speech, auditory icons, earcons, music, soundscapes, and sonifications. To make the workplace a more social and enjoyable place, they developed an audio awareness application that depicts the activity and person of each person of the work group as sound, such as the singing of the bird. We used a whispering sound effect as an awareness signal, similar to an earcon.

5.1   Setup and Method of the Study

In order to evaluate how participants would rate the kind and perception of the triggered signals, we run a Wizard-of-Oz (WoZ) study at a lab at the University of Oldenburg in April-May 2015. 17 subjects (11 female, 6 male) participated in the study (mean age 25). They were students of various disciplines (not computer science) and most of them computer-savvy; only one participant has never used a video communication software before. Each case study lasted about 45 min.

The participants were instructed to sit at a desk and watch a relaxing music video at low volume. Through this setting we tried to represent a situation at a working environment during a break, similar to the coffee lounge scenario described earlier. Then the investigator told them that there will be various signals in this environment and the participants should call the investigator through the communication software after they have been aware of a signal. The investigator, after receiving the call, would come into the lab and notify them that they are now going to test the next condition.

There were five settings with five different conditions tested:

1. Close light (lamp was next to the PC);
2. Distant light (lamp was on a chair on the participant's left side);
3. Sound (output of a wall-mounted speaker);
4. Combination of sound and light;
5. Absence of signals.

The investigator was at a surveillance room next to the lab where the study took place and triggered the light and sound remotely. The conditions were changed in random order, so that the training curve is not affected. The lamp used in the first, second, and fourth condition is a small lamp, ca. 30 cm high. It was illuminated white; no pulsing light or other light patterns. The investigator turned the lamp on and off with a time interval of 5 s. The light bulbs were from *Milight*, which offers an app for remote control. The aspect of colours and light patterns is currently out of the scope of the SOCIAL project. In the second condition, the lamp positioned left (ca. 90 degrees) from the user was placed at a chair which was of the same height as the chair where the participant was seated on. The sound (third and fourth condition) was a peripheral sound, triggered by an existing wall-mounted camera; it was a short "Psst...Psst" sound effect. The absence of the signals (fifth condition) was realized by the investigator calling the participants herself and not waiting for them to call the investigator, as in the other settings. With this condition we wanted to test how would the participants evaluate the transition from their activity to the communication, when they do not have the option to choose or give their consent if they want to communicate.

We selected two subjective evaluation measures: a think-aloud protocol during the experiment and a questionnaire at the end. For the design of the questionnaire, we adapted the following heuristics by Mankoff et al. [39] to our awareness and communication context: (i) peripherality of display, (ii) match between design of ambient display and environments (its design should not clash with its environment), (iii) easy transition to more in-depth information, (iv) visibility of state, and (v) aesthetic and pleasing design. The questionnaire consists of the following questions:

1. How easily perceptible was the signal?
2. How much did the signal distract you from your task?
3. How did you like the design/form of the signal?
4. How gradual was the transition from the task to communication?
5. Does the spatial position of the lamp influence its perception?
6. Which of the following signals do you prefer?
7. Evaluate the idea of using light, sound, and the combination of light and sound as awareness signals.

The pre-defined answers in the seventh question were on Likert scale from boring to interesting, familiar to unfamiliar, and unnecessary to necessary. At the end of the questionnaire, we also run a think-aloud protocol where the participants went through the study and described their thoughts.

5.2 Preliminary Results

Here we describe our three hypotheses along with the results of the questionnaire and the think-aloud protocol. The first hypothesis follows:

– *The spatial position of the signal's source influences its perception. A signal close to the user is more easily and faster receipted than a distant one.*

88,24 % of the participants stated that the spatial position of the lamp influences its perception. Figure 2a presents the options along the Likert scale. The close light was evaluated as the most easily perceptible signal with 94,12 % (scale 5-strongest perception) followed by the distant light with 64,71 % (scale 4). That means that the close light raised by far the strongest awareness of most participants compared to the other options, supporting this hypothesis. One participant said that he receipted the light much faster than the sound, arguing that the sound has to be repeated to be more perceptible.

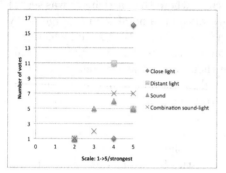

(a) Perception of signals

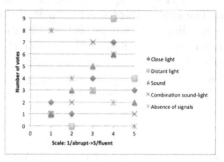

(b) Transition awareness-communication

Fig. 2. Perception and transition

- *The signal source, which is close to the communication medium, is better accepted by the users than the distant one. Moreover, the combination of two or more awareness signals is better than a single signal.*

Indeed, most participants preferred the distant to the close light, as the former was proved to distract less than the close one or the other signals (41,18 %-scale 2). A statement of the think-aloud protocol was: "the distant light provides a more discreet, background, and pleasant light, compared to the close light." Another participant noted that "it is easy to easy to blend the distant light out", showing that is up to the user's convenience to enter into communication. The rest of the participants, though, found the distant light distracting, as they had to turn their head to the light source and then continue with the actual task, i.e. to watch the music video and call the investigator.

As far as the second part of the hypothesis is concerned, most participants (64,71 %) preferred in general the situation-dependent option (i.e. light or sound) and not the combination of the signals (29,41 %). One participant stated "one signal is actually sufficient, as the combination leads to stimulus satiation". While many participants selected "light" as well (the questionnaire allowed multiple answers), remarkable is that only 5,88 % selected the sound. Most of the users described the selected sound effect as a "whisper" sound. Someone noted: "you can mistake the awareness sound with another sound or even imagine it, if you hear it often, specially if it is a short sound". They would rather prefer something like an alert tone, a bell sound, or typical mobile phone tones that most people are accustomed to. The fact that the signal which is close to the communication medium was not as much accepted as we expected might be justified because the close light was very eye-catching and "penetrative" according to the think-aloud protocol. To sum up, the first part of this hypothesis was proved wrong while the second part is partly confirmed.

- *Peripheral signals provide a more fluent transition to communication compared to signals close to our visual and/or auditory focus of attention.*

Figure 2b presents the questionnaire's results regarding this hypothesis. The absence of signals was ranked as the most abrupt (47,6 %-scale 1/most abrupt), whereas through the distant light as the most fluent (52,94 %-scale 4). The fact that the distant light distracted less than the close light, as mentioned above, affected also the evaluation of the transition from the awareness to communication state. This shows that the awareness signals are necessary for a fluent transition to communication.

With regards to the heuristics provided by [39], we can deduce from the study's results that peripheral signals, in our case, the distant light, is less distracting and better accepted than the close light; however, the distant one is not as easily perceptible as the close light. As for the match between design and environment, and the aesthetic aspect, the design of the lamp was considered as pleasing, as was said to be a mundane typical lamp. The transition from awareness to communication was more fluent with the distant light, as it was regarded as a "background light". Last but not least, the visibility of state was clear, as the triggered signal per se (be it light or sound) was explicit enough and made the state of the awareness system noticeable.

6   Summary and Future Work

In this paper, we introduced the project SOCIAL investigating spontaneous communication in spatially distributed groups. After a brief survey of related research fields, scenarios illustrating our vision of spontaneous communication and the process to realize them in a distributed setting were described. We presented a formal representation language for ambient intelligence, considering the capabilities of a system and its situational context. Furthermore, we showed how this language can be used to describe and detect specific situations and enable a system to react. As a starting point for our work, we presented a pilot study investigating the rise of awareness for the possibility of communication through visual and auditory signals. The results indicate that peripheral signals are more pleasant, i.e., user-friendly, than signals close to the user. They also provide fluency to the transition state from awareness to communication. On the other hand, close signals are more perceptible.

However promising the presented work is, we are only at the beginning of enabling seamless spontaneous communication in spatially distributed environments. We are working on a prototype system to study different possibilities of the interaction step in the real world with real people. Furthermore, we are looking for further and more complex examples of co-located situations, e.g., including multiple or moving people, containing spontaneous communication and research possibilities to compute respective comparable distributed situation descriptions. Another interesting aspect would be to limit spontaneous communication between specific individuals or groups on purpose for specific times to reduce distractions. On the other hand, we are also studying different technologies and methods to unobtrusively raise awareness and different kinds of communication modalities for specific situations.

In general, it is necessary to look at scenarios spanning more than just two physical locations to understand the potential for strongly distributed work groups. We plan a user study, with another scenario closer to the SOCIAL project (in a coffee lounge), with more fine-grained signals (light patterns, auditory icons, like the sound of the coffee machine), so that we can evaluate better the signals' purpose and usability. The load theory of attention by Lavie et al. [40] will be considered in order to focus on perceptual load and explore effective selective and focused attention in relation to awareness. Also, different kinds of groups should be considered, e.g., family members, friends, or general communities.

Acknowledgments. We acknowledge German Research Foundation (DFG) funding for project SOCIAL (FR 806/15-1 — BO 1645/12-1). We thank the four anonymous reviewers for their thoughtful and constructive comments.

References

1. Kiesler, S., Cummings, J.N.: What do we know about proximity and distance in work groups? a legacy of research. Distrib. Work **1**, 76–109 (2002)
2. Hinds, P.J., Bailey, D.E.: Out of sight, out of sync: understanding conflict in distributed teams. Organ. Sci. **14**(6), 615–632 (2003)
3. Kreijns, K., Kirschner, P.A., Jochems, W.M.G.: Identifying the pitfalls for social interaction in computer-supported collaborative learning environments: a review of the research. Comput. Hum. Behav. **19**(3), 335–353 (2003)
4. Hansen, M.T.: The search-transfer problem: The role of weak ties in sharing knowledge across organization subunits. Adm. Sci. Q. **44**(1), 82–111 (1999)
5. Kraut, R.E., Fussell, S.R., Brennan, S.E., Siegel, J.: Understanding effects of proximity on collaboration: Implications for technologies to support remote collaborative work. In: Hinds, P., Kiesler, S. (eds.) Distributed Work, pp. 137–162. The MIT Press, Cambridge (2002)
6. Watzlawick, P., Beavin, J., Jackson, D.: Some tentative axioms of communication. In: Communication Theory (2009)
7. Vinciarelli, A., Pantic, M., Bourlard, H.: Social signal processing: survey of an emerging domain. Image Vision Comput. **27**(12), 1743–1759 (2009)
8. Schmidt, A., Gellersen, H.W.: Implizite und situationsbezogene unterstützung von arbeitsprozessen. In: Proceedings of CSCW, München, pp. 1–4 (2000)

9. Streitz, N., Röcker, C., Prante, T., Stenzel, R., van Alphen, D.: Situated interaction with ambient information: Facilitating awareness and communication in ubiquitous work environments. In: Proceedings of HCI International (2003)
10. Vogel, D., Balakrishnan, R.: Interactive public ambient displays: transitioning from implicit to explicit, public to personal, interaction with multiple users. In: Proceedings of ACM Symposium on User Interface Software and Technology, pp. 137–146 (2004)
11. Weiser, M.: Ubiquitous computing. IEEE Comput. **27**(12), 1335–1346 (1993)
12. Ducatel, K., Bogdanowicz, M., Scapolo, F., Leijten, J., Burgelman, J.C.: Scenarios for ambient intelligence in 2010. Office for official publications of the European Communities (2001)
13. Augusto, J.C.: Ambient intelligence: the confluence of ubiquitous/pervasive computing and artificial intelligence. In: Schuster, A.J. (ed.) Intelligent Computing Everywhere, pp. 213–234. Springer, New York (2007)
14. Augusto, J.C., Nakashima, H., Aghajan, H.K.: Ambient intelligence and smart environments: a state of the art. In: Nakashima, H., Aghajan, H., Augusto, J.C. (eds.) Handbook of Ambient Intelligence and Smart Environments, pp. 3–31. Springer, New York (2010)
15. Cook, D.J., Augusto, J.C., Jakkula, V.R.: Ambient intelligence: technologies, applications, and opportunities. Pervasive Mobile Comput. **5**(4), 277–298 (2009)
16. Harrison, S.: Media Space 20+ Years of Mediated Life. Springer, London (2009)
17. Markopoulos, P., de Ruyter, B.E.R., Mackay, W.E. (eds.): Awareness Systems - Advances in Theory, Methodology and Design. Human-Computer Interaction Series. Springer, New York (2009)
18. Gutwin, C., Greenberg, S.: Workspace awareness for groupware. In: Proceedings of CHI, pp. 208–209 (1996)
19. Roussel, N., Gueddana, S.: Beyond "beyond being there": Towards multiscale communication systems. In: Proceedings of MULTIMEDIA, pp. 238–246. ACM, New York (2007)
20. Judge, T.K., Neustaedter, C., Kurtz, A.F.: The family window: the design and evaluation of a domestic media space. In: Proceedings of CHI, pp. 2361–2370 (2010)
21. de Greef, P., Ijsselsteijn, W.A.: Social presence in a home tele-application. Cyberpsy. Behav. Soc. Netw. **4**(2), 307–315 (2001)
22. Gaver, W.W., Moran, T.P., MacLean, A., Lövstrand, L., Dourish, P., Carter, K., Buxton, W.: Realizing a video environment: europarc's RAVE system. In: Proceedings of CHI, pp. 27–35 (1992)
23. Mackay, W.E.: Media spaces: environments for informal multimedia interaction. Comput. Support. Co-op. Work **7**, 55–82 (1999)
24. Karahalios, K., Donath, J.S.: Telemurals: linking remote spaces with social catalysts. In: Proceedings of CHI, pp. 615–622 (2004)
25. Dourish, P., Bly, S.A.: Portholes: supporting awareness in a distributed work group. In: Proceedings of CHI, pp. 541–547 (1992)
26. Romero, N.A., Markopoulos, P., van Baren, J., de Ruyter, B.E.R., Ijsselsteijn, W., Farshchian, B.A.: Connecting the family with awareness systems. Pers. Ubiquit. Comput. **11**(4), 299–312 (2007)
27. van de Ven, J., Schmid, F., Hesselmann, T., Boll, S.: A framework for communication and interaction in spatially distributed social groups. In: Proceedings of SISSI, Copenhagen, Denmark, pp. 73–82 (2010)
28. Ligozat, G.: Qualitative Spatial and Temporal Reasoning. Wiley, ISTE, London (2013)

29. Chen, J., Cohn, A.G., Liu, D., Wang, S., OuYang, J., Yu, Q.: A survey of qualitative spatial representations. Knowl. Eng. Rev. **30**(1), 106–136 (2015)
30. Hois, J., Dylla, F., Bhatt, M.: Qualitative spatial and terminological reasoning for ambient environments. In: Spatial and Temporal Reasoning for Ambient Intelligence Systems, p. 32 (2009)
31. Randell, D.A., Cui, Z., Cohn, A.G.: A spatial logic based on regions and connection. In: Proceedings of KR, pp. 165–176 (1992)
32. Moratz, R.: Representing relative direction as a binary relation of oriented points. In: Proceedings of ECAI, pp. 407–411 (2006)
33. Dylla, F., Kreutzmann, A., Wolter, D.: A qualitative representation of social conventions for application in robotics. In: AAAI Spring Symposium (2014)
34. Augusto, J.C., Nugent, C.D.: The use of temporal reasoning and management of complex events in smart homes. In: Proceedings of ECAI, pp. 778–782 (2004)
35. Sadri, F.: Ambient intelligence: a survey. ACM Comput. Surv. **43**(4), 36 (2011)
36. Schnoebelen, P.: The complexity of temporal logic model checking. In: Proceedings of Advances in Modal Logic, pp. 393–436 (2002)
37. Müller, H., Fortmann, J., Pielot, M., Hesselmann, T., Poppinga, B., Heuten, W., Henze, N., Boll, S.: Ambix: Designing ambient light information displays. In: Proceedings of Designing Interactive Lighting Workshop at DIS. ACM (2012)
38. Kainulainen, A., Turunen, M., Hakulinen, J.: Awareness information with speech and sound. In: Kainulainen, P., De Ruyter, B., Mackay, W. (eds.) Awareness Systems - Advances in Theory, Methodology and Design, pp. 231–256. Springer, New York (2009)
39. Mankoff, J., Dey, A.K., Hsieh, G., Kientz, J.A., Lederer, S., Ames, M.: Heuristic evaluation of ambient displays. In: Proceedings of CHI, pp. 169–176 (2003)
40. Lavie, N., Beck, D.M., Konstantinou, N.: Blinded by the load: attention, awareness and the role of perceptual load. Philos. Trans. R. Soc. Lond. B Biol. Sci. **369**(1641), 1–13 (2014)

Smart Tales: An Awareness Game for Ambient Assisted Living

Paolo Sernani[1]([⊠]), Fabiano Dalpiaz[2], Aldo Franco Dragoni[1],
and Sjaak Brinkkemper[2]

[1] Dipartimento di Ingegneria dell'Informazione, Università Politecnica
delle Marche, Ancona, Italy
{p.sernani,a.f.dragoni}@univpm.it
[2] Utrecht University, Utrecht, The Netherlands
{f.dalpiaz,s.brinkkemper}@uu.nl

Abstract. Despite the progress in ambient assisted living (AAL), the general audience is still mostly unaware of this term as well as of its purpose, enabling technologies, and potential. As a consequence, there are often misconceptions about AAL and smart homes, and the acceptance of AAL technologies is still too low. To cope with these problems, this paper presents a publicly available awareness game called *Smart Tales*, whose goal is to enhance the familiarity of its players with the notion and core concepts of AAL. In Smart Tales, the player has the role of an assisted patient in a smart home, and gets to learn about AAL and its technologies while trying to cheat the sensors that are placed in the house. In addition to presenting the design of the game following the Serious Games Design Assessment framework from the literature, we present results on engagement and learning that we obtained through a formative evaluation with ten users.

1 Introduction

The population ageing phenomenon [16] is expected to significantly increase the expenditures in healthcare [31] to assist elderly people all over the world. In this context, solutions are necessary to reduce these expenses, including the onerous costs for hospitalizing non-autonomous yet healthy elderlies. Ambient Assisted Living (AAL) comes to the rescue; its objective is to extend the time people can live in their preferred environment by increasing their autonomy, self-confidence and mobility [28].

Despite its promises, the acceptance of AAL and its technology is still unsatisfactory, and studies have shown a rather low intention of prospective users to adopt AAL techniques [2]. The reasons for low acceptance are many [14], and include technological concerns about the trustworthiness of AAL solutions [27] (in terms of functionality, reliability, usability) as well as ethical considerations such as the potential loss of privacy [2,4], dignity [8] and autonomy [30].

Our diagnosis is that low acceptance is often caused by the lack of awareness of the purpose of AAL and its enabling technologies. Although this is not the

© Springer International Publishing Switzerland 2015
Kameas et al. (Eds.): AmI 2015, LNCS 9425, pp. 187–204, 2015.
DOI: 10.1007/978-3-319-26005-1_13

only cause, we hypothesize that raising awareness could positively contribute to acceptance by avoiding misconceptions and by mitigating unjustified fears.

In this paper, we advocate the use of *awareness games* as a tool to deliver knowledge on the objectives and working principles of AAL. Awareness games are serious games [29] that aim at increasing awareness in a certain target audience about a given domain, in addition to providing engagement as a regular (video-)game. Awareness games have been proposed for several domains, including environmental issues [10], security engineering [21], and flooding policies [23].

Specifically, we present our developed game called *Smart Tales*, where the player impersonates an assisted patient living in a smart home, and gets to learn about AAL and its technologies while trying to cheat the sensors that are placed in the house. While doing so, the player collects informative cards concerning AAL, which are necessary to answer the knowledge quizzes at the end of each level so as to unlock further levels.

We make three main contributions to the literature:

- We argue for the importance of serious games to increase the acceptance of AAL and its enabling technologies;
- We systematically describe the design of Smart Tales, a game that focuses on increasing awareness on AAL in the context of smart homes;
- We present results from a formative evaluation with users, which shows promising results concerning the learning process, but also the need of improving engagement.

The remainder of the paper is structured as follows: Sect. 2 describes the relevant related work on the use of serious games and virtual worlds in AAL, healthcare, simulation and scenario visualization; Sect. 3 explains the goals of Smart Tales and describes its design using the Serious Games Design Assessment framework [20]; Sect. 4 reports on our evaluation of Smart Tales in terms of user engagement and learning effectiveness; finally, Sect. 5 concludes the paper and outlines future directions.

2   Related Work

The most common applications of serious games and virtual worlds in AAL concern motor and cognitive rehabilitation [24] and the improvement of social inclusion [3]. For example, Simmonds and Zikos [26] employ computer games in therapies for pain management, and their evaluation of two games shows improved pain threshold, mood and physical performance.

Game elements and virtual environments can be used for simulation purposes [25], in order to generate data to test artificial intelligence algorithms, e.g., for activity and behavior recognition. Godsey and Skubic [9] propose to simulate sensor networks using game engines, with the aim to reproduce data about the movements of a patient in a home environment. Exploiting the collision mechanism of the physics engine, the authors simulate passive infrared (PIR) sensors and test the correspondence of such a simulation with a real case.

A more advanced framework to collect data about patients' behavior is that by Kormányos and Pataki [13], which features three distinct models for the human, the environment and the motion sensor network. Their simulation generates logs about different variables (bed pressure, unwashed dishes in the sink, etc.) to train and test activity recognition algorithms. Zancanaro et al. [34] propose the SIMDOMO simulator of sensorized domestic environments to generate long-term data concerning human behavior.

Virtual worlds and 3D environments are applied also during the design, the engineering and the validation of AAL platforms. In designing AAL systems, the use of Interactive Scenario Visualization (ISV) based on 3D models can lead to the clarification of system functionalities, as well as to gain stakeholders' feedback [12]. Fernández-Llatas et al. [7] present a computer-aided tool to validate AAL platforms during design, which allows usability engineers to define the workflow of a simulation and to visualize the simulation in a 3D environment.

Smart Tales takes an orthogonal approach: its innovative soul is to use computer serious games to increase end-users' awareness towards ICT solutions for AAL. Smart Tales makes a step forward in the promising research direction of serious gaming to foster acceptance of smart homes, trying to break the learning barriers in the field [15].

3   Smart Tales

Smart Tales is a serious game that aims to raise awareness about the potential of Information & Communication Technology (ICT) solutions for AAL. The purpose of the game is to give the opportunity to end-users to learn about sensors that can be placed in a smart home, showing their capabilities as well as their weaknesses. The version of the game described in this paper is focused on motion detection and indoor positioning.

The player is the inhabitant of a smart home that is equipped with a number of sensors to detect the presence of the player's avatar, and to determine the room where the player is located. Three kinds of sensors are present in the virtual world: passive infrared (PIR) sensors for motion detection; active infrared sensors for passage detection; smart tiles for both motion and presence detection [22].

To engage the player, Smart Tales includes elements from different game genres: third/first person shooters, puzzle games and arcade games. The virtual environment of the game is in 3D (inside a dwelling) and the player controls an avatar through the arrow keys. The goals are to avoid being detected by the sensors in order to score points, and to progress to the next levels while gathering information about AAL and sensors. The player's goal is to provide evidence that some of the sensors are misplaced. In other words, the player is supposed to *cheat* the home, scoring points as much as he can. The game consist of levels: upon completing a level, the following level is unlocked.

The implementation relies on the Unity 3D (www.unity3d.com/) 4.6 game engine; 3D models of the smart home were built using Blender (www.blender.org/) and SweetHome3D (www.sweethome3d.com/).

3.1 Game Purpose

Being a serious game, the main goal of Smart Tales goes beyond pure entertainment [33]: the game is intended as a driver to achieve wider awareness and acceptance of ICT solutions for AAL by end-users. Thus, engagement and effectiveness of learning are the key determinants to assess the success of the game. To achieve such purpose, the design of Smart Tales takes into account multiple, partially conflicting requirements:

- Both technical and non-technical people need to be able to play the game. Hence, the controls should be easy to remember, minimal and intuitive;
- Information about AAL shall be delivered within the game mechanics in order to make the learning process lighter, using typical game features (such as providing challenges and goals, stimulating curiosity, cooperation, competition) to enhance user engagement and intrinsic motivation [17];
- The player shall be motivated to keep playing through all the levels, avoiding to overwhelm him with excessive information. Moreover, in line with the theory of flow [5] the game difficulty has to gradually increase, increasing the challenge but not the frustration, in order to reward the player for his progress and his learning.

The design of Smart Tales directly addresses its main purpose and these requirements, as explained in the next subsection.

3.2 Game Design

To describe the design of Smart Tales in a systematic manner we use the Serious Game Design Assessment (SGDA) framework, proposed by Mitgutsch and Alvarado [20]. This framework enables studying a serious game design in relation to the game purposes and intention: it allows to analyze a serious game investigating the cohesiveness of its *content and information, mechanics, fiction and narrative, aesthetics and graphics* and *framing*, and their coherence in relation to the game purpose.

Content and Information. In the SGDA framework, this aspect refers to the information and data provided during the game. We can distinguish between (a) the serious content that provides information about AAL and the sensors present in the virtual home, and (b) the information related to the game status.

The serious content relates to the core purpose of Smart Tales: in the game, the player has to collect informative cards (badges) about Ambient Assisted Living and the sensors present in the game levels. The player can read the collected badges in any moment of the game except while he is answering the quizzes at the end of each level, for the provided information is needed to correctly answer to the questions.

Figure 1 shows the information in one of the badges, that defines the notion of a "smart tile". The provided information is both textual and visual. The textual

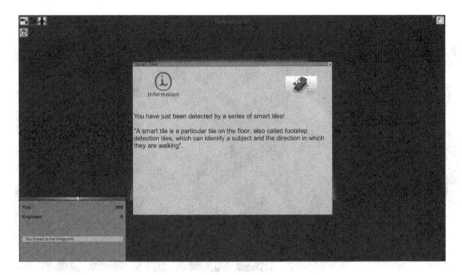

Fig. 1. Delivering awareness through badges: the definition of the sensor "smart tile".

information describes the content of the badge, while the visual information facilitates the recognition of the badge. The top-left "information logo" on the badge clarifies that the included information is useful to answer to the questions at the end of the level; the top-right logo identifies the main topic of the badge: there are different logos for badges on general information about AAL, PIR sensors, active infrared sensors and smart tiles.

In order to keep the player engaged in the game, to not overwhelm him with too extensive information and to make the learning process more effective, the information is split in nine cards. Furthermore, to ease the reading process, the content of the badges with longer content is presented in multiple pages.

During the game, the player can visualize data about the game status, including the time left to play the level, the earned points (and the points of his opponent, the engineer who configured the smart home, covered by the CPU) and the number of unread badges in the player's inventory. As depicted in Fig. 2, the player gets notified whenever he scores points. Such elements allow to keep the player focused on his goals in the game, pushing him to beat the home engineer, collecting and reading more badges, in order to foster engagement as a key factor in the learning process.

Game Mechanics. Mechanics are the various actions, behaviors and control mechanisms afforded to the player within a game context [11]. In the SGDA framework, the game mechanics involve the in-game goal of the game, the reward system, and the main playful obstacles/challenges. In Smart Tales, in order to advance to the next level, the player has to achieve three goals:

– Score more points than the home engineer;
– Collect all the badges within the level;

Fig. 2. In-game notification to the player: by exiting the hallway undetected for the first time in that level, the player scores 100 points. (Color figure online)

– Answer correctly to all the questions presented at the end of a level.

The first goal gives a challenge to the player: he needs to beat the engineer who configured the home. The difficulty increases with the levels, and the player has to carefully plan an effective path for his avatar to follow. To do so, the player can choose in which room he wants to place his avatar; some choices are better than others, and the right positioning can be crucial to pass the level. Thus, challenge and planning are instrumental to keep the player focused and engaged. The second goal pushes the player to collect all the badges with information about AAL. Finally, to unlock the next level, and thus to continue the challenge, the player needs to answer to three questions at the end of each level. The content in the badges is essential to answer correctly. In case wrong answers are given, the player does not unlock the next level.

To score points, the player needs to exit from the rooms of the smart home without being detected. When a sensor detects the presence of a player inside a room, the home engineer scores points. Consecutive actions give extra-bonus points, using a multiplier, as in arcade games, either to the player for having cheated the house, or to the CPU engineer for having kept track of the player. The basic action that the player can perform is to move his avatar in the 3D smart home, using the arrow keys, in order to avoid the placed sensors. The player is able to see the sensors' coverage before placing the avatar in the home; while playing, he can see the devices on the walls and doors, but not their sensing area. Moreover, the player gets bonus points by reading the informative badges: this mechanism gives an extra in-game incentive to read the AAL-related content. Another game mechanic is the time limit to play a level, for the player has one minute to complete the level and to achieve the first two objectives: to score more than the engineer and to collect all the badges. On the one hand, the time limit makes the level more challenging; on the other hand, keeping it low allows the player to not waste time waiting the quiz at the end of the level, in case he achieves the first two goals.

Fiction and Narrative. The fictional context of Smart Tales has the following logline: *an engineer equipped an assistive "unobtrusive" environment (a smart home), but the skeptical inhabitant does not consider the home that unobtrusive.* The player lives in the home and has to prove that the engineer has misplaced the sensors. The game takes place in a dwelling: the player has to place his avatar in a room and then he has to start moving, collecting badges and avoiding sensors.

The fictional context reflects the target environment of AAL: the home of an assisted person. The narrative introduces the player to the game challenges that will engage him in his learning process: the inhabitant does not consider the home unobtrusive, and his aim is to mislead sensors to proof they are misplaced.

Aesthetics and Graphics. To support the game purpose, Smart Tales uses basic 3D graphics to represent the smart home and the players avatar. A 3D environment gives additional opportunities to the player to avoid the sensors: in addition to moving inside the home, the avatar can walk crouched, jump and do small steps. To support the game mechanics, the main elements are highlighted in the user interface: the time is shown in red color on the top-center of the screen; the scores are on the bottom left of the screen (the player points are in green, the engineer points are in red). In addition, as per Fig. 2, a status bar shows whether the player is currently defeating the engineer, by positioning a cursor within a red-to-green scale (red = engineer is leading, green = player is leading). A green notification on the left side of the screen appears when the player scores points; a similar red-colored notification appears when the home engineer scores points on the right side of the screen. Finally, a set of icons allows the player to change the game camera (top-left of the screen) and to access the inventory of the collected badges (top right of the screen).

Framing. This element of the SGDA framework refers to the target group of a serious game. Since Smart Tales' purpose is to increase the awareness of ICT solutions for AAL, the target group is composed by people potentially interested in equipping a home with smart technology, such as the relatives of older adults who live alone. Hence, Smart Tales is mainly targeted to non-technical people and non-gamers. The complexity of the levels gradually increases in order to not overwhelm the player. In the first level, a few PIR sensors are available, and the badges are easy to collect. In the third and last level, both passive and active infrared sensors as well as smart tiles are present, and the player has properly plan beforehand on how to collect the badges, bearing in mind that he should score more points than the home engineer.

The controls of the game are easy to allow non-technical people to play: the avatar can be moved with the arrow keys (or the "WASD" keys) and the buttons on the screen are mouse-clickable. The default game camera is automatic and follows the avatars' movements, from a third person perspective. However, more skilled players can choose a manual camera that can be rotated with the mouse and can even use the "CTRL" key to make the avatar crouch, the "Q" key to do just a small step and the "space bar" to jump. A detailed tutorial explains all the controls of the game. As a reminder of the game controls, the player can always press the "question mark" button on the top-left of the screen: it shows the game controls and summarizes the level's goals.

4   Evaluation

We report on a preliminary evaluation concerning user engagement and learning effectiveness. Engagement is key to keep the player motivated to play, so that the entire (or at least most of the) gameplay is experienced. This is important because the serious purpose of the game—raising awareness on AAL—is delivered through the gameplay by collecting badges and answering to questions.

Our evaluation method involved user tests with ten people having different backgrounds, selected because of their inexperience in AAL. All the participants were from the same geographical area: the Netherlands. Eight participants were male and two were female. Nine of them had university level education in various fields of expertise including Mathematics, Psychology, Linguistics, Human/Economic Geography, Anthropology, Social Studies, Film Sciences, History and Electrical Engineering. One had secondary school education level. The age ranged from 21 to 30 years old. All but one finished the game and completed all the three levels of the tested version of Smart Tales.

We based the tests on the quasi-experimental research design model of Mayer et al. [19], and our study was conducted by three M.Sc. students. After an explanation of the game goals and of the evaluation's objectives, the participants filled in a short questionnaire to determine their prior knowledge on AAL and the sensors that Smart Tales features. Then, the participants were asked to play the three levels of the game, without imposing time limits. In the pre-game questionnaire, the users had to give yes/no answers to the following questions:

1. Do you know what is ambient assisted living?
2. Do you know what is a smart home?
3. Do you know what is a passive infrared sensor?
4. Do you know what is an active infrared sensor?
5. Do you know what is a smart tile?

As a double check, the questionnaire included five open questions that asked the participant an informal definition of the concepts of the previous five questions. Seven participants answered negatively to all of the questions; however, when asked to define AAL using their own words, they associated it to the concept of a "home technologically equipped to assist in some task and/or perform monitoring". One participant (with a background in Electrical Engineering) answered positively to the first four question, although he gave a wrong definition of infrared sensors. The last two participants knew what is a smart home; one of them answered "yes" on the last two questions, but actually gave a wrong definition of active infrared sensor and smart tile.

After the gameplay session, the participants had to fill in two questionnaires: the former measured user engagement, and was based on the User Engagement Scale (UES) proposed by Wiebe et al. [32] to assess engagement in video game-based environments; the latter focused on the assimilated knowledge by asking the same questions that were in the game, and was delivered thirty minutes after the end of the game session. The choice of relying on the same questions poses threats to the validity of the results, while it minimizes the chance of asking knowledge that the game did not deliver.

The tests were carried out in two sessions, at different stages of game development. Six participants tested an early version of the game, while four participants tested a revised version, including different textual and visual information. The early version displayed information on the badges without visual logos. Moreover, a clearer description of the in-game goals was added before the first level as well as in the game help. We performed this redesign after collecting feedback from the first six participants, in order to improve usability and limit confusion. In Sect. 4.2, we highlight the different results from the two test sessions.

4.1 Learning

In Smart Tales, the player has to answer three questions at the end of each level, in order to advance to the next one. The questions concern the serious information content that is contained in the badges collected in the level that was just played. The choice of including knowledge into artifacts is inspired by the *reified knowledge* game design pattern [18], in order to introduce knowledge into a game without disrupting the flow.

Figure 3 shows the questions at the end of the first level. These questions check the acquired knowledge on the concept of AAL and on the definition of PIR sensor; such topics are covered by the badges placed in the first level. While answering the in-game questions, the player is actually performing a self-assessment of his first-order learning. Visual feedback informs the player about the correctness of his answers: those highlighted in green are correct, while those in red are wrong (see Fig. 4). If wrong answers are given, the player has to replay the level and re-answer the questions, in order to unlock the next level. This is an incentive for learning the content in the badges.

During the users tests, we evaluated first-order learning: according to Mayer et al. [19], it is direct influence of playing the game on the individual, small group attitudes, knowledge, skills or behavior. We reused the nine questions that the player has to answer while playing Smart Tales (three per level): the questions were provided to the users as a questionnaire, thirty minutes after playing the game, in order to assess the effectiveness of the learning process.

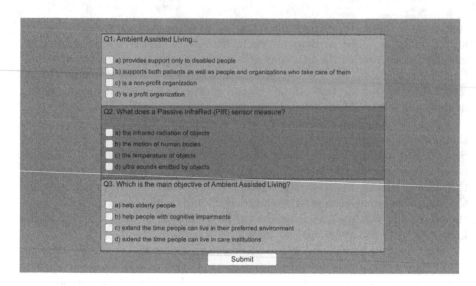

Fig. 3. The questions the player is confronted with at the end of the first level to unlock level two.

Table 1 includes the number of correct answers per player in the post-game questionnaire. Globally, 81 % of the answers given by the participants was correct: one player answered all the questions correctly, while five players gave just one wrong answer. However, one player was able to give only four correct answers. In fact, such player was not able to complete the second level, and gave up after five attempts; this means that he did not read all the badges and he did not learn enough to answer to more questions.

Table 1. Number of correct answers per player in the post-game questionnaire.

Player 1	6/9	Player 6	4/9
Player 2	8/9	Player 7	8/9
Player 3	8/9	Player 8	7/9
Player 4	9/9	Player 9	8/9
Player 5	7/9	Player 10	8/9

The approach that we employed in our preliminary evaluation of learning effectiveness does inevitably suffer from threats to validity:

– To adequately assess the learned knowledge, the time between the end of the game session and the post-questionnaire should be longer than thirty minutes. Further tests with an improved research protocol are essential;
– A comparison with traditional learning methods (for example reading books or papers) should be performed, in order to clearly evaluate whether our

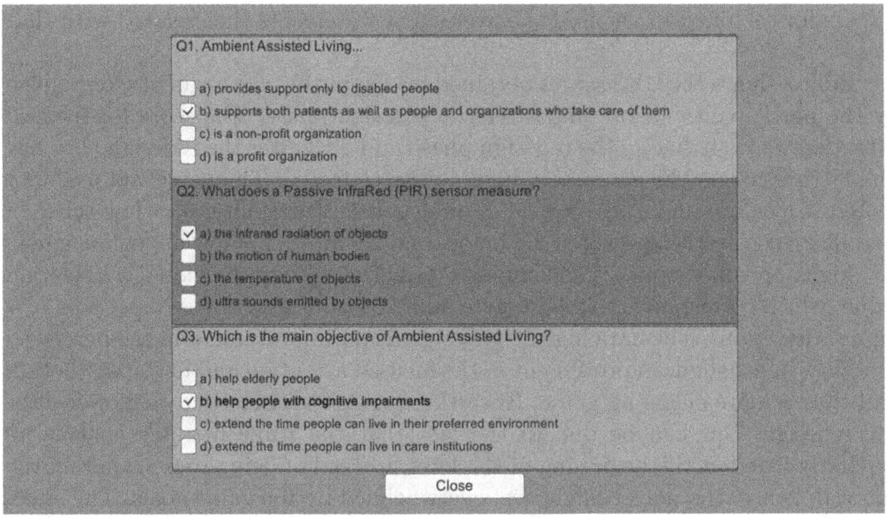

Fig. 4. The answers given by the player: the game provides a visual feedback on the correct answers (green) and on the wrong ones (red) (Color figure online)

awareness game is suitable for teaching the basics of AAL and its enabling technologies. This should involve a different research method where participants are allocated to either a treatment group (playing the serious game) or a control group (relying on other instructional techniques) [1].

- The post-questionnaire should be slightly different from the in-game questions, in order to be sure that the tester does not memorize the correct answer, but instead learns the information provided by the badges.

4.2 Engagement

To evaluate user engagement in Smart Tales, we used the User Engagement Scale (UES) proposed by Wiebe et al. [32] as a validated measure that is tailored for videogames. According to the UES, engagement is composed by four factors:

- *Focused attention*, based on the theory of flow [5], to evaluate the concentration, the temporal dissociation and the absorption of the player;
- *Perceived usability*, to evaluate affective (challenge/frustration) and cognitive (effortful) aspects of playing the game;
- *Aesthetics*, to evaluate the visual appearance of the game;
- *Satisfaction*, to evaluate the interest the game evoked, the fun of the gaming experience and the willingness to play it again (and to recommend the game to others).

The score each factor, we posed statements that the users could agree or disagree with using a 5-point Likert scale, where 1 corresponds to strong disagreement and 5 to strong agreement with the statement. In order to compute a score for each factor, we used the average of statements that related with that factor.

Table 2 shows the UES scores obtained by computing the mean of scores given by the participants, before and after the redesign phase. The score for focused attention was 2.42 before the redesign phase and 2.53 after the redesign (1 = low ability to focus on the game, 5 = high ability to focus). The perceived usability scored 3.4 before and 1.91 after (1 = high sense of usability, 5 = low sense of usability); the aesthetics scored 2.8 before and 2.9 after (1 = low appealing game, 5 = high appealing game). We combined these factors into the global satisfaction value, which corresponds to 2.64 before and 2.04 after (1 = low satisfaction, 5 = high satisfaction). The data highlights a significant improvement in the perceived usability, and a slight improvement in the focused attention and in the aesthetics, and thus a more engaging game. Nevertheless, user satisfaction was lower after the redesign: this can be due to the fact that the three in-game goals were explicitly listed at the beginning of the level, instead of being present just in the tutorial; hence, the player might feel overwhelmed by the game goals. The small number of subjects, however, does not allow to draw any statistically significant conclusion. Each factor is analyzed individually below.

Table 2. UES results for Smart Tales, before and after the minor redesign.

UES factor	Before	After
Focused attention	2.42	2.53
Perceived usability	3.40	1.91
Aesthetics	2.80	2.90
Satisfaction	2.64	2.04

Focused Attention. Table 3 lists the statements associated with the factor "Focused Attention". Before the performed redesign, all the statements scored between weak disagreement (2) and neutrality (3). The statements with the lowest score are those about the perception of time, while the statements about absorption and concentration got a score closer to neutrality (i.e., 2.67 and 2.83). While players need to concentrate to achieve the game goals, they seem not to lose awareness of the fact that they are performing a learning task. The redesign seems to have an impact on player absorption: the statement *I was absorbed in my gaming task* went from a value between weak disagreement and neutrality (2.33) to a value close to weak agreement (3.75); moreover, such impact is confirmed by the standard deviation of the answers, which diminished significantly with the redesign.

Perceived Usability. Table 4 includes the statements related to the factor "Perceived Usability": the mean of the scores before the redesign is in between neutrality (3) and weak disagreement (2), thereby calling for improving usability of the game. In particular, the participants felt frustrated: all the players but

Table 3. The average scores of the statements concerning focused attention ($\overline{x}$), before and after the minor redesign, as well as the related standard deviation (σ).

Focused attention statement	Before		After	
	$\overline{x}$	σ	$\overline{x}$	σ
When I was playing the game I lost track of the world around me	2.50	1.12	2.50	0.50
I blocked out things around me when I was playing the game	2.67	1.25	3.00	0.71
The time I spent playing the game just slipped away	2.17	1.07	2.25	0.43
I was absorbed in my gaming task	2.33	1.11	3.75	0.43
I was so involved in my gaming task that I lost track of time	2.00	1.00	1.50	0.50
During this gaming experience I let myself go	2.83	1.34	2.00	0.71
I lost myself in this gaming experience	2.33	1.11	1.75	0.43
I was really drawn into my gaming task	2.50	0.50	3.50	0.50

one weakly agreed with the sentence *I felt frustrated while playing the game* ($\sigma = 0.37$).

Follow-up interviews with the users revealed that the main reason was that players did not really know what to do due to ambiguous or missing feedback and a lack of instructions. The tutorial of Smart Tales includes written instructions given to the player using pop-ups. Most of the players found such instruction boring, and skipped the pop-ups before reading the content. Thus, a redesign might be needed, and tests with different techniques to give instructions should be carried out (for example we can consider to give audio instructions and to use subtitles).

However, as highlighted at the beginning of Sect. 4.2, the results on perceived usability after the redesign are encouraging: each statement gets a better score, and perceived usability globally scores 1.91. The sense of frustration was lower and all the participants agreed that they were able to do the things they needed to do in the game.

Aestethics. Table 5 shows the scores of the statements on factor "Aestethics". Users gave a positive score—between neutrality (3) and weak agreement (4)—to the statements on layout and graphics, which indicates that the basic graphics chosen for Smart Tales are appropriate for the purpose of the game. Nevertheless, the users did not define the game as very attractive (the statement on game attractiveness scored between weak disagreement and neutrality) since the graphics reminds third person shooter games, which typically have high-quality visual effects. This expectation can have a negative impact on global engagement: the statement *the game was aesthetically appealing* scored 2.67 before the redesign and 2.25 after the redesign; most of the participants (6 out of 10) weakly disagreed with the sentence, three were neutral and one agreed.

Table 4. The average scores of the statements concerning perceived usability ($\overline{x}$), before and after the minor redesign, as well as the related standard deviation (σ).

Perceived usability	Before		After	
	$\overline{x}$	σ	$\overline{x}$	σ
I felt discouraged while playing the game	3.83	1.50	1.07	0.50
I felt annoyed while playing the game	3.67	2.25	0.94	0.43
Playing the game was mentally taxing	2.83	1.75	0.69	0.43
I found the game confusing to use	3.83	2.50	1.07	0.50
I felt frustrated while playing the game	3.83	1.50	0.37	0.50
I could not do some of the things I needed to do in the game	2.83	1.00	1.21	0.00
The gaming experience was demanding	3.33	2.50	0.75	0.50
This gaming experience did not work out the way I had planned	3.00	2.25	1.15	0.43

Satisfaction. Table 6 includes the scores of the statements about factor "Satisfaction". Both before and after the redesign phase, the players indicated a low willingness to continue playing and to suggest the game to other people. In addition, all the participants to the tests performed after the redesign weakly disagreed with the sentence *Playing the game was worthwhile*. One reason for these issues is that the same home and sensors are present in all the three levels; thus, some players might find the game repetitive. Hence, a redesign might be needed, by adding levels with different home maps and more sensor types. The new redesign should address also players' curiosity and interest, since the participants were neutral toward these two aspect of the serious game.

Table 5. The average scores of the statements concerning aesthetics ($\overline{x}$), before and after the minor redesign, as well as the related standard deviation (σ).

Aesthetic statement	Before		After	
	$\overline{x}$	σ	$\overline{x}$	σ
I liked the graphics and images used in the game	3.17	4.00	1.34	0.71
The game appealed to my visual senses	2.50	2.75	1.26	0.83
The game was aesthetically appealing	2.67	2.25	0.75	0.43
The screen layout of the game was visually pleasing	2.83	3.50	0.90	1.12
The game was attractive	2.83	2.00	0.90	0.71

5   Discussion and Future Directions

In this paper, we presented the Smart Tales game that raises awareness on concept, objectives, working principles and enabling technologies of ambient assisted

Table 6. The average scores of the statements concerning satisfaction ($\overline{x}$), before and after the minor redesign, as well as the related standard deviation (σ).

Satisfaction statement	Before		After	
	$\overline{x}$	σ	$\overline{x}$	σ
The content of the game incited my curiosity	3.33	2.50	0.94	1.12
I would continue to play this game out of curiosity	2.00	1.25	1.00	0.43
I would recommend playing the game to my friends and family	2.17	1.75	1.21	0.43
Playing the game was worthwhile	2.33	2.00	1.25	0.00
I felt interested in my gaming task	3.00	2.50	1.15	0.50
My gaming experience was rewarding	2.33	2.00	0.94	0.71
This gaming experience was fun	3.33	2.25	0.94	0.43

living (AAL). Currently, the game has three levels as well as a tutorial for the user to learn about the game controls and objectives. The player impersonates an inhabitant of a smart home, and has to cheat the deployed sensors. While doing so, the player has also to collect informative badges about AAL and its technology, gaining the necessary knowledge to answer the quizzes at the end of each level, and advance to the next one.

We conducted a preliminary formative evaluation on learning effectiveness and user engagement with ten participants. Six participants played the game in its early stage, while the other four played an improved version, where we performed a minor redesign of the informative badges. The results concerning the learning process are promising and encourage the use of serious games to increase the end-users' knowledge on AAL and its enabling technologies: in the posttest questionnaires, 81 % of the answers were correct. Nevertheless, more extensive tests need to conducted: a comparison with a control group relying on traditional learning techniques can better validate the usefulness and effectiveness of serious games to increase awareness about AAL.

The tests on user engagement, based on the UES revised by Wiebe et al. [32], show clear room for improvement. On the one hand, the redesigned version obtained a perceived usability score of 1.91 in a scale from 1 to 5 (where 1 represents a high sense of usability and 5 a low sense of usability). On the other hand, focused attention, aesthetics and satisfaction obtained an average score at the middle of the scale: the repetitiveness of the levels needs to be reduced (e.g., by creating levels with different home maps and adding new sensors), to increase the players' curiosity and sense of fun; improving the graphics could lead to higher immersion and, thus, enhance the sense of flow.

Future work includes improving Smart Tales based on the outcomes of the formative evaluation, and to conduct further tests with users. Another direction concerns replacing the CPU-as-an-engineer gameplay with an additional role for the players, i.e., that of an engineer that has to properly configure a smart home. Future versions should also recognize that AAL and smart homes define *socio-technical systems* [6], rather than focusing only on the technological infrastructure.

Acknowledgments. The authors thank Brian Arendse, Mats Hofman and Lamia Soussi for their precious help in carrying out the users tests of Smart Tales.

References

1. Bellotti, F., Kapralos, B., Lee, K., Moreno-Ger, P., Berta, R.: Assessment in and of serious games: an overview. Adv. Hum. Comput. Interact. **2013**, 1:1–1:11 (2013)
2. Ben Allouch, S., van Dijk, J.A.G.M., Peters, O.: The acceptance of domestic ambient intelligence appliances by prospective users. In: Tokuda, H., Beigl, M., Friday, A., Brush, A.J.B., Tobe, Yoshito (eds.) Pervasive 2009. LNCS, vol. 5538, pp. 77–94. Springer, Heidelberg (2009)
3. Cascado, D., Romero, S., Hors, S., Brasero, A., Fernandez-Luque, L., Sevillano, J.: Virtual worlds to enhance ambient-assisted living. In: 2010 Annual International Conference of the IEEE Engineering in Medicine and Biology Society (EMBC), pp. 212–215 (2010)
4. Coughlin, J., D'Ambrosio, L., Reimer, B., Pratt, M.: Older adult perceptions of smart home technologies: Implications for research, policy & market innovations in healthcare. In: 29th Annual International Conference of the IEEE Engineering in Medicine and Biology Society, EMBS 2007, pp. 1810–1815 (2007)
5. Csikszentmihalyi, M.: Flow and the Psychology of Discovery and Invention. Harper Perennial, New York (1997)
6. Dalpiaz, F., Giorgini, P., Mylopoulos, J.: Adaptive socio-technical systems: a requirements-driven approach. Requirements Eng. **18**(1), 1–24 (2013)
7. Fernandez-Llatas, C., Mocholi, J., Sala, P., Naranjo, J., Pileggi, S., Guillen, S., Traver, V.: Ambient assisted living spaces validation by services and devices simulation. In: 2011 Annual International Conference of the IEEE Engineering in Medicine and Biology Society, EMBC, pp. 1785–1788 (2011)
8. Gaul, S., Ziefle, M.: Smart home technologies: insights into generation-specific acceptance motives. In: Holzinger, A., Miesenberger, K. (eds.) USAB 2009. LNCS, vol. 5889, pp. 312–332. Springer, Heidelberg (2009)
9. Godsey, C., Skubic, M.: Using elements of game engine architecture to simulate sensor networks for eldercare. In: Annual International Conference of the IEEE Engineering in Medicine and Biology Society, EMBC 2009, pp. 6143–6146 (2009)
10. Hildmann, H., Hirsch, B.: Raising awareness for environmental issues through mobile device based serious games. In: 4th Microsoft Academic Days, Berlin, Germany (2008)
11. Hunicke, R., Leblanc, M., Zubek, R.: MDA: a formal approach to game design and game research. In: Proceedings of the AAAI Challenges in Game AI Workshop. AAAI Workshop - Technical report, vol. WS-04-04, pp. 1–5 (2004)
12. van't Klooster, J.W., van Beijnum, B.J., Eliens, A., Hermens, H.: Interactive scenario visualization for user-based service development. In: 2012 International Conference on Collaboration Technologies and Systems (CTS), pp. 498–503 (2012)
13. Kormányos, B., Pataki, B.: Multilevel simulation of daily activities: why and how? In: 2013 IEEE International Conference on Computational Intelligence and Virtual Environments for Measurement Systems and Applications (CIVEMSA), pp. 1–6 (2013)

14. Lee, C., Coughlin, J.F.: Perspective: older adults' adoption of technology: an integrated approach to identifying determinants and barriers. J. Prod. Innov. Manage. **32**(5), 747–759 (2015)
15. Leonhardt, S., Kassel, S., Randow, A., Teich, T.: Learning in the context of an ambient assisted living apartment: including methods of serious gaming. In: Motta, G., Wu, B. (eds.) Software Engineering Education for a Global E-Service Economy. Progress in IS, pp. 49–55. Springer, Heidelberg (2014)
16. Lutz, W., Sanderson, W., Scherbov, S.: The coming acceleration of global population ageing. Nature **451**(7179), 716–719 (2008)
17. Malone, T.W., Lepper, M.R.: Making learning fun: a taxonomy of intrinsic motivations for learning. In: Snow, R., Farr, M.J. (eds.) Aptitude, Learning, and Instruction Vol. 3: Conative and Affective Process Analyses, pp. 223–253. Lawrence Erlabaum Associates, Hillsdale (1987)
18. Marne, B., Wisdom, J., Huynh-Kim-Bang, B., Labat, J.-M.: The six facets of serious game design: a methodology enhanced by our design pattern library. In: Ravenscroft, A., Lindstaedt, S., Kloos, C.D., Hernández-Leo, D. (eds.) EC-TEL 2012. LNCS, vol. 7563, pp. 208–221. Springer, Heidelberg (2012)
19. Mayer, I., Bekebrede, G., Harteveld, C., Warmelink, H., Zhou, Q., van Ruijven, T., Lo, J., Kortmann, R., Wenzler, I.: The research and evaluation of serious games: toward a comprehensive methodology. Br. J. Educ. Technol. **45**(3), 502–527 (2014)
20. Mitgutsch, K., Alvarado, N.: Purposeful by design? A serious game design assessment framework. In: Proceedings of the International Conference on the Foundations of Digital Games - FDG 2012, pp. 121–128. ACM Press (2012)
21. Newbould, M., Furnell, S.: Playing safe: a prototype game for raising awareness of social engineering. In: Australian Information Security Management Conference, pp. 24–30 (2009)
22. Rashidi, P., Mihailidis, A.: A survey on ambient-assisted living tools for older adults. IEEE J. Biomed. Health Inform. **17**(3), 579–590 (2013)
23. Rebolledo-Mendez, G., Avramides, K., de Freitas, S., Memarzia, K.: Societal impact of a serious game on raising public awareness: the case of floodsim. In: Proceedings of the 2009 ACM SIGGRAPH Symposium on Video Games, pp. 15–22. ACM (2009)
24. Rego, P., Moreira, P., Reis, L.: Serious games for rehabilitation: a survey and a classification towards a taxonomy. In: 2010 5th Iberian Conference on Information Systems and Technologies (CISTI), pp. 1–6 (2010)
25. Sernani, P., Claudi, A., Calvaresi, P., Accattoli, D., Tofani, R., Dragoni, A.F.: Using 3D simulators for the ambient assisted living. In: 3rd International Workshop on Artificial Intelligence and Assistive Medicine. CEUR Workshop Proceedings, vol. 1213, pp. 16–20 (2014)
26. Simmonds, M.J., Zikos, D.: Computer games to decrease pain and improve mood and movement. In: Proceedings of the 7th International Conference on PErvasive Technologies Related to Assistive Environments, pp. 56:1–56:4. ACM (2014)
27. Steinke, F., Bading, N., Fritsch, T., Simonsen, S.: Factors influencing trust in ambient assisted living technology: a scenario-based analysis. Gerontechnology **12**(2), 81–100 (2014)
28. Sun, H., De Florio, V., Gui, N., Blondia, C.: Promises and challenges of ambient assisted living systems. In: Sixth International Conference on Information Technology: New Generations, ITNG 2009, pp. 1201–1207 (2009)
29. Susi, T., Johannesson, M., Backlund, P.: Serious games: an overview. Technical report HS-IKI-TR-07-001, School of Humanities and Informatics, University of Skövde (2007)

30. Townsend, D., Knoefel, F., Goubran, R.: Privacy versus autonomy: a tradeoff model for smart home monitoring technologies. In: 2011 Annual International Conference of the IEEE Engineering in Medicine and Biology Society, EMBC, pp. 4749–4752 (2011)

31. Werblow, A., Felder, S., Zweifel, P.: Population ageing and health care expenditure: a school of 'red herrings'? Health Econ. **16**(10), 1109–1126 (2007)

32. Wiebe, E.N., Lamb, A., Hardy, M., Sharek, D.: Measuring engagement in video game-based environments: investigation of the user engagement scale. Comput. Hum. Behav. **32**, 123–132 (2014)

33. Winn, B.M.: The design, play, and experience framework. In: Ferdig, R. (ed.) Handbook of Research on Effective Electronic Gaming in Education, vol. 5497, pp. 1010–1024. IGI Global, London (2007)

34. Zancanaro, M., Marchesoni, M., Armellin, G.: SIMDOMO: a tool for long-term simulations of ambient-assisted living. In: Aarts, E., et al. (eds.) AmI 2014. LNCS, vol. 8850, pp. 47–50. Springer, Heidelberg (2014)

Context Recognition: Towards Automatic Query Generation

Marjan Alirezaie[✉], Federico Pecora, and Amy Loutfi

Applied Autonomous Sensor Systems, Department of Technology,
Örebro University, SE-701 82 Örebro, Sweden
{marjan.alirezaie,amy.loutfi}@oru.se, fpa@aass.oru.se
http://www.oru.se/aass/

Abstract. In this paper, we present an ontology-based approach in designing knowledge model for context recognition (CR) systems. The main focus in this paper is on the use of an ontology to facilitate the generation of user-based queries to the CR system. By leveraging from the ontology, users need not know about sensor details and the structure of the ontology in expressing queries related to events of interest. To validate the approach and demonstrate the flexibility of the ontology for query generation, the ontology has been integrated in two separate application domains. The first domain considers a health care system implemented for the GiraffPlus project where the query generation process is automated to request information about activities of daily living. The second application uses the same ontology for an air quality monitoring application in the home. Since these two systems are independently developed for different purposes, the ease of applying the ontology upon them can be considered as a credit for its generality.

Keywords: Query generation · Context recognition · OWL-DL ontology

1 Introduction

Context recognition (CR), and in particular recognizing Activities of Daily Living (ADL) has been addressed as an important challenge of ambient assisted living systems in a wide range of application areas such as elderly health care and smart homes. In general, this kind of CR system has at least two types of users: the primary user (service receiver), and the secondary user (service provider). For instance, in case of an elderly health care system, the primary user is the elderly person at home whose activities are monitored by a CR system, and the secondary user is a health professional that communicates with the primary user through the system. By increasing CR applications in different domains, the ease of communication between a CR system and its users becomes a very important matter of semantics.

In the literature, current approaches to the problem of activity recognition are categorized as data-driven and model-driven techniques. In this work, we focus

© Springer International Publishing Switzerland 2015
Kameas et al. (Eds.): AmI 2015, LNCS 9425, pp. 205–218, 2015.
DOI: 10.1007/978-3-319-26005-1_14

on model-driven approaches whereby patterns of changes in sensor observations are identified based on an abductive approach. In other words, changes in data are determined by hypothesizing the occurrence of specific activities. Due to this perspective, a model-driven CR system needs to also contain a domain knowledge where the activities along with their details including (pre)conditions are defined. However, providing domain knowledge is non-trivial for secondary users who are unfamiliar with the technical implementation of CR systems. Therefore, What is needed is an interface whereby secondary users can express situations which constitute an activity using natural language terms and also query the system in a similar manner. Therefore, for facilitating user interactions the users: (I) should not need to know the details of the sensors that are deployed in the environment, and (II) should be able to express queries in a flexible manner. For example, the user may be interested to query if *"John is awake during the night"*, where *John* is an elderly user. Another query could be *"How many times did John take his pills yesterday?"*. It is worth noting that specific activities such as *awake* or *taking pills* can be composed of several sub-activities. For instance *taking a pill* can be abductively inferred if the two activities of *opening the drug box* and *taking glass of water* are recently observed.

In this paper, we present an OWL-DL ontology as the knowledge representation model which is used for query generation. The structure of the ontology containing different abstraction levels satisfies the aforementioned criteria for the query language and hence becomes a key enabler to facilitate the communication between the CR system and its secondary user. Figure 1 represents an abstract view of a CR system with a query generator. Our focus in this work is on the role of the ontology in query generation process that enables the secondary user to interact with a given CR system. More specifically, in this work, we solve the problem of mapping high level user-entered queries into concepts and relations in an ontology and catch the time intervals during which the (secondary) user's

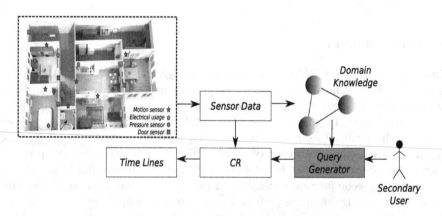

Fig. 1. The schema of a CR system. The query generation process provides an interface between the user and the CR system.

intended activities have occurred. We apply this ontology into an implemented health monitoring CR system, GiraffPlus [3] whose details are given in the paper.

Furthermore, in order to show how general and domain-independent the structure of the ontology is, we take another application of this ontology into account (air quality monitoring) where it has a different role in a different CR system [18].

This paper is organized as follows: Sect. 2 gives a brief overview about CR systems and their main features in terms of temporal relations. The details of the proposed knowledge model in this work are given in Sect. 3. Section 4 elaborates the applications of the ontology and shows how the query generation process can be facilitated by integrating the ontology with the CR systems. Discussion on the application is given in Sect. 5 where we also conclude the paper.

2   Context Recognition

A context is recognized based on a set of events or ADLs occurred during a specific period of time. Each ADL is composed of several sub-activities that depending on the context are performed at different times relative to the occurrence time of the ADL [2]. These sub-activities are divided into two groups based on the way that they are captured. First, the activities (events) that are seen as direct changes in sensor data (i.e., atomic activities), and second, the activities that are detected based on sequence of or concurrent atomic activities (i.e., complex activities). For instance, *being in bed* as an atomic activity, is simply detected by reading the pressure sensor attached to the bed, whereas,

Table 1. Allen's Temporal Relations. (t_i^s and t_i^e represent the lower and the upper bounds of the event E_i's time interval, respectively.)

#	Temporal relations	Illustration
1	E_1 before E_2	$t_1^e < t_2^s$
2	E_1 after E_2	$t_1^s > t_2^e$
3	E_1 meets E_2	$t_1^e = t_2^s$
4	E_1 met-by E_2	$t_1^s = t_2^e$
5	E_1 overlaps E_2	$t_1^s < t_2^s, t_1^e < t_2^e, t_1^e > t_2^s$
6	E_1 overlapped-by E_2	$t_1^s > t_2^s, t_1^e > t_2^e, t_1^s < t_2^e$
7	E_1 during E_2	$t_1^s > t_2^s, t_1^e < t_2^e$
8	E_1 contains E_2	$t_1^s < t_2^s, t_1^e > t_2^e$
9	E_1 starts E_2	$t_1^s = t_2^s, t_1^e < t_2^e$
10	E_1 started-by E_2	$t_1^s = t_2^s, t_1^e > t_2^e$
11	E_1 finishes E_2	$t_1^s > t_2^s, t_1^e = t_2^e$
12	E_1 finished-by E_2	$t_1^s < t_2^s, t_1^e = t_2^e$
13	E_1 equal E_2	$t_1^s = t_2^s, t_1^e = t_2^e$

being awake as a complex activity is captured when *being in the bed, leaving the bed* and *being at hall* are captured in order with certain time distances from each other.

A sub-activity alone does not add any meaning to the definition of an ADL unless a temporal relation between them are determined. In other words, what relates a complex activity to its sub-activities is a set of temporal relations that exist between them. Assuming that for each activity (event) E there is a time interval $[t^s, t^e]$ (where $t^s \leq t^e$), there are 13 possible qualitative temporal relationships between any two given events' intervals [1]. These relations known as Allen's temporal intervals are defined based on symbolic relations given in Table 1.

We have so far mentioned the two principal features of a context including (I) events with different types, and (II) temporal relations between events. These two features play a main role in construction of a knowledge model, and accordingly, in the query generation process as a communication interface between the secondary user and the CR system. In the next section, the structure of the proposed knowledge model is explained in terms of its concepts and their relations.

3   Knowledge Representation Model

In the literature, there are a number of works in activity recognition implemented based on model-driven approaches. Many of the research attempts in this area are increasingly focused on the use of knowledge models such as ontologies whereby semantics of activities and their relations to the environment can be declaratively expressed [5,6,9,10]. Applying ontologies, furthermore, enables CR systems to recognize activities using ontological reasoning techniques. Among the ontological languages, OWL-DL is highly used as it is suitably expressive and computationally decidable [8]. Moreover, due to the support of publicly used OWL-DL ontologies in the field of context recognition and semantic sensor networks such as SSN ontology [7], developing an ontology in OWL-DL can facilitate its integration with the available ones.

The knowledge model used in this paper is also represented within an OWL-DL ontology whose structure is illustrated in Fig. 2. This ontology consists of the representation of two types of knowledge, namely static knowledge and dynamic knowledge. The static knowledge represents time independent concepts which are related to observed phenomena (objects) and their properties in a given environment. In contrast, the dynamic knowledge represents time dependent concepts related to events. In the following, we go through the details of the knowledge structure in the ontology. As we will later show, due to its abstraction levels, the proposed ontology can be effortlessly used by various CR systems for different purposes.

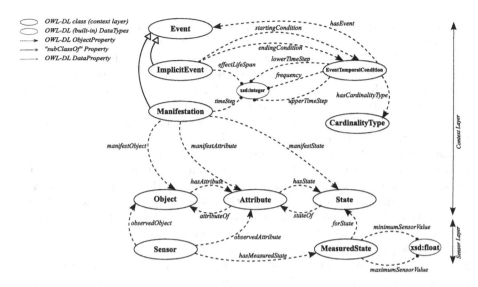

Fig. 2. The schema of the domain knowledge ontology composed of the two layers: Context Layer and Sensor layer.

3.1 Static Knowledge

As shown in Fig. 2, the structure of the ontology is composed of two layers: the context layer and the sensor layer. The former contains abstracted concepts about the context, whereas the later, as its name implies, contains sensor-related concepts with quantitative values.

Context Layer: The context layer is represented by 3 principal classes of *Object*, *Attribute* and *State*. The class *Object* refers to all the entities that are observed by a sensor and involved in a potential event in the environment. For instance, a fridge is defined as an object (*Fridge ⊑ Object*) since a sensor (e.g., a magnetic contact switch) can monitor it to see if there is any interaction with the environment. Moreover, a fridge and its interaction with the environment can be involved in a cooking process which is defined as an event.

Each object is defined based on a set of attributes whose states (which are monitored by sensors) are important factors in characterization of an event. For instance, the door of a fridge likewise its electric current are considered as its attributes (*Door ⊑ Attribute, ElectricCurrent ⊑ Attribute*). The states of attributes, furthermore, are defined as individuals of the class *State* that represent all the possible states (e.g., *cold ∈ State, warm ∈ State, dark ∈ State*) of an object's attributes.

Sensor Layer: The sensor layer, as mentioned before, contains sensor-related concepts. The class *Sensor* is responsible for holding sensors' information used for the observation process. Each sensor is decided to observe one state of an object's attribute. However, on the one hand, these states which are defined as individuals of the class *State*, can only explain the objects *symbolically* in terms of their attributes' situations. On the other hand, each (atomic) event is seen as a numeric (not symbolic) change captured in sensors' outputs. In order to establish a link between these two different concepts, the sensor layer, furthermore, contains another class called *MeasuredState*. As we can see in Fig. 2, this class is assumed to provide a link between numeric sensor data and their relevant symbolic states defined in the ontology.

Each individual of the class *MeasuredState* is assigned to a specific state via the object property *forState*. To be seen as an event, a numeric change in sensor data needs to be within a range of values. For this, each *MeasuredState* individual is also associated with two other properties, *minimumSensorValue* and *maximumSensorValue*, providing a range of values for a state. For instance, the triple *(min=1, max=3, forState=cold)* creates a *MeasuredState* individual related to a particular sensor via the *hasMeasuredState* property (see Fig. 2). Ranges of data that is set for a state depends on many factors including the type of sensor and the observed *object*. In other words, a particular state (e.g., *cold*) can be assigned to two different ranges depending on the type of objects. For example, range of values set for the *cold* state of a fridge is different than that of the *cold* state of a freezer.

3.2 Dynamic Knowledge

Dynamic knowledge refers to events in the environment that are whether directly or indirectly captured from sensor data. The class *Event* subsuming the two classes of *ExplicitEvent* and *ImplicitEvent* represents the symbolic concepts related to events (see Fig. 2). The former subclass, *ExplicitEvent* (which is also called *Manifestation*), indicates events that are directly detected from changes in sensor data, whereas the second subclass, *ImplicitEvent*, represents the events captured by a set of other events in the environment.

Manifestation: Once the knowledge model is populated with proper objects, attributes and their potential states, a set of subclasses of the *Manifestation* class is generated in the ontology. Each *Manifestation*'s subclass symbolically represents an event directly observed by sensors. The name of each subclass is generated by concatenating the name of the object, its attribute and state that are involved in the event. As an example of the *Manifestation* class we can refer to *Fridge-DoorOpen* indicating the occurrence of an event which is interpreted as *opening* the *door* of the *fridge*. Given the knowledge model, the CR system generates a manifestation instance such as *m:(fridge, door, open, t)*, whenever the sensor data says so. As we can see, this generated manifestation is free of the numeric sensor data that is set for the particular state. The last argument of the manifestation instance, t, represents the time point at which the manifestation is captured.

ImplicitEvent: The class *ImplicitEvent* addresses activities in the environment defined based on the occurrences of a set of whether implicit or explicit events.

Examples of implicit events include activities such as *Awake, Cooking, Eating,* etc. Each implicit event in the ontology is defined within a period of time (or time interval). To represent the time interval, each implicit event class is equipped with the two properties of *startingCondition* and *endingCondition* linking the implicit event to its conditions. By conditions we mean the required situations in the environment for inferring the starting and the ending point of the implicit event. Let's assume that an implicit event E_i occurs at time point t_i^s (as the starting time point), and ends at t_i^e. The two time points of t_i^s and t_i^e together represent a time interval, $[t_i^s, t_i^e]$, for the implicit event E_i. However, there are many events whose ending conditions do not need to be explicitly specified. These events to be represented, only need their starting condition to be taken into account meaning that their time interval is shrunk into a time point.

(Pre)conditions of an implicit event are represented within the class *Event-TemporalCondition* interlinked to the class *ImplicitEvent* via the two properties of *startingCondition* and *endingCondition* (see Fig. 2). A (pre)condition is identified in the form of an event in conjunction with a time interval. For this, the class *EventTemporalCondition* is related to the class *Event* via the property *hasEvent*. The two data properties, *lowerTimeStep* and the *upperTimeStep*, furthermore, relate the class *EventTemporalCondition* to two integer values indicating a time period during which the (pre)condition of the implicit event is expected to occur.

Temporal Relations: In this section, we show how the temporal relations between an implicit event and its (pre)conditions can be represented using the two aforementioned data properties, *lowerTimeStep* and *upperTimeStep*. As mentioned in the previous section, each event depending on its features can be defined either within a time interval or at a time point. For the ease of representation, we consider events as time-point events.

Let's assume that an implicit event E_i along with its (pre)condition event E_c are both time-point events which are occurred at time points T_i and T_c, respectively. Given these two time-point events, the 13 temporal relations between them listed in Table 1 are reduced into 3 temporal relations. Said differently, it is intuitive to say that the temporal relations `overlaps`, `overlapped-by`, `meets`, `met-by`, `contains`, `during`, `starts`, `started-by`, `finishes`, `finished-by` and `equal` will find the same meaning if the two events are time-point events, and therefore the three main relations will be:

E_c `before` E_i $\qquad\qquad\qquad\qquad\qquad \equiv \quad T_c < T_i$
E_c `after` E_i $\qquad\qquad\qquad\qquad\qquad\quad \equiv \quad T_c > T_i$
E_c `[meets | overlaps | during |... | equal]` E_i $\quad \equiv \quad T_c = T_i$

As shown in Fig. 3, given the implicit event E_i at time point T_i, the two numeric values of A and B (corresponding to the *upperTimeStep* and the *lowerTimeStep* properties) indicate a time interval including T_c. Regardless of the temporal relation between the events, it is always true to say that:

$$T_i - B \leq T_c \leq T_i - A$$

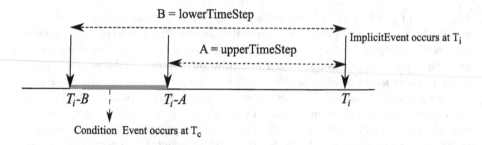

Fig. 3. The time interval set for the (pre)condition of an implicit event using the two properties of *upperTimeStep* and *lowerTimeStep*.

Given the above assumptions, equivalent relations to the aforesaid 3 temporal relations between the two numeric values A and B will be:

$$E_c \text{ before } E_i \qquad\qquad \Rightarrow \qquad 0 < A \leq B$$
$$E_c \text{ after } E_i \qquad\qquad \Rightarrow \qquad A \leq B < 0$$
$$E_c \text{ [meets | overlaps | during |... | equal] } E_i \quad \Rightarrow \quad A = B = 0$$

It is also possible to illustrate the inclusion of the two numeric values A and B in all the 13 relations, however as previously stated, for the ease of representation we have done so only for time-point events.

4   Applications of the Knowledge Model

The proposed OWL-DL ontology in this work, as said before, has been used as a context knowledge model for the two different CR systems explaining in the following subsections. The first CR system is an elderly health care monitoring [3] upon which our ontology is integrated to facilitate the query generation process for its users. The second system that is founded on the proposed ontology in this work is an air quality monitoring system whereby the cause of changes in the ambient air is explained by the system in terms of detected activities in the environment [18].

Since these two systems are independently developed with different ideas behind, the ease of applying our knowledge model[1] upon these two systems can be considered as a credit for its generality.

4.1   Application I: Query Generation for CR

The first system is called Giraffplus developed for an EU-FP7 founded project [3]. In this project a number of elderly people's accommodations were set up with different types of sensors monitoring both environmental and physiological

---

[1] The knowledge model ontology is downloadable from: http://aass.oru.se/~mae/files/ontologies/SmartEnvironmentOntology.

changes related to inhabitants. GiraffPlus also contains a context recognition system founded on a constraint-based reasoning approach [4] that accounts for human activity recognition at home. This system accepts as input an XML-based query expressing an activity and returns as output time lines during which this activity of interest has occurred. Figure 4 depicts a sample of the XML-based query asking the CR system for the time interval during which the (primary) user has been *Awake*. It is intended that secondary users (e.g., health professionals) can generate such queries. However, as seen in this figure, it is non-trivial for the user to know and state all dependencies of an activity (e.g., *Awake*) which are in terms of both sensors and atomic events information involved in the definition of the activity.

```
 1: <?xml version="1.0" encoding="UTF-8" ?>
 2: <rules xsi:noNamespaceSchemaLocation="rule_schema.xsd" xmlns:xsi="http://www.w3.org/2001/XMLSchema-instance">
 3:
 4:     <preproc name="TunstallTrueFalse" in="Bed - Bedroom @ testsite_se_2" out="_in_bed" args=""/>
 5:     <preproc name="TunstallPIRSimple" in="PIR - Hall @ testsite_se_2" out="_in_hall" args=""/>
 6:
 7:     <rule out="_awake">
 8:         <constraint from="_awake" type="during" args="" to="_in_hall" />
 9:         <constraint from="_awake" type="after" args="[0,1000]" to="_in_bed" />
10:     </rule>
11:
12: <extractor name="max" in="_awake" out="awake" />
13:
14: </rules>
```

Preprocessing — rule — extractor (margin labels)

Fig. 4. An XML-based query about the event *Awake*.

In this work, we apply our ontology to bridge between simple queries and XML-based queries used by the GiraffPlus system. Using the abstraction layers considered in the design of the proposed knowledge model, we show how the query generated by the (secondary) user can be free of both sensor details and the structure of the ontology. The secondary user is usually expected to know only about the implicit events. In other words, when the user is interested to know when the inhabitant was doing a certain activity, (s)he should not be concerned about how this activity (i.e., an implicit event) has been defined in the knowledge model, which sensors are involved in the process of capturing this activity and so on. For this, we provide an interface through which the user only needs to enter the name of the activity. Given the activity name, the query generation process (see Fig. 1) using the ontology (representing the domain knowledge) will catch all the required details of the activity to generate a query admissible by the reasoning process in the CR system.

Event's Details Retrieval: An XML-query asks for time-lines in which a user-entered event which is referred to as an implicit event, has occurred. As shown in Fig. 4, the XML-query is generated from three main sections including preprocessing, rule and extractor. The preprocessing section (lines 4–5) provides required information related to sensors that are involved in the process of capturing the implicit event. The second part of the XML query, the rule section (lines

7–10) in Fig. 4, is about the temporal relations between the given implicit event, and its correlated (whether implicit or explicit) events. The extractor section of the XML-based query (line 12) contains no information retrievable from the ontology except the name of the event entered by the user.

Given the populated OWL-DL ontology, the query generator (see Fig. 1), will generate a set of query expressions that can provide certain information to generate the XML-query executable by the constraint-based reasoning. The syntax of these query expressions is based on the OWL-DL Manchester syntax [15] processable by the OWL reasoners such as HermiT [14]. In the following, we represent a set of queries each is assumed to retrieve required information for a certain part of the XML-based query. In these queries, the variables are preceded by an underscore. The key-word **inverse** preceding a property name also indicates the inverted direction of the property.

Figure 5 represents an OWL-DL query retrieving all the sensor instances that are involved in capturing the user-entered implicit event ($\_implicitEvent$)[2]. The classes and properties involved in this query are labelled in red in the figure (beside the query). Starting with the class *ImplicitEvent* and following direction of properties mentioned in the query, we achieve the class *Sensor*. As mentioned in Sect. 2, an event can be whether atomic or complex. For this to be considered, the query in Fig. 5 contains a disjunction (the **or** constructor) where the first operand ($\_implicitEvent$) refers to the atomic event and the second operand (in blue) refers to the complex event.

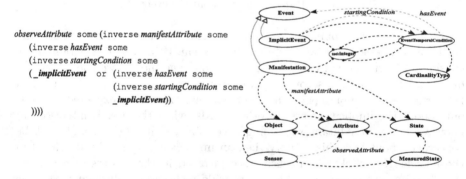

Fig. 5. Left: OWL-DL query capturing the sensor individuals involved in representation of a given implicit event. **Right:** The classes and properties involved in the query are labelled in red (Color figure online).

As said above, the rule section in the XML query (lines 7–10) indicates the temporal relations. The process of retrieving information required to construct this part contains two phases. The first phase is about finding the correlated events achieved by running the following query (see Fig. 2 to follow the direction of properties):

---

[2] The interested reader is referred to [16] for further information on OWL-DL and the query syntax.

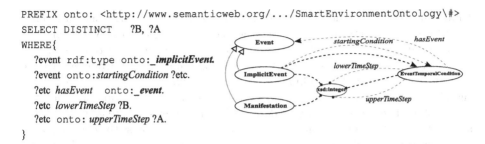

```
PREFIX onto: <http://www.semanticweb.org/.../SmartEnvironmentOntology\#>
SELECT DISTINCT    ?B, ?A
WHERE{
    ?event rdf:type onto:_implicitEvent.
    ?event onto:startingCondition ?etc.
    ?etc hasEvent  onto:_event.
    ?etc lowerTimeStep ?B.
    ?etc onto: upperTimeStep ?A.
}
```

Fig. 6. Left: SPAEQL query capturing the two integer values A and B that are representing the upper and lower time spaces set for an event. **Right:** The classes and properties involved in the query are labelled in red (Color figure online).

inverse *hasEvent* some

(inverse *startingCondition* _*implicitEvent*)

The mentioned above query results in a list of events that are interlinked to the _*implicitEvent*. At the second phase of the process, we need to retrieve for each event in this list (referred to as _*event*), the time distance to the _*implicitEvent* represented as a time interval in the form of lower and upper bounds. Due to involvement of data properties (*lowerTimeStep* and *upperTimeStep*) in representation of this information in the ontology, a SPARQL query [11] is applied to retrieve the required numeric values indicating the time interval. Figure 6 illustrates both the SPARQL query[3] as well as the marked classes and properties in the ontology that are involved in representation of the temporal relations between events.

Depending on the values of the two retrieved variables A and B that represent a time interval, a proper symbolic temporal relation mentioned in Sect. 3.2 will be used to express the temporal relation between a given implicit event and its conditions in the XML query.

As explained, health professionals only need to enter the name of an activity. The main query executable by the CR system is then automatically generated by the OWL-DL and SPARQL queries whose structures are not activity-dependent.

4.2   Application II: Monitoring System

The second application consists of a smart home environment to monitor air quality in the home. The output of the context recognition system is to provide a list of probable activities which has contributed towards the release of an odour in the home. Therefore, an activity recognition process is involved in the monitoring application, and the reasoner provides explanations in the form of activity (event) names detected in the environment. The environment is continuously observed with a set of sensors including an electronic nose[4].

---

[3] In SPARQL, variables are preceded by a question mark.

[4] An electronic node is a device that contains a set of chemical gas sensors. Sniffing the gases exposed to the sensors causes a number of chemical reactions whose numeric representations are considered as sensor outputs [17].

Unlike the first application explained in Sect. 4.1, in this scenario, one particular sensor (i.e., the electronic nose) is considered as a target sensor whose signals are annotated with the explanations provided by the context recognition. For example, a peak in the gas sensor signal can be annotated as "Cooking" which indicates occurrence of a cooking process. As shown in Fig. 7, since the target signal is pre-determined, the secondary user does not need to mention her/his events of interest. Once a change is detected in the target signal (e.g., the gas sensor data), the most relevant annotations are inferred to express the change based on the other isolated changes in other sensor signals and their time distances. The goal of this scenario in this paper is to use the same ontology populated in the same way, however for different purpose than query generation.

It is important to note that the context recognition process used here is associated with a reasoner that can handle the knowledge retrieval process incrementally. By incrementally, we mean that once an event (such as Cooking, Burning, etc.) occurs (e.g., at time $t = T$) it is captured as a likely cause of a tentative change in the target signal that may be detected later (at time $t \geq T$). The reasoner used in this scenario is based on an incremental version of Answer Set Programming (ASP) solver [12]. The reason why we chose ASP solver is out of the scope of this paper and we refer the reader to our previous work [18] for further details about the air monitoring application.

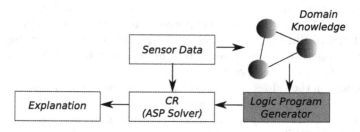

Fig. 7. The schema of a specific target-based CR system. Since the target signal is pre-determined (e.g., gas sensor data), the secondary user has no role in the system.

The ASP solver receives as input an ASP logic program[5]. In other words, in order to interpret the target signals, a logic program solvable by the incremental ASP solver has to be generated (see Fig. 7). This logic program that is composed of three types of rules, namely static, cumulative and volatile ones, is automatically generated by a logic program generator fed by the ontology (see Fig. 7). The static rules are generated based on the static knowledge in the ontology and both the cumulative and volatile rules which are time dependent are generated based on the dynamic knowledge (i.e., manifestations and implicit events).

---

[5] The interested reader is referred to [13] for further information about ASP logic programming.

5   Discussion and Future Work

If context recognition systems are to be accessible and usable by end users with little or no programming experience, the interface between such systems and the humans that use them must be intuitive. Being able to query a system using basic terms and having such queries translated in format which is compatible with the reasoning process of the system is essential. This paper has presented the application of an ontology for context recognition in the home which can be used to automate the translation from user requests e.g. "Is John Sleeping" into specifically formatted queries. We have demonstrated the application of this ontology on two different CR systems. The novelty in this work has been in providing a structure and framework in how events are interpreted and analysed by focussing on the knowledge model in a given CR system. We showed how the abstraction layers enable the ontology to be effortlessly integrated with two CR systems with different approaches. This was achieved by separating the sensor layer from the context layer as well as the static knowledge from the dynamic knowledge of the environment.

Although the query generator process at the moment accepts only the name of an activity, future work will investigate how to process more complicated user-entered terms (e.g., in the form of a sentence), and use natural language techniques that are able to parse the given sentence containing the activity name or its synonyms. For this, we will have to also provide an appropriate user interface through which the queries in the form of natural language are given to the system by the user.

Acknowledgments. This work and the authors are supported by the distributed environment Ecare@Home funded by the Swedish Knowledge Foundation 2015–2019.

References

1. Allen, J.F.: Maintaining knowledge about temporal intervals. Commun. ACM **26**(11), 832–843 (1983)
2. Saguna, S., Zaslavsky, A., Chakraborty, D.: Complex activity recognition using context-driven activity theory and activity signatures. ACM Trans. Comput. Hum. Interact. **20**(6), 32:1–32:34 (2013)
3. Coradeschi, S., Cesta, A., Cortellessa, G., Coraci, L., González-Jiménez, J., Karlsson, L., Furfari, F., Loutfi, A., Orlandini, A., Palumbo, F., Pecora, F., Rump, S.V., Stimec, A., Ulberg, J., Otslund, B.: Giraffplus: combining social interaction and long term monitoring for promoting independent living. In: 6th International Conference on Human System Interactions (HSI), pp. 578–585 (2013)
4. Pecora, F., Cirillo, M., DellOsa, F., Ullberg, J., Saffiotti, A.: A constraint-based approach for proactive, context-aware human support. J. Ambient Intell. Smart Environ. **4**(4), 347–367 (2012)
5. Chen, L., Nugent, C.D.: Ontology-based activity recognition in intelligent pervasive environments. Int. J. Web Inf. Syst. **5**(4), 410–430 (2009)

6. Chen, L., Nugent, C.D.: Is ontology-based activity recognition really effective? In: Pervasive Computing and Communications Workshops (PERCOM Workshops), pp. 427–431. IEEE (2011)
7. Compton, M., Barnaghi, P., Bermudez, L., Garca-Castro, L., Corcho, O., Cox, S., Graybeal, J., Hauswirth, M., Henson, C., Herzog, A., Huang, V., Janowicz, K., Kelsey, D., Le Phuoc, D., Lefort, L., Leggieri, M., Neuhaus, H., Nikolov, A., Page, K., Passant, A., Sheth, A., Taylor, K.: The SSN ontology of the W3C semantic sensor network incubator group. J. Web Semant. Sci. Serv. Agents World Wide Web **17**, 25–32 (2012)
8. Horrocks, I., Patel-Schneider, P.F., McGuinness, D.L., Welty, C.A.: OWL: a description logic based ontology language for the semantic web. In: Calvanese, D., McGuinness, D., Nardi, D., Patel-Schneider, P. (eds.) The Description Logic Handbook: Theory, Implementation, and Applications, 2nd edn. Cambridge University Press, Cambridge (2007)
9. Wongpatikaseree, K., Ikeda, M., Buranarach, M., Supnithi, T., Lim, A.O., Tan, Y.: Activity recognition using context-aware infrastructure ontology in smart home domain. In: International Conference on Knowledge, Information and Creativity Support Systems (KICSS), pp. 50–57. IEEE (2012)
10. Attard, J., Scerri, S., Rivera, I., Handschuh, S.: Ontology-based situation recognition for context-aware systems. In: International Conference on Semantic Systems, pp. 113–120 (2013)
11. Prud'hommeaux, E., Seaborne, A.: SPARQL query language for RDF. W3C Recommendation (2008)
12. Gebser, M., Kaminski, R., Kaufmann, B., Ostrowski, M., Schaub, T., Thiele, S.: Engineering an incremental ASP solver. In: Garcia de la Banda, M., Pontelli, E. (eds.) ICLP 2008. LNCS, vol. 5366, pp. 190–205. Springer, Heidelberg (2008)
13. Lifschitz, V.: What is answer set programming?. In: International Conference on Artificial Intelligence (AAAI), pp.1594–1597 (2008)
14. Shearer, R., Motik, B., Horrocks, I.: HermiT: a highly-efficient OWL reasoner. In: International Workshop on OWL: Experiences and Directions (OWLED EU), vol. 432, pp. 91–101 (2008)
15. Horridge, M., Drummond, N., Goodwin, J., Rector, A., Wang, H.: The manchester OWL syntax. Experiences and Directions (OWLED EU). In: International Workshop on OWL (2006)
16. Baader, F., Horrocks, I., Sattler, U.: Description logics as ontology languages for the semantic web. In: Hutter, D., Stephan, W. (eds.) Mechanizing Mathematical Reasoning. LNCS (LNAI), vol. 2605, pp. 228–248. Springer, Heidelberg (2005)
17. Pearce, T.C., Schiffman, S.S., Nagle, H.T., Gardner, J.W.: Handbook of Machine Olfaction: Electronic Nose Technology. Wiley-VCH, Hoboken (2003)
18. Alirezaie, M., Loutfi, A.: Reasoning for sensor data interpretation: an application to air quality monitoring. J. Ambient Intell. Smart Environ. (JAISE) **7**, 579–597 (2015)

Continuous Gait Velocity Analysis Using Ambient Sensors in a Smart Home

Ahmed Nait Aicha[1](✉), Gwenn Englebienne[2], and Ben Kröse[1,2]

[1] Department of Computer Science, Amsterdam University of Applied Sciences,
Amsterdam, The Netherlands
a.nait.aicha@hva.nl
http://www.digitallifecentre.nl
[2] Department of Computer Science, University of Amsterdam,
Amsterdam, The Netherlands

Abstract. We present a method for measuring gait velocity using data from an existing ambient sensor network. Gait velocity is an important predictor of fall risk and functional health. In contrast to other approaches that use specific sensors or sensor configurations our method imposes no constraints on the elderly. We studied different probabilistic models for the description of the sensor patterns. Experiments are carried out on 15 months of data and include repeated assessments from an occupational therapist. We showed that the measured gait velocities correlate with these assessments.

Keywords: Ambient assisted living (AAL) · Gait · Smart homes

1 Introduction

With the increasing number of older adults that live independently in their own homes, sensing systems that monitor someone's health are becoming popular. A wide range of sensor systems exists, often aimed at specific applications such as sleep monitoring or medicine intake monitoring. For more general lifestyle monitoring, ambient sensor networks consisting of motion and switch sensors mounted in the environment have been presented. In this paper, we focus on measuring gait velocity (walking speed) of elderly with such systems. Gait velocity is an important predictor of functional health; it is shown that it predicts the risk of falls [11,14], but also of hospitalization and survival [17]. For that reason, gait velocity is an important measure in comprehensive geriatric assessment in clinical settings.

The disadvantage of the clinical assessments is that the tests are usually carried out over a short period of time in an unnatural setting. In long term studies, regular measurements by a therapist are time consuming and therefore expensive. The measurements may also be subjective to the therapist taking the tests.

Continuous domestic monitoring may provide a clearer and more objective picture of a person's mobility. Systems have been presented that suggest specific

© Springer International Publishing Switzerland 2015
Kameas et al. (Eds.): AmI 2015, LNCS 9425, pp. 219–235, 2015.
DOI: 10.1007/978-3-319-26005-1_15

sensors in the home such as RGB-D cameras, radar sensors [20], motion sensors placed in an array [10], or use wearable sensors such as accelerometers [13].

We developed a system for measuring gait velocity from an existing ambient sensor network. Because the elderly are not instructed to follow predefined paths, the variations in walking patterns will be large. The contributions of this paper are: (1) we propose a method for automatically identifying useful paths for speed estimation, (2) we show that unconstrained daily activities result in non-trivial distributions over path durations and propose a model to deal with those (3) we investigate whether long paths or short paths provide a more consistent measurement of walking speed. Finally, we compared the results with measurements from an occupational therapist over a period of 15 months.

2   Related Work

Approaches for continuous walking speed assessment for elderly use either *wearable* sensors or *ambient* sensors. A review of wearable sensors for gait analysis is given in [18]. Apart from velocity, other characteristics of the gait may be measured such as under-foot pressure (the GaitShoe [2], the Smart Insole [21] and the In-Shoe device [5]) and rotation of the foot, that can be measured with gyroscopes. Pedometers are suitable for a long-term measurement of the physical activity. However, the accuracy of these pedometers is dependent of the implemented algorithm to count the steps. Furthermore, pedometers significantly underestimate the gait velocity of older adults [4]. The disadvantage of using wearable sensors in general for gate analysis is that the subject must not forget to wear the device and has to recharge it regularly. The acceptance of wearable sensor applications for long term monitoring is therefore low. Ambient pressure sensors can be used to build large sensor mats for the analysis of gait. GAITRite® is a portable electronic walkway of 0.89 m wide and between 5 and 8 m long where pressure sensors are embedded in a grid. This system is frequently used for clinical and research purposes [3,19]. Imaging devices such as the Microsoft Kinect have been presented to evaluate the gait [16]. The advantage of using the depth RGB-D is the ability to capture different parameters of gait such as walking speed, stride time and stride length. The disadvantages are, however, privacy related although only a silhouette of the subject is captured. An unobtrusive way for the continuous measurement of gait velocity is using motion sensors. A specific lay-out of motion sensors was used in [8], who mounted four motion sensors with a restricted view to ±4° in a line on the ceiling of a hallway with approximately 61 cm distance between them. The assumption of this method is that a long and narrow hallway is available to enforce the subject to walk in a line. This is not always the case in elderly apartments.

Frenken et al. [7] introduced a fully automated approach to calculate the Timed Up and Go (TUG), including the walking speed, using ambient sensors. These sensors consisting of force, light barriers and a Laser Range Scanner are incorporated in a chair to measure the walking direction and the speed. Both the

GAITRite® and the TUG-chair are suitable for periodic instrumented clinical tests, but the systems are expensive for continuous gait monitoring.

3   Sensor Data

We have continuously collected data, in several ambient assisted living apartments, for more than a year. The sensor networks used to collect data use the Z-Wave protocol and consist of off-the-shelf binary sensors that measure motion, pressure on the bed, toilet flush and the opening and closing of cabinets and doors. An overview of the location of the sensors in the apartment of one resident is shown in Fig. 1. The elderly are living their routine life and are not told to modify their behaviour in any way. The location of the sensors is chosen so that all the important rooms in the apartment are covered and so that the network does not affect the elderly's daily life. For instance, the pressure sensor for the bed is installed under the mattress and sensors in the kitchen are installed above the stove, under the freezer, etc. A list of the all the sensors installed in the apartement of volunteer A is shown in Table 1.

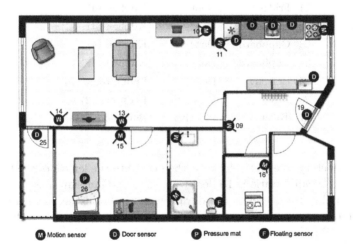

Fig. 1. A map of the apartment of volunteer A equipped with a wireless sensor network. Both apartments have the same basic size and layout. The number of used sensors, their types and their positions were kept as similar as possible between the two apartments.

4   Approach

To calculate the gait velocity, we collect the walking paths of the resident in his home during a period of time (*e.g.* week). We represent these walking paths by trajectories in a graph where the nodes represent sensors and the edges represent the distances between them, and calculate the corresponding durations. For each

Table 1. A list of the sensors (id, name, type and room) installed in the apartment of Volunteer A, as shown in Fig. 1. Cupboard1 contains coffee/tea items, cupboard2 contains spices and cupboard3 contains dinner dishes

Id	Sensor name	Sensor type	Room (number)
09	Hall	Motion	Hall (3)
10	Desk	Motion	Living room (6)
11	Kitchen	Motion	Kitchen (4)
12	Kitchen hob	Motion	Kitchen (4)
13	Living front	Motion	Living room (6)
14	Living back	Motion	Living room (6)
15	Bedroom	Motion	Bedroom (2)
16	Laundry	Motion	Laundry room (5)
17	Washbasin	Motion	Bathroom (1)
18	Shower	Motion	Bathroom (1)
19	Front Door	Door	Hall (3)
20	Freezer	Door	Kitchen (4)
21	Fridge	Door	Kitchen (4)
22	Cupboard1	Door	Kitchen (4)
23	Cupboard2	Door	Kitchen (4)
24	Cupboard3	Door	Kitchen (4)
25	Balcony	Door	Living room (6)
26	Bed	Pressure	Bedroom (2)
27	Toilet	Floating	Bathroom (1)

collected trajectory, the gait velocity is then equal to the length of the trajectory divided by its mean duration. To deal with the non-Gaussian noise in the data, we fit a probabilistic model to the durations and obtain the mean duration as an estimated parameter of the model. Before describing our approach in detail, we next describe the challenges involved.

4.1   Challenges

In instrumental tests, both the walking path and its duration are known. As the subject is instructed to walk without stopping, the gait velocity is therefore easy to compute. The calculation of the walking speed from ambient sensor data used for continuous monitoring is more challenging:

- The walking path is neither fixed nor precisely known, as the resident is not instructed to follow a specific walking path.
- The walking paths of the resident do not necessary follow straight lines.
- It is unknown if the resident's walking paths are interwoven with some other activity or not.

– Motion sensors do not provide us with accurate locations, and to save their batteries the sensors do not transmit every detection they make. The start time and location and the end time and location of the walking path are, therefore, not known precisely due to the nature of the sensors.
– There is more variation in the walking paths and speeds in natural conditions than during a controlled test.

4.2 Features

When the resident performs his activities of daily living during a period of time, the binary sensors generate a continuous stream of sensor-events. A sensor event $e_n = (t_n, s_n)$ is defined as a tuple consisting of the time stamp t_n of the sensor signal (ON or OFF) and the identity of the sensor that fired that signal, $s_n \in \{s_1, s_2, \ldots, s_{|S|}\}$[1]. The sequence of N sensor-events collected during some period of time can be represented as $e = <e_1, e_2, \ldots, e_N>$. The OFF-signals of the motion sensor correspond to the end of the sleep-time of the sensor. These OFF-signals are ignored as they do not necessarily correspond to the end of the movement of the resident. For the same reason, the OFF-signal of the float sensor is filtered out as this signal indicates the end of filling up the toilet water tank. Furthermore, if more than two consecutive sensor events come from the same sensor, only the first and last event are taken into account. The reason is that many consecutive events of a sensor usually do not correspond to a displacement of the resident, and we cannot associate any walking distance with them. For example, consecutive events of the bed sensor mean that the resident is changing his posture. Finally, the sensor events corresponding to visits to the resident are automatically detected and excluded from the data under consideration [12]. The method used, Markov Modulated Multidimensional non-homogeneous Poisson Process (M3P2), is an extension of the Markov Modulated Poisson Process (MMPP) to allow the incorporation of multiple feature streams. The periodic portion of these features is modeled using a non-homogeneous Poisson process, while the visits are modeled using a hidden state that varies according a Markov process.

To estimate gait velocity, we rely on sensor transitions $\tau_{ij}^{(n)}$ and their associated duration d_n. Let a transition between sensors i and j be a pair of consecutive sensor events e_n and e_{n+1}, where $s_n = i$ and $s_{n+1} = j$. The time stamp of the transition is chosen to be t_n and its duration is defined as $d_n = t_{n+1} - t_n$.

4.3 Model

We represent the walking paths of the resident in his home by trajectories in a graph. Figure 2 shows a graph of all possible walking paths of volunteer A. The node identities in this figure correspond to the sensors shown in Fig. 1. The sensor ids, indicating the location of the resident, are used as nodes and the

---

[1] The actual value of the event is not relevant to our purposes: we are interested in the knowledge that the resident is present at a certain location, not in their activity.

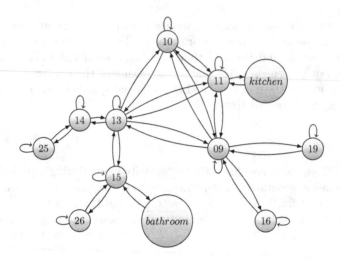

Fig. 2. A graph indicating the sensors that are topologically connected to each other. The node ids correspond to the sensor ids depicted in Fig. 1. The node kitchen (resp. bathroom) consists of six (resp three) sensors that are topologically connected to each other. These sensors are omitted to keep the overview of the graph clear

sensor-transitions, indicating the movement of the resident, are used as edges. As example, a trajectory corresponding to sensor sequence $< 15, 27, 17 >$ consists of three nodes and two edges. This trajectory represents the walking path 'bedroom-toilet-washbasin' resulted from a toileting activity.

The mathematical representation of the graph is $G = (V, E)$ where $V = \{s_1, s_2, \cdots, s_{|V|}\}$ and $E = \{(i, j) | \ i$ is topologically connected to $j\}$. To calculate the average gait velocity in a period of time, we assume that the average duration of typical paths in the house is representative of the person's gait velocity. For the calculation of the duration of the walking paths, we follow the approach:

1. We define a set of rules to create automatically extract valid walking paths (trajectories) from the sensor data and calculate the duration of the collected trajectories
2. Construct a model consisting of some (mixture of) probability distributions(s) to fit these durations (data points).
3. From this model, we extract the mean duration of each path and compute the corresponding walking speed.

Identification of Valid Trajectories: Given a sequence of sensor events $< e_1, e_2, \ldots, e_N >$ collected during a period of time T (e.g. a week), we need to identify subsequences that correspond to actual walking. We do this by cutting this sequence at edge $(n, n + 1)$ if its duration $d_n = t_{n+1} - t_n$ is larger than some threshold τ. Cutting the sequence at $(n, n + 1)$ means that one walking path ends with event e_n and a new path starts with event e_{n+1}. The variable τ

correspond to a 'rest moment' of the resident. This cutting action results in K sensor sequence segments. Some segments correspond to the movement of the subject in the same room and are therefore not suitable for the calculation of the gait velocity. Other segments, on the other hand, correspond to long and complex activities. These activities may contain walking paths that are suitable for the calculation of the gait velocity. Therefore, two possibilities to extract valid potential walking trajectories from theses segments have been investigated:

1. Automatically detect all trajectories that involve at least two rooms to ensure that the collected trajectories correspond to a movement of the resident and not to some activity in a room. These trajectories are referred as *auto-detected* trajectories.
2. Search within the K segments for some predefined walking trajectories. These predefined walking trajectories are as long and straight as possible. The objective is to collect trajectories similar to the walking path used by the therapist to measure the gait velocity. They are selected by manually inspecting the map of the apartment of the older adult. These trajectories are referred as *predefined* trajectories.

For all the collected trajectories, both auto-detected and predefined, the corresponding duration is calculated.

Modelling the Durations of the Trajectories: The Poisson is a widely used distribution to model time durations and is the correct model to use if our collected sequences all correspond to the same physical walking path in the space. We therefore selected this distribution as a candidate model for the duration of the collected trajectories. Some trajectories may, however, sometimes be interwoven with another trajectory, in which case a mixture of Poisson distributions would be a more accurate model. Trajectories may also be interwoven with one or more activities, whose duration is not adequately modelled by a Poisson distribution. We therefore also selected a mixture of a Poisson and a Normal distribution as a candidate model.

In our experiments we evaluated the following set of three candidate models:

1. a Poisson distribution with parameter $\Theta_1 = \lambda$,
2. a mixture of two Poisson distributions with parameters $\Theta_2 = (\alpha, \lambda_1, \lambda_2)$,
3. a mixture of a Poisson and a Normal distribution $\Theta_3 = (\alpha, \lambda, \mu, \sigma)$.

The probability distribution function (PDF) of a Poisson and a Normal distribution are given in Eqs. 1 and 2. The PDF of a mixture a Poisson and a Normal distribution is given in Eq. 3. The PDF of the mixtures of two Poisson distributions can be obtained in the same way.

$$P(k) = \frac{\lambda^k}{k!} e^{-\lambda} \tag{1}$$

$$P(k) = \frac{1}{\sigma\sqrt{2\pi}} e^{-(k-\mu)^2/2\sigma^2} \tag{2}$$

$$P(k) = \alpha \frac{\lambda^k}{k!} e^{-\lambda} + (1-\alpha) \frac{1}{\sigma\sqrt{2\pi}} e^{-(k-\mu)^2/2\sigma^2} \tag{3}$$

We estimated the parameters α, λ, λ_1, λ_2, μ, and σ maximizing the likelihood.

Calculate a Goodness of Fit Function of the Constructed Distributions: After fitting the durations with different probability distributions, the goodness of fit is calculated using the Akaike information criterion (AIC) and the Bayesian information criterion (BIC) metrics given by:

$$AIC = -2\log(\hat{L}) + 2K \tag{4}$$

$$BIC = -2\log(\hat{L}) + K\log(N) \tag{5}$$

In these equations, $\hat{L}$ represents the likelihood function of the model, K represents the number of parameters of the model and N is the number of observations. Both AIC [1] and BIC [15] metrics measure a penalised likelihood of the model. The penalty portion of AIC is only dependent of the number of the parameters of the model, while the penalty of the BIC is also dependent of the number of observations.

5   Experiments

5.1   Objectives

A set of three experiments is conducted to collect useful walking paths, to find the best model and to evaluate the resulting gait velocity. In the **first experiment**, we investigate the effect of varying the duration of the rest time on the resulting trajectories, and find the optimal value of τ for our dataset. Our hypothesis is that small values of τ will result in the collection of few useful trajectories (*i.e.*, trajectories involving at least two rooms), while large values of τ result in long sensor trajectories corresponding to walking paths with too many interwoven activities. We seek for a value of τ that results in sufficient useful trajectories, so that we can estimate our model parameters accurately, and that does not result in too many trajectories with interwoven activities.

In the **second experiment**, we show that the duration of the collected trajectories cannot be modelled optimally with a simple, unimodal distribution. Our hypothesis consists of two parts: on one hand, we expect the most frequently *auto-detected* trajectories to be short (between rooms) and therefore should be fitted by one probability distribution as these trajectories correspond to walking paths without interwoven activities. On the other hand, the *predefined* trajectories are long and may correspond to walking paths with interwoven activities and therefore need to be fitted using a mixture of probability distributions.

In the **third experiment**, we compare the walking speed measured occasionally by the therapist with the gait velocity estimated from the sensor data. Our hypothesis is that the walking speed measured by the therapist is higher than the gait velocity estimated from the sensor data, because the residents tend to improve their behaviour as a response of being watched. We also expect the estimated gait velocity to correlate with the motor Assessment of Motor and Processing Skills (AMPS) measured by the therapist.

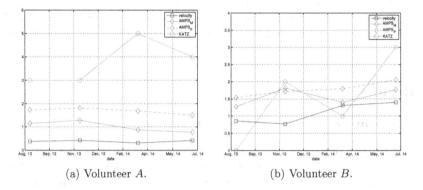

(a) Volunteer A.   (b) Volunteer B.

Fig. 3. Ground truth data consisting of the AMPS, KATZ and the gait velocity test over 3 m distance. The gait velocity (m/s) is rlepeated twice and the mean value is notated. An increase of the KATZ score $(\{0, 1, \ldots, 6\})$ indicates more need of assistance. A decrease of the AMPS $([-3, 4])$ indicates a decrease in the functional health. The exact assessment dates for both volunteers are '14-Aug-2013', '20-Nov-2013', '14-Mar-2014' and '27-Jun-2014'.

5.2 Sensor Data and Annotation

Two sensor datasets collected in our living labs are used to conduct the described experiments. The two sensor datasets are collected during 15 months between April 2013 and July 2014 in the apartment of two volunteers living alone. Volunteer A, a male of 84 years old, has difficulties with getting up from a chair and with walking. He occasionally walks in the apartment using a wheelchair as a support. Volunteer B, a female of 80 years old, has no difficulty with walking in her apartment. During this period, the two volunteers are visited by a therapist for the KATZ [9] and AMPS assessments [6]. The walking speed test taken over 3 meters is part of these assessments. The results of these assessments are given in Fig. 3. The KATZ-score varies between a minimum value of 0, indicating the subject needs NO assistance, and a maximum value of 6 indicating the subject is dependent of assistance for performing the Activities of Daily Livings (ADLs). Two values of the AMPS, the motor part $(AMPS_M)$ related to physical skills and the process part $(AMPS_P)$ related to cognitive skills, are calculated from the assessment. A decrease of the AMPS indicate a decrease in the functional health of the subject.

The assessment scores show an approximately stable functional health of volunteer A during this period of 15 months. This may be concluded from the gait velocity and the AMPS scores, which show no significant increase or decrease. For volunteer B, however, the assessment scores show an increase of the gait velocity and of the process AMPS, indicating the subject's functional health is improving. On the other hand, the increasing of the KATZ score indicates the subject needs assistance for preforming her ADLs, which is conflicting with the improvement of her functional health. Her motor AMPS is stable during this period.

6   Results

6.1   Experiment 1: Effect of the Rest Time τ

For each subject, we collected sensor data around the dates the therapist conducted the KATZ and AMPS assessments. We ensured that the selected weeks do not lack any sensor data. This resulted in 9 weeks of sensor data around the 4 assessment dates given in Fig. 3. From these 9 sequences of sensor readings, valid trajectories are extracted using the two proposed methods, *auto-detected* and *predefined* trajectories, as described in Sect. 4.

The frequency of the collected auto-detected trajectories as a function of the rest moment τ show that most auto-detected trajectories have a low frequency, which means that during a week, many unique trajectories are collected. For example, Fig. 4(a) shows that for $\tau = 10$ more than 96 % of the collected 713 trajectories have a frequency lower than 10. Comparable figures hold for the other values of $\tau \in \{5, 8, \ldots, 70\}$. The plot, given in Fig. 4(b), of the most frequently collected auto-detected trajectories (the peaks in the histograms) as a function of τ show that $\tau = 30$ gives us the largest number of auto-detected trajectories for which a good model fit can be expected.

Conducting the same experiment using the sensor data of volunteer A resulted in an 'optimal' value of $\tau = 60$ for collecting both auto-detected and predefined trajectories. Note that this higher values of τ for volunteer A compared to volunteer B correlates with the measured low walking speed of volunteer A compared to volunteer B.

6.2   Experiment 2: Modelling Trajectory Length

In this experiment, we have selected 9 weeks of sensor data similar to the first experiment and we used the 'optimal' values of τ found in experiment 1. For the collected trajectories, the durations are calculated and fitted to the selected three models. For each trajectory we calculated the AIC and BIC values. Figure 5 gives an example of the observed durations in a histogram and the fitted mixture of a Poisson and a Normal distribution.

Table 2 shows the AIC and BIC average values for the two most frequently auto-detected trajectories. These results show that the Poisson distribution fits

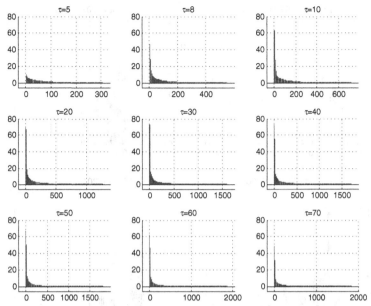

(a) Histogram of the durations of auto-detected trajectories using different values of τ.

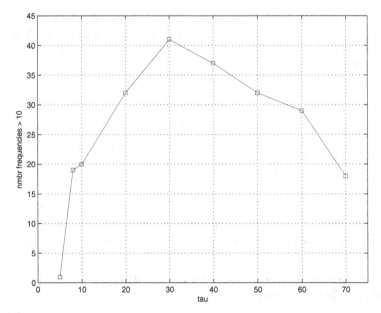

(b) Frequency of collected auto-detected trajectories, with at least 10 occurrences, versus τ.

Fig. 4. Visualisation of the collected auto-detected trajectories using different values of τ. Nine weeks of sensor data is used to collect these trajectories. The chosen weeks are around the assessment dates conducted by the occupational therapist.

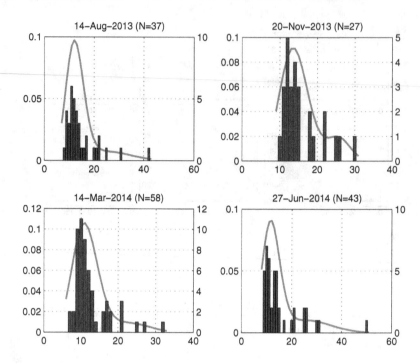

Fig. 5. A histogram of the duration of the collected *'living room back to kitchen'* trajectories. The data is fitted using a mixture of a Poisson and a Normal distribution. The X-axis denotes the durations, the Y-axis denotes the estimated probability and the Z-axis denotes the observed frequencies.

the calculated duration less well than the two mixtures of probabilities. We may conclude that the most frequently walked paths during a week are almost always interwoven with some other activity. We therefore reject the first part of our hypothesis that these auto-detected trajectories are best fit using one distribution.

Table 3 shows the average AIC and BIC scores for the four collected predefined trajectories. Overall, we see that the mixture of a Poisson and a Normal distribution gives the best fit. This is conform the second part of our hypothesis.

6.3   Experiment 3: Occasional Versus Continuous Measurement of the Gait Velocity

To compare the gait velocity measured occasionally by the therapist with the gait velocity estimated from the sensor data, we used sensor data collected during three weeks around the AMPS and KATZ assessment day: the week the assessment is conducted, the week before and the week after the assessment. This resulted in 12 weeks of sensor data for the 4 assessments dates given in

Table 2. Results of goodness of fit of the selected (mixture of) distributions applied to the collected top three *auto-detected* trajectories. The AIC and BIC values are calculated using 9 weeks of sensor data of volunteer A collected around the KATZ and AMPS assessment dates.

Collected trajectories	AIC and BIC of the model with parameter					
	$\Theta_1 = \lambda$		$\Theta_2 = (\alpha, \lambda_1, \lambda_2)$		$\Theta_3 = (\alpha, \lambda, \mu, \sigma)$	
Liv room front - kitchen	208.86	209.62	136.92	139.19	132.37	135.40
Toilet - bedroom	142.56	143.27	114.74	116.89	115.07	117.94
Kitchen - Liv room front	135.91	136.77	121.12	123.69	119.86	123.30

Table 3. Results of goodness of fit of the selected (mixture of) distributions applied to the collected *predefined* trajectories. The AIC and BIC values are calculated using 9 weeks of sensor data of volunteer B collected around the KATZ and AMPS assessment dates.

Collected trajectories	AIC and BIC of the model with parameter					
	$\Theta_1 = \lambda$		$\Theta_2 = (\alpha, \lambda_1, \lambda_2)$		$\Theta_3 = (\alpha, \lambda, \mu, \sigma)$	
Front door - Liv room back	162.71	155.52	120.96	118.21	113.65	115.89
Hall - Liv room back	347.17	348.22	229.97	233.12	196.58	200.78
Liv room back - Front door	178.86	171.26	117.18	115.02	112.40	114.38
Liv room back -Hall	469.79	471.16	283.17	287.26	250.17	255.63

Fig. 3. For this experiment, the value of τ and the probabilistic model found in the first two experiments are used, meaning that we fit a mixture of a Poisson distribution and a Normal distribution to the data. The value of λ, corresponding to the mean of the Poisson distribution, is used as the estimated duration. Using the distance of the collected trajectories obtained from the map of the apartment, we were able to estimate the average gait velocity from the sensor data.

Figure 6 gives the gait velocity estimated from twelve weeks of sensor data, its corresponding confidence interval and the walking speed measured by the therapist. The results show that, for volunteer A, the walking speed value measured by the therapist is higher that the average gait velocity estimated from sensor data. In two of the four measurements is this value significantly higher. For volunteer B, all measurements of the therapist are significantly higher than the gait velocity estimated from sensor data. These results are conform to our hypothesis that the subjects tend to improve their behaviour as a response of being assessed. Using a sample t-test, we tested the null hypothesis that the estimated gait velocity values come from independent normal distributions with equal means. The results ($p > 0.4$) show no significant increase of decrease of the gait velocity for both subjects during the period of 15 months, which is conform their motor AMPS.

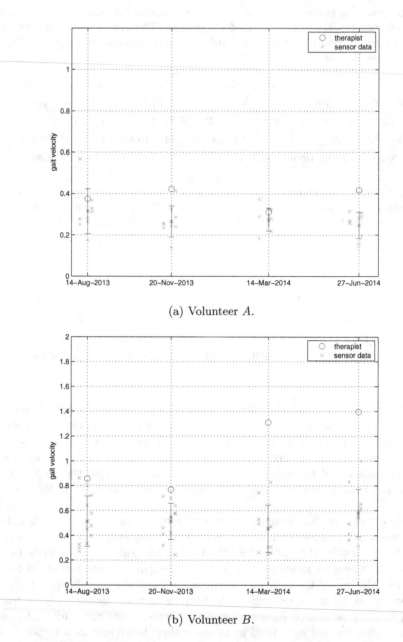

(a) Volunteer A.

(b) Volunteer B.

Fig. 6. Gait velocity measured by the therapist and estimated using a mixture of a Poisson and a Normal distribution with parameter $\Theta_3 = (\alpha, \lambda, \mu, \sigma)$. Each data point represents λ of one predefined trajectory collected during one week. The confidence interval of the estimated speed is also given. Four predefined trajectories and three weeks around the AMPS and KATZ assessment day are used.

7   Conclusion

This study shows the potential of continuously monitoring the indoor gait velocity of older adults living alone using a simple sensor network. We have shown that unconstrained behaviour leads to a multimodal distribution of path durations, as walking is interwoven with other activities. We have shown that we can nevertheless extract the gait velocity from unconstrained sensor data, by fitting a mixture model to the durations. In particular, the results show that the durations of the collected trajectories can be best fitted using a mixture of a Poisson and a Normal distribution as a model. Apart from the gait velocity, the method also allows us to detect the most recurrent indoor walking trajectories.

We applied this model to two sets of sensor data collected in a period of 15 months. Our results showed that the estimated gait velocity was conform the motor AMPS scores extracted from the assessments conducted by an occupational therapist. In accordance with the findings of [20], our results also show that the walking speed measured by the therapist is significantly higher than the average gait velocity. The subjects tend to improve their behaviour as a response of being assessed.

In a real-time situation, we could imagine a sliding window of one week needed to collect enough valid walking trajectories to be fitted by the model. In future work, we will extend the short period of 15 months during which data was collected, and during which the functional health of our volunteers did not change significantly. Moreover, the few assessments of the therapist do not provide a solid ground truth about the functional health of the resident. Currently, our group is involved in a monitoring older adults after having a hip surgery using comparable sensor networks. This project gives an opportunity to apply our findings to a new situation where we expect the walking speed to increase in a relative short period, as the functional health of these subjects gets better during the rehabilitation. It will be fascinating to have the same pattern from the gait velocity estimated from the sensor data. An interesting future challenge is the measurement of the gait velocity in a multi-person home setting.

Acknowledgments. This work is part of the research programs SIA-raak Smart Systems for Smart Services, Health-lab and COMMIT. The authors would like to thank the participants at Vivium Zorggroep Naarderheem.

References

1. Akaike, H.: A new look at the statistical model identification. IEEE Trans. Autom. Control **19**(6), 716–723 (1974)
2. Bamberg, S., Benbasat, A., Scarborough, D., Krebs, D., Paradiso, J.: Gait analysis using a shoe-integrated wireless sensor system. IEEE Trans. Inf. Technol. Biomed. **12**(4), 413–423 (2008)
3. Bilney, B., Morris, M., Webster, K.: Concurrent related validity of the gaitrite® walkway system for quantification of the spatial and temporal parameters of gait. Gait Posture **17**(1), 68–74 (2003)

4. Cyarto, E.V., Myers, A., Tudor-Locke, C.: Pedometer accuracy in nursing home and community-dwelling older adults. Med. Sci. Sports Exerc. **36**(2), 205–209 (2004)
5. De Rossi, S., Lenzi, T., Vitiello, N., Donati, M., Persichetti, A., Giovacchini, F., Vecchi, F., Carrozza, M.: Development of an in-shoe pressure-sensitive device for gait analysis. In: 2011 Annual International Conference of the IEEE Engineering in Medicine and Biology Society, EMBC, pp. 5637–5640. IEEE (2011)
6. Fisher, A.G., Jones, K.B.: Assessment of Motor And Process Skills. Three Star Press, Fort Collins (1999)
7. Frenken, T., Vester, B., Brell, M., Hein, A.: aTUG: fully-automated timed up and go assessment using ambient sensor technologies. In: 2011 5th International Conference on Pervasive Computing Technologies for Healthcare (PervasiveHealth), pp. 55–62, May 2011
8. Hagler, S., Austin, D., Hayes, T.L., Kaye, J., Pavel, M.: Unobtrusive and ubiquitous in-home monitoring: a methodology for continuous assessment of gait velocity in elders. IEEE Trans. Biomed. Eng. **57**(4), 813–820 (2010)
9. Katz, S., Ford, A.B., Moskowitz, R.W., Jackson, B.A., Jaffe, M.W.: Studies of illness in the aged: the index of adl: a standardized measure of biological and psychosocial function. Jama **185**(12), 914–919 (1963)
10. Kaye, J.A., Maxwell, S.A., Mattek, N., Hayes, T.L., Dodge, H., Pavel, M., Jimison, H.B., Wild, K., Boise, L., Zitzelberger, T.A.: Intelligent systems for assessing aging changes: home-based, unobtrusive, and continuous assessment of aging. J. Gerontol. Ser. B Psychol. Sci. Soc. Sci. **66**(suppl 1), i180–i190 (2011)
11. Montero-Odasso, M., Schapira, M., Soriano, E.R., Varela, M., Kaplan, R., Camera, L.A., Mayorga, L.M.: Gait velocity as a single predictor of adverse events in healthy seniors aged 75 years and older. J. Gerontol. Ser. A Biol. Sci. Med. Sci. **60**(10), 1304–1309 (2005)
12. Nait Aicha, A., Englebienne, G., Kröse, B.: Modeling visit behaviour in smart homes using unsupervised learning. In: Proceedings of the 2014 ACM International Joint Conference on Pervasive and Ubiquitous Computing, pp. 1193–1200. Adjunct Publication, ACM (2014)
13. Plasqui, G., Bonomi, A., Westerterp, K.: Daily physical activity assessment with accelerometers: new insights and validation studies. Obes. Rev. **14**(6), 451–462 (2013)
14. Quach, L., Galica, A.M., Jones, R.N., Procter-Gray, E., Manor, B., Hannan, M.T., Lipsitz, L.A.: The nonlinear relationship between gait speed and falls: the maintenance of balance, independent living, intellect, and zest in the elderly of boston study. J. Am. Geriatr. Soc. **59**(6), 1069–1073 (2011)
15. Schwarz, G., et al.: Estimating the dimension of a model. Ann. Stat. **6**(2), 461–464 (1978)
16. Stone, E., Skubic, M.: Evaluation of an inexpensive depth camera for in-home gait assessment. J. Ambient Intell. Smart Environ. **3**(4), 349–361 (2011)
17. Studenski, S., Perera, S., Patel, K., Rosano, C., Faulkner, K., Inzitari, M., Brach, J., Chandler, J., Cawthon, P., Connor, E.B., et al.: Gait speed and survival in older adults. Jama **305**(1), 50–58 (2011)
18. Tao, W., Liu, T., Zheng, R., Feng, H.: Gait analysis using wearable sensors. Sensors **12**(2), 2255–2283 (2012)
19. Van Uden, C.J., Besser, M.P.: Test-retest reliability of temporal and spatial gait characteristics measured with an instrumented walkway system (gaitrite). BMC Musculoskelet. Disord. **5**(1), 13 (2004)

20. Wang, F., Stone, E., Skubic, M., Keller, J.M., Abbott, C., Rantz, M.: Towards a passive low-cost in-home gait assessment system for older adults. IEEE J. Biomed. Health Inf. **17**(2), 346–355 (2013)
21. Xu, W., Huang, M.C., Amini, N., Liu, J.J., He, L., Sarrafzadeh, M.: Smart insole: a wearable system for gait analysis. In: Proceedings of the 5th International Conference on PErvasive Technologies Related to Assistive Environments, p. 18. ACM (2012)

ExerSeat - Sensor-Supported Exercise System for Ergonomic Microbreaks

Andreas Braun[1]([✉]), Ingrid Schembri[2], and Sebastian Frank[3]

[1] Fraunhofer Institute for Computer Graphics Research IGD, Darmstadt, Germany
andreas.braun@igd.fraunhofer.de
[2] Department of Industrial Engineering & Management,
Aalto University, Espoo, Finland
ingrid.schembri@aalto.fi
[3] RheinMain University of Applied Sciences, Mainz, Germany
SebastianFrank87@gmx.de

Abstract. The percentage of older adult workers in Europe has been increasing in the last decades. They are an important part of the work force, highly experienced and often hard to replace. However, their productivity can be affected by health problems, such as lower back pain. This increases the cost for employers and reduces the quality of life of the office workers. Knowledge workers that spend a large part of their day in front of a screen are particularly affected by pack pain. Regular exercise can help to mitigate some of these issues. This training can be performed in microbreaks that are taken at regular intervals during the work day. In this work we present ExerSeat, a combination of a smart sensing chair that uses eight capacitive proximity sensors to precisely track the posture of persons on or near an office chair. It is augmented by a desktop training software that is able to track exercises and training units during microbreaks, by analyzing frequency and form. We have performed a pilot over eight weeks with ten office workers. They performed training units at regular intervals during their work day. We report on the findings.

Keywords: Smart furniture · Capacitive proximity sensing · Office exercise · Microbreaks · Ergonomics · New Ways of Working · Well-being

1 Introduction

As a crucial component in tackling the challenges of population ageing in Europe, the Stockholm European Council agreed on increasing the employment rate of persons between 55–64 to 50 %. While this goal was not met, the overall rate rose from 37 % in 2000 to 46 % in 2010 [9]. Lower back pain correlates with age and a sedentary lifestyle [22]. Knowledge workers spend a considerable portion of their work time in front of a screen. Thus, older adult knowledge workers combine several risk factors.

© Springer International Publishing Switzerland 2015
Kameas et al. (Eds.): AmI 2015, LNCS 9425, pp. 236–251, 2015.
DOI: 10.1007/978-3-319-26005-1_16

To reduce the social and economic cost of ergonomic-related ailments, a variety of countermeasures have been proposed that range from standing desks and other ergonomic furniture, to general daily exercise sessions for all types of workers. A more individual solution are microbreak exercises [15]. During these breaks at regular intervals, the desk worker is asked to stop working for a few minutes and walk around or perform certain exercises. This has been proven effective in preventing lower back pain if performed regularly [16].

In this work we present ExerSeat, a work space exercise solution, based on a microbreak training application and a sensor-equipped smart chair. Using stored profiles and occupation, the application can launch various exercises at intervals of the worker's choice. The smart chair uses capacitive proximity sensing technology that detects the presence of a human body and determines postures with a high precision. ExerSeat encourages the user to perform simple exercises, while the software tracks the progress. Two microbreak triggers are presented: a fixed setting allowing the user to start exercises after a set time and a dynamic setting which is calculated after a certain time of occupation of the chair.

We contribute a novel method for sensing detailed posture on a smart chair. Using an idealized and simplified multi-volume body of the human body, we use a defined process to translate normalized sensor values into positions of joints. We show how this can be used to track a set of five exercises that can be combined to training units. ExerSeat has been evaluated over eight weeks in a pilot at a knowledge work environment in Finland. We present the setup and findings of this study.

2   Related Works

For this work we have considered three strands of related work. The domain of New Ways of Working explores processes and methods that improve modern work environments. Detecting human postures has been a research topic for many years. We present relevant works that use complex models for fitting a human body to known postures. Finally, the independent domain of smart furniture is strongly interlinked with ExerSeat. We present recent works in this area.

2.1   New Ways of Working

New Ways of Working (NewWoW) or Alternative Work Programs are becoming increasingly popular in Knowledge Work organizations both for cost motivations and for attracting new talent or retaining expert workers [1]. Most scholars and practitioners agree that Knowledge Work Environments are supported by enablers of the technological, physical and social kind. Recognizing working styles and providing suitable support for workers to comfortably and safely carry out their daily activities can help reduce the economic and personal cost of work injuries [8]. While salaries and benefits remain an organizations primary cost, it is a poignant reminder that a majority of office workers in the Western world have some time of absence from work due to poor ergonomic arrangements or inflexible work environments [1]. Desk workers are particularly affected by back pain caused from a sedentary working style. Physical activity during the day that is geared towards strengthening core muscles can contribute to increased well-being [16]. With regards to how the office chair contributes to well-being at work, Zemp et al. performed a meta-study that shows that pressure distribution is a good measure for comfort or discomfort, particularly peak pressure on the seat pan, pressure distribution on the back rest and changes in pressure patterns [23]. ExerSeat can be a technological enabler for a work environment that adapts to human and stimulates activity. Used alone or in combination with other enablers it can reinforce healthier working habits.

2.2 Posture Sensing

Harada et al. use a 3D representation of a statistically average human body that can freely move various joints [13]. This allows to detect a variety of postures, in this case using an iterative process based on potential energy, momentum and difference between the actual and simulated pressure distribution. Using such full body models, based on an internal skeleton of connected joints is also common in full body gesture tracking systems. However, while in those cases the volume of the body parts is important, there is typically no additional physical simulation of properties, such as weight and density [19].

Tan et al. have created a sensing chair that uses a pressure mat to detect posture [20]. They create pressure maps from the sensor data and calculate *eigenpostures*, which are eigenvectors calculated to best represent the variation between maps of the same posture. The system distinguishes 14 postures and uses training data collected from 20 users. The classification accuracy per posture is between 90.3 % and 99.8 %. Nazari et al. created the Aware Chair - a system based on eight binary pressure sensors that is able to distinguish eight postures of a user on an office chair [18]. Using a state-machine classification they were able to correctly identify 48 % of postures in a large study with 50 users.

2.3 Smart Furniture

Grosse-Puppendahl et al. have created a smart couch that infers body posture of one or two persons using hidden capacitive proximity sensors [12]. Eight sensors in the armrest, seat and back of the couch are sufficient to identify eight poses with a precision of 97 %. Based on the same technology Braun et al. created a smart floor system and a capacitive chair [3,5]. The latter places a combination of flexible, solid, and thread electrodes in seat, backrest and armrests. The sensor values are mapped to four postures using SVM classification. The achieved recall is 99 %. Another system in this domain is a bed frame equipped with capacitive sensors that detects posture of one or two occupants and estimates the strain on the spine using an approximated pressure distribution [4].

The Health Chair by Griffiths et al. uses pressure sensors in the backrest to detect the respiratory rate from chest movement and EKG electrodes on the armrests to measure the heart rate [10]. They performed a pre-study with several hundred users to find common sitting postures. They have optimized their data processing for detecting physiological signals of users in those postures. They conducted a study with 18 users that were taking poses on an equipped chair. The Health Chair was able to detect the heart rate in 32 % of the cases and respiratory rate 52 % of the time.

Liang et al. have investigated direct control of systems using smart pressure-sensitive cushions [14]. With a sparse collection of pressure sensors they are able to control a wheel chair by changing the body posture and a computer game.

3   Posture Recognition Using a Capacitive Chair

When acquiring capacitive proximity sensor data from physical objects, it is often difficult, or even impossible to analytically describe the resulting value. There are numerous environmental factors influencing the signal and the properties of the object might not be clearly determined [6]. Considering the human body, there is a mostly unconstrained number of sizes, shapes and biological properties that influence the response to an electric field. Thus, in order to fit sensor outputs to the potential object configurations, simplified models can be used that resemble the actual physical effects, yet can be described analytically. Models based on a single geometric object are considered single-body, while connected geometric objects that comprise a single model can be called multi-body.

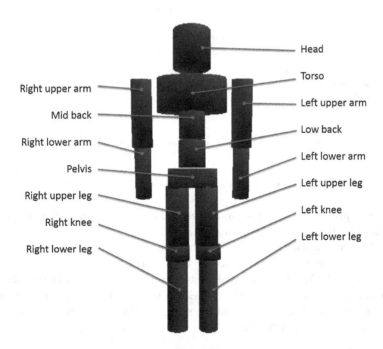

Fig. 1. ExerSeat skeleton model and associated body parts

Figure 1 shows the skeleton model used in ExerSeat. It is comprised of 15 groups. An unconnected model of 15 volumes that can translate and rotate freely has 90 degrees of-freedom (DOF). As the groups are connected to each other and we restrict the rotational freedom, the DOF are significantly reduced to just 10. Sensors close to the various body parts will modify the associated parts of the model. As an example, the distance of the left lower arm group is determined by the sensor in the left armrest. However, as the groups are connected, this will also modify the orientation of the left upper arm. Accordingly, if the sensor behind in the lower backrest detects a receding lower back, the position and orientation of the other back groups, head and arms are also modified. Thus, the fitting method attempts to place the groups of the model according to current sensor readings. A collection of rules is used that follows the flowchart outlined in Fig. 2.

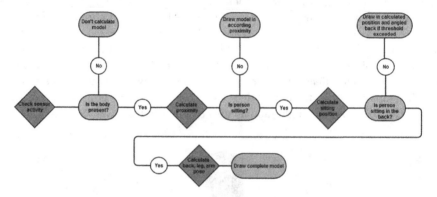

Fig. 2. Flowchart of the model fitting process of the grouped skeleton parts and performed calculations

The process for posture detection is following these steps:

1. *Check sensor activity* uses a threshold for each sensor to determine the presence of any objects in range. This can be used to identify a user approaching the chair.
2. *Calculate proximity* uses a second threshold for the sensors of the seat pan to distinguish sitting and non-sitting.
3. *Calculate sitting position* uses a weighted average of the seat pan sensors to determine if a person is sitting in the front of the back.
4. *Calculate back, leg, arm pose* calculates back pose by determining distance from different parts of the back to backrest sensors. Raise leg measures proximity to the sensors in the front of the seat pan. Calculate arm uses proximity to the sensors on the arm rests.

This method allows a fine-grained fitting of the model to the sensor values that closely resembles the pictures of a person moving in the chair. A number

Fig. 3. Screenshots of the ExerSeat application showing different poses of the skeleton model

of poses and the accordingly fitted 3D models using this method can be seen in Fig. 3. Exemplifying this process for the pose on the bottom right of Fig. 3. The sensors are active and a person is present. The person is sitting on the chair, as sensor values are high enough. The person is sitting on the back of the seat pan, as determined by the weighted average. The back is close to the backrest, the legs are put down on the seat pan. The left arm is raised and not on the arm rest.

4   ExerSeat Microbreak Training

The ExerSeat microbreak training system uses the posture recognition described in the previous section. The user has to take specific poses that are defined by the position of the joints. A single exercise is composed of poses that have to be taken by the user in order. Types of exercises and their number of repetitions can be freely combined to training units. These are triggered at regular intervals. We distinguish two types of triggers. Static triggers are executed after a certain amount of time. Dynamic triggers execute based on context, e.g. the time the chair has been occupied or level of work activity in a given period. ExerSeat currently supports the following five exercises that can be arbitrarily combined to training units:

- Back bend - a straight back is moved to the left and right with arms outstretched
- Back up - with a fixed sitting position lower the upper body to the legs - try to touch feet with hands and go back up
- Bicycles - sequentially raise the left and right leg from the chair
- Squat - with arms stretched to the front stand up from chair and sit back down
- Sit up - sitting upright on the front of the seat - lower straight back to the backrest and bring it back up

4.1   Modeling of Posture Based Exercises

As previously mentioned, the exercises are composed of poses that have to be taken in order. These poses are defined by joints of the fitted model, meeting certain criteria. These criteria and additional meta information are defined in XML files. The states are outlined in the following listing and an example is shown in Fig. 4 on the left.

- Preferred view matrix (so the user may better see certain aspects of the joint movements in 3D view
- Start pose specification as indicated by all joint positions defined via smaller than, larger than or equal to criteria
- Start pose specification as indicated by all joint positions defined via smaller than, larger than or equal to criteria

```
                                              <TrainingProgram >
                                                <trainingUnits>
                                                  <TrainingUnit>
                                                    <exercise>SQUAT</exercise>
                                                    <NumberOfReps>10</NumberOfReps>
                                                  </TrainingUnit>
<TrainingExerciseSpecification>                   <TrainingUnit>
  <direction>BIGGER_THAN</direction>                <exercise>SITUP</exercise>
  <jointValue>4</jointValue>                         <NumberOfReps>10</NumberOfReps>
  <jointName>LOWERBACK Y</jointName>              </TrainingUnit>
</TrainingExerciseSpecification>                </trainingUnits>
                                                <programName>SquatSit</programName>
                                              </TrainingProgram>
```

Fig. 4. Listings of joint posture specification for a specific exercise (left) and a training unit comprised of multiple exercises (right).

Multiple exercises comprise a training program that is defined in an XML file, using combinations of exercises. Figure 4 on the right shows a training unit comprised of 10 squat exercises and 10 sit ups.

4.2   Triggering of Training Programs

Microbreaks are interruptions of the work day occurring at regular intervals, e.g. hourly. There are numerous applications on the market that support a user in taking microbreaks [21]. However, these time intervals are set based on preference and do not consider any additional context. Therefore, they trigger statically. The capacitive sensors in ExerSeat are not only able to detect posture, but also occupation and work activity levels. This has been used in another capacitive seat by our team [3].

We can use this method to create a dynamic trigger for microbreaks. If the person was particularly active in the last hour, no training might be required. If the person was on the chair but has moved little in the past 30 min an exercise could be launched. For ExerSeat we are using three classes - not at chair, active work and inactive work. If the person is not on the chair no training is started - if the person has been on the chair continuously and has been working inactively an exercise is triggered after a certain time.

5   Prototype

The sensing chair is a regular office chair with armrests that is augmented with hidden capacitive proximity sensors (model Ikea Nominell). The hardware is based on the OpenCapSense rapid prototyping toolkit for capacitive proximity sensing applications [11]. It can interface eight sensors and supports three sensing modes. We have expanded the system for supporting wireless communication and battery operation, so the chair can be moved freely without attached cables. We chose Bluetooth as wireless technology, as it is supported by many PCs without additional hardware. For this the Bluetooth Mate Silver was attached to OpenCapSense. The battery is an off-the-shelf external charging kit for mobile

Fig. 5. Layout of the sensing kit (electrode positions in red, housing position in green). *left* is the plastic sheet that will later be glued to the backrest, *right* is the bottom of the seat pan (Color figure online).

devices. Despite the high energy consumption of OpenCapSense this enables a battery runtime of the system of about 20 h. This can be attributed to the non-optimized prototyping system. The required energy for the sensors is pretty low with about 2 mW each, however the powerful microcontroller requires more than 200 mW. An optimized system could use a less powerful chip and apply smart disabling of non-required sensors and reduction of the update rate. As long as no user is present a single sensor with low update rate on the seat area will suffice to notice an approaching person. Furthermore, switching to a Bluetooth Smart communication system can save additional energy.

The ExerSeat sensor layout is based on a single OpenCapSense board and eight electrodes. They are placed in two groups, one for the back rest and one for the seat area. Figure 5 shows the two groups, the position of the electrodes, and the position of the battery and board housing. The electrodes of the backrest have to be attached on the front of the chair. This was necessary, as metal parts in the chair were disturbing the signal in a way that made reliable readings impossible. Therefore, it is necessary to cut small holes in order to bring the wiring from the electrodes to the cover attached on the back of the chair. The group on the seat area is sensing from the bottom of the chair, as there are no disturbing materials in this case. The electrodes are fitted on a plastic sheet that is attached to the bottom of the seat pan.

5.1 Training Application

The ExerSeat training application is a microbreak program that allows the users to perform small exercises throughout the course of a work day. The software runs in the background and triggers microbreaks following the two triggering processes described earlier. The user can choose according to preference.

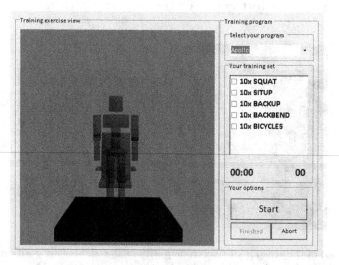

Fig. 6. Screenshot of ExerSeat training application

Once either trigger is hit, the program will ask the user if he wants to perform some exercise. If agreed the GUI shown in Fig. 6 appears. The user may select from trainings that have a flexible number of exercises and repetitions. A 3D view as shown in Fig. 6 on the left, displays the current pose of the user, the pose the user should take, and will give feedback if it was successfully performed. Once the exercise is complete, the user will get a success screen and the program disappears into the background. Additionally, the training can be aborted or marked finished (if there were technical issues and the user still wants to record the training as being successful).

The software collects debug information to identify occurring problems, provides an overview of the time until the next microbreak is due, and allows manual launch of training units. In order to evaluate the efficacy of the system we are creating extensive logs of the system operation. This includes timestamps of all events, type of training started, type of trigger, success of training, activity level by minute, results of a small daily usability survey, change of settings, logging of program activities, and occurring error messages.

6   System Piloting

ExerSeat has been evaluated in a pilot with desk workers at the VTT premises in Espoo, Finland. The primary purpose of the pilot was to test the viability of the ExerSeat concept. We selected from a group that had previous experience with other microbreak programs. From this group ten volunteers were chosen that had no planned vacation during the pilot period and could handle the required task. We wanted to know, how often and how well the training units were performed, if there is any preference for specific exercises, how usable the system is, and if there is room for improvement in future iterations. The initial prototype had to be modified with regards to the arm rests, as some participants preferred to work without. Thus, it was decided to have no sensors in the arm rests to have just a single prototype design. Ten female volunteers from office workers

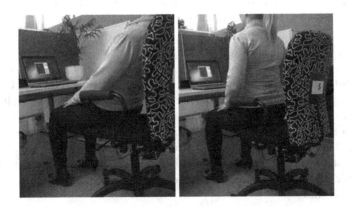

Fig. 7. Pilot participant performing a back up exercise.

Operations Support Services unit used ExerSeat during their regular working days hours - leading to an overall sample size of 42 work days (Fig. 7). All except one of the pilot volunteers had been daily users of a different ergonomic break computer application for nearly 2 years. This application uses a static triggering of exercises at user-defined intervals. If the user agrees on doing an exercise, a video shows of a coach doing a correct performance and encouraging the user to participate. The program has no capabilities of tracking if the workers actually performed the exercises. Five of the volunteers had previously participated in a flexible work pilot as part of an internal development initiative at the host organization, where they could work remotely, for instance from their home office. Nearly half of the volunteers were supplied with an adjustable height desk in their regular office work spaces, which they continued to use during the ExerSeat pilot. The participants work processes or tasks were not changed due to the pilot. Participation included using the chair, sending the automatically generated daily logs and giving feedback at the end of each of the 2 phases: static and dynamic setting.

No reward or incentive was initially offered to the study participants, thus relying only on motivated volunteers. However, after the pilot a coupon was handed to each, as a thank you.

The average age of the test users was 51.4, they are all female and have high experience with microbreak programs ($\mu = 8.7$, 1=no experience, 10=high experience). Five prototype systems were prepared and the pilot was performed in two stages. The first stage used a mandatory static triggering of the training units, whereas the users could select the interval. The second phase used an dynamic occupation-based trigger. Additionally between phases 1 and 2 the number of participants had to be reduced from 10 to 8, due to organizational changes and technical failure of one prototype. We fixed various bugs and improved the visual feedback of the exercises. During each phase the users had an ExerSeat system for two weeks. Overall this led to 42 work days of testing by our pilot participants.

The training units included the five basic exercises described previously with ten repetitions each, and combined exercises - squat & bicycles (5x, 10x), back bend & bicycles (5x, 10x), and squat & back bend (5x, 5x).

6.1   Training Results

The raw results of the training logging can be found in Table 1. Overall there were 1133 training units performed, 751 of which succeeded. There were a high number of manually triggered training units (603 manually started, 530 dynamically triggered). A fairly high number of training units were prematurely aborted (33.7 %). Only a small number of the triggered training units were denied (13.8 %).

The most popular exercise was the back bend with 37.4 % before bicycles with 21.2 %. The least popular were the combined bend & cycle (3.8 %) and squat & bend (3.3 %).

Table 1. Training results of ExerSeat in phase 1 and phase 2

Activity	Phase 1	Phase 2
Trainings triggered	420	110
Trainings accepted	358	99
Trainings denied	62	11
Overall trainings	779	354
Trainings succeeded	509	242
Trainings aborted	270	112
Back bend succeeded	171	78
Bicycles succeeded	96	45
Back up succeeded	57	26
Sit up succeeded	41	14
Squat succeeded	4	48
Squat & cycle succeeded	21	17
Bend & cycle succeeded	18	7
Squat & bend succeeded	15	7

6.2   SUS Usability Results

The System Usability Scale (SUS) is a common method to evaluate the usability of a system - that is its effectiveness, efficiency, and user satisfaction [7].

SUS has generally been considered as providing this type of high-level subjective view of usability and is thus often used in carrying out comparisons of usability between systems. Because it yields a single score on a scale of 0-100, it can even be used to compare systems that are outwardly dissimilar. This one-dimensional aspect of the SUS is both a benefit and a drawback, because the questionnaire is necessarily quite general. The SUS has been widely used in the evaluation of a range of systems [2].

The SUS questionnaire was performed after phase 1 of the piloting. Initially it was planned to have another SUS test after the second phase. However, due to the changes in pilot group size we refrained from that. The average SUS score was 52.5. However, there was a huge spread, with scores ranging from 20.0 to 85.0. We will discuss the implications in Sect. 7.

6.3   Questionnaire Results

The last part of the evaluation was an open questionnaire regarding positive and negative aspects of the system and potential improvements that should be considered in future iterations. We posed the following five questions:

- What did you like about the ExerSeat software?
- What did you dislike about the ExerSeat software?

- What did you like about the ExerSeat hardware?
- What did you dislike about the ExerSeat hardware?
- Do you have any suggestions for improving the system?

The users liked the simplicity and automatic triggering of the software. The large variety of exercises was appreciated. They disliked the graphical quality of the 3D models and that there were various technical issues that often prevented the system from working as planned. This is not surprising when considering the comparison that the volunteers made of ExerSeat against the sophisticated microbreak program, which they had been accustomed to using daily.

The hardware was not considered particularly comfortable by some users and the wires were too obvious. Many would have preferred to have the same functionality in their own chair. Although it is physically possible to wire the sensors into regular office chair, we preferred to cause the least inconvenience and cost to the hosting organization by supplying all the hardware needed for the trial via our dedicated project. The charging wires were often too short and the placement of the battery below the chair was unfortunate, since it made it more difficult to recharge the system and access it in case of issues. Additionally, there were several issues with some of the batteries. During the second phase we replaced the model of rechargeable battery of two faulty prototypes with more reliable varieties.

7   Discussion

During the piloting phase, we observed a high number of aborted training units (33.7 %). While the system was not able to directly identify the reason, we inquired about this behavior in the post-pilot interviews. The participants stated varying reasons. A main aspect was technical difficulties that made completing the training units difficult or impossible. Given the novelty of the application and possible differences in the setup on the users working desktops, it took some time for users to notice the application had already launched. It was common to discover that several sessions had been launched and therefore the application was stuck. The high level of incomplete training units was also due to parallel instances being launched. There were no complaints about the timing of the triggers. Apart from improving the stability of the system and allowing completion of the training units at all times, the user interface can be improved to prevent accidental triggering of a microbreak.

When evaluating the popularity of the exercises, we observed a strong correlation to their order in the GUI. The frequency of training units was in the same order as their listing in the program. We did not investigate if this was caused by the users actually not preferring specific exercises, or by other aspects of the system and piloting, e.g. not clearly explaining that users should do a specific exercise. This should be investigated in a follow-up study. We will consider a randomization of training units in the GUI to ensure more even training regimens. A required step in the future is a strong coordination with fitness trainers, to create a balanced fitness program in the office.

Regarding the system usability - it is difficult to grade the system in its current state. As there have been various technical difficulties and issues in getting the system to connect properly, some users were unable to use the system at certain days, when on-site support was not immediately available. The participants were overall not very satisfied with ExerSeat, given the low average SUS score of 52.5. The large spread strongly correlates with technical difficulties in using the system. One participant who did not like the level of comfort of the chair and had several technical difficulties graded the system with a 20.0. Another participant who liked the chair and had no technical issues graded a 85.0. It can be concluded that using a SUS on ExerSeat in its current state is a bit premature. The test should be repeated with a final system.

Regarding suggested improvements of the system, the main point was providing more robustness and stability. Particularly the communication between chair and computer was sometimes unstable. The second most common suggestion was to have better visuals that are more motivating, e.g. by having realistic 3D figures performing the exercises in front of nice scenery, accompanied by soothing music and gentle audio instructions. A further suggestion was that the system should be adaptable to more ergonomic chairs. Using a generally available system was deemed counter-productive, since it was less comfortable and probably less ergonomic than the existing chairs. Thus future versions should be adaptable to a larger variety of chairs or even any existing chairs. The system should be completely integrated and a battery solution has to be found that runs considerably longer and can be recharged more easily. Additionally, the system can be optimized using specific microcontrollers and disabling strategies, as previously explained. Finally, an improved version of the application should include more microbreak exercises that need to be performed while standing up, in order to give additional physical benefits to the user.

8   Conclusion

In this work we have presented ExerSeat, an exercise tracking system for the office, based on capacitive proximity sensors integrated into an office chair. We have presented a novel method for posture tracking that fits a simplified multi-body model of a human body according to the current sensor readings. The posture of an idealized model is calculated based on a set of processing steps and the normalized values of eight capacitive sensors placed around the chair. Using this posture tracking method, we can detect five single exercises and combinations thereof that comprise single training units. This system is used in the ExerSeat application that triggers training units during microbreaks on a typical office work day. In addition to time-based triggering of microbreaks, we present a method that dynamically triggers exercises, based on occupation and activity level of the person on the chair.

We have created several prototype systems that are composed of the ExerSeat chair with integrated sensors, battery, and communication facilities, as well as a software application that manages the microbreak training units. We conducted a pilot study with five ExerSeat systems that were used by ten users during 42 work days. Overall, 1133 training units were performed, 751 of which succeeded. For the most part, the participants were able to handle ExerSeat well, however had concerns regarding the usability and variability of the supported exercises.

We see several opportunities to improve ExerSeat. As our subjects would have preferred to use ExerSeat with their existing chairs, the system should be movable. We consider integrating the system into a flexible cushion that can be easily attached to most chairs, e.g. using wire electrodes, similar to the system presented by Rus et al. [17]. This would require specifically tailored sensors, as well as integrated battery and communication systems. The exercise tracking as of now is restricted to areas on or near the chair. It can be considered to add other types of sensors that are placed in the environment and allow better tracking of the upper limbs. This will enable exercises performed both on and off the chair. A good candidate is the Microsoft Kinect with its skeleton tracking capabilities. Finally, we would like to validate the supported exercises with professional fitness trainers, to guarantee a well-balanced training program for the users of ExerSeat.

Acknowledgments. We would like to extend our gratitude to the Operations Support Services Unit volunteers at VTT Espoo for participating in our pilot, providing detailed feedback and to their management for allowing our minor intervention to their daily office routine. This work was supported by EIT Digital under the project number SSP14267.

References

1. Aaltonen, I., Ala-Kotila, P., Järnström, H., Laarni, J., Määttä, H., Nykänen, E., Schembri, I., Lönnqvist, A., Ruostela, J.: State-of-the-Art Report on Knowledge Work (2012)
2. Bangor, A., Kortum, P.T., Miller, J.T.: An empirical evaluation of the system usability scale. Int. J. Hum. Comput. Interact. **24**(6), 574–594 (2008)
3. Braun, A., Frank, S., Wichert, R.: The capacitive chair. In: Streitz, N., Markopoulos, P. (eds.) DAPI 2015. LNCS, vol. 9189, pp. 397–407. Springer, Heidelberg (2015)
4. Braun, A., Heggen, H.: Context recognition using capacitive sensor arrays in beds. In: Proceedings AAL-Kongress (2012)
5. Braun, A., Heggen, H., Wichert, R.: CapFloor – a flexible capacitive indoor local-ization system. In: Chessa, S., Knauth, S. (eds.) EvAAL 2011. CCIS, vol. 309, pp. 26–35. Springer, Heidelberg (2012)
6. Braun, A., Wichert, R., Kuijper, A., Fellner, D.W.: Capacitive proximity sensing in smart environments. J. Ambient Intell. Smart Environ. **7**(4), 483–510 (2015)
7. Brooke, J.: SUS-A quick and dirty usability scale. Usability Eval. Ind. **189**(194), 4–7 (1996)
8. Davenport, T.H., Thomas, R.J., Cantrell, S.: The mysterious art and science of knowledge-worker performance. MIT Sloan Manag. Rev. **44**(1), 23–30 (2012)
9. European Foundation for the Improvement of Living and Working Conditions: Employment trends and policies for older workers in the recession. Technical report (2011). http://ec.europa.eu/social/BlobServlet?docId=9590&langId=en

10. Griffiths, E., Saponas, T.S., Brush, A.J.B.: Health chair: implicitly sensing heart and respiratory rate. In: Proceedings of the 2014 ACM International Joint Conference on Pervasive and Ubiquitous Computing - UbiComp 2014 Adjunct, pp. 661–671. ACM Press, New York, September 2014
11. Grosse-Puppendahl, T., Berghoefer, Y., Braun, A., Wimmer, R., Kuijper, A.: OpenCapSense: a rapid prototyping toolkit for pervasive interaction using capacitive sensing. In: 2013 IEEE International Conference on Pervasive Computing and Communications, PerCom 2013, pp. 152–159 (2013)
12. Große-Puppendahl, T.A., Marinc, A., Braun, A.: Classification of user postures with capacitive proximity sensors in AAL-environments. In: Keyson, D.V., et al. (eds.) AmI 2011. LNCS, vol. 7040, pp. 314–323. Springer, Heidelberg (2011)
13. Harada, T., Mori, T., Nishida, Y., Yoshimi, T., Sato, T.: Body parts positions and posture estimation system based on pressure distribution image. In: Proceedings 1999 IEEE International Conference on Robotics and Automation, vol. 2, pp. 968–975 (1999)
14. Liang, G., Cao, J., Liu, X., Han, X.: Cushionware: A practical sitting posture-based interaction system. In: CHI 2014 Extended Abstracts on Human Factors in Computing Systems, pp. 591–594 (2014)
15. McLean, L., Tingley, M., Scott, R.N., Rickards, J.: Computer terminal work and the benefit of microbreaks. Appl. Ergon. **32**(3), 225–237 (2001)
16. Robertson, M., Amick III, B.C., DeRango, K., Rooney, T., Bazzani, L., Harrist, R., Moore, A.: The effects of an office ergonomics training and chair intervention on worker knowledge, behavior and musculoskeletal risk. Appl. Ergon. **40**(1), 124–135 (2009)
17. Rus, S., Grosse-Puppendahl, T., Kuijper, A.: Recognition of bed postures using mutual capacitance sensing. AmI 2014. LNCS, vol. 8850, pp. 51–66. Springer, Heidelberg (2014)
18. Shirehjini, A.A.N., Yassine, A., Shirmohammadi, S.: Design and implementation of a system for body posture recognition. Multimedia Tools Appl. **70**(3), 1637–1650 (2014)
19. Shotton, J., Fitzgibbon, A., Cook, M., Sharp, T., Finocchio, M., Moore, R., Kipman, A., Blake, A.: Real-time human pose recognition in parts from single depth images. Commun. ACM **56**(1), 116–124 (2013)
20. Tan, H.Z., Slivovsky, L.A., Pentland, A., Member, S.: A sensing chair using pressure distribution sensors. IEEE/ASME Trans. Mechatron. **6**(3), 261–268 (2001)
21. TriSun Software Inc.: PC Work Break (2015). http://www.trisunsoft.com/pc-work-break/
22. Valat, J.P., Goupille, P., Védere, V.: Low back pain: risk factors for chronicity. Revue du rhumatisme (English ed.) **64**(3), 189–194 (1997)
23. Zemp, R., Taylor, W.R., Lorenzetti, S.: Are pressure measurements effective in the assessment of office chair comfort/discomfort? A review. Appl. Ergon. **48**, 273–282 (2015)

Persuasion Through an Ambient Device: Proof of Concept and Early Evaluation of CRegrette, a Smoking Cessation System

Alessandro Fenicio[1,2](✉) and Gaëlle Calvary[1,2]

[1] University of Grenoble Alpes, LIG, 38000 Grenoble, France
[2] CNRS, LIG, 38000 Grenoble, France
alessandrofenicio@gmail.com, Gaelle.Calvary@imag.fr

Abstract. Smoking cessation has become a real social challenge in healthcare domain and persuasive technologies combined with ambient intelligence figure as a possible approaches against this addiction. Choosing an effective persuasive design relies on different models and principles coming from several scientific contexts. We evaluate the triggers defined by the B.J.Fogg's model in different design strategies implementing three experiments: the first using smoking tools, the second with an Android application and a third one using the same application coupled with an Arduino-based ambient device. The CRegrette system's proof of concept suggests that statistics combined with an ambient device are more effective than notifications, mirroring and self-monitoring approaches. This article furthermore proposes some design strategies and research perspectives to support further research in the field of persuasion and ambient device design.

Keywords: Healthcare · Ambient intelligence · Smoking cessation · Persuasive technologies

1 Research Problem

Cigarette smoking is described by the World Health Organization as the single most preventable cause of premature death [1]. It is a well-established risk factor for all forms of stroke [2], increases myocardial sensitivity to ischaemia [3], and has been identified as a definite cause of cancer at many sites [4]. Preventing and curing smoking addiction has become a real social challenge and besides medical cures and group therapies, other solutions are being developed: electronic cigarettes (e-cigarettes), internet-based solutions, software for computers, ubiquitous systems and ambient intelligence. Nowadays computers support wellness and physical activity. Websites are able to give users more confidence when making decisions [5,6] and an increase in the development of mobile applications and software in this field has been registered. It has been proven, in fact, that mobile applications which support smoking cessation treatment have a positive impact on abstinence rates compared to a usual care approach [7]. "Persuasive

© Springer International Publishing Switzerland 2015
Kameas et al. (Eds.): AmI 2015, LNCS 9425, pp. 252–267, 2015.
DOI: 10.1007/978-3-319-26005-1_17

technology" is defined as the general class of technology that has the explicit purpose of changing human attitudes and behaviours [8] and has applications in public health, sales, diplomacy, politics, religion, military training and management. In this article an analysis of the persuasive principles at the base of the existing products has been performed from the perspectives of several scientific contexts: computer science, human computer interaction and psychology. We focused in particular on the perspective given by the behavioural change theories, which attempts to explain the stages and the factors that lead to a behaviour change. In this work we take into account the Transtheoretical model of behaviour change, the principles proposed by the professor Robert Cialdini and the model and perspectives suggested by B.J. Fogg, founder of the Stanford Persuasive Technology Lab. Our research has lead to the creation of a new persuasive system called CRegrette made by combining an Android application with an Arduino-based ambient device. The application relies on determined persuasive principles and interactions while the ambient device, which is wearable, is designed to be attached to the clothes as a badge. The ambient device makes tracking the user's habit easier and at the same time, through an RGB led, informs nearby people of the ambient air condition. In other words, it can be used by smokers as a facilitator but also by non-smokers as an indicator of the quality of air in their offices, apartments and environments in general. Moreover, a non-smoker wearing the ambient device can influence the behaviour of nearby smokers by allowing them to see a visual representation of their smoking.

2   State of the Art

Since persuasion is across several scientific contexts we looked at it from different scientific points of view: persuasion applied by principles as those of Robert Cialdini, the different stage of the process of a change as described in the Transtheoretical model of behaviour change, and finally by looking at factors leading to behavioural changes as depicted by B.J. Fogg in his model.

2.1   Robert Cialdini's Persuasive Principles

Robert Cialdini is the Regents' Professor Emeritus of Psychology and Marketing at Arizona State University and published the book "Influence: The Psychology of Persuasion" in 1984. He theorized six principles of persuasion: Consistency, Scarcity, Liking, Social Proof and Authority. These principles are currently used in several products in commerce. Taking, for example, one of the most downloaded smoking cessation Android applications, "QuitNow!"[1], we can find some of his principles applied. In QuitNow the "commitment and consistency" principle (people that commit an idea or a goal tend to respect their engagement) is implemented sharing objective and status on social networks while the "social proof" (people do things that they see other people or friends doing) and "liking"

---

[1] https://play.google.com/store/apps/details?id=com.EAGINsoftware.dejaloYa.

principles (users are more persuaded by people that they like) are implemented by allowing the user to see the progress of friends and contacts. Other applications implement the "authority" principle (obeying authority figures). This is the case for "Before I Eat"[2], which is designed for alimentary diseases and gives instant motivational text and audio messages to help control the user's insatiable desire during attacks.

2.2 Transtheoretical Model (TTM)

The Transtheoretical model (TTM) of behaviour change has been influential in research on smoking [9] and consists of four key constructs: stages of change, process of change, decisional balance and self-efficacy. There are six states of change: precontemplation (not ready to take action), contemplation (getting ready), preparation (ready), action (overt change), maintenance (sustained change) and relapse (resumption of old behaviors) [10]. In this work we consider the first three stages: "precontemplation" where individuals are not considered to be ready to quit smoking and unlikely to engage the change in the near future; "contemplation" where they are getting ready to change in the near future, appreciating the advantages of performing the change; and "preparation" in which they have the right motivations to change and they start to get information about the available techniques to quit smoking.

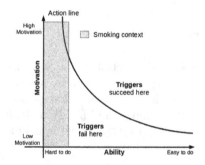

Fig. 1. Fog's Behaviour Model and smoking context

2.3 Fogg's Behaviour Model (FBM)

The FBM asserts that for a person performing a target behaviour, sufficient motivation, ability to perform the behaviour and a trigger are all required. These three factors must occur at the same moment, otherwise the behaviour will not happen [11]. In Fig. 1 the "action line" divides the regions in which giving the values of motivation and ability to change succeed or fail consequently on a trigger. A concrete application example could be to consider a person medically

² https://play.google.com/store/apps/details?id=com.standishmedia.BeforeIEat.

certified as "able to loose weight through diet". Taking as a trigger the death of a friend caused by bad eating habits (a "spark" trigger), the FBM states that in cases of sufficient motivation the person can change his behaviour, for example, choosing a healthier diet. If not motivated, the trigger will not have any impact. The participant's difficulty in considering this change has been depicted by the dashed area of the FBM, the zone in which just a small percentage of smokers, highly motivated to quit, succeed in this hard task.

The FBM introduces three different types of triggers: sparks, signals and facilitators:

- **Spark**: used to increase the motivation and can take the form of text, symbols or images.
- **Signals**: they do not seek to motivate people or simplify the task. They serve only as a reminder, just like road signals.
- **Facilitator**: used to trigger the behaviour-change, making it easier to do.

3 The CRegrette Vision

3.1 Characterization on the Fogg Model

It is possible to apply the Fogg model in the context of smoking addiction. In this case we are considering the part of graph with a low ability from the user's point of view (dashed area in Fig. 1). In this scenario, as we can see from Fig. 1, only a small percentage of people succeed in changing their behaviour, due to high motivations. Our research question was indeed to increase that percentage, shifting the action line curve towards the bottom-left of the plot, by using persuasive strategies. We emphasize that a shift of the curve in the downward direction is caused by an increase of motivation while a shift toward the left represents an increase in ability to accomplish the goal. In order to investigate this shift, we tested certain features of the system to see their effect on the Fogg behaviour model. In particular by implementing:

- **as sparks**: stickers with the "CRegrette" text positioned on the smoking gadgets and notifications provided by the CRegrette Android application;
- **as signal**: statistics provided by the CRegrette Android application;
- **as facilitators**: the CRegrette Android application (capable of keeping track of the smoking habits) and the CRegrette Arduino-based ambient device with a smoke detector (automating data-acquisition).

Our goal was to see the impact of these strategies and to infer an effective combination of them for maximizing the area above the aforementioned action line.

3.2 Inspiring Approaches and Related Works

It is possible to find in commerce products for wellness and health combining wearable biometric monitoring devices with mobile phone application. For example the "Fitbit"[3] technology uses a wearable device as a facilitator to count the

---

[3] https://www.fitbit.com/.

number of steps, providing statistics and notifications to the users to motivate them and to remind them to do their daily training. In this configuration (device plus application) in the smoking context few ideas were developed: mobile-phone-based Breath CO meters [16] such as the "Intelliquit" project[4] where users have to breath into the device to measure the CO level, "UbiLighter"[14] a system capable of making smokers aware of their daily smoking patterns, wrist accelerometers capable of recognizing hand to mouth (HGM) smoking gesture such as "Actigraph GT3X+"[17] or systems involving other kind of strategies such as the "Autosense sensor suite"[15] that includes ECG measurement and a Respiratory Inductive Plethysmograph (RIP) band to track relative lung volume and breathing rate. In this scenario we designed our system with the idea of "detect" and "present" but also "persuade". We wanted to count the number of smoked cigarettes as in UbiLighter and IntelliQuit using the smoke sensor to distinguish between an active or passive smoking activity. This detection in our system happens without interacting with the device as in the FitBit, Actigraph GT3X+ and in the Autosense systems but in addition, thanks to the visibility of the smoking detection system, a persuasive intent designed on the behavioural change theories is addressed to smokers and non smokers using the RGB Led and the Android application. This persuasion feature, does not involves just the person using the system but also nearby people made aware of the air situation in the ambient.

4   The CRegrette Persuasive Ambient System

4.1   Application

The main goals of the CRegrette Android application are to help users keep track of their smoking activity, to provide notifications and statistics related to their habit. The application's features include Bluetooth pairing and communication with the CRegrette device, access to GPS positions and to the internet in order to retrieve real addresses for those positions. When the application interacts with the ambient device, it is also capable of displaying information about the quality of the air. The application presents five main views:

- **Home**: in which participants can declare their behaviour. It has with two buttons: "I smoked" whose intent is to declare an active smoking activity and "I smelt smoke around me" to declare a passive smoking activity. Once one of these two buttons is pressed, data including the time, GPS position and the type of behaviour is stored in the phone's database. The information of the interface automatically updates when new data are stored [Fig. 2].
- **History**: with a list of months and an histogram reporting the number of cigarettes smoked per month and the daily average [Fig. 3 (left)]
- **Temporal view**: grouping the collected data to show the time during the day at which smoking activity reached its maximum frequency [Fig. 3 (center)]

---

[4] https://www.intelliquit.org/.

Fig. 2. Home view: declaring the smoking habit change the statistics

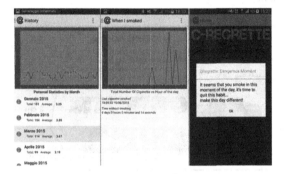

Fig. 3. History view (left), Temporal view (center), a notification example (right)

- **Spatial view 1**: tracking the environment where people declared to have smelt smoke.
- **Spatial view 2**: tracking the environment where people declared to have smoked.

These two last views [Fig. 4] are grouped by GPS coordinates with a range of 20 m × 20 m and ordered by total number of smoked cigarettes. The locations can be displayed in terms of GPS coordinates, real address or in a Google Map. We asked the participants to use the CRegrette mobile version for one week without informing them of the persuasive intent of the application. Finally, an ad-hoc procedure implemented in the application allowed participants to send feedback and the local database via email to our team.

4.2 Ambient Device

The CRegrette ambient device is composed of five main components: a battery, an Arduino Nano, a JY-MCU Slave Bluetooth module an MQ-2 smoke detector and an Adafruit NeoPixel RGB LED. The external box was printed using a 3D printer in order to have better space management of all the components. The battery capacity, 2600 mAh, has been chosen to provide 8 hours of autonomy

Fig. 4. Location represented by GPS coordinates (left), real addresses (center) and on the Google map (right)

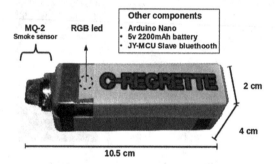

Fig. 5. The CRegrette device

to the device, rechargeable using a USB cable. The Arduino Nano is powered by the battery using its mini-B USB port and executes a program designed to read the data captured by the smoke sensor, process these values and determine the color of the RGB led. When this operation is completed, a Bluetooth message is sent by the JY-MCU module to the Android application, which uses it to compute and display information about the smoking activity. The device is designed to accomplish two main goals: inform the user and nearby people about the air condition using the LED, and transmit the information to the CRgrette mobile application. The Arduino program running on the device defines three values for the situations "no-smoking", "passive-smoking" and "active-smoking", respectively associated with green, orange and red continuous light emitted by the RGB led. Two thresholds define the minimum value perceived by the smoke sensor in order to distinguish between environment in which the air is healthy, foul or dangerous, respectively associated with green, orange and red blinking light emitted by the RGB led. The information related to the actual air condition is displayed afterwards also in the application (Fig. 5).

The CRegrette device has three uses showed in Fig. 6 :

Fig. 6. Device uses: (top) The device displays the air-condition while the user during the day, (center) a non-smoker wearing the device and a smoker being made aware of his behaviour, (bottom) the smoker wears the device, tracking his smoking activity

- **ambient monitoring**: it utilizes the LED colors to give instant information on the ambient air-condition [Fig. 6 (top)]
- **mirroring**: it mirrors the smoker's behaviour by using the LED's colors [Fig. 6 (center)]
- **facilitator**: it makes it easier for the smoker to keep track of their smoking habits [Fig. 6 (bottom)]

5   CRegrette Experimentations

This study aims to evaluate, using the FBM, the impact of our design strategies in the specific context of smoking cessation in order to give some findings to support the further development of technologies as ambient systems against smoking dependency. In particular, we investigated on the self-monitoring and mirroring techniques by providing some smoking tools, on the effect produced by statistics and notifications of the CRegrette Android application and on the impact of using the same application combined with the CRegrette electronic device. In the following subsections these experiments are described and completed with short evaluations which will form the basis of the final conclusions and perspectives of the article.

First Stage: Questionnaires and Recruitments. An initial stage of our experiments involved using general questionnaires to infer participants' phases of the TTM and their motivation to quit smoking. Participants were asked about previous attempts to quit in order to estimate their ability to do so and to identify the trigger that caused that attempt. The sample was composed of ten people that had already tried to quit, who were familiar with technology, and who are between 25–44 years of age, the most populated age-range for smokers [12]. We split the participants in three groups according to their everyday life activities and the availability of our kits: two CRegrette smoking tools(lighter and stickers), and one CRegrette electronic ambient device. A detail of this sample characteristics is showed by the table below. Despite our samples being small, it emerged that the participants were mostly in the contemplation phase, considering the idea of completely quitting smoking (medium motivation), and that about half of them actually tried to stop but had failed repeatedly (low ability). The attempt to stop their dependency was primarily motivated by health concerns and secondly by money.

Table 1. The participant sample

Experiment	Participant	Age	Sex	Occupation	Cigarette a day
1	P1	35	M	Bar tender	35 to 45
1	P2	44	M	Researcher	10 to 20
2	P3	32	M	Receptionist	less than 10
2	P4	30	M	Manager	10 to 15
2	P5	30	M	Student	less than 10
2	P6	28	M	Student	10 to 20
2	P7	27	M	Student	10 to 20
2	P8	28	F	Consultant	less than 10
2	P9	28	M	Manager	less than 10
2 and 3	P10	34	M	Researcher	18 to 22

5.1 Experiment 1: Self Monitoring and Mirroring

In this experiment we used some smoking tools [Fig. 7] to investigate the impact of self-monitoring and mirroring on the FBM and to validate the actual capability of smokers to autonomously keep track of their smoking habits. Our Hypothesis was that the participants may have falsely believed that they were aware of their habits and that through a mirroring technique, comparing their convictions with evidence, their motivation could be increased.

Fig. 7. First Experimentation Kit (Smoking tools)

During this experiment participants did not use any electronic device, but a lighter with the yellow text "CRegrette" and some additional stickers with the CRegrette logo to be attached on the cigarette packets as spark triggers [Fig. 7]. Once this equipment was provided to participants, they were asked to pay attention while smoking at to the time and place, and to count the number of cigarettes smoked within the day (self-monitoring). The experiment lasted three working days and three vacation days.

Evaluation. Participants during the working days were able to indicate the moments and places where they mostly smoked, while during vacation days they found it harder. In both cases participants used the amount of cigarettes remaining in the packet to indicate the number of cigarettes smoked, admitting a lack of accuracy in their estimation. Showing the incongruity between their affirmations and the declarations previously collected from the interviewees they declared to be surprised and "more motivated" (increase in motivation) proposing alternative solutions to improve their self-monitoring strategies. Their perception of the difficulties of quitting, on the other hand did not change (ability not affected) [Fig. 8].

5.2   Experiment 2: Notification and Statistics

In this experiment using the CRegrette Android application we investigated the impact of statistics as "signals trigger" and on notifications as a "spark trigger" on participants, relating the findings to the FBM. In order to do that, we implemented an Android application to provide participants with notifications and statistics during their smoking activity. The first trigger, notification, was represented by pop-up text messages. When a participant reached a place where they had already smoked, or a moment of the day in which they used to smoke, they were advised by a pop-up message containing the text *N1:"It seems that you smoke in this moment of the day, it's time to quit this habit...make this day*

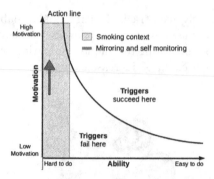

Fig. 8. Result of first experiment: increase in motivation

Fig. 9. Example of statistics and notification in the CRegrette application

different!" or *N2:"It seems that you smoke in this place. It's time to quit this habit...make this day different!".* Another pop-up informed participants when they were making progress, relating the moment of the day with the stored data: *N3:"You succeeded! Today you didn't smoke between <TIME> and <TIME>, your most difficult moment of the day. Keep going!".* These notifications were created by the system combining the data with an alarm strategy implemented in the application. The second trigger, statistics, was designed for participants in the pre-contemplation stage who could consider the idea to change their behaviour looking at the "History view" and at the average number of cigarettes smoked per month [Fig. 9 (left)]. In a second version of the application we improved the statistics, inserting text messages on the views concerning the actual behaviour of the user in each day: *S1:"You are improving your averages"*, *S2:"Your next cigarette will ruin your progress"* [Fig. 2] and *S3:"Time without smoking <TIME>"* [Fig. 3 (center)]

Evaluation. The participants pointed out that declaring their smoking habits was a demanding task, and that often they neglected to do it (P5, P6 Table 1).

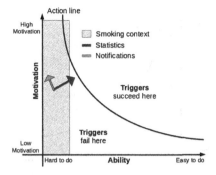

Fig. 10. Result of second experiment: motivation increased, ability increased by statistics but decreased by notifications

The "signal trigger" by statistics was appreciated by participants who declared to be more motivated. *P8: "I always declare my smoking activity because it is like a diary that show my progress"*. In particular, the feedback of the statistics on the History of cigarettes smoked made it easier for them to consider the idea of a change in behaviour *P9: "When I discover that my next cigarette will ruin my progress (S2 Experiment 2) I feel bad and I try to avoid smoking"*. The Place view was found useful to register the exact environments where the smoking activity happened. The signal triggers represented by notification via pop-up were not effective and, on the contrary, had the side effect of ruining the participants' progress by reminding them of smoking. *P10: "I was focused on my work. I received the notification (N3) which first motivated me but then I couldn't resist to the idea of smoke as soon as possible."* From the feedback that we obtained from this experiment, we were able to depict the impact of these two design strategies applied to smokers in the FBM as two oblique vectors, both increasing motivation. For the reasons described above, in the case of statistics we have also a positive increment of ability, while in the case of notifications we have a decrement in ability [Fig. 10].

5.3   Experiment 3: Facilitator by Electronic Device

In this experiment we used the CRegrette Android application with the CRegrette device to investigate the effect of providing an electronic device as facilitator trigger. Besides the facilitator's impact on the FBM, in this experiment we wanted also to show that the electronic device increases the credibility of statistics, making the triggers more effective. We asked the participant to use the CRegrette mobile version coupled with the CRegrette device for one week without informing them of the persuasive intent of the application. In particular we asked him to wear the device as a badge during the day and to recharge it during the night. We also asked the participant to collect any feedback from other people present during the experiment. Finally the same feature implemented in the previous experiment, allowed the participant to send feedback and the local database via email to our team.

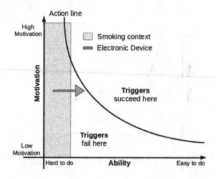

Fig. 11. Result of third experiment: ability increased

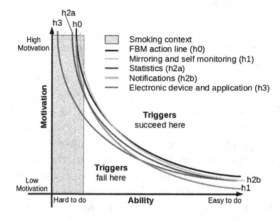

Fig. 12. CRegrette strategies on the FBM for the smoking context

Evaluation. The CRegrette Device acted as a facilitator trigger helping the participant to keep track of the smoking habits, causing an increment in his ability [Fig. 11]. The credibility of the statistics improved as well, but not as hypothesized due to some false or missed detections of the smoke sensor. The participant stated that the size of the device should be reduced since it was invasive in everyday life and he proposed different positioning of the device itself. People around him, moreover, asked about the purpose of the device and about the meaning of the LED, showing an interest in knowing the ambient air-quality.

6 Conclusion and Perspectives

6.1 Experiments Findings

Our experiments aimed to place the effect of the three different strategies in the Fogg Behaviour Model in order to design new effective technologies to support smoking cessation. Our three experiments modify the placement of the FBM "action line" with shifts. We depict an increase in motivation as a downward shift of the action line while an increase in ability shifts it towards the left. The action line shifts are computed relating the first stage questionnaires to post-interviews. In particular, we asked the participants to compare and quantify the difference between the different strategies they experienced and then we plotted the shifted action lines on the FBM on the base of their answers. We represent the results, we obtained the graph in Fig. 12. This early evaluation of the CRegrette system, suggests that the use of an electronic facilitator, able to detect the smoking activities, combined with a mobile phone application, capable of keeping track of statistics, produces the most effective shift of the action line on the FBM. This configuration is therefore identified as relevant strategy to support the behaviour change of smokers aiming to quit smoking. Furthermore, we propose some concrete design suggestions obtained from the interviewees and from the participants' feedback, which could support further development in persuasive technologies and ambient intelligence applied to smoking cessation.

6.2 Design Strategies and Perspectives

From the analysis conducted on the CRegrette system feedback, we suggest some design principles and strategies for persuasive technologies in the field of smoking addiction, concerning statistics, the displaying the feedback and the characterization of an ambient device.

Statistics. The more precise statistics are, the more they have a major impact on smokers' behaviour. In general, they are strongly recommended and relating them to variables other than the quantity of cigarettes smoked, such as the time and place, was shown to be appreciated and to be motivating. Further research experiments on statistics could evaluate whether a positive tracking of habits following the positive psychology[5] (e.g. time without smoking) is more effective than a negative one focused on the vice of the user (e.g. smoked cigarettes). We often registered a demand from participants to have, besides statistics, reminders of the benefits of not smoking (e.g. improvements in health that the smoker might have after a certain number of days without smoking). The impact of this strategy should be evaluated by new experiments.

Displaying the Feedback. The experiments show that statistics are more welcome and effective than notifications. From a human-interaction point of view, it is indeed advisable to design the persuasion strategy such that it must be checked by the user, rather than the user being automatically alerted by the system, which can result in annoying and affecting their everyday activities.

Ambient Device Characterization. The ambient device showed in the images has dimensions of $10.5 \times 4 \times 2$ centimetres. This is the size of the first proto-type but in future, for portability, it will have smaller dimensions thanks to an improved embedding of the components. This would allow an interactive envi-ronment in which ambient devices, measuring different data (e.g. quality of the

---

[5] https://en.wikipedia.org/wiki/Positive_psychology.

air, percentage of pollution, presence of virus or bacteria), are worn by people sharing real-time information about the environment.

The device's dimensions should strongly take into account human factors and ergonomic principles[6]. In particular the dimensions of the device should not affect ordinary everyday activities. Proposed examples to be evaluated are finger rings, bracelets, glasses or other wearable accessories that involve hand, wrist or head areas where the cigarette smoke is denser. From the smoking detector adjustment point of view we propose to add a sensor capable of only detecting carbon dioxide in order to decorrelate the data relative to smoke and to have a more precise data-capture, especially in closed environments. In addition, the final experiment's participant declared: *P10:"People around me noticed the device and I had to explain and show its functioning"*. This feedback opens the prospective of experimenting in exogenous persuasion (see [13]) related to the privacy of the user.

References

1. Paul, S.L., Thrift, A.G., Donnan, G.A.: Smoking as a crucial independent determinant of stroke. Tob. Induc. Dis. **2**(2), 67–80 (2004)
2. Organization, W.H.: Mortality country fact sheet, vol. 30, May 2006
3. Van Jaarsveld, H., Kuyl, J.M., Alberts, D.W.: Exposure of rats to low concentration of cigarette smoke increases myocardial sensitivity to ischaemia/reperfusion. Basic Res. Cardiol. **87**(4), 393–399 (1992)
4. Newcomb, P.A., Paul, P.: Carbone.: the health consequences of smoking. cancer. Med. Clin. North Am. **76**(2), 305–331 (1992)
5. Anhoj, J., Jensen, A.H.: Using the Internet for life style changes in diet and physical activity: a feasibility study. J. Med. Internet Res. **6**(3), 47–55 (2004)
6. Leslie, E., Marshall, A.L., Owen, N., Bauman, A.: Engagement and retention of participants in a physical activity website. Prev. Med. **40**(1), 54–59 (2005)
7. Gritz, E.R., Heather, E.D., Faith, E.F., Tami-Maury, I., Fingeret, M.C., King, R.M., Arduino, R.C., Vidrine, D.J.: Long-term outcomes of a cell phonedelivered intervention for smokers living with HIV/AIDS. Clin. Infect. Dis. **57**(4), 608–615 (2013)
8. IJsselsteijn, W.A., de Kort, Y.A.W., Midden, C., Eggen, B., van den Hoven, E. (eds.): PERSUASIVE 2006. LNCS, vol. 3962. Springer, Heidelberg (2006)
9. Prochaska, J.O., Velicer, W.F., Rossi, J.S., Goldstein, M.G., Marcus, B.H., Rakowski, W., Fiore, C., Harlow, L.L., Redding, C.A., Rosenbloom, D., Rossi, S.R.: Stages of change and decisional balance for 12 problem behaviors. Health Psychol. **13**(1), 39 (2004)
10. Prochaska, J.O., DiClemente, C.C.: Toward a comprehensive model of change. In: Miller, W.R., Heather, N. (eds.) Treating Addictive Behaviors. Applied Clinical Psychology, vol. 13, pp. 3–27. Springer, US (1986)
11. Fogg, B.J.: A behavior model for persuasive design. In: Proceedings of the 4th International Conference on Persuasive Technology, p. 40. ACM (2009)
12. Agaku, I.T., Brian, A.K., Shanta, R.D.: Centers for Disease Control and Prevention (CDC). Current cigarette smoking among adults United States, 2005–2012. MMWR Morb. Mortal. Wkly. Rep. **63**(2), 29–34 (2014)

---

[6] https://en.wikipedia.org/wiki/Human_factors_and_ergonomics.

13. Fogg, B.J.: Persuasive computers: perspectives and research directions. In: Proceedings of the SIGCHI Conference On Human Factors In Computing Systems, pp. 225–232. ACM Press/Addison-Wesley Publishing Co. (1998)
14. Scholl, P.M., Kücükyildiz, N., Laerhoven, K.V.: When do you light a fire?: capturing tobacco use with situated, wearable sensors. In: Proceedings of the 2013 ACM Conference on Pervasive and Ubiquitous Computing Adjunct Publication, pp. 1295–1304 (2013)
15. Ali, A.A., Hossain, S.M., Hovsepian, K., Rahman, M.M., Plarre, K., Kumar, S.: mPuff: automated detection of cigarette smoking puffs from respiration measurements. In: Proceedings of the 11th International Conference on Information Processing in Sensor Networks, pp. 269–280. ACM (2012)
16. Meredith, S.E., Robinson, A., Erb, P., Spieler, C.A., Klugman, N., Dutta, P., Dallery, J.: A mobile-phone-based breath carbon monoxide meter to detect cigarette smoking. Nicotine Tob. Res. **16**(6), 766–773 (2014)
17. Tang, Q., Vidrine, D.J., Crowder, E., Intille, S.S.: Automated detection of puffing and smoking with wrist accelerometers. In: Proceedings of the 8th International Conference on Pervasive Computing Technologies for Healthcare, pp. 80–87. ICST (Institute for Computer Sciences, Social-Informatics and Telecommunications Engineering) (2014)

Hidden Fatigue Detection for a Desk Worker Using Clustering of Successive Tasks

Yutaka Deguchi$^{(\boxtimes)}$ and Einoshin Suzuki

Department of Informatics, ISEE, Kyushu University, Fukuoka, Japan
yutaka.kyushu@gmail.com, suzuki@inf.kyushu-u.ac.jp

Abstract. To detect fatigue of a desk worker, this paper focuses on fatigue hidden in smiling and neutral faces and employs a periodic short time monitoring setting. In contrast to continual monitoring, the setting assumes that each short-*time* monitoring (in this paper, it is called a task) is conducted only during a break time. However, there are two problems: the small number of data in each task and the increasing number of tasks. To detect fatigue, the authors propose a method which is a combination of multi-task learning, clustering and anomaly detection. For the first problem, the authors employ multi-task learning which builds a specific classifier to each task efficiently by using information shared among tasks. Since clustering gathers similar tasks into a cluster, it mitigates the influence of the second problem. Experiments show that the proposed method exhibits a high performance in a long-*term* monitoring.

Keywords: Face monitoring · Anomaly detection · Incremental clustering · Multi-task learning

1   Introduction

In recent years, many desk workers suffer from fatigue which is induced by overwork and/or mental stress. For example, in Japan, the research of the Ministry of Health, Labour and Welfare showed that 34.6 % of laborers felt mental fatigue in visual display terminal (VDT) work in 2008. Fatigue causes drowsiness and physical weariness which practically decrease the ability for deskwork. In worse cases, it indicates a disease such as depression, anemia, sleep apnea and cancer. Therefore, it is important to detect high level fatigue in daily life.

In these years, many researchers tackled the problem of detecting fatigue. Among them, we especially focus on automatic fatigue detection. Ji et al. [10] developed a system which consists of two cameras to monitor fatigue of a driver. They extracted eyelid movement, gaze movement, head movement and facial expression and presented a Bayesian networks model to infer the fatigue from the observations. Hua and Zhang [8] presented a facial feature locating technology to detect fatigue. They used a parametric model which consists of 79 facial points to detect and track the eyes and the mouth to characterize the fatigue. In these

A part of this research was supported by JSPS KAKENHI 25280085 and 15K12100.

© Springer International Publishing Switzerland 2015
Kameas et al. (Eds.): AmI 2015, LNCS 9425, pp. 268–283, 2015.
DOI: 10.1007/978-3-319-26005-1_18

methods, fatigue was detected automatically without disturbing the work of the target person by using face monitoring systems.

However, the methods need to monitor the target person continuously so that they do not overlook behaviors related with fatigue: yawn and eye closure. It is uncomfortable for desk workers to be monitored continuously because they want to protect their privacy and confidential information of their work. Additionally, the monitored situation distracts some of desk workers from their work. In this paper, we employ a periodic short time monitoring setting for fatigue detection so that we do not interfere in their work and violate their privacy.

This paper consists of 7 sections. In the next section, we describe our periodic short time monitoring setting and a human monitoring system. In Sect. 3, we define our fatigue detection problem and the evaluation criteria. In Sect. 4, we propose our method which is a combination of multi-task learning, clustering and anomaly detection. Section 5 shows experimental results to evaluate our method. In Sect. 6, we describe some related works and we conclude in Sect. 7.

2 Periodic Short Time Monitoring

To detect fatigue of a desk worker, we employ a periodic short time monitoring setting: it takes less than 30 s to monitor a desk worker in 30 min. We define a short-*time* monitoring which continues for a short time, e.g., a few minutes. On the other hand, we define a long-*term* monitoring as a monitoring for a long time, e.g., more than a week, though the monitoring does not need to be continuous. We work on realizing a long-*term* monitoring which consists of short-*time* monitorings. Except during the short-*time* monitorings, our system stays outside the visual field of the desk worker and does not disturb him/her. This setting assumes that each of the monitorings is conducted during a part of a break time of the desk worker. We believe that the monitoring which continues for less than 30 s is short and does not affect him/her, if he/she is aware of it.

We employ a commercial robot, Kobuki with TurtleBot2[1,2], to realize our monitoring system. A mobile robot can move to outside the visual field of the desk worker, where it does not distract him/her from his/her work. The behavior of the system consists of two phases (Fig. 1): the monitoring phase and the waiting phase. In the monitoring phase, the robot moves to an optimal position to observe the face of the target person. After a short-*time* monitoring, it transits to the waiting phase. In the waiting phase[3], the robot stays outside the visual field of the target person and saves its power consumption. After 30 min have passed in the waiting phase, it transits to the monitoring phase[4].

---

[1] http://turtlebot.com/.

[2] The robot costs 649 euro and the docking station for the robot costs 45 euro (http://www.robotnikstore.com/robotnik/5121532/turtlebot-2.html, Aug. 24th, 2015).

[3] In this phase, the robot stays at a docking station and recharges its battery.

[4] In reality, we might need to modify our system so that the robot transits to the monitoring phase when ordered to do so by the desk worker.

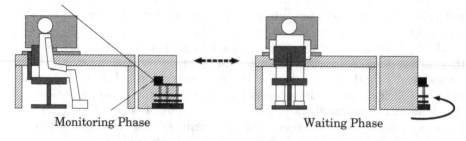

Monitoring Phase   Waiting Phase

Fig. 1. The overview of the behavior of our monitoring system

Table 1. Animation units of Kinect v2

ID	Name	ID	Name	ID	Name
0	JawOpen	6	LipCornerPullerRight	12	RightEyeClosed
1	LipPucker	7	LipCornerDepressorLeft	13	RightEyeBrowLowerer
2	JawSlideRight	8	LipCornerDepressorRight	14	LeftEyeBrowLowerer
3	LipStretcherRight	9	LeftCheekPuff	15	LowerlipDepressorLeft
4	LipStretcherLeft	10	RightCheekPuff	16	LowerlipDepressorRight
5	LipCornerPullerLeft	11	LeftEyeClosed		

Our robot is equipped with a Kinect for Windows v2[5] (Kinect v2) on the top to extract 17 animation units[6], which we use as facial features. The descriptions of the animation units are shown in Table 1. Each animation unit indicates the degree of a facial movement.

In a short-*time* monitoring, it is rare for a desk worker to show behaviors related with fatigue: yawn and eye closure. Thus we collect deliberate smiling and neutral faces with cooperation of the desk worker to detect hidden fatigue. Fatigue induces a significant decline in the smiling activity [1]. Neutral face is employed as the standard facial expression. Each label of facial data is input by the desk worker with a wireless mouse.

3   Hidden Fatigue Detection

Our problem is defined as an anomaly detection by using periodic short time monitoring to detect fatigue. The monitoring consists of short-*term* monitorings $\mathcal{Z} = \{Z^{(1)}, Z^{(2)}, ..., Z^{(T)}\}$, where T is the number of the short-*term* monitorings. We call each short-*time* monitoring a task. We assume that an anomaly detection method returns an anomaly measure e_t for $Z^{(t)}$, which is judged as anomalous if and only if e_t is greater than a threshold ψ.

To evaluate a fatigue detection method, we plot the receiver operating characteristic (ROC) curve and calculate the area under the curve (AUC) [2]. To plot

---

[5] http://www.microsoft.com/en-us/kinectforwindows/.

[6] We use Kinect for Windows SDK v2.0 1409 (http://www.microsoft.com/en-us/kinectforwindows/develop/downloads-docs.aspx) to build the animation units.

the ROC curve, we draw a graph of the true positive (TP) rate vs the false positive (FP) rate by varying the value of ψ. The TP rate measures the proportion of the tasks with fatigue that are correctly predicted. On the other hand, the FP rate measures the proportion of the tasks without fatigue that are incorrectly predicted. The ROC curve is plotted by sorting the pairs of the TP and FP rates in decreasing order of ψ and connecting each neighboring pair on the FP-TP rate plane.

The AUC is the area in the first quadrant under the ROC curve and it takes a value between 0 and 1. A high AUC indicates a high performance in discriminating tasks with fatigue from those without.

4   Proposed Method

4.1   Approach

In using the periodic short time monitoring, there are two problems. The first problem is that a short-*time* monitoring cannot have a large number of data because the monitoring continues for less than 30 s. It causes the scarcity of information about the task. The second problem is that the number of tasks increases over time, which increases the computational time of a fatigue detection method in a long-*term* monitoring.

To solve the first problem, we regard each short-*time* monitoring as a task and apply a multi-task learning (MTL) method to the tasks. MTL builds a classifier corresponding to each task by using information shared among tasks, which results from, for example, the skeleton of the face and the tendency of facial expressions of the target person. In using a MTL method, we use a task $Z^{(t)}$ which consists of facial data $\{\mathbf{x}_1^{(t)}, \mathbf{x}_2^{(t)}, ..., \mathbf{x}_{N(t)}^{(t)}\}$ and their labels $\{y_1^{(t)}, y_2^{(t)}, ..., y_{N(t)}^{(t)}\}$, where $N(t)$ is the number of data in $Z^{(t)}$. $y_n^{(t)} = 0$ indicates that $\mathbf{x}_n^{(t)}$ represents a neutral face and $y_n^{(t)} = 1$ indicates that $\mathbf{x}_n^{(t)}$ represents a smiling face. Since fatigue induces a significant decline in the smiling activity [1], the parameter vector $\boldsymbol{\theta}^{(t)}$ of a classifier which discriminates the two kinds of faces reflects fatigue effectively.

To solve the second problem, we employ a clustering method as a preprocessing of the anomaly detection. By using the parameter $\boldsymbol{\theta}^{(t)}$ as the feature vector of the task $Z^{(t)}$, a clustering method Γ clusters the tasks $\mathcal{Z}$ into a set of clusters $\mathcal{C} = \{c_1, c_2, ..., c_{M(\mathcal{Z}, \Gamma)}\}$, where $M(\mathcal{Z}, \Gamma)$ is the number of clusters. Since $M(\mathcal{Z}, \Gamma)$ is smaller than the number T of tasks, clustering mitigates the influence of the increasing tasks. In addition to solving the second problem, clustering has an advantage in detecting fatigue because fatigue is often chronic. In the case that tasks with similar fatigue are not small in number, they are not isolated. If the clustering gathers the tasks into a cluster, the anomaly detection by using clusters finds them as anomalies.

Our fatigue detection method by using the periodic short time monitoring is a combination of multi-task learning, clustering and anomaly detection. We employ an efficient lifelong learning algorithm (ELLA) [15] and balanced iterative reducing and clustering using hierarchies (BIRCH) [18] as the multi-task learning method and the clustering method, respectively. Since ELLA and BIRCH proceed incrementally when a new task is observed, our proposed method deals with the increasing number of tasks in a long-*term* monitoring effectively. We believe that incremental methods are effective to our problem because we succeeded to develop several human monitoring robot systems [6,13,16] by using BIRCH. The overview of the proposed method is shown in Fig. 2.

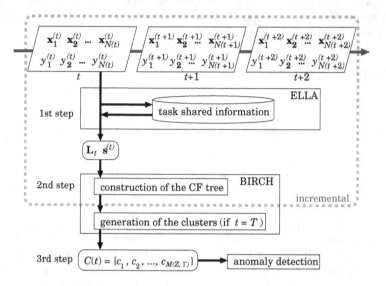

Fig. 2. The overview of the proposed method. The first and second steps are conducted incrementally when a new task is observed.

4.2   Prior Knowledge About Feature Vector

When a task $Z^{(t)}$ is observed, ELLA (refer to the Appendix A) learns the parameter $\boldsymbol{\theta}^{(t)}$ of the classifier for $Z^{(t)}$. $\boldsymbol{\theta}^{(t)}$ is represented as the product of $D \times k$ dictionary matrix $\mathbf{L}$ and $k \times 1$ coefficient vector $\mathbf{s}^{(t)}$, where D is the dimension of the parameter $\boldsymbol{\theta}^{(t)}$ and k is the number of the basis components of $\mathbf{L}$. $\mathbf{L}$ represents the information shared among the tasks.

The parameter $\boldsymbol{\theta}^{(t)}$ changes when a new task $Z^{(t)}$ is learnt because the matrix $\mathbf{L}$ is updated, thus $\mathbf{L}$ after $Z^{(t)}$ is learnt is denoted by $\mathbf{L}_t$. On the other hand, the vector $\mathbf{s}^{(t)}$ is determined by learning of $Z^{(t)}$ and then $\mathbf{s}^{(t)}$ does not change anymore.

4.3   Clustering of Task Parameters

We cluster each task $Z^{(t)}$ incrementally using BIRCH [18] (refer to the Appendix B) with respect to the parameter $\boldsymbol{\theta}^{(t)}$ of the corresponding classifier.

BIRCH consists of two phases: construction of the clustering feature (CF) tree and clustering its leaves. In using BIRCH in our method, there are two problems. The first problem is that the structure of the CF tree is broken if $\boldsymbol{\theta}^{(t)}$ is used directly as a feature vector of $Z^{(t)}$. The CF tree stores each example as a CF which is a representation of compressed data. However, $\boldsymbol{\theta}^{(t)}$ is updated when a new task is learnt. The second problem is that it is difficult to select two optimal values for thresholds τ (for the first phase) and ϕ (for the second phase) of BIRCH. It is difficult to foresee the values which discriminate tasks with fatigue from those without because there are individual differences in the facial expression.

Extended CF: Since the CF tree cannot store $\boldsymbol{\theta}^{(t)}$ as CFs, we take an approach that the $k \times 1$ vector $\mathbf{s}^{(t)}$ is stored instead of $\boldsymbol{\theta}^{(t)}$ and the corresponding CF of $\boldsymbol{\theta}^{(t)}$ is reconstructed from $\mathbf{L}$ and the CF of $\mathbf{s}^{(t)}$. We use an extended CF $(N, \mathbf{a}, \mathbf{B}) = (N, \sum_{i=1}^{N} \mathbf{s}^{(i)}, \sum_{i=1}^{N} \mathbf{s}^{(i)} \mathbf{s}^{(i)^{\top}})$; $\sum_{i=1}^{N} \mathbf{M}_i$ is equal to $\mathbf{M}_1 + \mathbf{M}_2 + \ldots + \mathbf{M}_N$, where $\mathbf{M}_i$ is a matrix. The extended CF uses the matrix $\sum_{i=1}^{N} \mathbf{s}^{(i)} \mathbf{s}^{(i)^{\top}}$ as the square sum instead of the scalar value $\sum_{i=1}^{N} \mathbf{s}^{(i)^{\top}} \mathbf{s}^{(i)}$ of the original CF. Since the square sum $\sum_{i=1}^{N} \mathbf{s}^{(i)^{\top}} \mathbf{s}^{(i)}$ is obtained by the diagonal sum of $\mathbf{B}$, the extended CF enables calculations of plural measurements [18] by using the original CF. The CF of $\boldsymbol{\theta}^{(t)} = \mathbf{L}\mathbf{s}^{(t)}$ is reconstructed as follows.

$$\left(N, \sum_{i=1}^{N} \mathbf{L}\mathbf{s}^{(i)}, \sum_{i=1}^{N} \mathbf{L}\mathbf{s}^{(i)} \left(\mathbf{L}\mathbf{s}^{(i)} \right)^{\top} \right)$$
$$= \left(N, \mathbf{L} \sum_{i=1}^{N} \mathbf{s}^{(i)}, \sum_{i=1}^{N} \mathbf{L}\mathbf{s}^{(i)} \mathbf{s}^{(i)^{\top}} \mathbf{L}^{\top} \right)$$
$$= \left(N, \mathbf{L}\mathbf{a}, \mathbf{L}(\mathbf{B})\mathbf{L}^{\top} \right) \tag{1}$$

Thus, we use the extended CF in BIRCH instead of the original CF.

Decision of Two Thresholds: The obtained clusters $\mathcal{C}$ depend on two kinds of thresholds τ (for each leaf in the CF tree) and ϕ (for clustering of the leaves) of BIRCH. It is difficult to find two optimal values for τ and ϕ. To mitigate this difficulty, we determine the values for τ and ϕ by using several tasks. Thus, we assume that the first K tasks are similar and not greatly affected by fatigue. It is not difficult to prepare a dataset which satisfies this assumption when K is small, e.g., when $K = 5$, the target person does not overwork for two and a half hours. We assume that the values for τ and ϕ are determined from the first K tasks.

Construction of the CF Tree: In the first phase in BIRCH, we calculate the diameter of a set which consists of an input example and examples in the nearest leaf on a scale of $\boldsymbol{\theta}_K^{(t)} = \mathbf{L}_K \mathbf{s}^{(t)}$. To judge whether the input example is absorbed into the leaf, the diameter is compared with an absorption threshold τ. In the

---

Algorithm 1. Decision of the absorption threshold τ (and the construction of the CF tree)

Input: weight vectors $\mathbf{s}^{(1)}, \mathbf{s}^{(2)}, ..., \mathbf{s}^{(K)}, ..., \mathbf{s}^{(T)}$, matrix $\mathbf{L}_2, \mathbf{L}_3, ..., \mathbf{L}_K$
Output: absorption threshold τ
 1: $\tau \Leftarrow \infty$
 2: $CreateRoot(\mathbf{s}^{(1)})$
 3: **for** $i = 2$ to T **do**
 4:     $j \Leftarrow i$
 5:     **if** $j > K$ **then**
 6:       $j \Leftarrow K$
 7:     **end if**
 8:     $\mathcal{E}_{\text{near}} \Leftarrow SearchCFtree(\mathbf{L}_j, \mathbf{s}^{(i)})$
 9:     $dist \Leftarrow Diameter(\mathbf{L}_j, \mathbf{s}^{(i)} \sqcup \mathcal{E}_{\text{near}})$
10:     **if** $\tau > dist$ **then**
11:       $\tau \Leftarrow dist$
12:     **end if**
13:     $InsertCFtreeAsLeaf(\mathbf{s}^{(i)})$
14: **end for**

---

construction of the CF tree phase, we do not gather the first K tasks because this phase cannot use the information shared among all tasks. Therefore we use a slightly smaller value to gather the first K tasks for τ.

Algorithm 1 determines the absorption threshold τ. $CreateRoot(\mathbf{s}^{(1)})$ generates the root node of a CF tree which consists of $\mathbf{s}^{(1)}$. $SearchCFtree(\mathbf{L}_j, \mathbf{s}^{(i)})$ searches the closest leaf $\mathcal{E}_{\text{near}}$ from $\mathbf{s}^{(i)}$ by using a distance on a scale of $\theta_j^{(t)}$. $Diameter(\mathbf{L}_j, \mathbf{s}^{(i)} \sqcup \mathcal{E}_{\text{near}})$ returns the diameter of $(\mathbf{s}^{(i)} \sqcup \mathcal{E}_{\text{near}})$ on a scale of $\theta_j^{(t)}$, where $(\mathbf{s}^{(i)} \sqcup \mathcal{E}_{\text{near}})$ is the merged set of $\mathbf{s}^{(i)}$ and examples in $\mathcal{E}_{\text{near}}$. $InsertCFtreeAsLeaf(\mathbf{s}^{(i)})$ inserts $\mathbf{s}^{(i)}$ in the CF tree as a new leaf. The Algorithm 1 outputs the maximum threshold τ that separates the first K tasks.

After the first K tasks are learnt, we use $\mathbf{L}_K$ to construct the CF tree because updated $\mathbf{L}$ changes $\boldsymbol{\theta}^{(t)}$ that breaks the structure of the CF tree. We use the "initializeWithFirstKTasks" option in ELLA and select $k = K$ so that $\mathbf{L}_j \mathbf{s}^{(i)}$ ($i \leq K$) is equivalent to $\mathbf{L}_K \mathbf{s}^{(i)}$ as follows.

$$\mathbf{L}_j \mathbf{s}^{(i)} = \mathbf{L}_i \mathbf{s}^{(i)} = \begin{pmatrix} l_1 \ ... \ l_{i-1} \ l_i \ \ * \ ... \ * \end{pmatrix} \begin{pmatrix} 0 \ ... \ 0 \ 1 \ 0 \ ... \ 0 \end{pmatrix}^\top = l_i \qquad (2)$$

$$\mathbf{L}_K \mathbf{s}^{(i)} = \begin{pmatrix} l_1 \ ... \ l_{i-1} \ l_i \ l_{i+1} \ ... \ l_K \end{pmatrix} \begin{pmatrix} 0 \ ... \ 0 \ 1 \ 0 \ ... \ 0 \end{pmatrix}^\top = l_i \qquad (3)$$

$\mathbf{L}_j$ ($j = i \leq K$) depends on how to decide $\mathbf{s}^{(i)}$. By using the "initializeWithFirstKTasks" option, $\mathbf{s}^{(i)}$ ($i \leq K$) becomes the unit vector in the direction of the i-th dimension. Since the i-th column of $\mathbf{L}_K$ is initialized by the i-th task only, the i-th column of $\mathbf{L}_j$ and $\mathbf{L}_K$ are equivalent as shown in Eqs. 2 and 3. Therefore the Algorithm 1 can also proceed correctly before $\mathbf{L}_K$ is obtained.

Generation of the Clusters: In the second phase in BIRCH, we can use $\mathbf{L}_T$, which reflects the information shared among all T tasks, to obtain clusters. To cluster

Algorithm 2. Decision of the threshold ϕ (and the generation of the clusters)

Input: leaves $\mathcal{E}_1, \mathcal{E}_2, ..., \mathcal{E}_{M'(\mathcal{Z},K)}$, matrix $\mathbf{L}_T$
Output: threshold ϕ

```
 1: φ ⇐ 0
 2: (v₁, v₂, ..., v_M'(Z,K)) ⇐ (0, 0, ..., 0)
 3: for i = 1 to M'(Z, K) − 1 do
 4:   if IncludeFirstK(Eᵢ) and vᵢ = 0 then
 5:     for j = i + 1 to M'(Z, K) do
 6:       if IncludeFirstK(Eⱼ) and vⱼ = 0 then
 7:         dist ⇐ Diameter(L_T, Eᵢ ⊔ Eⱼ)
 8:         if φ < dist then
 9:           φ ⇐ dist
10:         end if
11:         Merge(Eᵢ, Eⱼ)
12:         vⱼ ⇐ 1
13:       end if
14:     end for
15:   end if
16: end for
```

the leaves (subclusters) of the CF tree, we calculate the diameter of a merged set of examples in two subclusters on a scale of $\theta_T^{(t)} = \mathbf{L}_T \mathbf{s}^{(t)}$. The diameter is compared with a threshold ϕ to judge whether the subclusters are merged. We use ϕ which just gathers the first K tasks.

The threshold ϕ is determined by Algorithm 2. $(v_1, v_2, ..., v_{M'(\mathcal{Z},K)})$ is a vector of flags each of which indicates whether the corresponding leaf is merged into another leaf, where $M'(\mathcal{Z}, K)$ is the number of the leaves. $IncludeFirstK(\mathcal{E}_i)$ returns True when the leaf $\mathcal{E}_i$ includes at least one of the first K tasks, otherwise, it returns False. $Diameter(\mathbf{L}_T, \mathcal{E}_i \sqcup \mathcal{E}_j)$ calculates the diameter of $(\mathcal{E}_i \sqcup \mathcal{E}_j)$ on a scale of $\theta_T^{(t)}$, where $(\mathcal{E}_i \sqcup \mathcal{E}_j)$ is the merged set of examples in $\mathcal{E}_i$ and $\mathcal{E}_j$. $Merge(\mathcal{E}_i, \mathcal{E}_j)$ merges $\mathcal{E}_j$ into $\mathcal{E}_i$. This algorithm outputs the minimum threshold ϕ which gathers the first K tasks into a cluster.

4.4 Anomaly Detection with Respect to Clusters

To detect clusters which consist of tasks with fatigue, we apply anomaly detection to the clusters $\mathcal{C}$. To calculate an anomaly measure e_m of each cluster c_m, we use the centroids $\{\overline{\mathbf{x}}^{(1)}, \overline{\mathbf{x}}^{(2)}, ..., \overline{\mathbf{x}}^{(M(\mathcal{Z},K))}\}$ of clusters, their mean $\boldsymbol{\mu}$ and their unbiased estimator of a population variance $\boldsymbol{\sigma}^2$, where $M(\mathcal{Z}, K)$ is the number of clusters. In each dimension d, we calculate the Z-score $z_d^{(m)} = (\overline{x}_d^{(m)} - \mu_d)/\sigma_d$ and employ $\sqrt{\sum_{d=1}^{D} \left(z_d^{(m)} \right)^2}$ as the anomaly measure e_m, where $\overline{x}_d^{(m)}$, μ_d and σ_d are the d-th elements of $\overline{\mathbf{x}}^{(m)}$, $\boldsymbol{\mu}$ and $\boldsymbol{\sigma}$, respectively. $z_d^{(m)}$ shows that the distance between the centroid $\overline{\mathbf{x}}^{(m)}$ and the center of data distribution when the data follows the standard normal distribution. The Z-score is often used for normalization of features.

When the tasks in a cluster c_m are affected by fatigue, its anomaly measure e_m shows a higher value than other clusters. We set a threshold ψ to detect such clusters. When e_m is greater than ψ, it is considered that c_m consists of tasks with fatigue, otherwise, c_m consists of tasks without fatigue.

5   Experiments

5.1   Experimental Setting

To demonstrate the effectiveness of our method, we collected facial data of a desk worker for five days using our monitoring system. Since inducing fatigue deliberately gives a bad influence to the desk worker, it is difficult for us to prepare more datasets. The monitoring on each day started about 10:00 AM. There are about 35 facial data in each task. The details of the datasets are shown in Table 2.

Before the tasks 6, 14, 24 and 61, the target person did harder or more stressful work than usual. For the tasks 14 and 61, the person did deskwork in bad conditions for 30 and 20 min, respectively. In the condition, the display of his notebook PC was set to the lowest brightness and he worked without using his dominant hand. To induce fatigue for the task 24, he did the 2-back test [3] for 30 min. The test was used in [17] to induce fatigue. In the test, a letter is displayed for 2500 ms at 500 ms interval and the target person judges whether the current letter and the letter displayed at two back are same (the both letters are same at 33 %). The three tasks induced fatigue artificially. The task 6 induced mental stress which was caused by the situation that the target person ordered some products from an unfamiliar online store (the person knew the store on that day). He became nervous to think whether he might have made some mistakes in the order.

The proposed method (we call it **ELLA + BIRCH**) compared with three method. The first method **BIRCH(smile)** does not use any learning method. The method uses the means of 17 animation units in smiling faces as a feature vector for each task. In each dimension of the feature vector, the value is normalized using Z-score with the mean and the standard deviation which are calculated from the examples in the first K tasks. The second method **ELLA_only** does

Table 2. Facial data of the desk worker

Date	Feb. 19th	Mar. 5th	Mar. 6th	Mar. 9th	Mar. 10th
Number of tasks	14	14	12	11	12
TaskID	1–14	15–28	29–40	41–51	52–63
Number of data/task (mean)	33.2	36.7	32.6	38.1	35.1
Proportion of smile/task (mean)	47.7 %	47.1 %	48.3 %	47.5 %	46.7 %

not use BIRCH before anomaly detection. If clustering of tasks is not effective to detect fatigue, this method outperforms the proposed method. The third method **STL + BIRCH** uses a single task learner with the logistic regression setting instead of ELLA. This method spends shorter computational time than our method, however, this method cannot consider information shared among tasks.

In using BIRCH, we set $K = 2, 3, 4, 5$ (the number of the first tasks which are gathered into a cluster), because we considered that it is not difficult for a desk worker not to overwork for two and a half hours on the first day. In the proposed method, the number k of the latent basis for the dictionary matrix **L** in ELLA is equal to K to satisfy the condition for the Algorithm 1. Since **ELLA_only** is to confirm whether the clustering of the proposed method is effective, k in the method was set to K in the same way as the proposed method.

To evaluate the proposed method and the three compared methods, we conducted two kinds of experiments: each method is applied to (1) each dataset and (2) the combined set of all datasets. For the experiments (1), we selected the same parameter ψ in all datasets and applied the anomaly detection to the all clusters that were obtained from the datasets. This setting assumes the situation that we use an optimal threshold ψ in a dataset to detect fatigue in another dataset. The setting of the experiments (2) is more practical because a long-*term* monitoring is more suitable for fatigue detection of a desk worker than one-day monitoring.

5.2   Results

The results of the experiments (1) are shown in Fig. 3. Since **BIRCH(smile)** shows the lowest performance with all K, our setting that classifiers of smiling and neutral faces are employed as feature vectors is suitable for our prob-

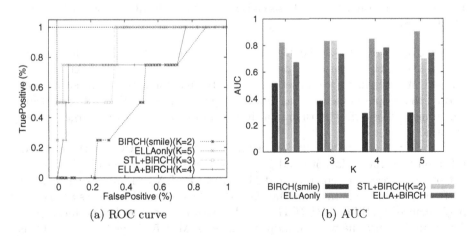

(a) ROC curve   (b) AUC

Fig. 3. ROC curve and AUC in the experiments (1). In the ROC curve, each method uses the best K.

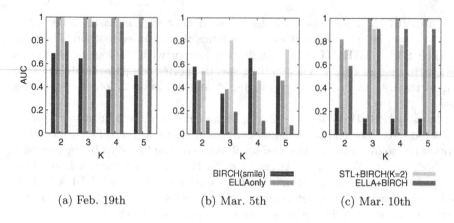

Fig. 4. AUC in the experiments (1) with the first approach.

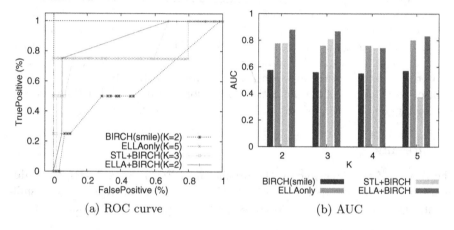

Fig. 5. ROC curve and AUC in the second experiment; in the ROC curve, each method uses the best K.

lem. **ELLA_only** shows the highest performance. In two out of four cases, **STL + BIRCH** outperforms our proposed method. These are because the number of tasks in each dataset is small (the maximum is 14). In such a situation, the proposed method has disadvantages because multi-task learning and clustering are less effective than in a situation in which there are a large number of tasks.

To analyze the details of the results, we verify the AUCs of the datasets taken on Feb. 19th, Mar. 5th and 10th. The AUCs are shown in Fig. 4. In seven out of eight cases on Feb. 19th and Mar. 10th, **ELLA_only** shows the highest performance. In the dataset on Mar. 5th, the proposed method shows a very low performance and **STL + BIRCH** and **ELLA_only** also show low performances. These are because the work to induce fatigue on Mar. 5th (the 2-back test) was as hard as daily deskwork and it is more difficult to detect the task 24 than the other three tasks with fatigue. In three out of four cases on Feb. 19th,

STL + BIRCH shows the highest performance. However, the method shows the lowest performance in the remaining case.

The results of the experiments (2) are shown in Fig. 5. In three out of four cases, the proposed method outperforms the three compared methods. In the experiments (2), the number of tasks is 63 which is greater than the one of each dataset in the experiments (1). In this situation, the proposed method has two advantages: multi-task learning clarifies differences among tasks using the information shared among tasks and clustering is effective in the preprocessing method for the anomaly detection. In $K = 4$, **ELLA_only** shows a higher evaluation value, however, there is no large difference between the proposed method and **ELLA_only**. Therefore, the proposed method is effective for fatigue detection in a long-*term* monitoring, where the number of tasks is large.

When we inspect the clusters, the tasks 61 (which is with fatigue), 62 and 63 often belong to the same cluster, e.g., in the experiments (1), the proposed method always gathers them. We consider that the tasks 62 and 63 were affected by the fatigue in the task 61 since the target person had not been recovered from the fatigue. In the end of Mar. 10th, the person was still feeling tired. Nevertheless we tackled detecting tasks just after the target worked to induce fatigue, the methods including clustering have a potential to detect other tasks which are affected by fatigue.

To discuss the computational time of the proposed method, we measured the processing time of two parts: the incremental part and the detecting part. The incremental part consists of learning a task in ELLA and constructing the CF tree in BIRCH and the part is conducted incrementally when a new task is observed. The detecting part consists of clustering the leaves of the CF tree in BIRCH and detecting anomalies and the part is conducted only when we need the result of the fatigue detection. To measure the processing times, we used the experiments (2) setting and the proposed method with $K = 2$. The mean of the processing time of the incremental part is 1.39×10^{-2} s and the mean of the processing time of the detecting part is 1.02×10^{-2} s[7]. Therefore our proposed system is fast enough to return the result in real time.

6   Related Works

In these years, many researchers tackled the problem of learning in non-stationary environments. Karnick et al. [12] presented an ensemble of classifiers based on an incremental approach. The classifiers are adapted to a concept drift by using a dynamically weighted majority voting. Kapp et al. [11] presented a dynamic optimization method to learn a support vector machine (SVM) classifier which efficiently predicts the class of an example. They proposed a particle swarm optimization (PSO) based framework to select optimal hyper-parameters of SVM in a dynamic environment. These methods are effective to adapt the learning models to the dynamic changes of the environments. We are motivated

---

[7] We use the notebook PC Panasonic CF-SX3BDCBP (Core i7 4650U 2.29 GHz, RAM 16.0 GB).

to describe the structure of the tasks explicitly. Thus we adopted such a multi-task learning (MTL) method.

Clustered multi-task learning (CMTL) is proposed as an extension of MTL. Jacob et al. [9] identified a cluster structure of different tasks and used it for MTL. They included a penalty term for the cluster structure in an objective function and proposed a method to compute the regularization of the function efficiently. Zhou et al. [19] adapted a convex relaxation to a CMTL method in which tasks are partitioned into a set of groups. They established an equivalence relationship between the method and the convex relaxation of alternating structure optimization (ASO), a popular MTL method proposed in [4]. Each of these works uses a convex relaxation to optimize its objective function efficiently. However, the incremental nature of our problem makes these methods unsuitable because they optimize their objective functions from scratch. Therefore we adopted an incremental MTL method, ELLA [15].

7   Conclusions

In this paper, we employed a periodic short time monitoring setting and proposed a method which is a combination of multi-task learning, clustering and anomaly detection to detect fatigue. This setting is effective for a desk worker who is often at his/her desk, e.g., a programmer and an office clerk. In contrast to continual monitoring, this setting avoids violating the privacy and practically decreasing the ability for deskwork of the desk worker. The experiments showed that our proposed method exhibited a high performance when the number of tasks was large. Although the dataset is small, it is considered that this paper indicates a new direction for fatigue detection.

In the future work, we will tackle other detection problems by using the periodic short time monitoring and the proposed method. For example, we will extend the proposed method to detect a change of emotion of a person which is related with faces and use it for human-centric applications.

Appendix

A   ELLA

ELLA [15] is a multi-task learning method using a parametric approach for a lifelong learning setting. Learning tasks $Z^{(1)}, Z^{(2)}, ..., Z^{(T_{\max})}$ are observed sequentially, where $T_{\max}$ is the number of tasks which is not known a priori. $Z^{(t)}$ is represented as $(\hat{f}^{(t)}, \mathbf{X}^{(t)}, \mathbf{y}^{(t)})$, where $\mathbf{X}^{(t)}$ is a set of examples, $\mathbf{y}^{(t)}$ is a set of labels and $\hat{f}^{(t)}$ is a hidden mapping from $\mathbf{X}^{(t)}$ to $\mathbf{y}^{(t)}$ in the task $Z^{(t)}$. Its goal is to construct classifiers $f^{(1)}, f^{(2)}, ..., f^{(T_{\max})}$ which approximate $\hat{f}^{(t)}$'s. The prediction function $f^{(t)}(\mathbf{x}) = f(\mathbf{x}; \boldsymbol{\theta}^{(t)})$ is specific to the task $Z^{(t)}$.

The model of ELLA is based on the GO-MTL model [14]. The parameter vector $\boldsymbol{\theta}^{(t)}$ is represented as a product of a matrix $\mathbf{L}$ and the weight vector $\mathbf{s}^{(t)}$, where $\mathbf{L}$ consists of k latent model components. The problem of minimizing the predictive loss over all tasks is realized by the minimization of the following objective function.

Algorithm 3. Learning a task in ELLA

Input: examples $\mathbf{X}^{(t)}$ and labels $\mathbf{y}^{(t)}$ of the task t
Output: dictionary matrix $\mathbf{L}$ and the weight vector $\mathbf{s}^{(t)}$ of the task t
 1: $T \leftarrow T + 1$
 2: $(\boldsymbol{\theta}_{\mathrm{STL}}^{(t)}, \mathbf{D}^{(t)}) \leftarrow singleTaskLearner(\mathbf{X}^{(t)}, \mathbf{y}^{(t)})$
 3: $\mathbf{L} \leftarrow reinitializeAllZeroColumns(\mathbf{L})$
 4: $\mathbf{s}^{(t)} \leftarrow \arg\min_{\mathbf{s}^{(t)}} \left(\mu \left\| \mathbf{s}^{(t)} \right\|_1 + \left\| \sqrt{\mathbf{D}^{(t)}} \left(\boldsymbol{\theta}_{\mathrm{STL}}^{(t)} - \mathbf{Ls}^{(t)} \right) \right\|^2 \right)$
 5: $\mathbf{A}_t \leftarrow \mathbf{A}_{t-1} + \left(\mathbf{s}^{(t)} \mathbf{s}^{(t)^\top} \right) \otimes \mathbf{D}^{(t)}$ $(\mathbf{A}_0 \leftarrow \mathbf{zeros}_{k \times d, k \times d})$
 6: $\mathbf{b}_t \leftarrow \mathbf{b}_{t-1} + \mathrm{vec}\left(\mathbf{s}^{(t)^\top} \otimes \left(\boldsymbol{\theta}_{\mathrm{STL}}^{(t)^\top} \mathbf{D}^{(t)} \right) \right)$ $(\mathbf{b}_0 \leftarrow \mathbf{zeros}_{k \times d, 1})$
 7: $\mathbf{L} \leftarrow \mathrm{mat}\left(\left(\frac{1}{T} \mathbf{A}_t + \lambda \mathbf{I}_{k \times d, k \times d} \right)^{-1} \frac{1}{T} \mathbf{b}_t \right)$

$$
e_T(\mathbf{L}) = \frac{1}{T} \min_{\mathbf{s}^{(t)}} \left\{ \frac{1}{n_t} \sum_{i=1}^{n_t} \mathcal{L}\left(f\left(\mathbf{x}_i^{(t)}; \mathbf{Ls}^{(t)} \right), y_i^{(t)} \right) + \mu \left\| \mathbf{s}^{(t)} \right\|_1 \right\} + \lambda \|\mathbf{L}\|_{\mathrm{F}}^2. \quad \text{(A.1)}
$$

where n_t is the number of examples in the task $Z^{(t)}$ and $\mathcal{L}$ is a loss function.

ELLA provides two approximations to optimize the objective function $e_T(\mathbf{L})$ efficiently and to proceed incrementally with respect to tasks. The first approximation uses the second-order Taylor expansion of $\frac{1}{n_t} \sum_{i=1}^{n_t} \mathcal{L}(f(\mathbf{x}_i^{(t)}; \mathbf{Ls}^{(t)}), y_i^{(t)})$ around $\boldsymbol{\theta} = \boldsymbol{\theta}_{\mathrm{STL}}^{(t)}$, where $\boldsymbol{\theta}_{\mathrm{STL}}^{(t)}$ is an optimal classifier learnt on only the training data for task $Z^{(t)}$. Using this approximation, the objective function does not depend on all of the previous training data through the inner summation.

The second approximation modifies the formulation to remove the minimization over $\mathbf{s}^{(t)}$. The previous tasks benefit from new tasks through modified $\mathbf{L}$ instead of updated $\mathbf{s}^{(t)}$. This choice to update $\mathbf{s}^{(t)}$ only when the task $Z^{(t)}$ is observed does not practically affect the quality of model fitting as the number of tasks grows large.

The overview of ELLA is shown in the Algorithm 3. T is the number of the observed tasks. At first, the parameter $\boldsymbol{\theta}_{\mathrm{STL}}^{(t)}$ and the Hessian $\mathbf{D}^{(t)}$ of the loss function $\mathcal{L}$ are calculated from the examples $\mathbf{X}^{(t)}$ and their labels $\mathbf{y}^{(t)}$. Before the calculation of $\mathbf{s}^{(t)}$, zero columns of $\mathbf{L}$ are reinitialized by using normal random numbers. In the line 4, $\mathbf{s}^{(t)}$ is calculated using lasso model fit with least angle regression (LARS) [7]. The matrix $\mathbf{A}_t$ and the vector $\mathbf{b}_t$ are used to update $\mathbf{L}$. This algorithm proceeds incrementally with respect to tasks.

The selection of $\mathbf{s}^{(t)}$ depends on $\mathbf{L}$. Before the first k tasks are learnt, some columns of $\mathbf{L}$ are invalid because they indicate initial values. The option "initializeWithFirstKTasks" decides how to choose $\mathbf{s}^{(t)}$ and $\mathbf{L}$ in the first k tasks. When the option is valid, $\mathbf{s}^{(t)}$ $(t \leq k)$ becomes the unit vector in the direction of the t-th dimension. In this case, the t-th column of $\mathbf{L}$ is initialized to be similar to $\boldsymbol{\theta}_{\mathrm{STL}}^{(t)}$ in the line 2 in the Algorithm 3. Otherwise, all elements of $\mathbf{L}$ are initialized by normal random numbers and $\mathbf{s}^{(t)}$ $(t \leq k)$ is selected by the line 4 in the Algorithm 3.

B   BIRCH

BIRCH [18] is a distance-based incremental clustering method. BIRCH consists of two main phases and two optional phases, though the latter two phases are out of the scope in this paper. The main phases of BIRCH are the construction of the clustering feature (CF) tree and the generation of the clusters. The CF tree gathers similar examples into its leaf which is called a subcluster and clusters are generated by clustering of the subclusters.

The CF tree is an index structure similar to B+ tree [5], which consists of CFs. For a set of examples $\mathcal{E} = \{e_1, e_2, ..., e_N\}$, the CF of $\mathcal{E}$ is a triplet $(N, \mathbf{a}, b) = (N, \sum_{i=1}^{N} \mathbf{e}_i, \sum_{i=1}^{N} \|\mathbf{e}_i\|^2)$. By using CFs, important statistics [18] about clusters such as the centroid $\overline{\mathbf{x}}$ and the diameter $D(\mathcal{E})$ of a set of examples $\mathcal{E}$ and the average inter cluster distance $D2(\mathcal{E}^{(k)}, \mathcal{E}^{(m)})$ of two sets of examples $\mathcal{E}^{(k)}$ and $\mathcal{E}^{(m)}$ are computed accurately as follows.

$$\overline{\mathbf{x}} = \frac{\sum_{i=1}^{N} \mathbf{e}_i}{N} = \frac{\mathbf{a}}{N} \tag{B.1}$$

$$D(\mathcal{E}) = \sqrt{\frac{\sum_{i=1}^{N} \sum_{j=1}^{N} (\mathbf{e}_i - \mathbf{e}_j)^2}{N(N-1)}}$$

$$= \sqrt{\frac{2Nb - 2\mathbf{a}^2}{N(N-1)}} \tag{B.2}$$

$$D2(\mathcal{E}^{(k)}, \mathcal{E}^{(m)}) = \sqrt{\frac{\sum_{i=1}^{N^{(k)}} \sum_{j=1}^{N^{(m)}} \left(\mathbf{e}_i^{(k)} - \mathbf{e}_j^{(m)}\right)^2}{N^{(k)} N^{(m)}}}$$

$$= \sqrt{\frac{N^{(m)} b^{(k)} + N^{(k)} b^{(m)} - 2\mathbf{a}^{(k)} \cdot \mathbf{a}^{(m)}}{N^{(k)} N^{(m)}}} \tag{B.3}$$

Note that CFs satisfy an additivity theorem, i.e., (CF of $\mathcal{E}^{(k)}$) + (CF of $\mathcal{E}^{(m)}$) = (CF of ($\mathcal{E}^{(k)} \sqcup \mathcal{E}^{(m)}$)), where ($\mathcal{E}^{(k)} \sqcup \mathcal{E}^{(m)}$) is the merged set of examples in $\mathcal{E}^{(k)}$ and $\mathcal{E}^{(m)}$. This theorem enables merging two sets of examples with the information of their CFs without using the original examples.

To construct a CF tree, two parameters are used: the branching factor β for an internal node and the absorption threshold τ for the diameter of a leaf. BIRCH searches the closest leaf of the CF tree from an input example and calculates the diameter of the CF which consists of the leaf and the example. When the diameter is less than τ, the example is absorbed into the leaf, otherwise, inserted in the CF tree as a new leaf, in a similar way as B+ tree [5]. In each leaf of the CF tree, similar examples are gathered, which is called a subcluster.

In the generation of the clusters phase, subclusters are clustered using a distance measure and a threshold ϕ. When the distance between two subclusters is less than ϕ, the subclusters are merged, otherwise, they are not merged. Since the number of subclusters is less than the number of examples, BIRCH is efficient for large datasets and real-time applications.

References

1. Brach, J.S., VanSwearingen, J.: Measuring fatigue related to facial muscle function. Arch. Phys. Med. Rehabil. **76**(10), 905–908 (1995)
2. Bradley, A.P.: The use of the area under the ROC curve in the evaluation of machine learning algorithms. Pattern Recogn. **30**(7), 1145–1159 (1997)
3. Braver, T.S., Cohen, J.D., Nystrom, L.E., Jonides, J., Smith, E.E., Noll, D.C.: A parametric study of prefrontal cortex involvement in human working memory. Neuroimage **5**(1), 49–62 (1997)
4. Chen, J., Tang, L., Liu, J., Ye, J.: A convex formulation for learning shared structures from multiple tasks. In: Proceedings of the 26th Annual International Conference on Machine Learning, ICML 2009, pp. 137–144 (2009)
5. Comer, D.: The ubiquitous B-Tree. ACM Comput. Surv. **11**(2), 121–137 (1979)
6. Deguchi, Y., Suzuki, E.: Skeleton clustering by autonomous mobile robots for subtle fall risk discovery. In: Andreasen, T., Christiansen, H., Cubero, J.-C., Raś, Z.W. (eds.) ISMIS 2014. LNCS, vol. 8502, pp. 500–505. Springer, Heidelberg (2014)
7. Efron, B., Hastie, T., Johnstone, I., Tibshirani, R., et al.: Least angle regression. Ann. Stat. **32**(2), 407–499 (2004)
8. Hua, C., Zhang, Y.: Driver fatigue detection based on active facial features locating. J. Simul. **2**(6), 335 (2014)
9. Jacob, L., Bach, F., Vert, J.-P.: Clustered multi-task learning: a convex formulation. Adv. Neural Inf. Process. Syst. **21**, 745–752 (2009)
10. Ji, Q., Zhu, Z., Lan, P.: Real-time nonintrusive monitoring and prediction of driver fatigue. IEEE T. Veh. Technol. **53**(4), 1052–1068 (2004)
11. Kapp, M.N., Sabourin, R., Maupin, P.: A dynamic model selection strategy for support vector machine classifiers. Appl. Soft Comput. **12**(8), 2550–2565 (2012)
12. Karnick, M.T., Muhlbaier, M.D., Polikar, R.: Incremental learning in non-stationary environments with concept drift using a multiple classifier based approach. In: 19th International Conference on Pattern Recognition (ICPR 2008), pp. 1–4 (2008)
13. Kondo, R., Deguchi, Y., Suzuki, E.: Developing a face monitoring robot for a desk worker. In: Aarts, E., et al. (eds.) AmI 2014. LNCS, vol. 8850, pp. 226–241. Springer, Heidelberg (2014)
14. Kumar, A., Daumé III, H.: learning task grouping and overlap in multi-task learning. In: Proceedings of the 29th International Conference on Machine Learning (ICML 2012), pp. 1383–1390 (2012)
15. Ruvolo, P., Eaton, E.: ELLA: an efficient lifelong learning algorithm. In: Proceedings of the 30th International Conference on Machine Learning, (ICML 2013), pp. 507–515 (2013)
16. Takayama, D., Deguchi, Y., Takano, S., Scuturici, V.-M., Petit, J.-M., Suzuki, E.: Multi-view onboard clustering of skeleton data for fall risk discovery. In: Aarts, E., et al. (eds.) AmI 2014. LNCS, vol. 8850, pp. 258–273. Springer, Heidelberg (2014)
17. Tanaka, M., Mizuno, K., Yamaguti, K., Kuratsune, H., Fujii, A., Baba, H., Matsuda, K., Nishimae, A., Takesaka, T., Watanabe, Y.: Autonomic nervous alterations associated with daily level of fatigue. Behav. Brain Funct. **7**, 46 (2011)
18. Zhang, T., Ramakrishnan, R., Livny, M.: BIRCH: a new data clustering algorithm and its applications. Data Min. Knowl. discovery **1**(2), 141–182 (1997)
19. Zhou, J., Chen, J., Ye, J.: Clustered multi-task learning via alternating structure optimization. Adv. Neural Inf. Process. Syst. **24**, 702–710 (2011)

Data-Analytics Based Coaching Towards Behavior Change for Dental Hygiene

Boris de Ruyter[✉]

Philips Research Europe, High-Tech Campus 36,
5656 AE Eindhoven, The Netherlands
boris.de.ruyter@philips.com

Abstract. Within the vision of Ambient Intelligence it is assumed that future electronic systems will be embedded into our lives and have different levels of intelligence. One class of systems that has reached such levels of embedding and intelligence are coaching systems for behavioral change. In this paper the findings of a field study are presented in which a coaching system is driven by data-analytics from sensor data. The study provides some first evidence that such coaching system is effective in guiding people to change their behavior. Additional, the study results enable the formulation of a statistical relationship between the test participant's behaviors and the achieved adherence to the coaching target.

1 Introduction

As outset in the vision of Ambient Intelligence (AmI), technology will become *embedded* into our daily life [2] and reach different levels of both *system-* and *social intelligence* [3]. As the Internet of Things (IoT) is expected to reach 50 billion Internet connected devices in just a couple of years from now [14] and as much as 60 % of the US population is tracking their weight, diet or exercise routines [15] through technologies embedded in their everyday life, it is acknowledged that the *embedding* of technology as described in Ambient Intelligence is no longer a vision of the future but has become part of reality.

With respect to the *intelligence* of technology applications embedded in our daily life it is often assumed that we have not yet reached all levels of intelligence (being: *context-aware, personalized, adaptive* and *anticipatory*). However, with the application of persuasive technologies in an AmI context [11], it is observed that all levels of system intelligence find their way in today's embodiment of the AmI vision.

In this paper a case study is presented of coaching users towards healthy habits using a rule-base coaching system that builds on data-analytics from ambient sensors in a home environment. More specific, the case study focussed on changing an *dental hygiene* related habit: brushing teeth before instead of after breakfast. This case study was selected as it involves the challenge of changing an existing habit while the outcome of such behavior change is of benefit to the end-user.

Kameas et al. (Eds.): AmI 2015, LNCS 9425, pp. 284–295, 2015.
DOI: 10.1007/978-3-319-26005-1_19

1.1   Dental Hygiene

Although the importance of proper tooth brushing habits seems widely accepted and well embedded into children's education, it seems that support on proper tooth brushing habits is missing [7]. In a longitudinal study on the tooth brushing habit of young teens more than 95 % of the participants reported daily brushing while in reality 20 % of the participants did not do it every evening [6]. Yet, studies have shown the effect of brushing frequency in caries reduction [8]. Besides tooth brushing frequency the brushing duration has been found to be of significant importance for plaque removal [10]. Clearly both having the correct habit (e.g. brushing in the evening) and the correct technique (e.g. brushing duration) are of great importance for dental hygiene.

An aspect that has received less attention is the timing of brushing teeth. Due to acidic foods and beverages (e.g. orange juice) that soften the enamel of teeth, it is recommended to brush teeth before meals as this can help preventing dental erosion. Yet, many people have developed the habit of brushing teeth after instead of before a meal.

1.2   Behavior Change

As society is confronted with many healthcare problems in general, it is widely accepted that many of these problems can be influenced, even prevented, by adequate human behavior. In fact, today's society does create awareness for the health related importance of, for example physical activity and nutrition, behavior in preventing healthcare problems. However, simply creating awareness for behaviors that influence the risk of developing a disease is rarely sufficient to change behavior [12]. Although raising awareness for the need to change behavior is of importance, it predicts only about 30 % of the variance in behavior change.

Within literature there are several theories on behavior change that model the relationship between behavior change and aspects such as for example, personal attitudes, social norms and perceived control over one's behavior. These theories act as a conceptual framework for designing behavior change programs. Some of the frequently used theories are the *Social Cognitive Theory* [5], the *Information-Motivation-Behavioral skills* model [9] and the *Trans-Theoretical Model* [13]. Based on the work of [4] the Social Cognitive Theory (SCT) focuses on the development of social behaviors and emphasizes that learning occurs in a social context using observation as a mechanism. Specifically attractive is that this theory combines *personal* (a person's own thought and self-beliefs), *behavioral* and *environmental* factors. The *Information-Motivation-Behavioral skills* (IMB) model relates three components:*information* (the knowledge required for changing behavior), *motivation* (the attitude towards changing the behavior) and *behavior skills* (the skills acquired that are necessary to maintain the behavior change). The consequence of using this model as a basis for designing a behavior change program is that, in order to achieve behavior change, one must focus on all three components. Important to note is that changing behavior is not a momentary event but requires longitudinal coaching programs to achieve success.

Models such as the *Trans-Theoretical Model* (TTM) of health behavior change propose a sequence of phases people go through as behavior is changed [13]. For each of these phases different techniques are available to promote that people progress to the next phase in the behavior change model. Such dynamic requires the deployment of adaptive systems that can be tailored to the behavior change phase a person is going through.

The behavior change theories have resulted in a rich set of behavior change techniques that can be readily deployed in coaching programs [1]. In the present study a selection of those techniques are used to design a coaching program (see further).

1.3   Data-Analytics Based Coaching

In this study a data-analytics based approach to coaching people towards behavior change is evaluated. More specific, a number of sensors will be placed in test participant's homes and will provide raw sensor data to a data-analytics backend. The interpreted data will serve as facts upon which a rule-engine can reason to generate coaching guidance (through personalized advice messages) for the test participant. The sensors will provide some basic contextual information from which the rule-engine can infer participant's habits and behavior change. This study is not focusing on the design of innovative coaching techniques but rather on the potential of a data-analytics approach for supporting the deployment of a coaching program designed on the basis of existing coaching techniques (for an extensive overview of coaching strategies see [1]). In the next sections the empirical study and its results will be presented and discussed.

2   Method

2.1   Participants

The study sample consisted of 25 healthy individuals (e.g. no medical conditions such as diabetes or heart diseases) between the ages of 18 and 65 who do not wear complete or partial dentures. The study was approved by an ethics committee to be in accordance with the ethical standards of the responsible committee on human experimentation and with the American Psychology Association.

2.2   Apparatus

An overview of the technical setup for the study is provided in Fig. 1. The study relies on three systems:

1. An *Android App* on the test participant's smartphone
2. A *sensor system* collecting contextual data at the participant's home
3. A *backend system* for collecting and processing data and running a coaching engine

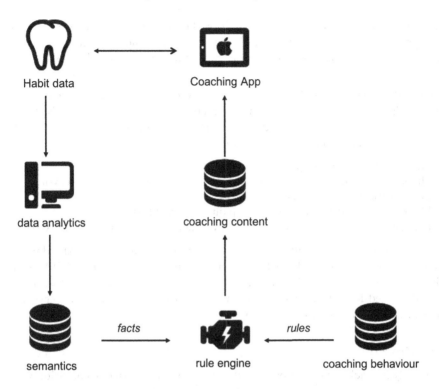

Fig. 1. System setup

Android App. Throughout the study several types of information (i.e. statistics in a dashboard, educational messages, personal advice and reminder messages) should be delivered to the test participants. For this a dedicated App is developed using the Cordova framework. The App receives information in JSON format from the backend server and sends logging information (of the App's usage) in JSON format to the backend server. Due to the cumbersome process for distributing iOS Apps, it is decided to compile the App for the Android platform only.

In order to preserve the test participant's privacy, no private personal related information is required. Upon first time use of the App after installation, the App requests a unique device ID from the Google Cloud Messaging service. Test participants are requested to enter the ID number of the data collection unit they received (the units are handed out without the test leader being aware of which ID number is given to which participant). As part of the App's activation both the GCM unique device ID and the data collection unit's ID number are sent to the backend server. With that the backend can link the data provided by the data collection unit to the App and send messages to the related user's App.

Sensor System. Contextual data is collected using the NetICHome system (http://netichome.com). This system provides a central unit that can be paired with several Z-wave sensors and actuators. The sensor system collects data on the participant's presence in the bathroom, bedroom and kitchen as well as the use of a kitchen appliance (used during breakfast) and the tooth brush.

Backend System. The backend system (standard LAMP infrastructure) collects all data as uploaded by the sensor systems in a MySQL database for further processing. With this data the data-analytics backend (consisting of a number of compiled MATLAB scripts) calculates:

- The time that the test participant wakes up every day
- The times at which the test participant brushes his/her teeth everyday
- The duration of each brushing session
- The times at which the test participant has breakfast
- The time at which test participant leaves/enters the home on a daily basis.

These calculations result in a series of facts that are stored in the database for the rule-engine to work with. The rule-engine is a standard CLIPS engine with forward chaining. Using a CRON job, the CLIPS engine is called and its output is used for actions such as setting new facts, modifying facts, activating rules or sending messages to the App.

2.3 Procedure

The study is a field study (maximum duration 5 weeks) with one condition where all test participants will follow the same study design (see Fig. 2). While sensor data will be collected throughout the entire study, the data-analytics will provide two types of facts to the rule-engine: (i) statistics about the habits waking-up, having breakfast, brushing teeth and leaving home for work, and (ii) actual behavior (i.e. no statistical average) about the toothbrushing habit. More specific, the data-analytics will calculate statistics and, as soon as these are considered reliable, present these to the test participant in the App (presented as a personal dashboard) during the *informing* phase. After one week of personal statistics (updated daily) the App will present educational messages as part of the *informing* phase. During the *advising* phase the data-analytics will generate facts of the participant's daily behavior that are used by the rule-engine to generate personalized coaching advice that is presented as messages in the App. During the *reminding* phase test participants will receive generic reminders for behavior change.

Test participants are recruited through an agency and have been screened for a set of exclusion criteria and for having the habit to brush their teeth after breakfast. Hence, all test participants are assumed to have an dental hygiene habit that we are aiming at to be changed during the study. The data collection during the learning phase (before the coaching starts) confirmed that at the offset of the study all participants did indeed brush their teeth after breakfast.

During a plenary intake session the test participants are informed about the objective of the study and any remaining questions are answered. After signing the informed consent form a download link to install the coaching App is

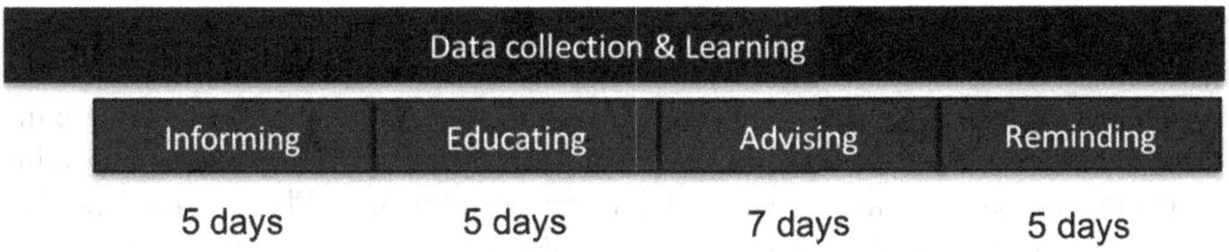

Data collection & Learning			
Informing	Educating	Advising	Reminding
5 days	5 days	7 days	5 days

Fig. 2. Study design showing the different phases of the study

provided. The App is installed during the intake to ensure that all participants managed to activate the App. As part of the intake sessions all participants receive a package with the sensor system and instructions to install the sensors in their home by themselves. The maximum duration of the test will be five weeks. It should be noted that throughout the study only weekdays will be taken into account. The argument for this is that it is expected that participants have a regular daily pattern during the week while weekends might reflect more divers en irregular patterns.

Test participants are asked to ensure that the data collection system is well-installed and to check messages that are sent to the App. No instructions with respect to behavior change are given and participants are informed that the objective of the study is to validate a data analytic approach for collecting contextual data. Hence, test participants were not made aware that the actual aim of the study was to influence their behavior.

Coaching Strategy. The coaching strategy consists of four consecutive phases (implemented on weekdays only) during which different types of information will be presented to the test participants. The types of information are:

1. *Informing.* As soon as the data analytics system has identified some contextual information (e.g. wake-up time, breakfast time, time of tooth brushing and the leave home time) statistics are provided in the App's dashboard. The statistical information is personal and calculated per test participant from the sensor data. It typically takes a couple of days before such personal statistics are available. An example of such awareness information if presented in Fig. 3.
2. *Educating.* After one week of awareness information through the dashboard, a daily educational message is sent to the App. Like in an email client the test participant receives a notification when such message is delivered and can view the message using the App. The messages are general and not related to the test participant's specific context. All educational messages relate to general good dental healthcare behavior (e.g. brushing immediately after drinking a soda was found to be harmful in a controlled study). An example of an educational message would be: *"Brushing at the wrong time, particularly within 30 min of finishing a meal, can erode the teeth far faster than they would have by themselves"*.

3. *Advising.* After one week of receiving educational messages the test participant would receive a daily advice message generated by a coaching plan. The
advice is adapted according to the contextual data from that test participant
and relates to the behavior of the test participant (in contrast to the educational messages that are general for the population). The personal advice
messages are timely delivered (e.g. first thing after waking up). The coaching
plan is fixed in time and terminated after 7 weekdays of coaching. Hence, if
a participant did not manage to change behavior, the coaching plan would
still be terminated after 7 days of providing personal advise. An example of a
personal advice message would be: *"It looks like yesterday you did not manage to brush before instead of after breakfast. While it is not an easy habit
to change, you did manage in the past to brush before breakfast. I am con-
vinced that today you will manage to brush before breakfast instead of after
breakfast"*.
4. *Reminding.* Once the coaching plan is completed the test participants receive
a generic reminder messages on a daily basis for one week. These messages
contain no new information other than reminding the test participant to continue brushing before breakfast. The reminder message is static and would be:
"Don't forget that it is important to brush before instead of after breakfast".

It should be noted that the *awareness information* and *personal advice messages* are personal as these are based on the participant's own behavior while
the *educational messages* and *reminders* are generic and not specific for the test
participant's context.

Coaching Plan. A dedicated coaching plan for several days was designed and
is deployed in the personal advice messages phase. This plan represents the
behavior change approach for guiding people to change the dental hygiene habit
from brushing after breakfast to brushing before breakfast. The messages during
the personal advice phase are following a number of behavior change techniques.
The deployed techniques are:

- *Provide general information on consequences of behavior (individual)*: provide
information about the benefits and costs of action or inaction to the person
- *Provide general encouragement*: praising or rewarding the person for effort or
performance without this being contingent on specified behaviors or standards
of performance
- *Set graded tasks*: set easy tasks, and increase difficulty until target behavior is performed. Breaking down the desired behavior into smaller easier to
achieve tasks and enabling the person to build on small successes to achieve
the desired behavior. This may include increments towards the desired behavior, or incremental increases from baseline behavior
- *Provide contingent rewards*: praise, encouragement or material rewards that
are explicitly linked to the achievement of specified behaviors
- *Provide information about behavior health link*: general information about
behavioral risk, e.g., susceptibility to poor health outcomes or mortality risk
in relation to the behavior

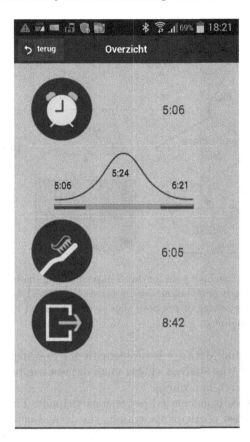

Fig. 3. Awareness information on the App

– Fear arousal: involves presentation of risk information relevant to the behavior as emotive images designed to evoke a fearful response

An example of the coaching plan is presented in Fig. 4. Note that the coaching plan adapts to the person's specific contextual behavior. For example, the difficulty of the graded task that is set in day 2 of the program depends on previous behavior of the person: if the person did manage to change the behavior in the past then the difficulty of the graded task is raised (e.g. higher consecutive number of times showing the desired behavior).

2.4   Results

From the total of 25 test participants 24 actually deployed the systems. From those 24 deployed systems only 12 provided complete data suitable for statistical analysis. Although the data collection resulted in a large data set (91 GB), only participants with data from both the breakfast and brushing sensors available for each day during the entire study are involved in the analysis.

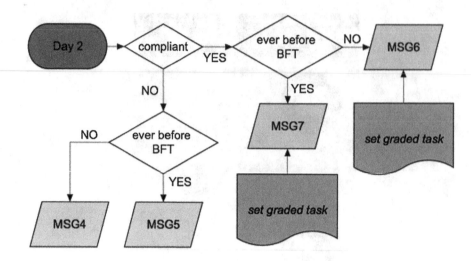

Fig. 4. Example of the coaching plan for day 2 implementing the behavior change techniques (in green) through personal advice messages (in yellow) based on the person's behavior (compliant to advice of previous day or ever brushed before breakfast time (BFT)) (Color figure online)

Obviously such small data set is problematic for drawing reliable statistical conclusions. However, the analysis of this small dataset can be used to formulate rather than test research hypothesis.

An adherence score is calculated per test participant. This score is the proportion of times the test participants exhibits the desired behavior (i.e. brushing before breakfast) during the total period in which information regarding the desired behavior is given (i.e. the educational, advice and reminder messages). This score ranges from 0 to 1.

Overall (except for participant 3, 6, 10 and 11) compliance is reasonable and most participants managed to adopt to some extent the desired behavior (see Fig. 5). This interpretation is qualitative as there is no normative data for deciding what the minimal success rate for the coaching approach should be.

In further exploring the data set (using the frequency of viewing the different types of information as independent variables and the adherence score as dependent variable) it is found that the adherence score is very well related ($r = 0.73$, $p < 0.01$) to the frequency of viewing the personal advice messages (see Fig. 6).

Although the data set is small, a regression analysis is performed to further understand the relationship between the adherence score and the frequency of viewing the dashboard, the educational messages, the personal advice messages and the reminder messages. The Durbin-Watson test indicates that there is no correlation among the residuals ($p = 0.69$). Additional, the Variance Inflation Factor (VIF) indicates that there is no problematic (highest VIF is 1.45) multicollinearity.

The regression model predicting the adherence score from the dashboard, educational, advice and reminder messages is significant ($p = 0.005$) and explains

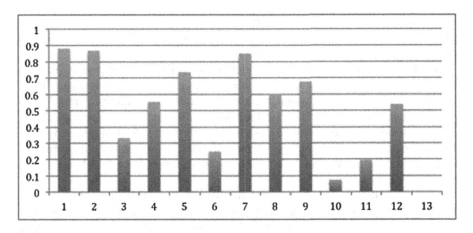

Fig. 5. Adherence scores (Y-axis) per subject (X-axis)

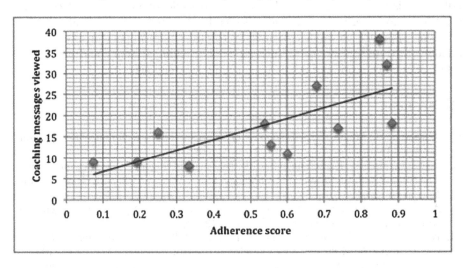

Fig. 6. Correlation between the frequency of reading the personal coaching advice messages (Y-axis) and the adherence score (X-axis)

76 % of the variance (adjusted R^2). Interesting in this model is that both the dashboard and personal advice messages contribute significantly (p <0.05) to the model while the educational and reminder messages do not contribute significantly.

3   Discussion

Overall, it can be concluded that behavior change was induced to some extent with the test participants. Interesting is the correlation between the participant's adherence and the frequency of viewing the personal advice messages.

Additional, a statistical significant regression model could be fit onto the data and predicts (from the frequency of consulting the personal dashboard and the coaching messages) the achieved adherence score for 76 % correctly.

This leads to the hypothesis that information related to the person (such as the dashboard of a person's behavior and the personal advice messages based on the person's context) has an important (statistical significant) relation to the adherence score, more than general information (such as educational and reminder messages). Future research should clarify if the effect of person related information and messages is independent of general information. The current study design does not exclude the presence of such cross-over effect between the two types of information.

As noted before, these conclusions are not decisive but can be the basis for formulating interesting research hypothesis and should be further investigated in follow-up studies. Given that there would be significant differences between types of coaching content (generic versus personal) and their relation to the person's adherence is very insightful for developing more effective and efficient coaching solutions. Modeling these relationships could be an interesting instrument for a coaching approach to tailor dynamically towards more impact on the person's adherence. More specific, using such model a coaching system could predict the user's adherence score and adapt its coaching strategy accordingly.

References

1. Abraham, C., Michie, S.: A taxonomy of behavior change techniques used in interventions. Health Psychol. **27**(3), 379–387 (2008)
2. Aarts, E., Harwig, R., Schuurmans, M.: Ambient Intelligence, The Invisible Future: The Seamless Integration of Technology into Everyday Life. McGraw-Hill Inc, New York (2001)
3. Aarts, E., de Ruyter, B.: New research perspectives on Ambient Intelligence. J. Ambient Intell. Smart Environ. **1**(1), 5–14 (2009)
4. Bandura, A.: Social Learning Theory. Prentice Hall, Englewood Cliffs (1977)
5. Bandura, A.: Self-Efficacy: The Exercise of Control. Freeman, New York (1997)
6. Bruno-Ambrosius, K., Swanholm, G., Twetman, S.: Eating habits, smoking and toothbrushing in relation to dental caries: a 3-year study in Swedish female teenagers. Int. J. Paediatr. Dent. **15**(3), 190–196 (2005)
7. Blinkhorn, A.S.: Influence of social norms on toothbrushing behavior of preschool children. Commun. Dent. Dental Epidemiol. **6**(5), 222–226 (1978)
8. Chestnutt, I.G., Schfer, F., Jacobson, A.P.M., Stephen, K.W.: The influence of toothbrushing frequency and post-brushing rinsing on caries experience in a caries clinical trial. Commun. Dent. Dental Epidemiol. **26**(6), 406–411 (1998)
9. Fisher, W., Fisher, J., Harman, J.: The information-motivation-behavioral skills model: a general social psychological approach to understanding and promoting health behavior. In: Suls, J., Wallston, K. (eds.) Social Psychological Foundations of Health and Illness, pp. 82–106. Blackwell Publishing Ltd., Malden (2003)
10. Honkala, E., Nyyssönen, V., Knuuttila, M., Markkanen, H.: Effectiveness of children's habitual toothbrushing. J. Clin. Periodontol. **13**(1), 81–85 (1986)
11. Kaptein, M., Markopoulos, P., De Ruyter, B., Aarts, E.: Persuasion in ambient intelligence. J. Ambient Intell. Hum. Comput. **1**(1), 43–56 (2010)

12. Leventhal, H., Benyamini, Y., Brownlee, S., Diefenbach, M., Leventhal, E.A., Patrick-Miller, L.: Illness representations: theoretical foundations. In: Petrie, K.J., Weinman, J.A. (eds.) Perceptions of Health and Illness. Harwood, Amsterdam (1997)
13. Prochaska, J.O., Velicer, W.F.: The transtheoretical model of health behavior change. Am. J. Health Promot. **12**(1), 38–48 (1997)
14. Swan, M.: Sensor mania! The internet of things, wearable computing, objective metrics, and the quantified self 2.0. JSAN 2012 **1**(3), 217–253 (2012)
15. Swan, M.: The quantified self: fundamental disruption in big data science and biological discovery. Big Data **1**(2), 85–99 (2013)

Experience-Driven Design of Ambiences for Future Pop Up Workspaces

Aino Ahtinen[(✉)], Jenni Poutanen, Maiju Vuolle, Kaisa Väänänen, and Sanna Peltoniemi

Tampere University of Technology, Tampere, Finland
{aino.ahtinen,jenni.poutanen,maiju.vuolle,
kaisa.vaananen,sanna.peltoniemi}@tut.fi

Abstract. Knowledge work is in transformation and new means for supporting workers' wellbeing and productivity are needed. Pop Up workspaces are temporary and often social working environments where people can modify their environment to suit their current work mode. The aim of the present research was to explore the opportunities of future Pop Up workspaces, and specifically their technology-mediated ambiences that can provide meaningful experiences for the workers. We employed the Experience-Driven Design (EDD) approach to gain insights of the desired experiences in Pop Up workspaces. We first conducted three participatory group sessions to ideate experience types for Pop Up workspaces. We then run a multidisciplinary concepting workshop in which we designed concepts for technology-mediated ambiences. Five experience categories for worker mindsets were identified, namely Liberty, Fellowship, Determination, Retreat and Recovery. We present ambience concepts that utilise the mindsets and related target experiences, and how they can be supported by ambient technologies.

Keywords: Pop up workspaces · Knowledge work · Workspace ambiences · Experience-driven design · User experience · Space design · Ambient technologies

1 Introduction

Knowledge work is facing a crisis – knowledge workers face challenges in managing the amount of the workload, cognitive load, competence challenges and time pressure, and at the same time, the feeling of not being productive enough. The work is changing rapidly due to the emergence of novel technologies and applications, leading to more flexible, mobile and collaborative work practices and spaces, e.g., [1, 2]. At the same time, the demands for the knowledge workers related to the self-development and productivity are constantly rising, often at the cost of the individual worker's wellbeing. In addition, the sedentary nature of contemporary office work has serious impact to the health of the workers [3].

Our definition for *Pop Up workspaces* is the following: Pop Up workspaces are workspace designs that are temporary, modifiable and often social. Such workspaces aim at increasing both wellbeing and productivity by allowing workers to manipulate their work environment. Wellbeing and work productivity are usually tied together – the

© Springer International Publishing Switzerland 2015
Kameas et al. (Eds.): AmI 2015, LNCS 9425, pp. 296–312, 2015.
DOI: 10.1007/978-3-319-26005-1_20

better the wellbeing of the worker, the more productive she is supposed to be. Experimental Pop Up spaces can also be seen as a method of participatory design including user feedback on space development [4]. Designing Pop Up workspaces requires a multidisciplinary approach, as knowledge work is conducted in a system where the physical, virtual, social and emotional work environments meet, e.g., [5]. In order to develop understanding about novel work environments we combine the viewpoints of user experience (UX) design, architecture and knowledge management.

The aim of the research presented in this paper is to explore what kind of experiences people expect in Pop Up workspaces, and how those experiences could be supported by ambience design. The research approach is based on *experience-driven design (EDD)* of Pop Up workspaces. EDD means designing for particular experiences evoked by the usage of everyday products [6]. In this case, the goal is to design workspaces and enable experiences that will increase workers' wellbeing and productivity. We first conducted a participatory design study with brainstorming sessions to ideate meaningful experience types for workspaces. After that, we run a multidisciplinary concepting workshop in which we designed early-phase concepts for the experiences that emerged in the participatory design study.

The resulting concepts take the form of *workspace ambiences* that can be generated with the means of architectural space design and ambient technologies. By ambience we mean the atmosphere of the space. The Pop Up aspect in technologically enabled ambiences is that the atmosphere of the space can be changed based on the user's needs, work task, feelings and other changing aspects of work. It gives more flexibility for the workspaces. Our vision is that the users could select a suitable ambience for their current work mode. The variety of ambiences may support people in getting pleasurable experiences in the workspace, as novelty and change are among the human needs for the good product user experience [7].

As far as we are aware, the experience-driven design approach has so far not been utilized in the design of workspace ambiences. The research questions of this study are the following:

1. *What are the meaningful experiences in Pop Up workspaces for knowledge work?*
2. *How can those experiences be supported with ambiences, which are designed as desired combinations of ambient technology, real-world objects and spatial design?*

2   Related Work

2.1   Workspace Design for Knowledge Workers

Contemporary knowledge work is related to the great variety of skills and the demand of those, such as creativity, innovativeness, focus, task management, sociability, flexibility, adaptability, presentation. Knowledge work needs specific support for various activities, such as the information gathering, storage, transfer, use and application, as well as learning and organizing [8]. Work tasks can range from routine to creative work, include both face-to-face interaction and technology-mediated work with customers or colleagues, as well as require individual working time and concentration. Due to the independency of time, place and utilization of technology, knowledge work can be done in multiple spaces beyond the traditional office environment. Therefore, there is a need to design more multi-use, multi-purpose workspaces to support interaction, creativity, as well as concentration, in order to improve wellbeing and productivity [2].

The previous demands have lead to the development of the increasingly popular activity-based office concept, where employees can choose a workstation most functional for their current activity, but which also matches their preferences [9]. According to Värlander [10], the spatial design of work environments is consisted of *affordances*, which may allow or incline certain behaviors and actions rather than others, and then again may inhibit others. During the nonroutine phases of knowledge work, the layout of work environment can indirectly contribute to productivity, as the sharing of ideas, communication and shared search for alternative solutions are facilitated [11]. However, the lack of possibilities for *personifying* one's workplace is one of the known disadvantages of activity-based offices [9]. It is also noteworthy, that employees' personal preferences influence greatly how certain type of workplaces are used, rather than the ergonomics and ICT facilities [9].

2.2   User Experience and Experience-Driven Design

User experience (UX) has become a mainstream in the design of interactive products and services. The user experiences of products and services are supposed to be pleasurable or satisfying as a result of an UX design process and practises. According to Hassenzahl [12], the product user experience consists of pragmatic and hedonic attributes. By pragmatic attributes, he refers to the functional usability and usefulness of the product, while the hedonic attributes relate to the non-instrumental and emotional needs of the people using the product. Hedonic attributes are strong potentials for pleasure [13].

Experience-driven design (EDD), i.e. *how to design for particular experiences*, is a more scarce approach for product design, although its popularity is rising [14]. In EDD, a specific user experience, or a set of them, form the basis and target of the design process [6, 15]. EDD intends to evoke particular experiences. Product experience is a multifaceted phenomenon; the first layer is the degree to which the senses are gratified (aesthetic experience), the second consists of the meanings that the users attach to the product (experience of meaning), and the third layer is about the feelings and emotions that are elicited (emotional experience) [6].

Playful experiences framework (PLEX) is a model that consists of 22 playful experience categories [16]. Examples of experience categories of PLEX are *captivation* (forgetting one's surroundings), *discovery* (finding something new or unknown), *nurture* (taking care of oneself or others) and *subversion* (breaking social rules and norms). Many experiences that are included in PLEX are also applicable in wider context of design than just designing interactive products.

2.3   Experience-Driven Space Design

According to Norberg-Schulz [17], the character of a space is essential part of experiencing a place. The character of spaces similar to each other can differ greatly according to the elements defining the spaces. Light, materials, form and structure define the character of a space or place, hence affecting the experience. Essential is also how these elements are constructed. Thus a phenomenology of place, an everyday experience, has to consist of basic modes of construction and their relation to formal expression [17].

Now, we present a prior design case, where experience-driven design approach has been applied to the space design. A new type of a hospital waiting room was created by Marcus Boesenach [6]. Based on an exploratory study of being ill, the target experiences were defined as following: *pride (self-esteem)*, *peacefulness*, *confidence* and *acceptance*. The final concept design created a synthesis between a spatial unit and a piece of furniture. The new waiting area was supposed to invite the patients to discover its different possibilities of functionality and meaning. The product offered different ways of using it. For example, the design supported for the patient to choose her own level of privacy or openness. Thus, the patient could discover her own personal area and create space that fitted in within her personal concerns.

2.4   Ambience Design

The dictionary definition for 'ambience' is *"the atmosphere of the place"* (dictionary.com). Furthermore, 'atmosphere' is defined as follows: *"a surrounding or pervading mood, environment, or influence"* (dictionary.com). According to these definitions, ambience involves a place, space or environment, which is surrounded by a certain atmosphere, mood or influence. A concept called *Ambience Design* has been presented by Karjalainen et al. [18]. One of their projects was built around the idea of involving multi-sensory experiences of people into comprehensive environmental design. They describe the concept of Ambience Design, e.g., with the following aspects; it is cross-disciplinary, collaborative, and design for the multi-sensory environment. Ambience Design is also design of atmosphere, which means putting focus on experiences and phenomenality, and it utilizes ubiquitous technology. Adjustability, modifiability, modularity and individuality are the central themes of Ambience Design [19]. These aspects match well with our definition on ambience.

In this article, ambience is defined as *"a multisensory atmosphere and character of space, which is created by the means of ambient technologies, real world objects and spatial design to evoke particular user experiences"*. The technology components that can be utilized when designing multisensory ambiences include, e.g. screens to display visual materials (images, videos, colors, shapes); lighting; speakers for the auditory stimuli; vibration and intelligent materials for the sense of touch; aroma dispensers for the olfactory sense. With the means of above mentioned ambient technologies it is possible to create a space that enables varying ambiences.

In the literature, there exists some cases to present technology-enabled ambiences. For example, Wisneski et al. [20] advocated for moving personal computing interfaces from small screens towards the comprehensive experience in physical environment with nature-simulating effects. Especially their development, *the ambientROOM*, which "surrounds the user within an augmented environment", houses similar ideas and ambient experiences to ours. Furthermore, *LiveNature* [21] is an interactive system that connects people with their remote cherished places. The system captures live video streaming and weather data from a cherished place and presents the "sense" of the place in an ambient, aesthetic way on screens in the user's location. *Scented Pebbles* [22] is a set of interactive lighting objects to create multisensory ambience of light and smell. The lighting objects, pebbles, emit smells and control the lighting conditions to evoke sensorial imagination and generate unique ambiences, such as Hawaiian Sunset or Japanese Onsen. Ip and Kwong [23] present *Smart Ambience Games* for children with learning difficulties. In the smart ambience game, the learners interact through the body movements in a virtual environment that provide visual and auditory stimuli. The learning environment was used, e.g. for virtual painting, experiencing virtual environments, building a favorite surrounding, and dancing. Furthermore, Kuijsters et al. [24] state that changes in light characteristics (tone, color, illuminance) influence the atmosphere and thus, the affective experience of the room. They present work of *affective ambiences created with lighting* for older people visiting care centres, to reduce negative feelings and enhance wellbeing by creating cosy and activating ambiences.

3 Methodology

There were two phases in our study, which followed the challenges of EDD: (1) *to determine what experience(s) to aim for* and (2) *to design the product that is expected to evoke that experience* [6]. Designers and users usually co-create the experiences [25]. Understanding the context, interpretative approach for research and participatory design are among the main issues in defining the experiences [25].

3.1 Participatory Design Study – Exploring User Needs and Determining Experiences

A participatory design (PD) study was arranged *to understand the user needs towards the future Pop Up workspaces and based on them, to determine the meaningful experiences in them*. 14 individuals (F = 10, M = 4) participated in three brainstorming sessions (4–6 persons/session). They were employees (researchers, secretaries) and students (architecture, pervasive computing and electrical engineering) in one of the largest universities in Finland. They were recruited with email and social media advertisement. The criterion was that they should be knowledge workers, which in this context involved also students. Most participants were 20–35 years old, and three were older than that. All of them used mobile phone, email and internet in a daily basis.

The study consisted of a task that was carried out prior to the group session, where the participants imagined the Pop Up workspace of their dreams. They were guided to write a short description of the space, e.g.: What adjectives describe the space? How does the space look like? How does it sound like? Three brainstorming sessions were arranged to discuss participant's expectations, as well as to construct and try out some aspects of the Pop Up workspaces. In the session, the participants presented their expectations towards Pop Up workspaces, and after that, they collectively formulated a

Pop Up space where they would like to work. The space they formulated could include aspects from all participants' expectations. The sessions took place in a room equipped with stimulus materials (furniture, folding screens, cardboard, papers, pens, mockups of devices, drawable walls etc.). The participants were asked to use their imagination and modify the space according to their expectations on Pop Up spaces, and think aloud at the same time. Also, if some aspect they wanted to include in the space was not actually available, they were asked to imagine it and describe it with words, or sketch it. The purpose of the construction task was to activate participants to do a hands-on experiment. The hands-on experiment was expected to free their minds more than just participating a discussion. In the end of the session, there was a wrap-up discussion, where the insights gained during the session were discussed. The participatory design study generated data about the user needs (perceptions, expectations) towards future Pop Up workspaces.

The data of the participatory study was analyzed with the content analysis method [26]. The data was first transcribed word for word and the researcher went through the data and tracked the emerging themes of the meaningful experiences of future workspaces, and their higher-level categories, which we call mindsets. Next, the data was more systematically coded on a spreadsheet. In the analysis, the main question for the data was *"What are the meaningful experiences in future Pop Up workspaces?" (research question 1)*. After the systematic coding of data, the researcher conducting the analysis labeled the mindsets and the related meaningful experiences with descriptive names (Table 1).

Table 1. The five mindsets and the related meaningful experiences in Pop Up workspaces.

Liberty	Fellowship	Determination	Retreat	Recovery
Creativity	Encounter	Focus	Independency	Recreation
Inspiration	Being part	Concentration	Peacefulness	Peace of mind
Exploration	Collaboration	Conventionality	Concentration	Wellbeing
Innovation	Closeness	Formality	Safety	Escape
Expression	Connectedness	Peacefulness	Selection	Captivation
Sensation	Cosyness	Discreetness	Feeling connected	Safety
Freedom	Equality	Being part		Activation
Feeling energized		Beauty		Nature experience
Activation				
Variation				
Being part				
Connectedness				

3.2 Concepting Workshop – Designing for Experiences

In the concepting workshop, five researchers representing UX, architectural space design and knowledge management, participated in conception. Their titles varied from the doctoral student to professor.

The workshop aimed at conception of early phase example solutions for the meaningful experiences and mindsets of Pop Up workspaces: *"How can those experiences be created with ambiences which are designed as desired combinations of ambient technology, real world objects and space design?" (research question 2).* For each mindset, we designed an example ambience that aims at enabling experiences that were involved in that specific mindset. Concerning ambient technologies, the purpose was to utilize the appropriate combinations of existing technological components, and not to design new technological solutions as such.

The moderator first presented the results of the PD study, and presented the definition of the "ambience", as well as a list of possible technologies for ambience design. A moment was first spent for individual ideation, after which the ideas were collectively gone through. A list of ambience enablers for each mindset was created. Finally, the moderator summarized the ideas. According to those summaries, the visualizations representing each ambience were created afterwards. The summarized data and the visualization of each mindset describe the example ambiences.

4 Findings of the Participatory Study

This section presents the main results analyzed from the participatory study. The data revealed *five experience categories, here called mindsets*, namely *Liberty, Fellowship, Determination, Retreat* and *Recovery*. Those involve the meaningful experiences in the future Pop Up workspaces. The mindsets and experiences are summarized in Table 1. Authentic participant citates are provided in italics.

4.1 Mindset 1: Liberty

The first mindset for knowledge work is called *Liberty* intended *for creative, and inspirational, most often collective work.* The Liberty involves the freedom for creative expression (**Creativity**), as well as the feeling of being inspired (**Inspiration**): *"There should be freedom to do!"* (female, 26–30 years). It also includes the experiences of exploring an object, situation or task (**Exploration**), as well as finding a solution for the problem or inventing something new (**Innovation**). The Liberty also involves the freedom to express oneself without the fear of being judged of one's thoughts in the first phase (**Expression**), as people may feel vulnerable when they are creative: *"When one really wants to throw oneself to the topic, the space needs to create a feeling of safety. Normal official one does not do that."* (male, 21–25 years).

The space for Liberty is interesting, tempting and casual, calling for individuals to come by. It offers stimulation for all senses (**Sensation**) with the variety of materials, shapes, visuals, colors, sounds and scents: *"The space should take into account different senses, and inspire through them."* (female, 31–35 years); *"The world of scents could support the characteristics of the space."* (female, 31–35 years).

The space for Liberty is an environment to feel spaciousness and lightness (**Freedom**): *"There should be space for thoughts."* (female, 26–30 years). It is full of sunshine. The space makes one to become mentally active (**Feeling energized**): *"Full of light and sunny, somehow energetic. One would be like, oh, there are good energies to work."* (female, 26-30 years).

In the space for Liberty, there is freedom to work in an active and large way (**Activation**). The participants wished for more activating working habits and a possibility to decrease the amount of sitting during the workday: *"It is somehow old-fashioned way to sit all the time at work."* (female, 50+ years). Working in this space happens mostly by standing and moving in the space. The space supports walking, taking different positions, locations and points of view: *"I agree that one needs to be able to move (in the space). That opens up the creativity."* (male, 21–25 years); *"It should be so that you can physically change your position once in awhile."* (female, 26–30 years).

In addition, the space for Liberty is also strongly associated with the possibility and permission of modification and changing the space (**Variation**). The workspace for Liberty is flexible and allows for modifications for different work tasks, purposes, sizes of groups and moods. The objects, furniture, materials and tools in space can be modified by the workers: *"As people start to use these kinds of novel workspaces, they could be suggested to think a meaningful way of working. They would be given a moment to do that."* (female, 41–45 years); *"It makes you relaxed if you have a permission to change."* (male, 26–30 years).

One participant visioned a workspace that could be modified by pushing a button. He imagined to be able to change the appearance and atmosphere of the space very easily, including the visual appearance as well as the soundscape of the space. Also, another participant was talking about changing the mode of the space with different kind of music: *"The walls could be covered with display panels. As you push a button, you would be in Florida or somewhere else. My vision is a very much modificable. One can change the wall from wood to ceramics... And if you push a button, it takes you into the jungle, and there would be a soundscape of the jungle. And up on a mountain there would be another soundscape."* (male, 26–30 years); *"One can change the mode of the space with music."* (female, 31–35 years).

Creativity, inspiration and innovation is often social in nature. The space of Liberty allows for being connected with people working in the same space (**Being part**). On the other hand, it is not isolated from the outer world either (**Connectedness**). A view for the hustle and bustle outside of the workspace, i.e. "bringing the outer world to the workspace" creates feelings of belonging. Connectedness to the outer world is provided in a discreet way that to maintain the concentration to the ongoing task: *"I would say that the space (for ideation) would exist a bit higher. In a way that one could see people down there.."* (male, 21–25 years).

4.2   Mindset 2: Fellowship

The second mindset is called *Fellowship*. Fellowship is a mindset *for sudden encounter and collaborational work*. In the space of Fellowship the atmosphere enables sudden encounter between people who might not necessarily meet otherwise (**Encounter**). The space prevents isolation and calls for meeting people and communicating with them (**Being part**): *"The space encourages to see and meet people in a comfortable way."* (male, 21–25 years). The space is a place for co-operation between people (**Collaboration**). The space makes it possible for being close to other people (**Closeness**).

In addition to being part of the work community or other people in the space, there is also a need for being connected to the outer world (**Connectedness**). The atmosphere in this space is homely and relaxed (**Cosyness**) That is created with soft materials such as carpets, and the overall friendly and welcoming atmosphere: *"Yes, so that it would be homely, a little bit of soft material here and there."* (male, 26–30 years); *"It makes you relaxed if there is homely atmosphere."* (female, 31–35 years).

In the space of Fellowship, there are no hierarchies between people, and the titles and authorities are forgotten (**Equality**). The space mixes people from different levels and backgrounds, e.g., student, teachers, researchers and company workers. The space is defined by multidisciplinary approach and learning from others: *"Students see professors only in certain situation of authority, and vice versa. Meeting in other situations might generate new ideas."* (male, 21–25 years).

4.3 Mindset 3: Determination

The mindset called *Determination* is *for focused, conventional work, which usually takes places in a group*. It is characterized by doing focused task completion (**Focus**). In the space for Determination people concentrate on specific task (**Concentration**). In addition, the work takes places in a conventional way (**Conventionality**) and deals with formal issues (**Formality**). There is no need for the space to provide additional inspiration or stimulation. The space offers ideal settings for sitting down, focused communication and making decisions: *"The strategy meeting of a company, for that a discreet atmosphere would do, restrained colors. People would be sitting. I would say that there one would not sit on beanbags in a relaxed way."* (female, 41–45 years).

The atmosphere in the space for Determination enables the work in silent and peaceful settings (**Peacefulness**). The space is characterized with neutral colors and materials (**Discreetness**). The space keeps the work situation as a harmonized and focused experience: *"If one needs to talk about serious things, and for example decide something, I would say that it would not be very successful in a very colorful space."* (female, 41–45 years); *"When one wants to keep focused and make decisions, then a colorless surrounding would do."* (female, 50+ years).

The workspace is closed for the participating individuals and thus, it enables being connected (**Being part**) with relevant others. There is no need for connections to outer world, except maybe a video conference option for another worksite or a colleague who exists elsewhere. On the other hand, there is no reason why the space for Determination could not include some beautiful elements (**Beauty**), such as nice curtain or some pieces of art, to provide aesthetic experience of in the middle of the focused work: *"It could be in a space which would have some arts, flowers, nice curtains and so forth."* (female, 50+ years).

4.4 Mindset 4: Retreat

The fourth mindset is called *Retreat* and it is *for individual, concentrated work*. The Retreat provides personal space for the individual work when needed (**Independency**).

Some work tasks, such as writing, require peaceful settings (**Peacefulness**) and a possibility to concentrate on specific task (**Concentration**): *"If one wants to read book, concentrate, or just be quiet, there could be own spot where to go."* (female, 36–40 years). Sometimes people want to spend time with their own thoughts. For that purpose they need a space where they would feel safe (**Safety**): *"You would be safe (in that space), but not in an isolated cellar."* (male, 26–30 years).

The Retreat enables selecting the distance to the others (**Selection**): *"In the group occasion, there could be small spaces where one could escape with one's own thoughts. One could decide the distance to the rest of the group, to close oneself or be more open to others."* (female, 26–30 years). Sometimes the work task or certain mood demand for a total isolation from the group. However, sometimes people need to work alone, but still having the feeling of not being in isolation (**Feeling connected**): *"One could just turn towards the forest - now you focus."* (female, 26–30 years).

4.5   Mindset 5: Recovery

The fifth mindset discovered in this study is called *Recovery*. It is a mindset *for recreation during the break, either individually or collectively*. The space for Recovery aims at getting relaxed and "recharging batteries" (**Recreation**). It happens mostly through activities that are not direct work activities, but more more related to having a break. The space enables returning the mental balance (**Peace of mind**) after intensive work: *"To retreat and be quiet would be very good. One can sit, pray, meditate or whatever one wants to do."* (male, 26–30 years). Especially in this space, people feel well and good (**Wellbeing**). It enables forgetting the demands and requirements of work for a while (**Escape**): *"A space to retreat from the normal hustle and bustle."* (male, 26–30 years). The space also makes it possible to forget one's physical sur-roundings for a while (**Captivation**): *"The space would disappear for a while and one could hear the relaxational soundscape, whatever it is. One could get the mind out of the thing that she has been concentrating for the whole day, for a short moment."* (female, 41–45 years). In the space, one can feel safe (**Safety**). Recovery can happen in personal space or in a social setting.

In the space for Recovery, the workers are able to do their own things. On the other hand, it can be resting or meditation, but on the other hand it can be an active moment of including physical activity or stretching (**Activation**): *"I could go and have a walk in nature for 10 min."* (female, 50+ years).

The wish and importance for being able to work in nature and outdoors, or in the settings that people of nature (**Nature experience**), is closely linked to the Recovery. The nature experience means either being in nature or bringing the elements of nature to the workspace, in form of materials, landscapes, soundscapes, fresh air and natural light: *"An indoor space where one can see a great view. A magnificent and big window."* (female, 50+ years); *"I miss to be able to open a window, to hear sounds from nature, even the smallest blaster."* (female, 41–45 years).

5   Concept Design of Ambiences for Pop Up Workspaces

In this section, we present the early phase examples of ambiences that were designed for the mindsets in a multidisciplinary concepting workshop. The ambiences were created as combinations of ambient technologies, space design and physical objects. Two of the ambiences are presented with example visualizations.

5.1   Ambience for Liberty

The space of Liberty (Fig. 1) can be best characterized with the following adjectives: rough, workshop-like, activating and modifiable. The appearance of the space is incomplete and raw, which gives workers freedom and courage to make modifications and test out things. The floor can be made of, for example, concrete, which gives an unfinished perception. It is possible to paint the space, for example paint the electronic wall paper with virtual colors. The space is spacious, i.e. there is plenty of space to do and modificate. There are also bright lights in the space.

Fig. 1. An example visualization of the ambience for Liberty. **Sources:** Room: http://pixabay.com/p-597166/?no_redirect; Display: http://pixabay.com/p-160135/?no_redirect; Light bulbs: http://www.jisc.ac.uk/rd/get-involved/research-data-spring; People sitting: http://pixabay.com/p-703002/?no_redirect; Beanbag chairs: http://pixabay.com/p-21493/?no_redirect; Melody: http://pixabay.com/p-148443/?no_redirect; People walking: http://pixabay.com/p-609640/?no_redirect; Man painting graffiti:© Bogdan/Wikimedia Commons/CC-BY-SA-3.0/GFDL http://commons.wikimedia.org/wiki/File:Graffiti-Bucharest.jpg; Man sitting in a beanbag chair: © Dave Morris/CC-BY-2.0 https://www.flickr.com/photos/12771303@N00/4455307; City: © Adam J. W.C./CC-BY-SA-2.5 http://commons.wikimedia.org/wiki/File:City_of_sydney_ from_the_balmain_wharf_dusk_cropped2.jpg; Street artist: © K. C. Tang/CC-BY-SA-3.0/GFDL http://commons.wikimedia.org/wiki/File:Street_artist_Centre_Pompidou.jpg. **Full licence details:** GFDL (GNU Free Documentation License): http://en.wikipedia.org/wiki/Wikipedia:Text_of_the_GNU_ Free_Documentation_License; CC-BY-SA-3.0: http://creativecommons.org/licenses/by-sa/3.0/; CC-BY-SA-2.5 http://creativecommons.org/ licenses/by-sa/2.5/deed.en; CC-BY-2.0: http://commons.wikimedia.org/wiki/Category:CC-BY-2.0; CC-BY-3.0: http://creativecommons.org/ licenses/by/3.0/deed.en; Pixabay: http://pixabay.com/en/service/terms/#download_terms

The space and the furniture can be changed and molded by the workers. The material of the furniture is intelligent – it returns itself to the original shape by itself. There is a culture of being in courage in the space and not being limited by "the big brother". The space provides plenty of different materials to be used, and removable walls to "construct the space" again and again. The space is like a testing platform where almost everything is possible to do. The modifications can stay in the space and the following users can see them as there is no need to reset the modifications after work.

Different viewpoints and stimulation are provided via a virtual window, which is a wall-sized display. From the virtual window, the workers are able to see wonderful still pictures or video from the metropolitan cities, their hustle and bustle and people coming and going. This reminds them of freedom, as in big cities there is a sense of freedom to be what you are. The soundscape that is created with 3D speakers matches with the view to the metropolis – the workers can hear a realistic hum of city: people talking, shoes knocking, cars driving and honking. The space smells like fresh air, and every now and then a refreshing breeze whisks through the space.

The space motivates to be on the move and work actively. The work is usually not done in the sitting mode, but by standing, moving, taking different positions and viewpoints. This is enabled with a dynamic floor. Like in the stage of a theater, the floor rotates. The dynamic floor can be used as a treadmill, or as a source for dynamic thinking and taking different points of view.

5.2 Ambience for Fellowship

The space for Fellowship is an open space, visible from different directions. It is a space where sudden encounters take place, and where people are naturally located close to each other. The furniture is homely, and the atmosphere reminds of the living room. The lightning is warm and an electronic fire place brings cozy atmosphere. The space smells like coffee, bun and strawberry.

There are special, playful furniture in the space. The furniture discuss by sounds with each other, which may trigger conversation between the workers, too. In addition, as the user sits down on the chair, the chair makes noise. In the space, there are sympathetic animal robots that can be hugged.

The electronic board on the wall shows some information of the people who are in the space, which can trigger discussion. In the space, there is equipment for visualizing and writing the upcoming ideas collectively, for example on the drawing board that saves the outputs in a cloud service.

5.3 Ambience for Determination

The ambience for Determination can be described as "non-ambience". It is a conventional space with neutral materials and minimal extra stimulus, meant for focused work. The appearance is almost ascetic, and the furniture is ergonomic for doing work in the sitting mode, but they also allows for adjusting the working position. The main focus in the space is in the focused task completion. The work happens discreetly and productively. The lightness of the space is like a natural light. A *pomodoro method* for working is in use (25 min of work and 5 min of break), and it is moderated via the loudspeakers of the space. During the break, the space generates mild surprises, for example a prompt to stand up and make some stretching or simple gymnastic exercises.

The virtual window (display) of the space does not show any external stimulus, but it is meant for presenting factual information, e.g. task related information visualizations, charts, presentations, to do-lists, proceeding in the task, etc. As the ongoing task is completed, a tangible smart object on your desk cheers your completion in a discreet way.

5.4   Ambience for Retreat

The space for Retreat (Fig. 2) is surrounded by intelligent glass walls, whose transparency can be adjusted by the worker. The worker can set the walls as transparent when she or he wants to be closer to others and visible for them. By setting the walls as non-transparent the worker is able to achieve a total privacy. Also, different levels of semi-transparency are available depending on how "close" the user wants to be in relation to people around. The transparency of the space reveals worker's availability for others – if they can see the user, she or he is more available than in the situations when the user has set the walls as non-transparent. This brings safety for the user, as she or he can be sure about not being disturbed by others. In the space of retreat there is a permission to be "offline", i.e. not available for others.

In the space for Retreat, the atmosphere is cosy and peaceful, and it is created with a limited amount of space and height. The space reminds the user of a nest. The ambience in this space is personalized for the worker. Depending on the worker's profile, the lightness of the space is adjusted. A personally meaningful landscape or object is visible on the virtual window. There can be a view for, e.g. a favorite nature place. Also the soundscape comes from the personal profile, i.e. user-defined music, sounds or silence is played.

5.5   Ambience for Recovery

The space for Recovery provides contrast for the work task that the worker has done lately. It is a space to escape the work demands. If the worker has conducted intensive, creative ideation in a group, she would most probably want to be alone for a while, in a peaceful and safe ambience. For those purposes, the space for Recovery adjusts the lightness as dark, and the worker can have a massage in a chair meant for that, or she can swing in the chair in prone position. The soundscape of the space is peaceful, either a total silence or peaceful music or sounds, for example noise of sea. The atmosphere is relaxing. On the ceiling of the space, a sky with stars is made of optical fibre. The space smells like fresh nature. The relaxational ambience is created in closed, safe space, which can be locked and which is not transparent for others.

On the other hand, if the worker has done concentrated work alone, she or he might most probably want to have an activating moment of Recovery with other people around. The social and active recovery might well take place in the space for

Fig. 2. An example visualization of the ambience for Retreat. **Sources:** Glass cube: © Hubert Berberich/CC-BY-3.0   http://commons.wikimedia.org/wiki/File:Glass_Cube_Mannheim_night. jpg; Office:© Foundation7/CC-B Y-SA-3.0 http://commons.wikimedia.org/wiki/File:The_Park_ Northpoint_-_Open_Plan_Office_Space.jpg; Rain water dripping: © Horia Varlan https://www. flickr.com/photos/horiavarlan/4303835161/in/gallery-dentonpotter-72157635510954827/; Working by the beach: © Yuvi Panda/CC-BY-3.0 http://commons.wikimedia.org/wiki/File: Yuvi_working_on_beach_1.jpg; Glass texture: http://pixabay.com/en/glass-texture-window-reflection-163865/. **Full licence details:** GFDL (GNU Free Documentation License): http://en. wikipedia.org/wiki/Wikipedia:Text_of_the_GNU_Free_Documentation_License; CC-BY-SA-3. 0: http://creativecommons.org/licenses/by-sa/3.0/; CC-BY-SA-2.5 http://creativecommons.org/ licenses/by-sa/2.5/deed.en; CC-BY-2.0: http://commons.wikimedia.org/wiki/Category:CC-BY-2. 0; CC-BY-3.0: http://creativecommons.org/licenses/by/3.0/deed.en; Pixabay: http://pixabay.com/ en/service/terms/#download_terms

Fellowship, by having a possibility to chat freely with others in a lively atmosphere. One possibility, which would offer contrast for focused work would be to take a short bike ride on a stationary bike, which would be located in front of a virtual window. From the window, the user could see a nice view to a cozy village, and she would feel as if she was biking in a village. The soundscape would match with the view.

6 Discussion and Conclusions

Ambient technologies which can be embedded in the space, for example screens and projectors, loudspeakers, sensors and small robots, provide novel possibilities for increasing the flexibility of the space, and the development of different ambiences for the future Pop Up workspaces. Knowledge work is an area that can benefit from the modifiability of the space, as the work practices are changing rapidly towards more collaborative, flexible and mobile (e.g., [1, 2]). Drawing on Gibson's concept of affordances [27], where the perceived properties of objects and environments allow or hinder certain actions or behavior relative to the individual, Pop Up spaces can be seen as affordances for experiences and ambiences supporting knowledge work. Allowing workers to adjust their work environment ambiences according to their tasks or preferences has a potential to increase their job satisfaction. Contextual individual flexibility is connected to organizational flexibility too, and "individuals' preconception, meanings, and views of that environment affect their behaviour" [10].

Through the experience-driven design process consisting of the participatory design study and a concepting workshop, we have resulted in a set of potentially meaningful experiences of future Pop Up workspaces, divided in five experience categories that we call mindsets. The set of experiences has similarities to as well as differences with the experiences listed in the PLEX model [16]. In addition, we have created initial concepts of workspace ambiences (or atmospheres) for the five mindsets. The ambiences were designed as versatile combinations of ambient technologies, real-world objects and space design. The presented ambiences have confluences with the concept of Digital Territory, which introduces the notions of personal and public spaces, and the blurring boundaries between those, in the Ambient Intelligence environment [28]. Our future vision is that the workers the workspace could modify the workspace by selecting the ambience of the space according to their work task, mood, etc. The ambiences would increase the flexibility of the space, thus supporting the productivity and wellbeing of the workers.

As our research consists of qualitative methods and thus, limited amount of data sources (participants), the validity and generalisability of the results are limited. However, this early-phase research aimed to be explorative and generative rather than reveal statistically proved facts. We will continue our work by validating the meaningful experiences for future Pop Up workspaces, as well as testing the future possibilities and limitations of our concepts of workspace ambiences. We will also test different possibilities of ambient technologies to construct the Pop Up workspaces described in this paper.

References

1. Coenen, M., Kok, R.A.: Workplace flexibility and new product development performance: the role of telework and flexible work schedules. Eur. Manage. J. **32**(4), 564–576 (2014)
2. Waber, B., Magnolfi, J., Lindsay, G.: Workspaces that move people. Harvard Bus. Rev. **92**(10), 68–77 (2014)
3. Dantzig, S., Geleijnse, G., Halteren, A.T.: Toward a persuasive mobile application to reduce sedentary behavior. Pers. Ubiquit. Comput. **17**(6), 1237–1246 (2013)
4. Poutanen, J.: Pop-up spaces: from prototyping to a method of revealing user-attitudes. In: Chudoba, M., Joachimiak, M., Laak, M., Lehtovuori, P., Partanen, J., Rantanen, A., Siter, N. (eds.) ATUT Proceedings, 5th Annual Symposium of Architectural Research, Architecture and Resilience, pp. 13–23 (2013)
5. Vartiainen, M.: Hindrances and enablers of fluent actions in knowledge work. In: Sachse, P., Ulich, E. (eds.) Psychologie menschlichen Handelns: Wissen und Denken – Wollen und Tun, Pabst Science Publishers, pp. 95–111 (2014)
6. Desmet, P., Schifferstein, R. (eds.): A Collection of 35 Experience-Driven Design Projects. Eleven International Publishing (2012)

7. Logan, R.J., Augaitis, S., Renk, T.: Design of simplified television remote controls: a case for behavioral and emotional usability. In: Proceedings of the 38th Human Factors and Ergonomics Society Annual Meeting, Human Factors and Ergonomics Society, vol. 38, no. 5, pp. 365–369 (1994)

8. McIver, D., Lengnick-Hall, C., Lengnick-Hall, M., Ramachandran, I.: Understanding work and knowledge management from a knowledge-in-practice perspective. Acad. Manage. Rev. **38**(4), 587–620 (2013)

9. Appel-Meulenbroek, R., Groenen, P., Janssen, I.: An end-user's perspective on activity-based office concepts. J. Corporal Real Estate **13**(2), 122–135 (2011)

10. Värlander, S.: Individual flexibility in the workplace: a spatial perspective. J. Appl. Behav. Sci. **48**(1), 33–61 (2012)

11. Peponis, J., Bafna, S., Bajaj, R., Bromberg, J., Congdon, C., Rashid, M., Warmels, S., Zhang, Y., Zimring, C.: Designing space to support knowledge work. Environ. Behav. **39** (6), 815–840 (2007)

12. Hassenzahl, M.: Hedonic, emotional, and experiential perspectives on product quality. In: Ghaoui, C. (ed.) Encyclopedia of Human Computer Interaction, pp. 266–272. Idea Group Reference, Hershey, PA, USA (2006)

13. Hassenzahl, M.: The thing and I: understanding the relationship between user and product. In: Blythe, M.A., Overbeeke, K., Monk, A.F., Wright, P.C. (eds.) Funology, from Usability to Enjoyment, pp. 31–42. Kluwer Academic Publishers, Norwell, MA, USA (2003)

14. Olsson, T., Väänänen-Vainio-Mattila, K., Saari, T., Lucero, A., Arrasvuori, J.: Reflections on experience-driven design: a case study on designing for playful experiences. In: Proceedings of the 6th International Conference on Designing Pleasurable Products and Interfaces, pp. 165–174 (2013)

15. Hassenzahl, M.: Experience Design, Technology for All the Right Reasons. Morgan & Claypool, San Rafael (2010)

16. Arrasvuori, J., Boberg, M., Holopainen, J., Korhonen, H., Lucero, A., Montola, M.: Applying the PLEX framework in designing for playfulness. In: Proceedings of the 2011 Conference on Designing Pleasurable Products and Interfaces (DPPI 2011). Article 24, 8 p. (2011)

17. Norberg-Schulz, C.: Genius Loci – Towards a Phenomenology of Architecture. Rizzoli International Publications, New York (1980)

18. Karjalainen, T-M., Koskinen, J., Repokari L.: Ambience design: creating multi-sensory moods within built environments. In: Conference Presentation at HAAMAHA (2005)

19. Koskinen, J.: Ambience Design Notes. Service Design: On the Evolution of Design Expertise. Lahti University of Applied Sciences Series A, Research reports, part, vol. 16, pp. 155–165 (2012)

20. Wisneski, C., Ishii, H., Dahley, A., Gorbet, M., Brave, S., Ullmer, B., Yarin, P.: Ambient displays: turning architectural space into an interface between people and digital information. In: Yuan, F., Konomi, S., Burkhardt, H.-J. (eds.) CoBuild 1998. LNCS, vol. 1370, pp. 22–32. Springer, Heidelberg (1998)

21. Wang, J., Mughal, M.A.: LiveNature: connecting people with their cherished places. In: Proceedings of the Companion Publication on Designing Interactive Systems, pp. 113–116 (2014)

22. Cao, Y.Y., Okude, N.: Scented pebbles: interactive ambient experience with smell and lighting. In: Proceedings of the Ninth International Conference on Tangible, Embedded, and Embodied Interaction (TEI 2015), pp. 409–410 (2015)

23. Ip, H.H.-S., Kwong, B.: Smart ambience games for children with learning difficulties. In: Pan, Z., Aylett, R.S., Diener, H., Jin, X., Göbel, S., Li, L. (eds.) Edutainment 2006. LNCS, vol. 3942, pp. 484–493. Springer, Heidelberg (2006)

24. Kuijsters, A., Redi, J., de Ruyter, B., Seuntiëns, P., Heynderickx, I.: Affective ambiences created with lighting for older people. In: Lighting Research and Technology (2014)
25. Wright, P., McCarthy, J.: Experience-Centered Design - Designers, Users, and Communities in Dialogue. Morgan & Claypool, San Rafael (2010)
26. Zhang, Y., Wildemuth, B.M.: Qualitative analysis of content. In: Applications of Social Research Methods to Questions in Information and Library Science, pp. 308–319 (2009)
27. Gibson, J.J.: The Ecological Approach to Visual Perception. Houghton Mifflin, Boston, MA (1979)
28. Daskala, B., Maghiros, I.: Digital territories. IET Int. Conf. Intell. Environ. 2, 221–226 (2006)

Designing an Application Store for the Internet of Things: Requirements and Challenges

Simon Stastny[1], Babak A. Farshchian[2(✉)], and Thomas Vilarinho[2]

[1] Norwegian University of Science and Technology, Trondheim, Norway
stastny.simon@gmail.com
[2] Stiftelsen SINTEF, Trondheim, Norway
{babak.farshchian, thomas.vilarinho}@sintef.no

Abstract. Although things in the Internet of Things contain considerable amounts of software, developers of such software have no standardized means of maintaining, improving and sharing this software as they can do, e.g., with applications on a smart phone. This limitation can hamper user-driven innovation. In this paper we evaluate the usefulness of the "app store" metaphor as a means of sharing and deploying Internet of Things software among makers. We did a set of interviews and a questionnaire-based survey with a sample of makers in various maker communities. We used this data to extract requirements for an application store, using the common "app store" metaphor as a starting point. The app store concept was developed as a proof of concept implementation, and evaluated through feasibility evaluation and focus group evaluation methods. Our findings show that although the app store metaphor is familiar and easy to grasp, there are some fundamental challenges when adapting the metaphor: (1) The difficulty of supporting the diversity in the software and hardware vendor market, (2) The tension between context awareness and the need for pre-configuration and pre-packaging, and (3) usability challenges related to the number of devices and apps.

Keywords: Internet of things · IoT · App store · Application repository · App installation · App deployment · App sharing · Ambient intelligence · Ubiquitous computing · Pervasive computing

1 Introduction

The Internet of Things (IoT) is defined as *"the pervasive presence around us of a variety of things or objects –such as...tags, sensors, actuators, mobile phones [that] are able to interact with each other and cooperate with their neighbors to reach common goals"* [1]. IoT can be seen as the enabling technology for many of the applications that are envisioned by the Ambient Intelligence (AmI) community. The exponential growth of the IoT can therefore be seen as an opportunity to realize some of these visionary scenarios.

When talking about IoT, the obvious thing that comes to our mind is the *thing* or the physical object. But we should not forget that IoT's value propositions are equally based on the software that runs these things. This software can be present in many forms: embedded, middleware, applications, service composition logic, and management

© Springer International Publishing Switzerland 2015
Kameas et al. (Eds.): AmI 2015, LNCS 9425, pp. 313–327, 2015.
DOI: 10.1007/978-3-319-26005-1_21

tools [1, 2]. Our interest in this study is related to the embedded software and the management tool used to share, distribute and deploy this software. Using popular denotations from the smartphone domain, we call the collection of these management tools the *IoT app store*. We also call the embedded software that resides in the things for *IoT app*.

IoT apps are in a transition from being "embedded" into IoT things—i.e. being inseparable from and secondary to the thing itself—to becoming an independent and central business asset. In many domains nowadays "firmware upgrades" start getting more attention than product releases—see for instance firmware upgrades for Leica digital cameras. Software engineering practices related to maintaining, upgrading and releasing "firmware" are becoming important topics even in industries such as automotive, where the physical product plays a central role [3]. Some have even gone so far to consider the physical product—the thing—as being secondary to the software that runs on it [4].

When the IoT app becomes a separately tradable asset, it becomes also interesting to look into tools that can support its trade. We already have the popular example of smartphone application stores such as those of Apple, Google and Amazon [5]. These stores have played a central role in grassroots and third-party initiated innovation in the area of smartphone apps [6]. User-driven innovation in IoT apps can be a strong vehicle for a wider uptake of AmI. Preparing a marketplace for sharing such innovation is crucial for nurturing and promoting this innovation [7]. However, due to limitations and complexities that exist in current tools and technologies, such innovation is mostly happening in specialized communities such as among researchers [8, 9] and maker/hackers [10]. As researchers, our interest is drawn to maker/hacker communities, and how their members share their innovations. We believe maker communities, being early adopters [11], can provide us with important insights into how the IoT app landscape will look like in the near future.

In this paper we will present a study of how the app store metaphor might be adapted to IoT. Our research question is *"what are the requirements and challenges for an app store for IoT?"* We have studied a number of makers in order to understand the challenges they face when packaging, sharing and deploying IoT apps. We have used the findings to extract requirements for an IoT app store concept called UbiBazaar. The concept was developed as a paper prototype, evaluated in a focus group, and later implemented as a proof-of-concept prototype. The paper will describe this study by first discussing our method, data and findings from user studies. We will then present the UbiBazaar proof-of-concept implementation, and discuss our findings.

2 Method and Approach

Our study uses the design science research methodology [12], where the research activities are divided into the three cycles of *rigor*, *relevance* and *design* [13]. Here we will shortly describe how we have taken these three aspects of the methodology into account.

To ground our research in existing theory and related work and to clarify our contribution (the rigor cycle in design science) we conducted a systematic literature review. We ran a query in *Scopus* based on common phrases such as IoT, AmI, Pervasive and Ubiquitous computing, software deployment, installation etc. We ended up with 164 hits (October 2014). Ten of these papers were retained after a screening based on title and abstract [inclusion criteria: (1) paper is about deployment in IoT, (2) paper is about app stores in IoT]. In addition, we have studied a number of other papers based on other informal search and snowballing from references in the included papers. Details about the literature study can be found in [14].

In order to increase the relevance of our research (the relevance cycle in design science research) we conducted interviews and a survey with makers. Based on the findings from the literature we conducted four in-depth semi-structured interviews with four experienced makers and developers of IoT projects and software. The interview topics were related to the nature of the IoT projects the interviewees were working on, the methods they used to develop and deploy software, and the challenges they face in the process. Details about the interviews, the interview guide and transcriptions can be found in [14].

Based on the findings from the literature and the interviews we designed and published an online questionnaire. We sent the questionnaire to a number of maker communities (in total 8 communities) and asked their members to participate. In this questionnaire we wanted to investigate the means of software deployment, distribution, and collaborative development. We also wanted to know which IoT platforms are popular among makers. A total of 11 members from these communities responded to the questionnaire, and one of them was further interviewed by us.

Based on these results we designed a paper prototype and a proof of concept implementation of an IoT app store called UbiBazaar (the design cycle in the design science research). The paper prototype was evaluated in a focus group workshop with four experts, the results of which guided the development of the software prototype.

The results from these studies will be presented in the following sections. Section 3 documents the literature study. Section 4 discusses our findings from the interviews and the survey. Sections 5 and 6 discuss the results from designing and evaluating UbiBazaar.

3   Related Work

In this section we present an analysis of our findings from the literature. The section is divided into three sub-headings: (1) general discussion of motivation and challenges of using app stores in IoT and similar domains, (2) the challenge of the heterogeneity of platforms and ecosystems, and (3) the challenge of changing context and configuration.

3.1   Software Deployment in IoT

Most non-technical people, when buying an intelligent "thing" or device, never update or change the IoT app that comes with it. This has disadvantages because outdated apps can mean outdated devices. Therefore maintaining, sharing and deploying IoT apps are becoming increasingly common activities. These activities are mostly done in three ways: (1) through proprietary "firmware upgrades", (2) through source code sharing in open communities, and (3) through proprietary app stores.

Firmware upgrades are proprietary and cumbersome methods for updating IoT apps. Most firmware upgrades require a high level of technical knowledge, such as downloading and unpacking files and specialized tools, and transferring files to devices using specialized cables. Many companies are secretive about protocols used to do firmware upgrades and don't allow third parties to develop firmware because of commercial or security concerns. Some industries have been involved in attempts to standardize and open up the firmware upgrade process. Makowski et al. [15] describe a standardized method for upgrading firmware in the Telecommunications Computing Architecture (xTA). Another example is the OSGi platform—used in e.g. automotive industry—that has for many years provided advanced means for deploying so-called bundles onto an OSGi runtime platform [16]. A recent standardization effort is based on using Docker[1], a deployment tool, together with Raspberry Pi. This Docker-based method is demonstrated in our concept of UbiBazaar, to be discussed later.

IoT and its physicality have been a contributing factor to the emergence of strong maker/hacker and Do-It-Youself (DIY) communities in recent years [10]. These communities have gradually developed their own channels of sharing and deploying IoT apps. One of the major channels used is configuration management tools such as Git. Github and specialized portals—such as those of Arduino and Raspberry Pi—are used as channels for distributing open source code for IoT apps. Although popular among makers and DIY communities, this is a complicated method for many people as it involves interacting with code repositories, and configuring and compiling code. As we will see later, the makers we interviewed were looking for better ways of distributing their IoT apps than through code repositories.

The third method of deploying software—i.e. using app stores—is gaining in popularity as app stores in general have become a common household tool for everyone including users [5] and developers [6]. What is probably the main advantage of app stores is their user-friendliness both for providing and consuming packaged apps. App stores are suggested by others as means of deploying IoT apps to general public [7, 17, 18] or for research purposes [9, 19]. There are emerging initiatives for building such app stores (see for instance "The Pi Store" for Raspberry Pi[2] or Android Market for Wear[3]). These existing initiatives are mainly attempts to repeat the success of smartphone app stores, but do not take into consideration the challenges of IoT, pervasive and ubiquitous computing and AmI such as the heterogeneity of platforms and the context-awareness of IoT apps.

3.2   Heterogeneous Platforms and Ecosystems

The most frequently mentioned challenge in the literature we studied was the heterogeneity of the IoT environments [17, 18, 20, 21]. This heterogeneity is regarded as an issue that is harming the further uptake of IoT innovations, and leading to "a solution that may be outdated quickly" [18]. This heterogeneity makes software deployment

---

[1] www.docker.com.

[2] store.raspberrypi.com.

[3] www.android.com/wear/.

harder, as the way a software artifact is deployed or even packaged is in many cases platform-specific. Some works suggest this is the reason why we do not have standardized distribution channels for IoT apps [17]: "The IoT industry doesn't have a unified hardware and software platform [which] greatly complicates the creation of distribution channels for software applications."

3.3   Configuration and Context Awareness

A challenge facing IoT app deployment is the need for local configuration of IoT apps due to their varied and changing context. IoT systems are formed by a number of interconnected things, which need to be paired, registered, or configured in order to be able to work together [1]. This configuration is unique for each situation, which makes it difficult to distribute pre-packaged standard IoT apps.

Some researchers [20–23] suggest addressing the challenge of configuration by employing runtime self-configuration mechanisms [24]. Self-configuration can be achieved through context- awareness, i.e. automatically reacting to changes in other parts of the system and the operational environment.

Another approach to configuration and context awareness is to allow users do the configuration through e.g. end user configuration [25, 26]. Both end user configuration and automatic configuration are promising approaches that provide valuable input to how an app store concept can deal with specific context of use for IoT apps. Our approach when developing the concept for UbiBazaar has been to define part of the context—i.e. the device capabilities—handled by the app store, while letting IoT app developers chose the means to configuring the apps once installed.

4   Findings from the Interviews and the Survey

Our informants were involved in IoT projects making systems as diverse as sensor systems for collecting data from crisis situations, ubiquitous smart home systems for monitoring energy consumption, wearable fall detection systems for elderly, and devices augmented with social computing features. Data from 5 in-depth interviews and 11 answers to survey questionnaires were analyzed using topic-based qualitative data analysis. From this analysis three topics emerged, partly overlapping with our findings from the literature: (1) diversity of deployment platforms, (2) cumbersome distribution and deployment channels, and (3) context awareness vs. pre-configuration.

4.1   Diversity of Deployment Platforms

Most of our respondents use multiple hardware platforms in their projects, including Arduino and Raspberry Pi as the most prolific. The respondents also mentioned other platforms. See Fig. 1 for an overview of reported platform in our survey.

Another finding is the large number of device variants. A number of these devices— such as Arduino and Raspberry Pi—consist of generic "boards" that can be equipped

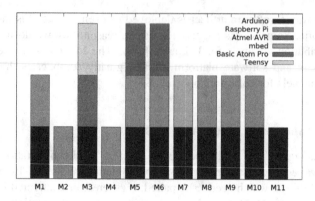

Fig. 1. Overview of the survey informants' usage of hardware platforms.

with sensors, actuators and other peripherals of choice. This means that there is no standard "Arduino device" or "Raspberry Pi device". Each device is potentially unique. Most of the respondents also mentioned that they use multiple platforms within the same project.

The wide variety of hardware platforms results in an even wider variety of deployment tools and mechanisms. While some platforms require use of specialized tools to program a device—e.g. Arduino—other platforms require users to come up with their own ad hoc means of deployment. Some platforms also require physical access to the device—e.g. using a USB cable—while others support remote deployment over wireless network.

4.2   Cumbersome Distribution and Deployment Channels

The difficulty of distributing and deploying IoT apps was mentioned by a number of our informants. In a number of cases the informants were working with projects where the devices were not in their physical vicinity. This meant that they had invented ad hoc means for remote installation of software, which did not seem to be so user-friendly:

- *"I do all deploying myself, in this moment. But I do not have physical access to all of those controllers..."*
- *"It would be nice if this [deployment] could be done wirelessly."*
- *"...I really could see wireless deployment of upgrades coming down from the cloud, that could be user-transparent, to be useful"*

The informants had some thoughts about scalability of their home-grown deployment methods:

- *"If the prototype gets further developed and maybe commercialized, of course we would need a tool or a procedure to upload a new firmware to the Arduino"*
- *"It would be nice to automate build and deploy updates for the microcontroller..."*
- *"What would be useful is a dedicated server wrapping the build tool that would provide building remotely as a service."*

Some commented how the IoT apps could be packaged in order to facilitate their sharing and deployment:

- *"If you're going to produce thousands of Raspberry Pis that are customized for this project then you would produce them all with this image that already has this house-monitoring software installed. The other case is when you have someone who wants to create their own application and deploy it in the Raspberry Pi."*
- *"Typical deployment takes about six hours [...].If you already have a prepared image for the Raspberry Pi, then the entire deployment takes about one hour"*
- *"[the application on Raspberry Pi] could be Dockerized, The Java component, the GUI, the application that stores the different power which is a web application written in PHP. This all can be packaged as a Docker file, kind of an installation script and then once someone takes a Raspberry Pi and installs Docker and get this Docker file, he will have the service running. However there is still pairing with the smart plugs to be done."*

Sharing of IoT apps with others is done manually through uploading, downloading and compiling source files. This means that the recipient manually fetches the software—downloads a binary package or source code—and then configures it as wished—typically deploying the software, or doing changes to source code and then building and deploying.

All the informants reported that they use source code repositories to share source code of their software. Some use private code repositories, while others use it as a way of releasing the sources for use by the general public. In addition to using popular services such as Github, respondents frequently mentioned that they share the software on community forums or through their personal website or blogs.

Some respondents mentioned distributing software in form of binaries or built packages. While these are easier for an end user to use, often they cannot be configured. Two of the respondents also mentioned they publish their software on software store such as the Pi Store.

4.3   Context Awareness vs. Pre-configuration

Local configuration emerged as a topic in our findings. In particular, network context for the IoT apps was mentioned:

- *"The mobile talks to Arduino via Bluetooth and sends commands to it."*
- *"In one deployment, the cottage, there is a Raspberry Pi connected with WiFi USB connector to the WiFi network. In other deployments, Raspberry Pi is connected with a network cable to the router."*

Other types of configuration mentioned included new sensors or actuators getting connected to a board:

- *"When you deploy for the first time the system needs to be manually configured before you can use it."*

– *"[when a new plug is connected] user needs to assign it in the web interface."*

A related topic that has to do with local configuration is the awareness that our informants had of the fact that they were part of a DIY prototyping community. They were very clear about the fact that what they did was not commercial product development, that they developed a personal prototype for their personal use, and that –when shared –the product had to be customized by its new users:

– *"If the prototype gets further developed and maybe commercialized, of course we would need a tool or a procedure to upload a new firmware to the Arduino"*
– *"One of the ideas of Arduino is really just prototyping. In essence you use Arduino to easily build your prototype, but afterward if you want to sell a product, you go industrial-wise and you have sort of a personalization process [...] You program the firmware to the board in the factory and you're done."*
– *"It depends on in which moment you want to do [deployment] - if you want to do this on the prototyping level, or the production level."*

5   UbiBazaar: A Proof of Concept App Store for IoT

In order to further test our findings through design we developed a proof-of-concept implementation of an IoT app store called UbiBazaar. UbiBazaar is based on a focus group evaluation of an early paper prototype. The paper prototype was based on our findings from literature and user studies. We first describe UbiBazaar in this section, before we return to the paper prototype evaluation in the next section.

#	Requirement	Rationale
1	UbiBazaar should support the basic functionality and concepts found in popular application markets such as instant wireless installation of apps, and easy-to-use interfaces for developers to share apps	Since we are testing the usefulness of the "app store" metaphor, it is important that test users can find UbiBazaar concepts similar to those in common app stores, and as easy to use
2	UbiBazaar should support multiple deployment platforms, and be extensible to other existing or emerging platforms	Both the literature and our informants point to the fact that IoT consists of multiple hardware and software platforms
3	UbiBazaar should be aware of and manage the capabilities of the devices belonging to a user	Our findings show that IoT applications are context-aware. A part of the context that we think can be used by an app store is that of a user's existing devices and their capabilities such as on-board sensors, actuators and network interfaces

5.1 Start Page and Basic Functionality

As we are using the app store metaphor as the underlying concept, it is important that the users can get a feeling of visiting an app store when they visit UbiBazaar. The basic functionality for enabling this feeling includes the ability to browse IoT apps and their description, to search for IoT apps based on app category and other criteria, to log in and store a personal profile, including personal apps and devices. In addition, in order to allow support for multiple platforms, the apps are categorized based on the hardware platform they are designed for.

5.2 Sharing New IoT Apps as Developer

After a user registers, he/she can share IoT apps. The sharing process consists of two steps (see Fig. 2): (1) define the basic metadata about the IoT app, and (2) select the hardware platform the app can run on.

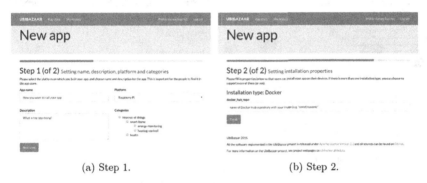

(a) Step 1.   (b) Step 2.

Fig. 2. Adding a new IoT app consist of two steps: (1) provide common metadata, and (2) select hardware platform.

5.3 Maintaining a Set of Device Definitions

UbiBazaar allows the user to maintain a set of devices (see Fig. 3). The devices are given a name and a description and are assigned a platform type, e.g. Arduino or Raspberry Pi. Upon the registration of a device, a pairing and authentication process is performed. It consists of installing an *installation manager* on the device (see later section on the UbiBazaar architecture), and pairing this installation manager with UbiBazaar server. After this pairing is done, the device can communicate with Ubi-Bazaar in order to query for content and to install/uninstall apps.

5.4 Installing an App on a Device

UbiBazaar allows the user to browse for IoT apps that are compatible with a specific platform—e.g. Raspberry Pi—and chose a device of that type to install the app

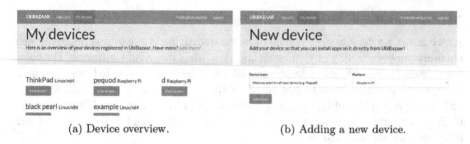

(a) Device overview.   (b) Adding a new device.

Fig. 3. Defining and maintaining a set of devices.

(see Fig. 4). UbiBazaar also allows the user to maintain the apps that are installed on each device. Some devices, such as Raspberry Pi, allow multiple IoT apps on-board while others—e.g. Arduino—do not.

(a) App detail.   (b) Device detail.

Fig. 4. Installing an IoT app on a device.

5.5   UbiBazaar Architecture

Figure 5 shows UbiBazaar's architecture. It consists of a central *UbiBazaar server* hosting a number of services for maintaining users and their personal profiles such as apps and devices (upper part of the figure). The server also includes the *web front-end* that was described in the previous sections. In addition to the server, a number of *installation managers* are being developed. Installation managers are responsible for implementing the communication between the devices—the things—and UbiBazaar. This communication is necessary for querying the devices about their capabilities and about the IoT apps they host. Figure 5 shows how the installation managers for Raspberry Pi and Arduino are implemented. Since Raspberry Pi is a full-fledged Linux-based device with network capabilities, the device (thing) itself can host the installation manager. Arduino is a much simpler device and for this reason we have implemented the installation manager for Arduino as an Android app [27]. This app then communicates with Arduino devices, using Bluetooth to send IoT apps to these devices [28]. We have emphasized the definition and use of open APIs for

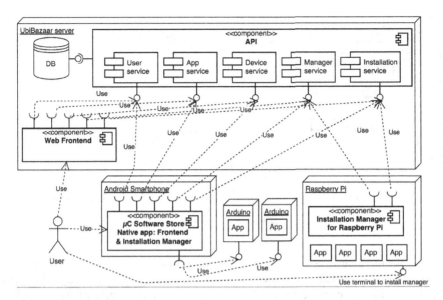

Fig. 5. UbiBazaar architecture.

communication between the components. These APIs are defined and documented in the project web site [29].

6   Evaluation

Based on findings from our field and literature studies, the initial concept of UbiBazaar was developed as a paper prototype using the Balsamiq tool[4]. This prototype was evaluated by a focus group of four makers (different than those who were initially interviewed). The results from this focus group were used to refine the concept before it was implemented as a reference implementation that was described in the previous section. This section will provide an overview of the findings from this evaluation of the paper prototype. The main concepts of IoT apps and devices were already demonstrated in this paper prototype. In addition, we also demonstrated the installation and pairing with devices of the type Raspberry Pi.

Streamlining of Concepts and Terminology. One of the main findings from the evaluation was the need to simplify the concepts used in the prototype. For instance, we eliminated the use of the concept "Deploy" and "Download" and used instead concepts such as "Install". See Fig. 6.

Device Pairing and Authentication. The way UbiBazaar handles the first time pairing with devices was discussed by the focus group. The discussion was due to the difficulty of the concept, but also due to practical issues such as firewall configurations.

---

[4] http://balsamiq.com/.

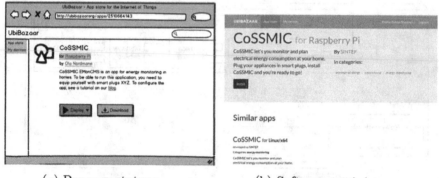

(a) Paper prototype.   (b) Software prototype.

Fig. 6. Moving from "Deploy" and "Download" to "Install".

The original mechanism of device pairing and authentication was based on downloading a generic installer, installing the software and then configuring it manually. The focus group found this too complicated for the user and suggested to simplify the process. For the final solution, installation script with built-in credentials and auto-configuration were used. For Arduino, Standard Bluetooth pairing is done on the Android device [28].

Managing Devices. The participants discussed how it will look like when the user has many devices that can communicate with each other. Currently UbiBazaar maintains a flat list of devices. Specifying device capability is not supported. The participants wished to see some way of allowing the user tell UbiBazaar what devices can communicate with each other and how.

Trust and Security Concerns. Trustworthiness in IoT app stores has been addressed by previous research [30] and was also a big concern for the focus group participants. IoT has a potential to influence our daily lives in ways we may not even be able to imagine yet. It is necessary to ensure that IoT apps, many of which will handle our personal data and control our lives to a certain extent, are to be trusted and prevent misuse by third parties. Although simple authentication is implemented in our proof of concept, more research needs to be done in this area.

Social and Collaborative Aspects. The participants meant that UbiBazaar should not only be an app catalogue but also a social platform with features such as ratings and comments. Since IoT apps need local customizations much more than current smartphone apps, the participants envisaged a more central role for social and collaborative aspects in order to support collaborative customization.

7   Discussion

Using the app store metaphor in the context of IoT is an attractive idea, as witnessed by both commercial and research-based initiatives discussed in this paper. The need for an app store-like tool was raised in our user studies. UbiBazaar concept was easily understood and appreciated by our focus group participants. The metaphor is familiar, and has shown to be successful in creating and maintaining sustainable ecosystems. It is therefore natural to think about reusing the concept in the IoT domain. In particular, some properties of IoT—e.g. large numbers of devices, devices without a management interface, the need for remote management and so on [31]—would mean that a management tool such as an app store is the answer. However, our study shows that there are some fundamental challenges facing this hypothesis.

The first challenge is that of the heterogeneity of hardware and software platforms. Compared to the heterogeneity that we can see in IoT, even the smartphone platform market seems very homogeneous. After more than a decade of smartphone development we have not yet arrived at a common platform. So the journey towards a common platform might be much longer for IoT. There are strong commercial interests connected to app stores and the ecosystem surrounding them [32] that point in the direction of even stronger proprietary ecosystems in the future. This will be a challenge for an IoT app store that aims to support a heterogeneous set of things running different software platforms. UbiBazaar architecture is a step in bridging the gap, but will have limitations in supporting commercial, proprietary platforms.

The second challenge is that of context awareness. Smartphone context can arguably be said to be much simpler than that of a typical IoT system consisting of tens of devices each running various IoT apps. Uncritical application of app store concept to such scenarios will mean users will get overloaded with configuration and re-configuration tasks. We need to build on findings from both context-aware and autonomous computing [24], but also use research done in the area of end user programming and end user configuration [26]. The answer will probably lie in combining what the app store can support, what the user can configure, and what the IoT system can/should automate. The goal should be to work on a usable and useful tool for the user. Our approach in UbiBazaar has been to keep UbiBazaar in charge of maintaining device capabilities, and allow app developers decide the type of context-awareness and end user configuration at the app level.

Our study has resulted in findings related to usability. What does it mean to deploy, install or update an IoT app? How do we update remote devices? How do we know which device we are updating? See [33] for a wide range of such issues that can apply to IoT app stores. More research is needed within IoT app store usability.

We believe that maker communities form an ideal setting to do further research on these issues. We see a need for an IoT app store among the makers we have talked to. We also see makers as early adopters of technologies that will be available in every household in the not so far future.

8 Conclusions

In this paper we have studied IoT apps and IoT app stores. We have presented empirical evidence from user studies and the literature about the feasibility of using the app store metaphor in the IoT domain. We have presented a proof-of-concept implementation of an IoT app store called UbiBazaar. UbiBazaar is implemented as an open source project [29] and will be used as platform for further research in this area.

Our surveys (n = 11) and interviews (n = 5) should be repeated in order to refine and generalize the findings. We believe however that the nature of the practices we have studies is such that that most makers will have the same challenges as those we have studied. Our future research will include studies of how UbiBazaar will be used by makers.

We have focused our empirical investigations towards maker communities. Our assumption has been that the needs of makers, being early adapters, can be generalized to those of non-makers. We believe this is a hypothesis that can be tested in future research, by evaluating UbiBazaar and related concepts with non-makers.

Our reference implementation UbiBazaar is only an early proof-of-concept prototype and needs to be extended in a number of directions. Of most interest for us are the addition of support for collaboration, and the addition of functionality for specifying device capabilities in a more detailed manner as a means for specifying a context for IoT apps. We also think it will be important to add support for a wider variety of platforms, in particular full support for Arduino.

Acknowledgements. This research was funded by the European FP7 projects OPTET (317631) and CoSSMic (608806). We thank AmI 2015 reviewers for constructive comments to the draft of the paper.

References

1. Atzori, L., Iera, A., Morabito, G.: The internet of things: a survey. Comput. Netw. **54**, 2787–2805 (2010)
2. Ebert, C., Jones, C.: Embedded software: facts, figures and future. IEEE Comput. **4**, 42–52 (2009)
3. Broy, M.: Challenges in automotive software engineering. In: Proceedings of 28th International Conference Software Engineering, pp. 33–42 (2006)
4. Shih, W.C.: Does hardware even matter anymore? Harv. Bus. Rev. (2015). https://hbr.org/2015/06/does-hardware-even-matter-anymore.
5. Cuadrado, F., Dueñas, J.: Mobile application stores: success factors, existing approaches, and future developments. IEEE Commun. Mag. **50**, 160–167 (2012)
6. Holzer, A., Ondrus, J.: Mobile application market: a developer's perspective. Telemat. Inform. **28**, 22–31 (2011)
7. Kortuem, G., Kawsar, F.: Market-based user innovation in the Internet of Things. In: 2010 Internet Things, pp. 1–8 (2010)
8. Gellersen, H., Kortuem, G., Schmidt, A., Beigl, M.: Physical prototyping with smart-its. IEEE Pervasive Comput. **3**, 74–82 (2004)
9. Cramer, H., Rost, M., Belloni, N., et al.: Research in the large. using app stores, markets, and other wide distribution channels in Ubicomp research. In: Proceedings of 12th ACM International Conference on Adjunct Papers on Ubiquitous Computing - Ubicomp 2010, p 511. ACM Press, New York, USA (2010)
10. Lindtner, S., Hertz, G.D., Dourish, P.: Emerging sites of HCI innovation: hackerspaces, hardware startups and incubators. In: Proceedings of SIGCHI Conference on Human Factors Computing Systems, pp. 439–448 (2014)
11. Rogers, E.M.: Diffusion of Innovations. Simon and Schuster, New York (2010)

12. Hevner, A.R., March, Salvatore T., Park, J., Ram, S.: Design science in information systems research. MIS Q. **28**, 75–105 (2004)
13. Hevner, A.R.: A three cycle view of design science research. Scand. J. Inf. Syst. **19**, 87–92 (2007)
14. Stastny, S.: UbiBazaar - app store for the Internet of Things. Student thesis, Norwegian University of Science and Technology, Trondheim, Norway (2014)
15. Makowski, D., Jab, G., Perek, P., et al.: Firmware upgrade in xTCA systems. IEEE Trans. Nucl. Sci. **60**, 3639–3646 (2013)
16. Parrend, P., Frenot, S.: Supporting the secure deployment of OSGi bundles. In: 2007 IEEE International Symposium on a World Wireless, Mobile Multimedia Networks, vol. 33, pp. 1–6 (2007)
17. Munjin, D., Morin, J.-H.: Toward Internet of Things application markets. In: 2012 IEEE International Conference on Green Computing and Communications, pp. 156–162 (2012)
18. Svendsen, R.M., Castejon, H.N., Berg, E., Zoric, J.: Towards an integrated solution to Internet of Things - a technical and economical proposal. In: 2011 15th International Conference on Intelligence Next Generation Networks, pp 46–51. IEEE (2011)
19. Davies, N.: Beyond prototypes, again. IEEE Pervasive Comput. **10**, 2–3 (2011)
20. Medvidovic, N., Malek, S.: Software deployment architecture and quality-of-service in pervasive environments. In: International Workshop on Engineering of Software Services, pp 47–51. ACM Press, New York, USA (2007)
21. Hoareau, D., Mahéo, Y.: Middleware support for the deployment of ubiquitous software components. Pers. Ubiquitous Comput. **12**, 167–178 (2006)
22. Zheng, D., Wang, J., Han, W., et al.: Towards a context-aware middleware for deploying component-based applications in pervasive computing. In: 2006 Fifth International Conference on Grid and Cooperative Computing, pp 454–457. IEEE (2006)
23. Sung, B.Y., Kumar, M., Shirazi, B.: Flexible and adaptive services in pervasive computing. Adv. Comput. **63**, 165–206 (2005)
24. Kephart, J.O., Chess, D.M.: The vision of autonomic computing. Computer **36–1**, 41 (2003)
25. Danado, J., Paternò, F.: Puzzle: a mobile application development environment using a jigsaw metaphor. J. Vis. Lang. Comput. **25**, 297–315 (2014)
26. Paternò, F., Tetteroo, D., Markopoulos, P., et al.: End-user development in the Internet of Things Era. In: CHI 2015 Extended Abstract (2015)
27. Eriksen, J., et al.: mC Software store. Student report, Norwegian University of Science and Technology, Trondheim, Norway (2013)
28. Eie, A.B., et al.: oSNAP- Open Social Network Arduino Platform. Student report, Norwegian University of Science and Technology, Trondheim, Norway (2012)
29. Stastny, S.: UbiBazaar project at Github.com (2015). http://ubibazaar.github.io/
30. Kang, K., Pang, Z., Da, XuL, et al.: An interactive trust model for application market of the Internet of Things. IEEE Trans. Ind. Informatics **10**, 1516–1526 (2014)
31. Andersson, J.: A deployment system for pervasive computing. In: Proceedings of the International Conference on Software Maintenance ICSM-94, pp. 262–270. IEEE Computer Society Press (2000)
32. Eaton, B., Elaluf-Calderwood, S., et al.: Distributed tuning of boundary resources: the case of apple's iOS service system. MIS Q. **39**, 217–243 (2015)
33. Bellotti, V., Back, M., Edwards, W.K., et al.: Making sense of sensing systems: five questions for designers and researchers. In: Proceedings of the SIGCHI Conference on Human Factors Computing System. Changing Our World Changing ourselves CHI 2002, pp 415–422 (2002)

Evaluation of a Mobile Home Care Platform

Lessons Learned and Practical Guidelines

Christos Panagopoulos[1(✉)], Eirini Kalatha[2],
Panayiotis Tsanakas[3], and Ilias Maglogiannis[2]

[1] Bioassist S.A., Patras, Greece
cpan@bioassist.gr
[2] University of Piraeus, Piraeus, Greece
ekalatha@hotmail.com, imaglo@gmail.com
[3] National Technical University of Athens, Athens, Greece
panag@cs.ntua.gr

Abstract. As the population of the industrialized world is aging, the field that deals with seniors' adoption of technology has gained ground in the scientific community. Recent advances in technology have allowed the development of sophisticated telecare systems that support the independent living of seniors, with communication, remote health monitoring and emergency response services. However, usability issues often prevent elderly people from enjoying the benefits of modern technology, despite the amount of research to understand their needs in system design. In this work, we have performed a usability assessment of the "BioAssist" system, which is an integrated home care platform that incorporates both communication and health monitoring features. A comparative evaluation with the "iTriage" application, followed by a series of interviews and qualitative analysis have provided us with valuable insights and guidelines for designing home care systems for seniors.

Keywords: Home care · Usability · Older adults · Technology adoption

1 Introduction

Technology has become a dominant and integral part of our society, due to the fact that it is pervasive across all domains of life. As the population of the industrialized world is aging, the body of literature associated with seniors adopting technology and the benefits of this adoption is increasing [1–6].

The majority of older adults prefer to live independently, in their own homes and modern technology can be a key element to their support and well-being. Use of ICT services can enhance social engagement, help seniors remain updated about current affairs, eliminate loneliness, bridge the generation gap, and provide lifesaving alert systems [2–6]. Moreover, advances in the field of medical sensors have enabled us to remotely monitor and manage health conditions and diseases. Older adults can benefit from such technologies, as they have an increased chance of facing chronic conditions,

© Springer International Publishing Switzerland 2015
Kameas et al. (Eds.): AmI 2015, LNCS 9425, pp. 328–343, 2015.
DOI: 10.1007/978-3-319-26005-1_22

such as diabetes (34 % of adults aged 65 or older report having at least one health condition or disability) [1].

Telecare and telehealth applications are becoming increasingly popular, because they have the potential to reduce the enormous healthcare and elderly care costs for many developed countries [1]. This has led to a significant increase of research and development of many new applications. Many seniors acknowledge the benefits of such systems and are willing to adopt new technologies [1]. However, uptake is still low, as certain usability issues are still unresolved.

Much work has been done on identifying the constraints that older users face in learning or using modern ICT products. The most significant and easy to identify are inaccessibility and physical limitation constraints, such as visual impairments. In addition, there are psychological barriers, such as limited self-confidence, hesitance and feelings of anxiety when beginning to learn how to use ICT applications. Lastly, there are environmental factors, such as lack of support [2, 3, 7–9]. While many researchers have proposed certain guidelines to address these issues, there is still a gap of knowledge about the real needs of the ageing population, especially regarding psychological and environmental parameters [10–14].

A case study of a typical home care system, designed for the elderly, can highlight good practices and explore innovative solutions to overcome some of the aforementioned issues. In this work, we have performed a usability assessment of the "BioAssist" home care platform, which is a technology solution for independent living that provides advanced communication and health monitoring features. Our study was implemented in two phases. The first phase involved the use of the SUS method [19], which is a popular usability testing method that provides a high-level overview of usability by gathering data from potential typical users. Based on the results of the first phase, we conducted a series of interviews to further explore open issues and validate good practices.

2 Related Work and Background Information

2.1 State-of-the-Art in Home Care and Related Monitoring Applications

Home care refers to the application of telemedicine in the home environment [4]. The main aims that contributed to the development and evolution of this field are divided to financial, medical and personal. As far as financial aims are considered, it is a fact that the cost of senior care has increased significantly, especially in developed counties where the population is aging faster [5]. Early diagnosis, which can be achieved by continuous health monitoring, can reduce the cost of medical care. Furthermore, the remote monitoring of seniors who live alone may contribute to the improvement of their health and achieve early detection of potential relapses [4, 5]. For example, detection of falls, poor medication adherence, changes in sleep patterns, changes in physiological parameters or cognitive abilities represent critical information about an elderly person's health status.

At first, home care services were developed for chronic patients that required support at home, but soon expanded to address the needs of other vulnerable groups and to enhance the quality of life of seniors, by assisting their independent living [4]. Modern home care systems usually include three types of services:

- *Communication and social networking:* Many home care platforms include functionalities that support communication (e.g. videoconferencing or email) of seniors with their family members and friends or their doctor, keeping up with community events and staying connected with their loved ones by sharing content, such as photos. These features promote social engagement and help seniors overcome loneliness, boredom and depression, while maintaining a network of support. An example of a commercially available system that offers such services is "Claris Companion" [15], which is a retail service that aims to socially interconnect elderly people with their friends and family. The platform features videoconferencing and email capabilities, reminders to support daily activities and tasks such as medication intake, photo sharing for connected users, wellness surveys and a newsfeed.
- *Health monitoring:* Home care systems exploit medical sensors (e.g. pulse oximeters, glucometers, etc.) and various other devices that measure physiological parameters at home, to record and transmit real-time information about a senior's health and well-being. This information can be evaluated by healthcare professionals to create a customized care plan, while anomalies can be detected automatically, to identify possible deterioration of the patient's health status. A widely used system that offers this type of services is "BePatient", which is a telecare platform the supports remote monitoring of patients in homes before and after surgery [16]. The platform incorporates user interfaces for patients and healthcare professionals and tools to implement care coordination procedures and to analyze patient data. It includes features, such as monitoring of biosignals and physical activity and an electronic health record that can be accessed by the patient, family members and doctors.
- *Emergency response:* Many systems focus on emergency event management, by incorporating a "red button" service, smart home sensors and location tracking, to identify potentially dangerous situations and provide the necessary support. A commercially available solution of this type is "BeClose", which is a home monitoring solution that combines smart home enabled alarms and sensors, to analyze daily activity patterns and alert caregivers for abnormalities [17]. The system can also provide doctors with data on behavioral health, daily routines and care plan compliance.

For our study, we have selected the "BioAssist" home care platform which incorporates the widest selection of the above features and services, allowing us to explore all possible use cases, and has been designed with an emphasis on usability. The "BioAssist" platform is described in detail in the next section.

2.2   Methodologies for Usability Assessment

Usability evaluation aims to identify how well the potential users of a system can learn and use it, as well as how satisfied they are with that process. There is a variety of methods that are used for assessing a system's usability, at different stages of the design and development process. Some of these methods rely on data from actual users, while others rely on usability experts, and they can be classified into three main categories [18]:

1. Inspection methods: Methods that involve observation of users by an expert. These methods do not usually involve users directly. Well-known methods of this type are heuristic evaluation, ethnography, pluralistic inspection and consistency inspection.
2. Inquiry methods: Methods that involve the collection of qualitative data for users and include focus groups, interviews and surveys.
3. Testing methods: Methods that involve gathering quantitative data from typical users in a realistic environment. Common methods of this type include remote usability testing, the Think Aloud protocol and benchmark testing.

In this work, we used two assessment methods. First, we applied a testing method, which involves quantitative data collection via a questionnaire. This provided us with a quick, initial evaluation of the overall design of the selected home care platform, as well as some indications of issues that remain unresolved. To further explore these unresolved issues and gain insights on ways to overcome them, we also conducted interviews with users and performed a qualitative analysis.

Some of the most widely used and reliable questionnaires for usability assessment are the System Usability Scale (SUS) [19–21], the Website Analysis and Measurement Inventory (WAMMI) [22] and the Questionnaire for User Interaction Satisfaction (QUIS) [23]. We have chosen the SUS questionnaire for our study, because it can be used on a variety of products and services, including software applications, mobile apps, hardware consumer products and others types of systems, as it is technology-agnostic, and it has been used for the evaluation of telehealth systems [29–31]. Additionally, it is nonproprietary, cost effective and also easy for study participants to complete. Most importantly, it has been found that the SUS is robust and highly reliable [20].

The SUS gives a high-level subjective view on usability and is often used for comparisons of usability between systems, even dissimilar ones [20]. In order to better understand how various systems are evaluated on the SUS, we decided to conduct an additional assessment for another system, during the first phase of our study, to compare the results. For this task, we opted for a more mature system that is considered acceptable by many users. Since similarity between the two systems was not necessary, we chose the well-known "iTriage" application.

2.3 The "iTriage" Application

The "iTriage" system [24] enables users to look up symptoms and derive possible causes, treatment options procedures and common complications. Medical content in iTriage is created by physicians and reviewed by the Harvard Medical School. Users can select a body part according to the symptom they are experiencing or browse from an alphabetical list. They can also search for specific medications, possible side effects, usage instructions and overdose information and can even find nearby hospital ER's, physicians, urgent care centers, retail clinics, pharmacies, outpatient clinics and book an appointment.

Finally, users are able to store and manage personal health, such as insurance information, preferred doctors and facilities, appointments, medication and dosage information, diagnosed conditions, test results or procedures and even set prescription refill reminders. The system is available as a web-based application, but also as an app for Android and iOS devices (Fig. 1).

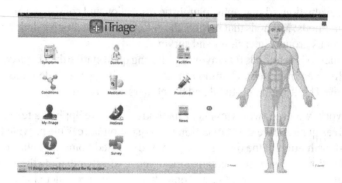

Fig. 1. "iTriage" app home screen and body part selection screen

3   Description of the "BioAssist" Platform

3.1   General Description

"BioAssist" is a technology assisted independent living platform that delivers superior monitoring and communication services [25]. The platform facilitates the creation of a patient-oriented social and support network of healthcare professionals, relatives and friends, and also provides the framework and the required services for effective communication and management of a wide range of wearable devices and sensors, which enable constant monitoring of the patient's biosignals and activities.

Each patient is provided with biosignal recording devices, a smartwatch and a tablet or other smart device (e.g. set-top box). The patient's doctor can use the platform tools and access the patient's PHR (medical history, laboratory test results, medication and allergies, etc.), assess his/her health condition using the platform analysis services and visualization features and define a monitoring and treatment schedule. This schedule includes a timeline of biosignal measurements, respective thresholds for each biosignal, as well as the prescribed medication and the timeline of its reception. Compliance to this schedule is enforced via reminders. Whenever a measurement exceeds the respective threshold, the doctor is automatically notified.

Real-time analysis algorithms are fused with data from various sources such as biosignal measurements and data from the patient's PHR, so as to provide continuous treatment assessment, and also to detect anomalies and emergency conditions (e.g. detect potential falls, based on the smartwatch accelerometer data). For the latter, a helpdesk service is automatically notified to provide the appropriate form of assistance.

3.2   System Architecture

The "BioAssist" homecare environment (Fig. 2) consists of four main sub-systems: an application for smart devices, a web-based application, a helpdesk application and a cloud back-end platform. The system follows a service-oriented architectural design, exploiting the evolution and flexibility of cloud computing, and implements modern UIs for all types of users. A combination of Java and JavaScript technologies and frameworks are used for implementation and communication of the various application components and services, while the video-conferencing functionality is implemented with the WebRTC protocol [26].

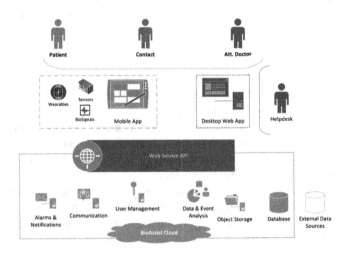

Fig. 2. "BioAssist" environment

The mobile application incorporates the required functionality for communicating with the cloud-based platform services and also acts as a platform gateway to the various sensors and smartwatches. The user interface is realized as a mobile web application, which is practically nested within the native application using "CrossWalk" [27], which creates a placeholder for HTML5 and JavaScript content that is dynamically served to the smartphone or tablet of the patient, allowing high flexibility and compatibility across devices.

The web-based application includes the core functionality for interacting with all user types. In contrast to the mobile application, which is lightweight and simplified so as to ease the interactivity with the elderly users and patients, the web application has a rich user interface for configuring the user and application parameters, and also for visualizing biosignals and health records.

The helpdesk application is accessible by healthcare operators, who receive the emergency requests from patients and trigger appropriate actions to deal with each situation. It incorporates the same technologies with the web-based application, in a suitable user interface.

The "BioAssist" platform back-end is a set of cloud-based services and components. Most of its features are exposed to the aforementioned applications through web services. In addition, communication with external healthcare providers is available for updating the patient's PHR in case new data is available.

3.3 Functionalities

Patients can access the system through the mobile application (Fig. 3), which provides the following functionalities:

1. *Contact management and videoconferencing:* Each user can manage a list of contacts, which include friends and family members, as well as their doctors. Contacts are displayed with their name and profile photo. The user can initiate a video call to a contact with a single touch or send a push notification to ask a contact for a callback.
2. *Reminders:* Patients or their caregivers can set reminders, for tasks such as doctor appointments, or non-medical tasks, such as social engagements. Also, reminders regarding medication intake and biosignal measurements are automatically created by the system, based on the schedule set by the patient's doctor. The user receives reminder notifications both from the tablet and the smartwatch.
3. *Personal health record and biosignals:* Patients can view and update their personal health record, which includes lab test results, medications and allergies. They can also view recorded physical activity data or biosignal measurements and record new measurements from interconnected sensors.
4. *Gallery:* Patients can view photos of their contacts and also upload photos of their own. While the application remains idle, the photos are displayed in a slideshow.
5. *Emergency Call:* In case of emergency, patients can contact the service's helpdesk, with a single touch, to receive assistance and medical advice.

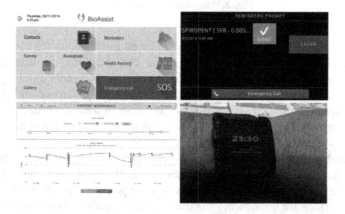

Fig. 3. "BioAssist" mobile application home screen, reminder notification screen, doctor's view of biosignal measurements and smartwatch

3.4 Applied Usability Principles

Considering the needs and limitations of seniors, "BioAssist" has been designed according to the following guidelines:

- *User Interface:* The user interface of the mobile application has been designed with consideration of well-known rules of usability for seniors and people with sensory impairments, including large buttons and fonts, icons and consistent use of colors [11].
- *Devices:* Preferences in devices vary among different people and this can greatly affect how comfortable a user is when using a system, as seniors tend to prefer devices that they already feel comfortable using [12]. The "BioAssist" application can run on various devices, such as smartphones, tablets, but also on TVs, depending on the user's preferences.
- *Multimodality:* Addressing the needs of people with sensory impairments requires the use of multiple modalities [11, 12]. For this reason, notification and reminders are presented with audio and visual alerts on the tablet, as well as vibration alerts on the smartwatch.
- *Understandability:* The interface consists of only a few buttons, while nested menus have been avoided, to simplify navigation and make the application easier to understand.
- *Automation:* Many tasks are automatically executed by the system (e.g. automatic medication reminders, recording measurements from wireless sensors, auto-answer for video calls) or assigned to caregivers (e.g. biosignal measurement schedule). This minimizes the level of action required from the patient and ensures simplicity of use. Furthermore, the application incorporates mechanisms that enable automatic connection with sensors, automatic reconnection with the service in cases of communication loss, as well as automatic relaunch of the application in case of unexpected faults.
- *Motivation:* Users are motivated to engage with the system and use it regularly, by incorporating enjoyable features, such as the gallery functionality. Sharing content and communicating with relatives and friends also promotes social engagement for chronic patients.

4 Usability Evaluation

4.1 Set up and Methodology

Our sample comprised of 26 senior adults, between the ages of 60 and 83, with equal representation of men and women. Some of them face serious chronic diseases such as heart problems, autoimmune problems or cancer. From this sample, 9 women and 11 men eventually accepted to respond to the questionnaire, while the rest denied for reasons such as ignorance or indifference.

First, we presented the platform and its features to each respondent. Before the evaluation, the respondents were given some time (approximately 15 min) to use the system. They were asked to perform simple tasks (such as initiating a video call), with minimum assistance, in order to explore the platform's various features. Afterwards, we interviewed each participant and asked them to respond to the SUS questionnaire (Fig. 4). The SUS questionnaire, is based on a Likert psychometric scale and consists of 10 questions, which can provide a high-level subjective view of usability [19, 20].

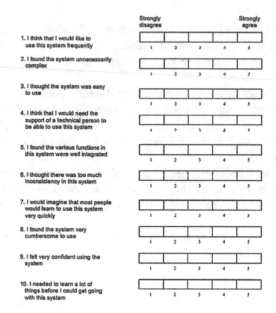

Fig. 4. SUS Questionnaire (Source: Brooke, J.: SUS - A Quick and Dirty Usability Scale. http://cui.unige.ch/isi/icle-wiki/_media/ipm:test-suschapt.pdf)

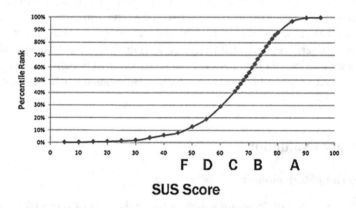

Fig. 5. Percentile rankings of SUS scores (Source: Brooke, J.: SUS: A Retrospective. In: Journal of Usability Studies, vol. 8, no. 2, pp. 37)

The SUS evaluation gives a score that ranges from 0 to 100. This score is calculated as follows [19]:

1. Calculate the individual score for each item.
   (a) For items 1, 3, 5, 7 and 9 the score is equal to the numerical value of the answer (1 to 5) minus 1.
   (b) For items 2, 4, 6, 8 and 10 the score is 5 minus the numerical value or the answer.
2. Sum the scores of all items.

3. Multiply the sum by 2.5, to obtain the total SUS score.

Using the following graph (Fig. 5), we can obtain the corresponding percentile rank of usability for our score, and a grade between A and F. For example, for a SUS score of 74, the corresponding percentile value is 70 % and the grade is B. Any system that has a SUS score greater than 74 is marked as 'Good' and is considered acceptable in terms of usability (Fig. 6).

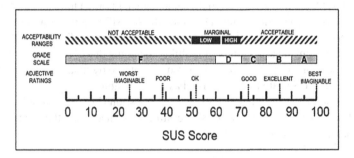

Fig. 6. Grade rankings of SUS scores (Source: Brooke, J.: SUS: A Retrospective. In: Journal of Usability Studies, vol. 8, no. 2, pp. 36)

4.2 Results and Comparison with ITriage

The scores we obtained from the evaluation ranged between 60 and 92.5 (average = 75, median = 72.5) for female respondents and between 52.5 and 82.5 (average = 70.68, median = 72.5) for male respondents. The overall score is 72.84, which is within the acceptable range, corresponding to the grade C. Even though the score ranges are slightly different for male and female participants, there were no significant differences in the attitude of the responses based on gender (i.e. both male and female respondents tended to agree or disagree on the same questions). An overview of the participants' answers to each question is presented in Fig. 7.

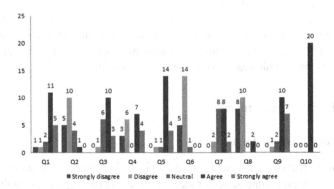

Fig. 7. "BioAssist" - SUS questionnaire responses

As mentioned before, in order to better understand the meaning of the SUS scores and ratings, we also conducted a usability evaluation of the well-known "iTriage" application, for a comparative assessment. The process that we followed and the participants were the same. To minimize potential bias in the results, the order in which the systems were presented to and evaluated by each participant was randomly selected.

The results of the evaluation for "iTriage" ranged between 42.5 and 77.5 (average = 63.3, median = 55) for female respondents and between 30 and 85 (average = 64.09, median = 70) for male respondents, giving a total score of 63.71 and the grade D. Overall, we can comment that the "BioAssist" system has a more successful design, in terms of usability. Also, the results for "iTriage" indicate that this method gives a rather pessimistic assessment of usability, meaning that even systems which have been in use for a long time and are considered acceptable by many users may receive a low score on the SUS scale and be marked as unacceptable.

A comparison of the average scores on each question (Fig. 8), can indicate in what ways the "BioAssist" platform is more successfully designed than other systems, as well as issues that have not been solved.

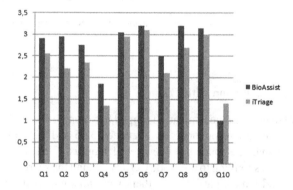

Fig. 8. Comparison of average scores for each question

Based on the scores for questions 2, 3, 6 and 8, we can conclude that most users found both systems consistent, but thought "BioAssist" is simpler and more straightforward. Most participants answered that they felt confident using both systems. However, the scores for questions 4 and 10 indicate that most of them would require training and perhaps assistance to use either system, despite the fact that some of them believe other people would learn to use the system very quickly.

5   Qualitative Assessment

5.1   Set up and Methodology

For the second part of our study, we conducted 6 interviews with senior adults (summary in Table 1). We used the same quota for the recruitment of participants, as in the previous phase. However, most people aged over 75 were unwilling to participate. In the end, our sample mostly included people between the ages of 60 and 70. A few of them have some experience in using computers.

Table 1. List of interviews conducted

A/A	Participant	Health condition	Computer experience
1	Female, 63, lives alone	Diabetes type 2, visual impairment	Some experience from work
2	Male, 65, lives alone	Diabetes type 2, hypertension	None
3	Male, 70, married	Hypertension	Some experience from work
4	Male, 65, married	–	Uses computer for simple tasks
5	Female, 68, married	–	None
6	Female, 78, lives alone	Arthritis, hearing impairment	None

The interviews were semi-structured, following a discussion guide that started with broad questions regarding the participants' attitude and experiences towards technology, as well as potential physical and psychological barriers they face when using computers and ICT systems and their views on home care systems. The participants were then presented with the "BioAssist" platform. Each feature was showcased, explained and discussed in detail, progressively focusing on more specific issues, depending of the respondents' answers, but also examining issues that were revealed in the previous phase. Qualitative analysis on the data was performed using the Framework Approach [28].

5.2 Findings and Insights

The second phase of our study highlighted some good practices that have been applied on the "BioAssist" platform and successfully fulfill certain categories of requirements for ageing usability, as well as some ideas for improvement.

User Interface Design. All participants gave positive feedback on the user interface, describing it as "simple" or "not confusing" compared to other systems, mainly because of the small number of buttons on the home screen. They also appreciated the size of the buttons (large enough to view comfortably) and the use of icons, as they reduced the need to read text on the screen and helped them remember the functionality associated with each button.

Some of the respondents commented on the use of color. One of them expressed the need for brighter colors and higher contrast, but mostly for aesthetic appeal, as they found the current color scheme easy to view. Another participant commended the meaningful use of color (i.e. red colored emergency button, green colored confirmation buttons, etc.).

Finally, some respondents mentioned that they would like to be able to change the font size.

Devices. Most participants found tablets to be the best device option for the application, even though some of them have been hesitant to use tablets until now or had never considered getting one. The reasons were mostly associated with the device's size and portability. When presented with the idea of having the application run on a TV, some of them found it confusing, as they could not visualize it or could not imagine how they would operate the system.

The use of sensors presented no difficulty for any of the respondents, even if they were not used to daily measurements of vital signs, as connectivity is automated. In fact, participants with diabetes found this easier than recording measurements on paper every day.

Device control and manual data input, however, appears to be an important unresolved issue. All respondents stated that they are averse to touch screens, for reasons such as reduced sense of touch, higher chances of making mistakes, frustration and loss of patience, especially when using touch screen keyboards. A couple of them also mentioned that they consider touch screen devices to be too advanced for their generation. Those with some experience in using computers would prefer the use of a regular keyboard for typing and suggested adding a dock for the tablet, with a small keyboard, to the system. Others responded well to the idea of a remote control, but expressed concerns of losing it or confusing it with remote controls of other devices. All users consider simple voice commands as the best solution.

Functionality. Respondents found the functionalities of the system useful and well integrated and appreciated the small number of steps required to perform even complicated tasks, such as creating reminders or recording biosignal measurements.

Most of them commented the reminders feature. One participant characterized the automated functionality of reminders with positive remarks, such as "leaves no room for error", "someone else can do it for me" and "it would be someone else's responsibility", explaining that he finds stressful the idea of having to input himself important data for fear of making mistakes. Similarly, all respondents appreciated the incorporation of mechanisms that automate the communication with the various sensors and the cloud platform, and the automated handling of networking problems. Many respondents also said that they find the gallery feature "enticing" and that it would probably encourage them to use the device more.

Overall, video calls, reminders and the gallery were the features that the participants appreciated the most and believe that they would use more regularly. A couple of them mentioned that they probably wouldn't use the health record functionality and thus would prefer if it was not visible. Other respondents also mentioned that they would like a customizable home screen, which would allow them to remove buttons that they don't use.

Understandability. All participants found the platform and the various functionalities fairly easy to understand, after it was explained to them, but still thought that they would require some training or assistance to use it. Some mentioned that the sequence of steps to perform tasks was easy to remember, especially compared to performing tasks on a computer, but they would need some time to gain confidence in using the system. They all agreed that short and simple audio or animated instructions could be a helpful feature.

A significant finding that emerged is that senior users need to feel in control of the system. One of the respondents mentioned that it is important for him to know how every feature that is visible operates. In that sense, he appreciated that no visible feature was too complicated for him to understand. Other respondents commented that they feel calmer and more confident when using this system, in comparison to using a computer, because it appears simple, regardless of how complicated it actually is.

Motivation to Adopt. An important part of the discussions was based on identifying reasons that would motivate the respondents to adopt home care technology. Some participants stated that the most important motivation to adopt any technology is that it fulfills a need and so they would use a home care system if they felt they needed it. One of them further commented that a major health incident would have to occur before she felt the need for health monitoring.

All of the participants, however, found very appealing the fact that their doctor would be able to monitor their health status and that they would have an easy way to communicate with their caregivers. As one participant commented, "it makes you feel more secure, that someone cares and is in charge". This highlights the importance of incorporating communication features between the various stakeholders.

Finally, some of the respondents mentioned that they would be motivated to use technology for entertainment and thus would appreciate features such as multimedia players or games. The addition of a serious games module could be a valuable step in that direction.

6   Conclusion and Future Directions

In this paper, we have conducted a usability evaluation of the "BioAssist" platform, a home care system that offers communication, health monitoring and emergency response features. The system has been designed according to some well-known requirements for ageing usability. Usability testing with the SUS method has provided us with an overall evaluation of the system's design. Qualitative research has given more insights on the needs and preferences of seniors and has highlighted some good practices regarding user interface design and functionalities that appeal to senior users, and some ways to make the seniors' interaction with the system more convenient for them. Our findings have illustrated the importance of incorporating communication features in home care systems, as well as features that can make the system more attractive, in order to motivate elderly people to use them on a regular basis.

An ethnography could give us a much better understanding of how well would seniors be able to use the system in real conditions. Future work should also include the perspective of the rest of the stakeholders, as they can provide a more comprehensive view on this strategic application domain.

References

1. Mitzner, T.L., Boron, J.B., Fausset, C.B., Adams, A.E., Charness, N., Czaja, S.J., Dijktra, K., Fisk, A.D., Rogers, W.A., Sharit, J.: Older adults talk technology: technology usage and attitudes. Comput. Hum. Behav. **26**(6), 1710–1721 (2010)

2. Selwyn, N.: The information aged: a qualitative study of older adults' use of information and communications technology. J. Aging Stud. **18**(4), 369–384 (2004)
3. Lee, B., Chen, Y., Hewitt, L.: Age differences in constraints encountered by seniors in their use of computers and the Internet. Comput. Hum. Behav. **27**(3), 1231–1237 (2011)
4. Botsis, T., Demiris, G., Pedersen, S., Hartvigsen, G.: Home telecare technologies for the elderly. J. Telemedicine Telecare **14**(7), 333–337 (2008)
5. PACITA Project: EU stakeholder involvement on ageing society. Telecare Technology for an ageing society in Europe. Current State and Future Developments. http://wp6.pacitaproject.eu/wp-content/uploads/2014/02/Telecare-description-web.pdf. Accessed 20 June 2015
6. Ojel-Jaramillo, J.M., Cañas, J.J.: Enhancing the usability of telecare devices. Hum. Technol. Interdisc. J. Hum. ICT Environ. **2**, 103–118 (2006)
7. Renaud, K., Van Biljon, J.: Predicting technology acceptance and adoption by the elderly: a qualitative study. In: Proceedings of the 2008 Annual Research Conference of the South African Institute of Computer Scientists and Information Technologists on IT Research in Developing Countries, pp. 210–219. Riding the Wave of Technology (2008)
8. Wagner, N., Hassanein, K., Head, M.: Computer use by older adults: a multi-disciplinary review. Comput. Hum. Behav. **26**(5), 870–882 (2010)
9. Gatto, S.L., Tak, S.H.: Computer, Internet, and e-mail use among older adults: benefits and barriers. Educ. Gerontol. **34**(9), 800–811 (2008)
10. Patsoule, E., Koutsabasis, P.: Redesigning websites for older adults: a case study. Behav. Inf. Technol. **33**(6), 561–573 (2014)
11. Salama, M., Shawish, A.: Taxonomy of usability requirements for ageing. In: Proceedings of the 13th International Conference on Software Engineering, Parallel and Distributed Systems (2014)
12. McGee-Lennon, M.R., Wolters, M.K., Brewster, S.: User-centred multimodal reminders for assistive living. In: Proceedings of the SIGCHI Conference on Human Factors in Computing Systems, pp. 2105–2114 (2011)
13. Karahasanović, A., Brandtzæg, P.B., Heim, J., Lüders, M., Vermeir, L., Pierson, J., Lievens, B., Vanattenhoven, J., Jans, G.: Co-creation and user-generated content – elderly people's user requirements. Comput. Hum. Behav. **25**(3), 655–678 (2009)
14. Lindberg, T., Näsänen, R., Müller, K.: How age affects the speed of perception of computer icons. Displays **27**(4–5), 170–177 (2006)
15. Claris Companion Official Website. http://www.clariscompanion.com/
16. BePatient Official Website. http://www.bepatient.com/
17. BeClose Official Website. http://beclose.com/
18. Genise, P.: Usability Evaluation: Methods and Techniques: Version 2.0, University of Texas (2002)
19. Brooke, J.: SUS - a quick and dirty usability scale. http://cui.unige.ch/isi/icle-wiki/_media/ipm:test-suschapt.pdf. Accessed 20 June 2015
20. Brooke, J.: SUS: a retrospective. J. Usability Stud. **8**(2), 29–40 (2013)
21. Bangor, A., Kortum, P., Miller, J.: Determining what individual SUS scores mean: adding an adjective rating scale. J. Usability Stud. **4**(3), 114–123 (2009)
22. WAMMI Official Website. http://www.wammi.com/
23. QUIS Official Website. http://www.lap.umd.edu/quis/
24. iTriage Official Website. https://www.itriagehealth.com/
25. BioAssist Official Website. https://bioassist.gr/
26. WebRTC Official Website. http://www.webrtc.org/
27. CrossWalk Official Website. https://crosswalk-project.org/

28. Smith, J., Firth, J.: Qualitative data analysis: the framework approach. Nurse Researcher **18**(2), 52–62 (2011)
29. Dhillon, J.S., Wünsche, B.C., Lutteroth, C.: An online social-networking enabled telehealth system for seniors: a case study. In: Proceedings of the Fourteenth Australasian User Interface Conference, vol. 139, pp. 53–62 (2013)
30. Stojmenova, E., Imperl, B., Žohar, T., Dinevski, D.: Adapted user-centered design: a strategy for the higher user acceptance of innovative e-health services. Future Internet **4**(3), 776–787 (2012)
31. Bozkurt, S., Zayim, N., Gulkesen, K.H., Samur, M.K., Karaagaoglu, N., Saka, O.: Usability of a web-based personal nutrition management tool. Inform. Health Soc. Care **36**(4), 190–205 (2011)

Determining Field of View in Outdoors Augmented Reality Applications

Vlasios Kasapakis[1,2(✉)] and Damianos Gavalas[1,2]

[1] Department of Cultural Technology and Communication,
University of the Aegean, Mytilene, Greece
{v.kasapakis,dgavalas}@aegean.gr
[2] Computer Technology Institute and Press 'Diophantus' (CTI), Patras, Greece

Abstract. The use of augmented reality (AR) becomes increasingly common in location based application development. A situation often encountered in AR applications is the -partial or full- occlusion of virtual objects by physical artifacts; if not appropriately handled, the visualization of occluded objects often misleads users' perception. This paper presents a Geolocative Raycasting technique aiming at assisting developers of outdoors augmented reality applications into generating a realistic field of view for the users by integrating real time building recognition, so as to address the occlusion problem.

1 Introduction

Augmented reality (AR) requires only a limited amount of the user's field of view to be rendered with computer-generated graphics with the major part of the user's view covered by the physical world [2]. The allowance of users to view the physical world provides them a better sense of where they are and what is around them. Nevertheless, cases often occur that a physical object occludes a virtual object; like when surrounding buildings exist and are highly likely to occlude a point of interest. Then, the overlaying of the augmented image may cause confusion to users' perception. This incorrect display contributes to misconceptions and wrong pursuance of tasks amongst users [1, 3]. The problem of occlusion in AR can be observed in a variety of location-based applications. TripAdvisor[1] is a popular mobile travel application which provides reviews of travel-related content. Recently, TripAdvisor added an AR projection mode for points of interest (POIs), superimposing AR markers upon the smartphone's camera views. A similar technique is followed in mTrip[2], another popular, commercial mobile tourism route planner. The occlusion problem is also common in pervasive games utilizing AR, affecting the players' immersion when virtual characters are not hidden when located behind surrounding buildings [4].

In classic video games, the visibility of virtual objects is estimated utilizing the raycasting technique. Raycasting is the act of casting imaginary light beams (rays) from a source location (typically the point of view of the character or object controlled by the

---

[1] www.tripadvisor.com.
[2] www.mtrip.com.

© Springer International Publishing Switzerland 2015
Kameas et al. (Eds.): AmI 2015, LNCS 9425, pp. 344–348, 2015.
DOI: 10.1007/978-3-319-26005-1_23

player) and recording the objects hit by the rays. Herein, we extend this idea in outdoors AR applications wherein, unlike video games, the virtual space is integrated with the physical one, is not pre-registered and occlusion is typically caused by surrounding buildings. In particular, we introduce a *Geolocative Raycasting* technique that allows augmented reality application developers to detect buildings or custom-generated obstacles in location-based and AR game environments, thereby reliably resolving the object occlusion issue.

2   Preparing the Building Data and Performing Raycasting

In order to perform geolocative raycasting, the information about the location of buildings surrounding the user should be available. In our approach the building data is yield from the Overpass Turbo API[3], where the latitude and longitude points of every building polygon are utilized to generate a list of polygons[4] and LatLngBounds[5] (i.e. rectangular bounding boxes utilized to approximate the coordinates of the building's center). The building polygons are drawn on the OSM map[6]. Next, the accelerometer and magnetometer sensors[7] of the user's Android smartphone are enabled to extract the azimuth from the rotation matrix of the device[8], determining the device's orientation (taking into account the device inclination and remapping the axis when needed). The device's bearing is calculated utilizing the azimuth measurement. An extract from our raycasting algorithm implementation is listed in Fig. 1 below.

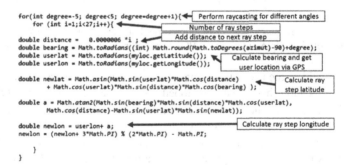

Fig. 1.   Extract from the raycasting algorithm implementation.

---

[3] http://overpass-turbo.eu/.

[4] https://github.com/sromku/.

[5] developer.android.com/reference/com/google/android/gms/maps/model/LatLngBounds.html.

[6] https://code.google.com/p/osmdroid/.

[7] developer.android.com/guide/topics/sensors/sensors_overview.html.

[8] http://developer.android.com/reference/android/hardware/SensorManager.html.

The raycasting algorithm utilized in our work[9] generates virtual locations along a straight line (26 points, each positioned ~3.8 m further from the previous one, resulting in a 100 m ray) towards the user's facing direction, until one of the ray steps (i.e. virtual location) is found to lie inside a polygon (building) of the above mentioned polygon list. Upon detecting such event, it is realized that the ray has been blocked by a building; hence generating further ray steps along that line is unnecessary. Since a single ray is insufficient to accurately estimate the user's field of view, the above detailed process is executed every second degree (note that in the implementation of the raycasting is performed for every one degree of the field of view), in a range of −5 to +5°, considering the current bearing of the device as central direction (10 raycasts in total, resulting into a 10° degrees angle field of view). The above described method is illustrated in Fig. 2a, where 10 raycasts determine the 10° users' field of view in an area featuring buildings stored in the OSM database (red-colored dots denote points invisible from the device's current location).

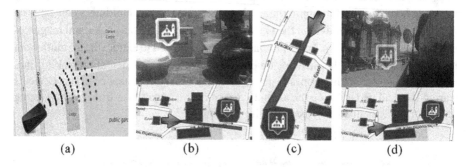

| (a) | (b) | (c) | (d) |

Fig. 2. (a) multi-angle raycasting generating users' field of view; (b) POI outside the users' field of view; (c) field of view representation; (d) POI partially inside the users' field of view.

In order to validate the raycasting approach presented in this work, a simple mobile tourist AR application has been developed as a case-study utilizing OSM and BeyondAR[10] framework. The application included a POI church building which was represented by a marker on OSM maps and an augmented reality marker in BeyondAR framework. When the building polygon of the POI is out of the user's field of view, a grey-colored AR marker is used to denote the location of the church. (Figure 2b) When the ray steps hit the POI building, the point of impact of the blocked ray is saved in an array; upon the completion of the raycasting process, those impingement points are utilized to draw a polygon on the OSM map, providing a visual representation of the users' field of view (Fig. 2c). Finally when the POI is inside the users' field of view the church icon turns from grey to red, informing the user that she has eye constant with it (Fig. 2d). Also the total number of the rays which hit the building were utilized to adjust

---

[9] The formula for calculating a virtual point in front of the user utilizing her current locations' latitude and longitude, along with her device direction may be found at http://www.movable-type.co.uk/scripts/latlong.html.

[10] http://beyondar.com/.

the augmented reality marker transparency, visualizing this way the percentage of the field of view of the user where the POI was included[11].

A factor largely affecting the performance of raycasting is the number of buildings examined (among those returned from the Overpass Turbo API). To limit that number we have applied a distance threshold (representing the ray's reach) around the user's location. The distance is calculated from the user's current location to the center of every building (i.e. the center of the LatLngBounds bounding box). Nearby buildings are re-calculated upon every change on the user's position. The application of a distance threshold slightly longer than the length of the ray ensured that the corners of buildings whose centers are slightly further from the ray's reach are also detected. In order to evaluate the sufficient preface of the raycasting method presented in this work for real time building recognition a full performance test has been conducted.

The test space (see Fig. 3 below) has been set in the center of Athens (Greece), as the OSM database contains a large number of registered buildings in that area. The size of the test area has been set to 707 m^2, adjusting the ray to the same settings as presented above. Updates of the nearby buildings list have been triggered every 2 s by applying a distance threshold of 120 meters. The device was constantly rotated throughout the test (approximately 25 rotations in a 60 s testing session). The total number of buildings within the 120 m radius was 266 with a mean of 43 buildings taken into account by every ray cast. A total number of 457 raycastings were executed, with a mean of 7.6 raycastings per second and an execution mean of 131.2 ms per raycast, providing sufficient evidence that the presented technique would be sufficient for location-based AR applications with real time performance requirements.

Fig. 3. Athens test area.

3   Conclusion

In this article a geolocative raycasting technique has been proposed to detect buildings in real-time, aiming to help future developers into addressing the occlusion problem which is common in location-based AR applications.

---

[11] A video presenting the performance of the test application can be found at https://youtu.be/ zCoI0RW1CcI.

A prototype location-based AR tourist guide application has been used as a case study to showcase the validity of our approach. The performance evaluation of the above application revealed its efficiency which makes it appropriate for relevant location-based outdoors AR applications, wherein marked POIs are commonly occluded by surrounding buildings.

References

1. Shah, M.M., Arshad, H., Sulaiman, R.: Occlusion in augmented reality. In: 2012 8th International Conference on Information Science and Digital Content Technology (ICIDT), pp. 372–378. IEEE (2012)
2. Thomas, B.H.: A survey of visual, mixed, and augmented reality gaming. ACM Comput. Entertainment **10**, 1–33 (2012)
3. Tian, Y., Long, Y., Xia, D., Yao, H., Zhang, J.: Handling occlusions in augmented reality based on 3D reconstruction method. Neurocomputing **156**, 96–104 (2015)
4. Wetzel, W., Blum, L., McCall, R., Oppermann, L., Broeke, T.S., Szalavári, Z.: Final Prototype of TimeWarp application, IPCity (2009)

Standalone Sound-Based Mobile Activity Recognition for Ambient Assistance in a Home Environment

Svilen Dimitrov[(✉)], Norbert Schmitz, and Didier Stricker

DFKI, Kaiserslautern, Germany
{svilen.dimitrov,norbert.schmitz,didier.stricker}@dfki.de

Abstract. Developments of ambient assistance systems and energy consumption optimization in home environments are one of the main goals of ambient intelligent systems. In this work we propose a wearable standalone solution, which combines the assistance task and the energy optimization task. For this purpose we develop a real-time mobile sound-based device and activity recognizer that senses the audible part of the environment to support its owner during his daily tasks and to help him optimize them in terms of resource consumption.

Keywords: Smart home · Sound-based recognition · Wearable · Ambient intelligence · Ambient assistance · Power optimization

1 Introduction

In our daily life we perform activities using devices, which consume resources like electricity and water. A way to optimize the resource consumption is to perform our tasks in efficient ways such that we utilize the devices in optimal way, like avoiding leaving them idling unsupervised or forgotten. Ambient Intelligent Systems support us for that purpose in various ways. To do so however, such systems should first sense us and our environment to recognize our actions and guess our intentions.

Sound-based context recognition is a natural way of environment sensing by anticipating its ambient sounds. First sound-based recognition systems date from roughly 10 years ago and use both wearable [1] and static [2] microphone placements. Recently, there are developments done with different sound setups and sensing aspects of the environment, like distress event detection [3] and device recognition [4] in a home environment or general context mobile recognition [5].

In this work we synthesize the mentioned approaches with an implementation of a standalone system for smartphones. We advance the research state by not only recognizing devices, but their states too, as well as other audible user activities in a home environment. The application further lists the different activities recognized during its execution and also issues various notifications to the user concerning its observations, including popping up warnings for electrical devices left running for long periods of time. The latter is of special interest for users with hearing impairments, while other users can profit from such application by receiving vital device usage information and use it to optimize their electrical or other resource consumption.

© Springer International Publishing Switzerland 2015
Kameas et al. (Eds.): AmI 2015, LNCS 9425, pp. 349–352, 2015.
DOI: 10.1007/978-3-319-26005-1_24

2 Architecture and Environment

The process from an activity to its corresponding device recognition starts with the environment where some activity occurs. Its sounds are captured by a smartphone and used to extract a desired set of features to classify the ongoing activities and their corresponding devices (see Fig. 1).

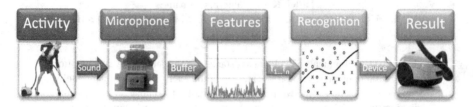

Fig. 1. Illustration of the process from activity to its corresponding recognition.

This study seeks to provide wearable activity recognition in a smart home so the architecture and the implementation are centralized on a home environment (see sample setup in Fig. 2). Our design requires a mono recording functionality – a capability of all smartphones, and if more audio input channels are present, we mix their input into a single processing channel. The latter enables switching between different on-body positioning setups without computational overhead. We assume there is only one activity running at a time, performed by a user with or without device, or the device doing its periodic miscellaneous tasks alone. Due to the nature of our design that exploits existing smartphone hardware, we consider our installation to be low cost and feasible for every user.

Fig. 2. Illustration of a sample usage scenario in a home environment – a user with hearing impairment receives sound-based recognition ambient assistance during his daily routines.

3   Sound-Based Activity Recognizer Implementation

Our implementation of a sound-based activity recognizer consists mainly of two components. The first one is a sound processing component, which records a mono sound with 32 bit depth at 44100 Hz and uses Fast Fourier transformation with Hamming window, to extract 8 features as described in [6]. The second one is a machine learning component, which classifies the different activities according to their sound-based fingerprint using the Nearest Neighbor algorithm. Both of the components require only standard smartphone hardware and are implemented in a highly optimized way in order to allow a real-time recognition combined with a low-battery consumption. We also implement a model of an incremental learning system, which relies on user input to build its activity database and to receive feedback about the recognition accuracy while running.

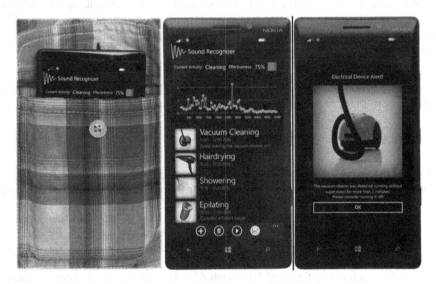

Fig. 3. On-body placement of the smartphone (left) with the application running (middle) and a sample alert (right) after leaving electrical device running longer than desired.

The application itself is capable of running in live recognition mode and provides its recognition results (see Fig. 3) at different possible rates starting at 10 Hz. It enumerates the different activities, which it recognizes and can also display both power/time and frequency/power representations of the sound, so that if the user has hearing impairment he can see the sound picture of his home. This graphical representation of the sound is also useful for a user to decide whether some activity can be captured by the device clear enough so that it makes sense to add it to its activity list. The application can also issue different warnings via vibration on different events like leaving the vacuum cleaner or blender running for too long, or notifications for washing machine or coffee pot ready. The latter might be crucial since one can forget his coffee on the heating element for long periods of time and thus expose themselves to potential danger. Furthermore, notifications about various possible misuses of electrical and other devices are important for several reasons, including electrical and other resource usage optimization, and extending the lifetime of those devices.

4 Conclusion and Future Work

Our main contribution in the field of sound-based context recognition is creating a wearable standalone system for device and activity recognition. It further can recognize the states of some devices, which allowed us to explore application opportunities beyond the recognition-only task. On top of the recognition functionality we implemented an ambient assistance application, which issues different activity-related notifications, besides the automatic creation of an activity schedule.

We plan to extend our working prototype with a communication interface to make the application accessible by other sensor nodes and to increase its intelligence in terms of being integral part of a wireless body sensor network for activity recognition. The latter is also an important step for evaluating and comparing the implementation with other ambient recognition techniques.

Acknowledgement. This work has been partly developed for the EASY-IMP[1] project funded by the European Union under grant agreement No 609078.

References

1. Stager, M., Lukowicz, P., Troster, G.: Implementation and evaluation of a low-power sound-based user activity recognition system. In: Eighth International Symposium on Wearable Computers, 2004. ISWC 2004, vol. 1, pp. 138–141. IEEE (October 2004)
2. Vuegen, L., Van Den Broeck, B., Karsmakers, P., Vanrumste, B.: Automatic monitoring of activities of daily living based on real-life acoustic sensor data: a preliminary study. In: Proceedings of Fourth Workshop on Speech and Language Processing for Assistive Technologies (SLPAT), pp. 113–118 (2013)
3. Istrate, D., Vacher, M., Serignat, J.-F.: Embedded Implementation of distress situation. identification through sound analysis. J. Inf. Technol. Healthc. 6(3), 204–211 (2008)
4. Dimitrov, S., Britz, J., Brandherm, B., Frey, J.: Analyzing sounds of home environment for device recognition. In: Aarts, E., etal. (eds.) AmI 2014. LNCS, vol. 8850, pp. 1–16. Springer, Heidelberg (2014)
5. Rossi, M., Feese, S., Amft, O., Braune, N., Martis, S., Troster, G.: AmbientSense: a real-time ambient sound recognition system for smartphones. In: 2013 IEEE International Conference on Pervasive Computing and Communications Workshops (PERCOM Workshops), pp. 230–235. IEEE (March 2013)
6. Peeters, G.: A large set of audio features for sound description (similarity and classification) in the CUIDADO project. Institut de Recherche et Coordination Acoustique/Musique, Analysis/Synthesis Team. IRCAM, Paris, France (2004)

[1] EASY-IMP is a European research project aiming to develop methodologies, tools and platforms for the design and production of personalized meta-products, combining wearable sensors embedded into garment with mobile and cloud computing (www.easy-imp.eu).

Gamification Techniques for Rule Management in Ambient Intelligence

Francesco Benzi[1], Federico Cabitza[2], Daniela Fogli[1(✉)],
Rosa Lanzilotti[3], and Antonio Piccinno[3]

[1] Dipartimento di Ingegneria dell'informazione, Università degli Studi di Brescia, Brescia, Italy
{f.benzi,daniela.fogli}@unibs.it
[2] Dipartimento di Informatica, Università degli Studi di Milano-Bicocca, Milan, Italy
cabitza@disco.unimib.it
[3] Dipartimento di Informatica, Università di Bari "Aldo Moro", Bari, Italy
{rosa.lanzilotti,antonio.piccinno}@uniba.it

Abstract. This paper discusses the application of gamification techniques in the Ambient Intelligence context. A three-layer framework for ambient intelligence based on the concept of interconnection among all actors involved in the intelligent environment is first delineated. Then, mechanisms for user-driven creation and modification of environment behavior are advocated in the user layer. For this purpose, event-condition-action rules are promoted in literature. With this position paper we would like to suggest that user interfaces for rule construction must be integrated with proper techniques for user engagement and motivation, such as those proposed in the gamification theory.

Keywords: Rule-based system · Smart home · Sustainability · Gamification

1 Introduction

Gamification is "the use of game design elements in non-game contexts" [1] and is recently considered a useful technique for one's own business or organization [2]. Indeed, the introduction of gamification elements such as points, badges and leaderboards – the so-called PBLs elements in [3] – has proven to be a successful solution to support collaborative work, increase sells in e-commerce web sites, and foster participation in social networks. The term "gamification" is sometimes controversial, but the definition given above and the survey provided in [1] clarify that "gamified" applications are different from (video) games, serious games or just software applications that provide a playful interaction, like those considered in [4].

This paper investigates the introduction of gamification elements in the frame of Ambient Intelligence (AmI) to support the participation of end users in the configuration and continuous development of an AmI environment. The idea stems from the consideration that, in order to adapt the behavior of such environments to the needs and preferences of their inhabitants, one has to provide not only usable user interfaces, but also sustain users through engaging features and tools. With this position paper we suggest that the proposals arising in the gamification research area could inspire the design of such features and tools.

© Springer International Publishing Switzerland 2015
Kameas et al. (Eds.): AmI 2015, LNCS 9425, pp. 353–356, 2015.
DOI: 10.1007/978-3-319-26005-1_25

2 A Conceptual Framework for AmI

We are currently working on a conceptual framework for AmI based on the concept of *interconnection* [5] among all actors involved in the intelligent environment. The main point of this metaphor is that an AmI environment cannot be simply considered the aggregation of computational devices and human actors endowed with perceptual and effectual capabilities, bound together by functional relations. Rather what emerges from this aggregation is something new, i.e., an environment where some *states* and *conditions* are visible and available (e.g., the temperature of the room, if the light is on, if the door is open) and some *actions* are feasible (e.g., raise the room temperature, switch off the light, call the security). And, last but not the least, where "intelligent inference" is kept in the loop between conditions and actions.

This brings to conceive an AmI architecture as structured in three layers: (1) the *physical layer*, where devices operate, with their perceptual and effectual capabilities, and inter-operate, through a shared information space that collects their states and acts as a communication medium; (2) the *inference layer*, where logical reasoning is automatically carried out to link perceptions to actions; (3) the *user layer*, where people are called on not only to act in the environment, also in response to state changes and/or ambient conditions, but above all to manipulate the "logic" (i.e., rules, policies, behaviors) their ambient should follow to either assist or satisfy their (situational) needs.

Literature of AmI provides plenty of solutions for the physical layer [6], while the inference layer can be easily realized through the adoption of artificial intelligence techniques (e.g., [5, 7]). In particular, rule-based approaches are often proposed, where event-condition-action (ECA) rules are stored in a proper rule base and managed by a rule engine. More recently, attention is paid to the user layer as well. This requires providing end users with an easy way to interact and live in an intelligent environment, and to adapt the environment behavior to their own needs and preferences. This objective can be achieved by designing proper mechanisms for ECA rule creation and modification by end users. However, even though there are some works in the AmI area, which propose user interfaces based on the ECA paradigm (e.g., [8]), there is no study that demonstrates the acceptability and actual usage of this approach by users without competencies in information technology. Furthermore, users' motivations fostering rule creation and modification over time are usually not considered. This leads to address new issues that we denote as the perception of relative advantage and long-term sustainability. The *perception of relative advantage* regards a known principle from the diffusion of innovation model theory [9]: for an innovation to have an impact on the daily life of its users it is important that these latter ones perceive the new thing as giving them a clear advantage with respect to the traditional counterparts whatever these are. The *long-term sustainability* is closely related and regards the fact that users should find convenient using and adapting their intelligent environments even after that the thrill for the technology novelty and curiosity have faded out and, most notably, after that some expert, be this a professional or simply an enthusiast acquaintance of theirs, has gone away and left the lay user alone with her/his own computational support. This means that a careful design of the user-related layer is needed, so that an AmI environment can co-evolve over time with the users' needs and technologies available [10]. In the following, we suggest the adoption of gamification techniques to address the above issues.

3 The Role of Gamification in AmI: A Scenario

In [3], a gamification framework is proposed encompassing three types of elements: dynamics, mechanics and components. Dynamics are the highest-level elements that provide motivations for participation, such as *emotions* or *progression*. Mechanics are the elements that drive player involvement and allow implementing the dynamics; they are for example *challenges, rewards, competition, cooperation,* etc. Components are the low-level tools that allow making the mechanics concrete; they include a variety of elements that are usually introduced in the user interface of a gamified system, such as *avatars, badges, leaderboards, levels, points, quests,* and many others [2]. Overall, these elements contribute to create an *experience* that engage users and foster their participation. In the following, we propose the use of game components in a user interface supporting the collaborative creation of ECA rules for smart home configuration and adaptation. This user interface is currently under development.

We suppose that our smart home system allows managing different set of rules, each one associated to a home inhabitant and that some rules are associated to "all users", because they are managing shared spaces such as the living room or the garden. The list of rules associated to all users could be endowed with gamification components that stimulate social interaction, cooperation and possibly competition. For example, this part of the interface could show not only a way to add a new rule, but also components to post requests for creating new rules or improving existing rules that anyone in the family could satisfy. **Prizes** may be offered to motivate the satisfaction of such requests, where the prize mechanism could be managed by means of **points** that could be gained when someone satisfies a request. For instance, mum might post the request "please make the vacuum cleaning robot work at night", and one of her children could create a suitable rule and thus gain points to get the prize. Rule modification by someone that is not the rule creator could be submitted to a **poll** before becoming effective. In this case, some voters could have higher priority with respect to the rest of users; for instance, the **mayor** concept could be used to endow some users with more power. A mayor could be in fact associated to every single place and be represented by the registered user who spent most time in that place. **Levels** could also be introduced to evaluate rules and their creators over time. For instance, a rule could gain experience every time it is activated with positive side effects (e.g., energy saving), and eventually reach an upper level. On the contrary, when a rule does not behave as some user expected, that user could notify it with a special annotation. In this way, every time the rule is activated it will lose experience, until reaching a so-called "defective" level, where the rule cannot be activated anymore. The inhabitants of the smart home should be motivated to modify the rules, even after they have completed the configuration of the smart home. To this end, **quests**, such as "Consume less than X kilowatts in a week period", may be generated automatically by the system or set by an administrator. Indeed, quests may provide the users with difficult goals to achieve, which may require an unusual set of rules and an increased living effort by all the family. Completed quests could give virtual **rewards** that can be redeemed in the form of real goods or discounts on real stuff.

4 Conclusion and Future Work

We have presented some proposals for "gamifying" the user interface supporting a smart home configuration and adaptation. Obviously, different solutions should be identified depending on the chosen AmI context (smart hospital, smart city, etc.). The aim of this position paper is just promoting a "contamination" between the gamification and AmI research areas. In the future, we plan to develop and experiment the approach in different case studies, in order to derive a general design methodology.

Acknowledgments. This work is supported by the Italian Ministry of University and Research (MIUR) under grant PON 02_00563_3470993 project "VINCENTE".

References

1. Deterding, S., Dixon, D., Khaled, R., Nacke, L.: From game design elements to gamefulness: defining "gamification". In: 15th International Academic MindTrek Conference: Envisioning Future Media Environments, pp. 9–15. ACM, New York, NY, USA (2011)
2. Werbach, K., Hunter, D.: The Gamification Toolkit: Dynamics, Mechanics, and Components for the Win. Wharton Digital Press, Philadelphia (2015)
3. Werbach, K., Hunter, D.: For the Win: How Game Thinking Can Revolutionize Your Business. Wharton Digital Press, Philadelphia (2012)
4. Alis Salah, A., Schouten, B.A.M., Göbel, S., Arnrich, B.: Playful interactions and serious games. J. Ambient Intell. Smart Environ. **1**, 1–5 (2014)
5. Cabitza, F., Dal Seno, B., Sarini, M., Simone, C.: "Being at one with things": the interconnection metaphor for intelligent environments. In: Proceedings of IEE International Workshop on Intelligent Environment, pp. 63–73. IEE, Colchester, UK (2005)
6. Sadri, F.: Ambient intelligence: a survey. ACM Comput. Surv. **43**(4), 1–66 (2011)
7. Augusto, J.C., Nugent, C.D.: The use of temporal reasoning and management of complex events in smart homes. In: Proceedings of ECAI 2004, pp. 778–782. IOS Press (2004)
8. García-Herranz, M., Haya, P., Alamán, X.: Towards a ubiquitous end-user programming system for smart spaces. J. Univers. Comput. Sci. **16**(12), 1633–1649 (2010)
9. Emani, S., Yamin, C.K., Peters, E., Karson, A.S., Lipsitz, S.R., Wald, J.S., Williams, D.H., Bates, D.W.: Patient perceptions of a personal health record: a test of the diffusion of innovation model. J. Med. Internet Res. **14**(6), e150 (2012)
10. Cabitza, F., Fogli, D., Piccinno, A.: Fostering participation and co-evolution in sentient multimedia systems. J. Vis. Lang. Comput. **25**(6), 684–694 (2014)

Happy Running?

Using an Accelerometer to Predict the Affective State of a Runner

Joey van der Bie[✉] and Ben Kröse

Amsterdam University of Applied Sciences, Wibautstraat 2-4,
1091 GM Amsterdam, The Netherlands
{j.h.f.van.der.bie,b.j.a.krose}@hva.nl

Abstract. This paper explores a method for deducing the affective state of runners using his/her movements. The movements are measured on the arm using a smartphone's built-in accelerometer. Multiple features are derived from the measured data. We studied which features are most predictive for the affective state by looking at the correlations between the features and the reported affect. We found that changes in runners' movement can be used to predict change in affective state.

Keywords: Affect · Emotion · Accelerometer · Smartphone · Physical activity

1 Introduction

Knowing how an athlete feels can help a sports coach in communication and setting up a more tailored training schedule. Also a continuous measurement of the affective state would be advantageous for a automatic digital coaching system (coaching-app). Affective experiences in activities are usually measured using video recordings [1]. This is unpractical for everyday use. It would be more practical to use a smartphone worn by the athlete, making it possible for a coaching-app to use its affective state. We are developing a system that infers the affective state of a runner from the movement characteristics measured by the accelerometer sensor of a smartphone mounted on the arm. In this paper we present our work on the analysis of the accelerometer data: which movement features from the data correlate best with the perceived affective state?

2 Related Work

Recent studies have shown that spatio-temporal body features are indicative for the affective state of a person [1].

In the field of running intensity has an influence on the affective state. Continuous running above the ventilatory threshold (the point during exercise at which respiration starts to increase at a faster rate) changes the affective experience negatively. Running below the ventilatory threshold has little influence on the affective state [2].

© Springer International Publishing Switzerland 2015
Kameas et al. (Eds.): AmI 2015, LNCS 9425, pp. 357–360, 2015.
DOI: 10.1007/978-3-319-26005-1_26

Accelerometers can be used at various places on the body to determine type of activity. The raw signal can be transformed into features and used as an indicator for an activity [3].

3   Experimental Set-Up and Data

We created a dataset consisting of accelerometer data from a smartphone worn by the runners and affective state reported by the runners. Test subjects ran on a treadmill on their ventilatory threshold until they were tired. The threshold was determined for each runner separately in a previous session based on the method of Bood et al. [4]. Running speed, heart rate, movement, ability to talk, perceived exertion and perceived affective state are measured. The data collection was part of a larger experiment. This study uses the accelerometer data and perceived affective state.

Movement was measured using a smartphone's (Google Nexus 5) three degrees of freedom accelerometer (with a sample rate of 100 Hz), worn by the runner in a band on the left arm. The phone's X-axis measured forward movement, the Y-axis measured vertical movement and the Z-axis measured sideways movement. Perceived affective state was measured with the 11-point Feeling scale [5] by verbal expression of the subject once every two minutes while running. The questionnaire was displayed on a screen in front of the user.

Eighteen runners participated, four male, fourteen female, with an average age of 23 years (STD 3 years). They ran an average of 16.6 min (STD 5 min) of which an average of 8 min at a constant speed. In total 96 affective responses were given while running at constant speed.

4   Feature Extraction

We were interested in features related to the intensity of the movement and to the regularity of the movement. Corresponding to each affective response a data sample of 12000 data points (two minutes of data) was created from the movement signal. The data was transformed with a Hanning-window. For each sample the mean of the signal, the variance of the signal and the entropy of the Fourier transform were determined. We used the individual X-, Y- and Z-axes of the accelerometer as signals. In total we had nine features (three axes times three features) for every time sample.

5   Results

Figure 1a shows the reported affect for the participants as a function of time during the eight minutes of constant speed. All participants show the expected tendency towards negative affect as described by [2]. However, we also observe inter-person differences: some participants report a structural higher affect than others.

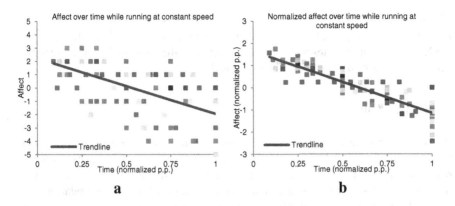

Fig. 1. (a) Affective responses as a function of time. (b) Normalized affective responses as a function of time.

In our first approach we determine correlations between the reported affect and the nine accelerometer features. We determined the p values using an independent sample size of 18 (the total number of participants). Overall the correlation values are low. The highest correlation value can be found in the mean of the X-axis (-0.20) with a p value of 0.42. The correlation values are displayed in Table 1. One reason for the low correlation can be the inter-person differences, both in affect as in feature values.

Table 1. Correlation of features with affect. r = correlation value. p = significance

Feature	r	p	Feature	r	p	Feature	r	p
Mean X	-0,2	0,42	Mean Y	0,05	0,85	Mean Z	-0,07	0,79
Variance X	-0,17	0,51	Variance Y	-0,005	0,98	Variance Z	0,01	0,97
Entropy X	0,09	0,72	Entropy Y	-0,01	0,98	Entropy Z	-0,19	0,46

Table 2. Correlation of normalized features with normalized affect. r = correlation value. p = significance

Feature	r	p	Feature	r	p	Feature	r	p
Mean X	-0,07	0,78	Mean Y	0,27	0,28	Mean Z	0,25	0,32
Variance X	-0,52	0,03	Variance Y	-0,38	0,12	Variance Z	-0,74	4,03×10-4
Entropy X	-0,11	0,66	Entropy Y	-0,03	0,89	Entropy Z	-0,03	0,91

In order to filter out individual characteristics, the feature values and affect values are standardized using Z-score normalization for each individual participant. Normalized affective responses are depicted in Fig. 1b. We determine the most likely indicative features by calculating the correlation between each feature and the affective response.

The highest correlation value can be found in the variance of the Z-axis (which indicates the sideways movement of the phone) with a p value of 4.03×10^{-4} and the variance of the X-axis (which indicates the forward movement of the phone) with a p value of 0.03. The correlation values are displayed in Table 2.

6   Conclusion

We observe that the inter-person characteristics on affective response are large and that the absolute affect is hard to predict from the accelerometer data. When using normalized response data, a strong inverse correlation between affective state and the runners' forward and sideways movement characteristics is observed. The low correlation values of the Y-axis features show that vertical movement characteristics do not change sufficiently in relation to affective state.

We measured movement on the arm and not on other parts of the body, therefore we cannot determine if the movement is specific for the arm or for the whole body.

Concluding, our model can be used to detect changes in affective state based on changes in movement. Using the accelerometer sensor of a smartphone, our model can be applied in a digital coaching-app.

Acknowledgments.   We thank the participants, the Radboud University, the University of Twente and the VU University of Amsterdam for making the creation of the dataset possible.

This publication was supported by the Dutch national program COMMIT and the Amsterdam Creative Industries Network.

References

1. Kleinsmith, A., Bianchi-Berthouze, N.: Affective body expression perception and recognition: a survey. IEEE Trans. Affect. Comput. **4**(1), 15–33 (2013)
2. Ekkekakis, P., Parfitt, G., Petruzzello, S.J.: The pleasure and displeasure people feel when they exercise at different intensities. Sports Med. **41**(8), 641–671 (2011)
3. Bicocchi, N., Mamei, M., Zambonelli, F.: Detecting activities from body-worn accelerometers via instance-based algorithms. Pervasive Mob. Comput. **6**(4), 482–495 (2010)
4. Bood, R.J., Nijssen, M., van der Kamp, J., Roerdink, M.: The power of auditory-motor synchronization in sports: enhancing running performance by coupling cadence with the right beats. PLoS ONE **8**(8), e70758 (2013)
5. Hardy, C.J., Rejeski, W.J.: Not what, but how one feels: the measurement of affect during exercise. J. Sport Exerc. Psychol. **11**(3), 304–317 (1989)

Web Based Monitoring and Irrigation System with Energy Autonomous Wireless Sensor Network for Precision Agriculture

Georgios Mitralexis[✉] and Christos Goumopoulos

School of Science and Technology, Hellenic Open University, Patras, Greece
mitralexis.georgios@mfa.gr,goumop@aegean.gr

Abstract. The use of Precision Agriculture systems is in its infancy in Greece, because of the high fragmented land and the adherence of farmers to traditional farming methods. This paper presents the design, implementation and performance evaluation of an integrated agricultural monitoring and irrigation system using energy-autonomous wireless sensors and actuators. Monitoring and irrigation of the field are carried out through a web application that collects data from a Wireless Sensor Network deployed in a cultivation and displays relative information in real time. Furthermore, the system can operate proactively based on user-defined rules that can decide when the farm should be irrigated. The system is easy to use by farmers who look for a first contact with Precision Agriculture applications. Our results have revealed the possibility to develop a robust, fully-automated, solar powered, and low cost monitoring and irrigation system that suits to the socio-economic conditions of small scale farms in countries like Greece.

Keywords: Wireless sensor/actuator network · Precision agriculture · Rule based irrigation · Outdoor deployment · Energy harvesting

1 Introduction

In the last decades in Greece, but also worldwide, has been observed a reduction and ageing of the rural population, while the climate change and the destructions that will cause, are expected to endanger global agriculture production. Farmers, in order to meet future challenges, must improve the efficiency and the quality of agricultural production, with the growth of "Precision Agriculture" (PA) [1]. Despite the possibilities offered by the current technological progress in the manufacture and development of wireless sensor networks, Greek farmers do not embrace with proportional rhythms innovative applications in the production process. The majority of Greek farmers have small scale cultivations, low educative level and deficit of technological skills, so they hesitate to invest in modern agricultural production methods.

In this paper we present the design, implementation and performance evaluation of an energy autonomous monitoring and culture irrigation system via Internet. Our system, because of its low cost and user-friendly interface of the web application, can be easily adopted by small farmers who want to use PA practices at an introductory level without

© Springer International Publishing Switzerland 2015
Kameas et al. (Eds.): AmI 2015, LNCS 9425, pp. 361–370, 2015.
DOI: 10.1007/978-3-319-26005-1_27

having to invest in new technologies. The system developed is based exclusively on open source tools (programming languages, software and hardware) so that a low-cost but efficient and relatively simple to install system can be implemented. The system by exploiting a wireless sensor/actuator network, can provide multiple benefits both in terms of crop yield and in terms of better management and protection of natural resources.

The rest of the paper is organized as follows. Section 2 discusses related work. The design choices of our system are explained in Sect. 3. The implementation of the system in terms of the wireless sensor network, the irrigation system and the web application are discussed in Sect. 4. Section 5 presents a real deployment of our system followed by the experimental results collected and our conclusions.

2 Related Work

In recent years, a wide diversity of applications that follow PA practices in cultures, using WSNs have been presented. Four indicative examples of using WSNs for crop cultivation are in vineyard farms in Galicia [2], in potato plantation in India [3], in cotton crop in USA [4] and in potato cultivation in Egypt [5]. The approach followed in by the example systems in Galicia and Egypt include the use of a WSN and the creation of decision tools in order the farmer to better plan the irrigation and fertilization of the crop in addition to the ability to forecast the occurrence of diseases as demonstrated in [2]. In both implementations the remote monitoring of the crop via Internet was possible, but there was not a subsystem that controlled irrigation of the fields, which continued to be performed in a traditional way. On the other side, the example systems in India and USA have used the WSN technology to gather the required information needed by an irrigation system to determine and implement the automated watering strategy. In both cases, an application for remote monitoring and control of systems was missing.

The system presented in this paper, combines all the individual features demonstrated by the above examples, with the addition of more advanced features, as the exploitation of solar panels to achieve the energy autonomy of the WSN nodes and the browser-based access to the system from any device, anywhere.

3 System Design

The aim of the system is to monitor in "real-time" via Internet selected plant and environmental conditions in the field and irrigate it when it is necessary. The system architecture consists of three subsystems (Fig. 1). The first one is a *wireless sensor network* which is installed in the field, collects sensor measurements and then uploads the data in the Cloud Database. The components of the WSN include a coordinator node and two sensor nodes that communicate in a star topology with protocol ZigBee Pro (v.2007). The sensor nodes include temperature, relative humidity, soil moisture and leaf wetness sensors. The second subsystem manages irrigation using an *irrigation controller* that is being administered by the web application. The irrigation controller controls two solenoid valves that are connected in two respective irrigation lines. The system configuration is completed by the presence of a *web application* which stores sensors measurements in a database, presents them to the user in various forms and controls the irrigation subsystem of the field.

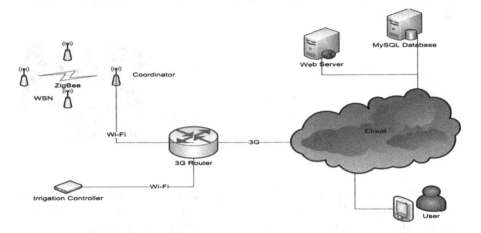

Fig. 1. System architecture

Irrigation can be performed either manually or automatically by the system, based on rules activated when the soil moisture values exceeds a specific threshold. More advanced rules can be specified based on crop expert advisement. The role of the coordinator node is to receive sensor data from end devices, process and send them to the database with HTTP via the 3G router, which is the Gateway of the system to the Internet via the mobile telephony network. The coordinator is connected to the 3G router with Wi-Fi and the irrigation controller with Ethernet or Wi-Fi, respectively (Fig. 1). In automatic mode, when the system receives a measurement by a soil moisture sensor, it calculates the mean from the last ten measurements of the node. A mean filter is implemented in order to avoid random noise that it would trigger the irrigation accidentally. If the average of the last 10 measurements of the soil moisture sensor exceeds the threshold, the system activates the irrigation line for a predetermined period of time.

4   System Implementation

4.1   Wireless Sensor Network

Nodes wireless communication is based on ZigBee Pro protocol which is characterized by very low power consumption and wide-range coverage. ZigBee Pro emits in 2.4 GHz band with 250 kbps data transfer speed. A star network topology is used along with the CSMA-CA access method in order to avoid collisions when the sensor nodes send packets to the coordinator. The WSN nodes used are based on the Waspmote by Libelium which are characterized by their very low energy consumption and modular architecture. In the decreased energy consumption contribute the embedded Real Time Clock (RTC), which allows Waspmote to enter in low power mode (Deep Sleep and Hibernate) and to wake up in a scheduled time. All nodes have ZigBee modules to communicate with each other and are powered by battery Li-Ion 6600 mAh. For recharging the batteries each node is connected to a solar panel 7 V-500 mA. An Expansion Radio Board and a Wi-Fi module are installed on the Coordinator node (Fig. 2) in order to communicate with the 3G router.

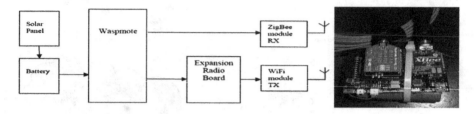

Fig. 2. Coordinator architecture

The WSN terminal nodes (Fig. 3) have an Agriculture Sensor Board that mount the sensors of the system. The sensors used in each node are Temperature (MCP9700A), Humidity (808H5V5), Soil Moisture (Watermark 200SS) and Leaf Wetness.

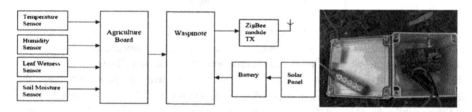

Fig. 3. Sensor node architecture

4.2 Irrigation System

The irrigation controller consists of an Arduino board with integrated microcontroller ATmega644, which is running open source software OpenSprinkler. The irrigation controller is able to be connected with up to 8 solenoid valves 24 V. Also, there is a built-in Web Server for remote communication and management. The irrigation board is connected to the 3G router via Ethernet or Wi-Fi adapter.

4.3 Web Application

The Web Application has been developed with web technologies such as PHP, HTML, Javascript and jQuery and is compatible with any kind of device (PC, tablet, smartphone etc.). The application presents the sensors data in real-time in numerical and graphical format. Also the user will be able to download a csv file of historical data, to create graphs and to manage the irrigation controller and the irrigation mode (Manual or Automatic). The Web application has a friendly Graphical User Interface that can be used by a simple smartphone user, requiring no previous experience.

5   Experiment

The experimental system deployed in the Social Vegetable Garden of Agioi Anargiroi Municipality for 31 days (17/5–16/6/2015). A software program was developed and uploaded into the sensor nodes to allow them to measure temperature, relative humidity, soil moisture, leaf wetness, battery level, and RSSI (Received Signal Strength Indicator) at time intervals of 15 min (duty cycle 6.66 %) for the 1st node and 30 min (duty cycle 3.3 %) for the 2nd node. The scope of the experiment was to test the reliability and functionality of the system in real conditions. At the same time, we examined the energy consumption of sensor nodes and various factors that affect the quality of wireless links of the network.

6   Results

6.1   Battery Level

To study the WSN energy behavior, the nodes were connected to solar panels for the first seven days, where the batteries level was steadily between 96 % and 97 %. The solar panel was disconnected for a period of 21 days and the sensor nodes were powered exclusively by batteries. During this period, the daily discharge rate stood at 0.38 % (25,08 mAH per day about) and the level fell from 96 % to 88 % for both nodes. On the 29th day of experiment, the solar panels were reconnected to the nodes; within 7 h of plenty sunshine, the batteries covered the energy losses of the previous 21 days. The charging rate fluctuated 528 mAH per day, proving that in a country with high level of sunshine (like Greece), the nodes of the system can operate until battery lifetime is exhausted and the battery is not able to be charged anymore (Figs. 4 and 5).

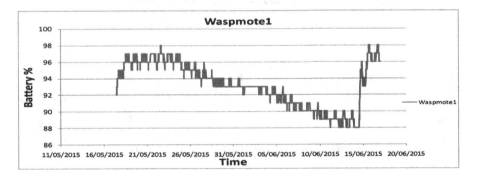

Fig. 4. Battery level timeline of 1st sensor node

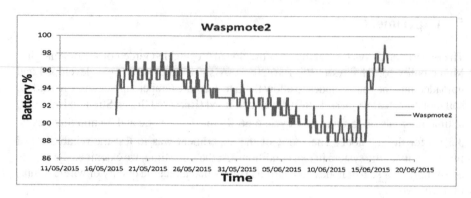

Fig. 5. Battery level timeline of 2nd sensor node

6.2 RSSI and Battery Level

Throughout the duration of the experiment, RSSI measurements were collected by the two nodes and then the correlation between battery level and temperature was studied (Figs. 6 and 7). As shown in Fig. 6, the RSSI level of the 1st node remains stable between −45dbm and −55dbm as long as the battery level is above 90 %. When it reaches at 90 %, we see a visible drop in signal strength levels between −55dbm and −80dbm. With the beginning of battery charge from the solar panel, we observe that the signal strength increases gradually until it stabilizes at the previous levels between −45 and −55dbm.

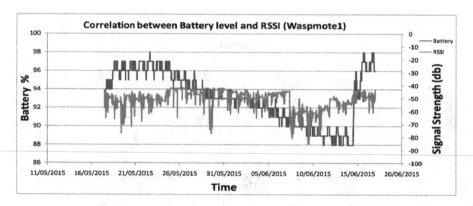

Fig. 6. Correlation between battery level and RSSI in 1st node

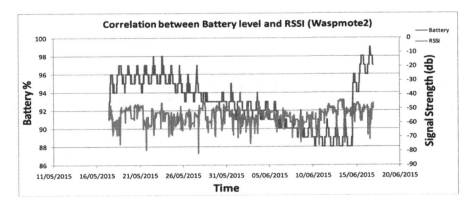

Fig. 7. Correlation between battery level and RSSI in 2nd node

Finally, there is a significant correlation between battery level and the quality of the wireless links of the network. A fully charged battery helps nodes to have better and more constant power signal. In our system this goal is achieved by uninterrupted charging of node batteries using solar panels, strengthening the robustness of network.

6.3 RSSI and Temperature

The correlation between temperature and RSSI has been studied thoroughly [6–8]. Despite the controversial results, the dominant conclusion is the negative impact of high temperature on RSSI [6, 7]. Observing Figs. 8 and 9 a visible inverse pattern between temperature and signal strength on both nodes is noticed, indicating a negative correlation. At midday, when the outdoor temperature reached the higher values (above 30° C), the RSSI values fell, respectively. The reduction of RSSI is linear and inversely proportional to the increase of temperature. On the contrary, during the night when the temperature lowers, the signal strength is stronger, characteristically.

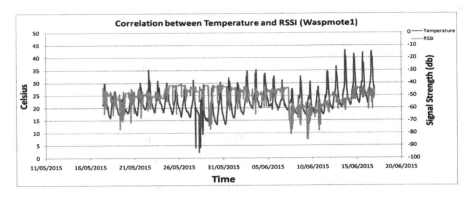

Fig. 8. Correlation between temperature and RSSI in 1st node

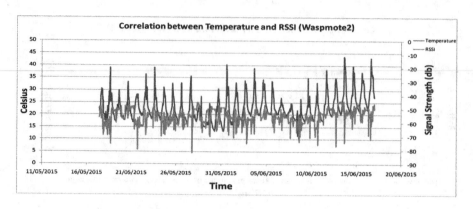

Fig. 9. Correlation between temperature and RSSI in 2nd node

The explanation of the correlation of temperature with RSSI lies in the sensitivity of hardware. Specifically, the high temperature creates leak current in semiconductors and in the transceiver which results in a drop of the signal strength. The negative effect of high temperatures from the sun, it should be taken seriously into account during deployment of nodes in a WSN. Their placement should be in shady places, in protective boxes having proper heat insulation. Also, we should keep in mind that if the wireless links of a WSN are unstable, reliability can be improved deferring communication between nodes during cooler periods (evening or night).

6.4 Packet Delivery Ratio and Packet Loss Rate

An interesting metric was the measurement of the Packet Delivery Ratio (PDR) of the system, which is defined as the number of packets received by the destination node (cloud database) compared to the number of packets that have been sent out by the WSN nodes. The higher the value of PDR, the better the system performance. We note in Table 1 that the PDR and PLR vary at satisfactory levels for both nodes, so that do not cause problems in system operation and the immediate and accurate information to the user.

Table 1. Packet delivery ratio and packet loss rate

	Waspmote1	Waspmote2
Duty cycle	6.66 %	3.3 %
Tx packets	2867	1428
Rx packets	2708	1357
Lost packet	159	71
Packet delivery ratio	94.454 %	95.028 %
Packet loss rate	5.545 %	4.971 %

7 Conclusions and Future Work

The proposed system is a low cost PA system that can be easily deployed, as our experimental prototype demonstrated, in any small or large scale cultivation. The monitoring subsystem enables the precise observation of the real conditions in the cultivation. The web application provides a handy tool for remote and active crop protection, helping the farmer to prevent adverse situations (frost, diseases, sub-irrigation etc.) and to manage effectively required resources (water and fertilizer). Finally, the irrigation subsystem relaxes the requirement for farmer's continuous presence (often on a daily basis) to irrigate the cultivation. At the same time, the system provides the ability to irrigate the crop precisely depending on local context of the field (soil composition, crop type, area exposure to natural phenomena etc.). With respect to irrigation we should also emphasize the ability of the system to operate proactively, based on user's defined rules.

The experiment proved that the proper placement of the nodes is crucial. The nodes must be protected as much as possible from high temperatures. It is useful before the final placement, to make an assessment of the conditions that could affect the wireless sensor network (temperature, humidity etc.) by studying historical data of the region, in order to properly prepare the network taking into account the conditions that it will likely meet.

For future work, we propose a large scale deployment with more nodes and use of the Cluster Tree topology. Also it would be interesting to use a wider variety of sensors and to improve the autonomous irrigation based on more detailed rules or rules that the system learns by applying machine learning techniques [9]. In future expansion of the system, we will replace the ZigBee communication protocol with 6LoWPAN, so each node of the network (sensor nodes, coordinator, router, irrigation controller) will have a public IPv6 address, directly accessible from the Internet.

The reader can visit the web application and the components of the system in the website www.smartfield.eu.

References

1. Srinivasan, A. (ed.): Handbook of Precision Agriculture Principles and Applications. Haworth Press, New York (2006)
2. Bielsa, A.: Smart agriculture project in Galicia to monitor vineyards with Waspmote, 8 June 2012. http://www.libelium.com/smart_agriculture_vineyard_sensors_waspmote. Accessed 28 June 2015
3. Shinghal, K., Noor, A., Srivastava, N., Singh, R.: Wireless sensor networks in agriculture for potato farming. Int. J. Eng. Sci. Technol. 2(8), 3955–3963 (2010)
4. Vellidis, G., Tucker, M., Perry, C., Kvien, C., Bednarz, C.: A real-time wireless smart sensor array for scheduling irrigation. Comput. Electron. Agric. **61**, 44–50 (2008)
5. El-kader, S.M.A., El-Basioni, B.M.M.: Precision farming solution in Egypt using the wireless sensor network technology. Egypt. Inform. J. **14**(3), 221–233 (2013)
6. Bannister, K., Giorgetti, G., Gupta, S.K.S.: Wireless sensor networking for hot applications: effects of temperature on signal strength, data collection and localization. In: Proceedings of the 5th Workshop on Embedded Networked Sensors (HotEmNets) (2008)

7. Boano, C., Brown, J., He, Z., Roedig, U., Voigt, T.: Low-power radio communication in industrial outdoor deployments: the impact of weather conditions and ATEX-compliance. In: Proceedings of the 1st International Conference on Sensor Networks Applications, Experimentation and Logistics (SENSAPPEAL) (2009)
8. Thelen, J., Goense, D., Langendoen, K.: Radio wave propagation in potato fields. In: Proceedings of the 1st Workshop on Wireless Network Measurement (WiNMee) (2005)
9. Goumopoulos, C., O'Flynn, B., Kameas, A.: Automated zone-specific irrigation with wireless sensor/actuator network and adaptable decision support. Comput. Electron. Agric. **105**, 20–33 (2014)

Author Index

Printed in the United States
By Bookmasters